Paper MA

ACCA

Management Accounting

> Welcome to Emile Woolf's study text for
> Paper *Management Accounting* (MA) which is:
> - Written by tutors
> - Comprehensive but concise
> - In simple English
> - Used around the world by Emile Woolf Colleges including China, Russia and the UK

Fifteenth edition published by
Emile Woolf International Limited
Bracknell Enterprise & Innovation Hub
Ocean House, 12th Floor, The Ring
Bracknell, Berkshire, RG12 1AX United Kingdom
Email: info@ewiglobal.com
www.emilewoolf.com

© Emile Woolf International Limited, June 2022

All rights reserved. No part of this publication may be reproduced, stored in a retrieval system, or transmitted, in any form or by any means, electronic, mechanical, photocopying, recording, scanning or otherwise, without the prior permission in writing of Emile Woolf International Limited, or as expressly permitted by law, or under the terms agreed with the appropriate reprographics rights organisation.

You must not circulate this book in any other binding or cover and you must impose the same condition on any acquirer.

Notice
Emile Woolf International Limited has made every effort to ensure that at the time of writing the contents of this study text are accurate, but neither Emile Woolf International Limited nor its directors or employees shall be under any liability whatsoever for any inaccurate or misleading information this work could contain.

British Library Cataloguing in Publications Data
A catalogue record for this book is available from the British Library.

ISBN: 978-1-84843-681-7

Printed and bound in Great Britain.

Acknowledgements
The syllabus and study guide are reproduced by kind permission of the Association of Chartered Certified Accountants.

Applied Knowledge
Management Accounting (MA)

Contents

	Page
Syllabus and study guide	v
Formulae sheet and tables	xix
Chapter 1: The nature and purpose of cost and management accounting	1
Chapter 2: Cost classification	25
Chapter 3: Cost behaviour	47
Chapter 4: Presenting information	55
Chapter 5: Forecasting techniques	63
Chapter 6: Simple and weighted index numbers	105
Chapter 7: Summarising and analysing data	119
Chapter 8: Accounting for materials	147
Chapter 9: Accounting for labour	179
Chapter 10: Accounting for overheads	193
Chapter 11: Accounting for costs: ledger entries	233
Chapter 12: Marginal costing and absorption costing	249
Chapter 13: Job costing, batch costing and service costing	267
Chapter 14: Process costing	277
Chapter 15: Alternative costing systems	313
Chapter 16: Budgeting	339
Chapter 17: Capital budgeting and discounted cash flows	379
Chapter 18: Standard costing and variance analysis	411
Chapter 19: Performance measurement	459
Answers to exercises and practice multiple choice questions	509
Practice questions	537

	Page
Answers to practice questions	555
Index	579

Applied Knowledge
Management Accounting (MA)

Syllabus and study guide
September 2022 to August 2023

Aim

To develop knowledge and understanding of management accounting techniques to support management in planning, controlling and monitoring performance in a variety of business contexts.

Main capabilities

On successful completion of this paper, candidates should be able to:

- **A** Explain the nature, source and purpose of management information
- **B** Explain and apply data analysis and statistical techniques
- **C** Explain and apply cost accounting techniques
- **D** Prepare budgets for planning and control
- **E** Compare actual costs with standard costs and analyse any variances
- **F** Explain and apply performance measurements and monitor business performance.

Rationale

The syllabus for *Management Accounting (MA)/FMA*, introduces candidates to elements of management accounting which are used to make and support decisions.

The syllabus starts by introducing the nature, the source and purpose of management information followed by the statistical techniques used to analyse data. Then the syllabus addresses cost accounting and the costing techniques used in business which are essential for any management accountant.

The syllabus then looks at the preparation and use of budgeting and standard costing and variance analysis as essential tools for planning and controlling business activities. The syllabus concludes with an introduction to measuring and monitoring the performance of an organisation.

Detailed syllabus

A   The nature, source and purpose of management information
1. Accounting for management
2. Sources of data
3. Cost classification
4. Presenting information

B   Data analysis and statistical techniques
1. Sampling methods
2. Forecasting techniques
3. Summarising and analysing data
4. Spreadsheets

C   Cost accounting techniques.
1. Accounting for material, labour and overheads
2. Absorption and marginal costing
3. Cost accounting methods
4. Alternative cost accounting principles

D   Budgeting
1. Nature and purpose of budgeting
2. Budget preparation
3. Flexible budgets
4. Capital budgeting and discounted cash flow
5. Budgetary control and reporting
6. Behavioural aspects of budgeting

E   Standard costing
1. Standard costing system
2. Variance calculations and analysis
3. Reconciliation of budgeted and actual profit

F   Performance measurement
   1.   Performance measurement - overview
   2   Performance measurement - application
   3   Cost reductions and value enhancement
   4.   Monitoring performance and reporting

Approach to examining the syllabus

The syllabus is assessed by two-hour computer-based examination. Questions will assess all parts of the syllabus and will test knowledge and some comprehension or application of this knowledge. The examination will consist of two sections. Section A will contain 35 two-mark objective test questions (OTs). Section B will contain 3 ten-mark multi-task questions (MTQs) each of which will examine Budgeting, Standard costing and Performance measurement sections of the syllabus.

Note: Budgeting MTQs in Section B can also include tasks from B2 Forecasting techniques. B4 Spreadsheets could be included in any of the MTQs, as either the basis for presenting information in the question scenario or as a task within the MTQ.

Study Guide

A   THE NATURE, SOURCE AND PURPOSE OF MANAGEMENT INFORMATION

1. Accounting for management

a) Describe the purpose and role of cost and management accounting within an organisation.

b) Compare and contrast financial accounting with cost and management accounting.

c) Outline the managerial processes of planning, decision-making and control.

d) Explain the difference between strategic, tactical and operational planning.

e) Distinguish between data and information.

f) Identify and explain the attributes of good information.

g) Explain the limitations of management information in providing guidance for managerial decision-making.

2. Sources of data

a) Describe the three main data sources: machine/sensor, transactional and human/social.

b) Describe sources of information from within and outside the organisation (including government statistics, financial press, professional or trade associations, quotations and price lists).

c) Explain the uses and limitations of published information/data (including information from the internet).

d) Describe the impact of the general economic environment on costs/revenue.

3. Cost classification

a) Explain and illustrate production and non-production costs.

b) Describe the different elements of non-production costs - administrative, selling, distribution and finance.

c) Describe the different elements of production costs - materials, labour and overheads.

d) Explain the importance of the distinction between production and non-production costs when valuing output and inventories.

e) Explain and illustrate with examples classifications used in the analysis of product/service costs including by function, direct and indirect, fixed and variable, stepped fixed and semi variable costs.

f) Explain and illustrate the use of codes in categorising transactions.

g) Describe and illustrate, graphically, different types of cost behaviour.

h) Explain and illustrate the concept of cost objects, cost units and cost centres.

i) Distinguish between cost, profit, investment and revenue centres.

j) Describe the differing needs for information of cost, profit, investment and revenue centre managers.

4. Presenting information

a) Prepare written reports representing management information in suitable formats according to purpose.

b) Present information using tables, charts and graphs (bar charts, line graphs, pie charts and scatter graphs).

c) Interpret information (including the above tables, charts and graphs) presented in management reports.

B DATA ANALYSIS AND STATISTICAL TECHNIQUES

1. Sampling methods

a) Explain sampling techniques (random, systematic, stratified, multistage, cluster and quota).

b) Choose an appropriate sampling method in a specific situation. (Note: Derivation of random samples will not be examined)

2. Forecasting techniques

a) Explain the structure of linear functions and equations.

b) Use the high low method to separate the fixed and variable elements of total costs including situations involving semi variable and stepped fixed costs and changes in the variable cost per unit.

c) Explain the advantages and disadvantages of using the high low method to estimate the fixed and variable elements of costing.

d) Construct scatter diagrams and lines of best fit.

e) Analysis of cost data.
   i) Explain the concepts of correlation coefficient and coefficient of determination.
   ii) Calculate and interpret the correlation coefficient and the coefficient of determination.
   iii) Establish a linear function using regression analysis and interpret the results.

f) Use linear regression coefficients to make forecasts of costs and revenues.

g) Adjust historical and forecast data for price movements.

- h) Explain the advantages and disadvantages of linear regression analysis.
- i) Explain the principles of time series analysis (cyclical, trend, seasonal variation and random elements).
- j) Calculate moving averages.
- k) Calculate the trend, including the use of regression coefficients.
- l) Use trend and seasonal variation (additive and multiplicative) to make budget forecasts.
- m) Explain the advantages and disadvantages of time series analysis.
- n) Explain the purpose of index numbers.
- o) Calculate simple and multi-item (weighted) index numbers for one or more variables, including Laspeyre and Paasche indices.
- p) Describe the product life cycle and explain its importance in forecasting.

3. Summarising and analysing data

- a) Describe the five characteristics of big data (volume, variety, velocity, value and veracity).
- b) Explain the three types of big data: structured, semi-structured and unstructured.
- c) Describe the main uses of big data and data analytics for organisations.
- d) Describe the two types of data: categorical (nominal and ordinal) and numerical (continuous and discrete).
- e) Explain the terms descriptive analysis and inferential analysis.
- f) Calculate the mean, mode and median for ungrouped data and the mean for grouped data.
- g) Calculate measures of dispersion including the variance, standard deviation and coefficient of variation both grouped and ungrouped data.
- h) Calculate expected values for use in decision making.
- i) Explain the properties of a normal distribution.
- j) Interpret normal distribution graphs and tables.

4. Spreadsheets

- a) Explain the role and features of a computer spreadsheet system.
- b) Identify applications for computer spreadsheets and their use in data analysis, cost and management accounting.

C COST ACCOUNTING TECHNIQUES

1. Accounting for material, labour and overheads

a) Accounting for materials

i) Describe the different procedures and documents necessary for the ordering, receiving and issuing of materials from inventory.

ii) Describe the control procedures used to monitor physical and 'book' inventory and to minimise discrepancies and losses.

iii) Interpret the entries and balances in the material inventory account.

iv) Identify, explain and calculate the costs of ordering and holding inventory (including buffer inventory).

v) Calculate and interpret optimal reorder quantities.

vi) Calculate and interpret optimal reorder quantities when discounts apply.

vii) Produce calculations to minimise inventory costs when inventory is gradually replenished.

viii) Describe and apply appropriate methods for establishing reorder levels where demand in the lead time is constant.

ix) Calculate the value of closing inventory and material issues using LIFO, FIFO and average methods.

b) Accounting for labour

i) Calculate direct and indirect costs of labour.

ii) Explain the methods used to relate input labour costs to work done.

iii) Prepare the journal and ledger entries to record labour cost inputs and outputs.

iv) Describe different remuneration methods: time-based systems, piecework systems and individual and group incentive schemes.

v) Calculate the level and analyse the costs and causes of labour turnover.

vi) Explain and calculate labour efficiency, capacity and production volume ratios.

vii) Interpret the entries in the labour account.

c) Accounting for overheads

i) Explain the different treatment of direct and indirect expenses.

ii) Describe the procedures involved in determining production overhead absorption rates.

iii) Allocate and apportion production overheads to cost centres using an appropriate basis.

iv) Reapportion service cost centre costs to production cost centres (including using the reciprocal method where service cost centres work for each other).

v) Select, apply and discuss appropriate bases for absorption rates.

vi) Prepare journal and ledger entries for manufacturing overheads incurred and absorbed.

vii) Calculate and explain the under and over absorption of overheads.

2. Absorption and marginal costing

a) Explain the importance of, and apply, the concept of contribution.

b) Demonstrate and discuss the effect of absorption and marginal costing on inventory valuation and profit determination.

c) Calculate profit or loss under absorption and marginal costing.

d) Reconcile the profits or losses calculated under absorption and marginal costing.

e) Describe the advantages and disadvantages of absorption and marginal costing.

3. Cost accounting methods

a) Job and batch costing:
  i) Describe the characteristics of job and batch costing.
  ii) Describe the situations where the use of job or batch costing would be appropriate.
  iii) Prepare cost records and accounts in job and batch costing situations.
  iv) Establish job and batch costs from given information.

b) Process costing
  i) Describe the characteristics of process costing.
  ii) Describe the situations where the use of process costing would be appropriate.
  iii) Explain the concepts of normal and abnormal losses and abnormal gains.
  iv) Calculate the cost per unit of process outputs.
  v) Prepare process accounts involving normal and abnormal losses and abnormal gains.
  vi) Calculate and explain the concept of equivalent units.
  vii) Apportion process costs between work remaining in a process and transfers out of a process using the weighted average and FIFO methods.
  viii) Prepare process accounts in situations where work remains incomplete.

ix) Prepare process accounts where losses and gains are identified at different stages of the process.

x) Distinguish between by-products and joint products.

xi) Value by-products and joint products at the point of separation.

xii) Prepare process accounts in situations where by-products and/or joint products occur. (Situations involving work-in-process and losses in the same process are excluded).

c) Service/operation costing

i) Identify situations where the use of service/operation costing is appropriate.

ii) Illustrate suitable unit cost measures that may be used in different service/operation situations.

iii) Carry out service cost analysis in simple service industry situations.

4 Alternative cost accounting principles

a) Explain activity-based costing (ABC), target costing, life-cycle costing and total quality management (TQM) as alternative cost management techniques.

b) Differentiate ABC, target costing and life cycle costing from the traditional costing techniques (note: calculations are not required).

D BUDGETING

1. Nature and purpose of budgeting

a) Explain why organisations use budgeting.

b) Describe the planning and control cycle in an organisation.

c) Explain the administrative procedures used in the budgeting process.

d) Describe the stages in the budgeting process (including sources of relevant data, planning and agreeing draft budgets and purpose of forecasts and how they link to budgeting).

2. Budget preparation

a) Explain the importance of the principal budget factor in constructing a budget.

b) Prepare sales budgets.

c) Prepare functional budgets (production, raw materials usage and purchases, labour, variable and fixed overheads).

d) Prepare cash budgets.

e) Prepare master budgets (statement of profit or loss and statement of financial position).

f) Explain and illustrate 'what if' analysis and scenario planning.

3. Flexible budgets

a) Explain the importance of flexible budgets in control.

b) Explain the disadvantages of fixed budgets in control.

c) Identify situations where fixed or flexible budgetary control would be appropriate.

d) Flex a budget to a given level of volume.

4. Capital budgeting and discounted cash flows

a) Discuss the importance of capital investment planning and control.

b) Define and distinguish between asset and expense items.

c) Outline the issues to consider and the steps involved in the preparation of a capital expenditure budget.

d) Explain and illustrate the difference between simple and compound interest, and between nominal and effective interest rates.

e) Explain and illustrate compounding and discounting.

f) Explain the distinction between cash flow and profit and the relevance of cash flow to capital investment appraisal.

g) Identify and evaluate relevant cash flows for individual investment decisions.

h) Explain and illustrate the net present value (NPV) and internal rate of return (IRR) methods of discounted cash flow.

i) Calculate present value using annuity and perpetuity formulae.

j) Calculate NPV, IRR and payback (discounted and non-discounted).

k) Interpret the results of NPV, IRR and payback calculations of investment viability.

5. Budgetary control and reporting

a) Calculate simple variances between flexed budget, fixed budget and actual sales, costs and profits.

b) Discuss the relative significance of variances.

c) Explain potential action to eliminate variances.

d) Define the concept of responsibility accounting and its significance in control.

e) Explain the concept of controllable and uncontrollable costs.

f) Prepare control reports suitable for presentation to management (to include recommendation of appropriate control action).

6. Behavioural aspects of budgeting

a) Explain the importance of motivation in performance management.

- b) Identify factors in a budgetary planning and control system that influence motivation.
- c) Explain the impact of targets on motivation.
- d) Discuss managerial incentive schemes.
- e) Discuss the advantages and disadvantages of a participative approach to budgeting.
- f) Explain top down and bottom up approaches to budgeting.

E STANDARD COSTING

1. Standard costing

- a) Explain the purpose and principles of standard costing.
- b) Explain and illustrate the difference between standard, marginal and absorption costing.
- c) Establish the standard cost per unit under absorption and marginal costing.

2 Variance calculations and analysis

- a) Calculate sales price and volume variance.
- b) Calculate materials total, price and usage variance.
- c) Calculate labour total, rate and efficiency variance.
- d) Calculate variable overhead total, expenditure and efficiency variance.
- e) Calculate fixed overhead total, expenditure and, where appropriate, volume, capacity and efficiency variance.
- f) Interpret the variances.
- g) Explain factors to consider before investigating variances, explain possible causes of the variances and recommend control action.
- h) Explain the interrelationships between the variances.
- i) Calculate actual or standard figures where the variances are given.

3 Reconciliation of budgeted and actual profit

- a) Reconcile budgeted profit with actual profit under standard absorption costing.
- b) Reconcile budgeted profit or contribution with actual profit or contribution under standard marginal costing.

F PERFORMANCE MEASUREMENT

1. Performance measurement - overview

- a) Discuss the purpose of mission statements and their role in performance measurement.
- b) Discuss the purpose of strategic, operational and tactical objectives and their role in performance measurement.

c) Discuss the impact of economic and market conditions on performance measurement.

d) Explain the impact of government regulation on performance measurement.

2 Performance measurement - application

a) Discuss and calculate measures of financial performance (profitability, liquidity, activity and gearing) and non-financial measures.

b) Perspectives of the Balanced Scorecard
   i) discuss the advantages and limitations of the balanced scorecard.
   ii) describe performance indicators for financial, customer, internal business process and innovation and learning.
   iii) discuss critical success factors and key performance indicators and their link to objectives and mission statements.
   iv) establish critical success factors and key performance indicators in a specific situation.

c) Economy, efficiency and effectiveness
   i) explain the concepts of economy, efficiency and effectiveness.
   ii) describe performance indicators for economy, efficiency and effectiveness.
   iii) establish performance indicators for economy, efficiency and effectiveness in a specific situation.
   iv) discuss the meaning of each of the efficiency, capacity and activity ratios.
   v) calculate the efficiency, capacity and activity ratios in a specific situation.

d) Unit costs
   i) describe performance measures which would be suitable in contract and process costing environments.

e) Resource utilisation
   i) describe measures of performance utilisation in service and manufacturing environments.
   ii) establish measures of resource utilisation in a specific situation.

f) Profitability
   i) calculate return on investment and residual income.
   ii) explain the advantages and limitations of return on investment and residual income.

g) Quality of service

   (i) distinguish performance measurement issues in service and manufacturing industries.

   (ii) describe performance measures appropriate for service industries.

3. Cost reductions and value enhancement

a) Compare cost control and cost reduction.

b) Describe and evaluate cost reduction methods.

c) Describe and evaluate value analysis.

4 Monitoring performance and reporting

a) Discuss the importance of non-financial performance measures.

b) Discuss the relationship between short- term and long-term performance.

c) Discuss the measurement of performance in service industry situations.

d) Discuss the measurement of performance in non-profit seeking and public sector organisations.

e) Discuss measures that may be used to assess managerial performance and the practical problems involved.

f) Discuss the role of benchmarking in performance measurement.

g) Produce reports highlighting key areas for management attention and recommendations for improvement.

Applied Knowledge
Management Accounting (MA)

Formulae sheet and tables

Regression analysis

$y = a + bx$

$a = \dfrac{\sum y}{n} - \dfrac{b \sum x}{n}$

$b = \dfrac{n \sum xy - \sum x \sum y}{n \sum x^2 - (\sum x)^2}$

$r = \dfrac{n \sum xy - \sum x \sum y}{\sqrt{(n \sum x^2 - (\sum x)^2)(n \sum y^2 - (\sum y)^2)}}$

Economic order quantity

$= \sqrt{\dfrac{2 C_0 D}{C_h}}$

Economic batch quantity

$= \sqrt{\dfrac{2 C_0 D}{C_h \left(1 - \dfrac{D}{R}\right)}}$

Arithmetic mean

$\bar{x} = \dfrac{\sum x}{n}$ $\qquad \bar{x} = \dfrac{\sum fx}{\sum f}$ (frequency distribution)

Standard deviation

$\sigma = \sqrt{\dfrac{\sum (x - \bar{x})^2}{n}}$ $\qquad \sigma = \sqrt{\dfrac{\sum fx^2}{\sum f} - \left(\dfrac{\sum fx}{\sum f}\right)^2}$ (frequency distribution)

Variance

$= \sigma^2$

Coefficient of variation

$CV = \dfrac{\sigma}{\bar{x}}$

Expected value

$EV = \Sigma px$

Present value table

Present value of 1 i.e. $(1+r)^{-n}$

where r = discount rate

n = number of periods until payment

Periods					Discount rate (r)						
(n)	1%	2%	3%	4%	5%	6%	7%	8%	9%	10%	
1	0.990	0.980	0.971	0.962	0.952	0.943	0.935	0.926	0.917	0.909	1
2	0.980	0.961	0.943	0.925	0.907	0.890	0.873	0.857	0.842	0.826	2
3	0.971	0.942	0.915	0.889	0.864	0.840	0.816	0.794	0.772	0.751	3
4	0.961	0.924	0.888	0.855	0.823	0.792	0.763	0.735	0.708	0.683	4
5	0.951	0.906	0.863	0.822	0.784	0.747	0.713	0.681	0.650	0.621	5
6	0.942	0.888	0.837	0.790	0.746	0.705	0.666	0.630	0.596	0.564	6
7	0.933	0.871	0.813	0.760	0.711	0.665	0.623	0.583	0.547	0.513	7
8	0.923	0.853	0.789	0.731	0.677	0.627	0.582	0.540	0.502	0.467	8
9	0.914	0.837	0.766	0.703	0.645	0.592	0.544	0.500	0.460	0.424	9
10	0.905	0.820	0.744	0.676	0.614	0.558	0.508	0.463	0.422	0.386	10
11	0.896	0.804	0.722	0.650	0.585	0.527	0.475	0.429	0.388	0.350	11
12	0.887	0.788	0.701	0.625	0.557	0.497	0.444	0.397	0.356	0.319	12
13	0.879	0.773	0.681	0.601	0.530	0.469	0.415	0.368	0.326	0.290	13
14	0.870	0.758	0.661	0.577	0.505	0.442	0.388	0.340	0.299	0.263	14
15	0.861	0.743	0.642	0.555	0.481	0.417	0.362	0.315	0.275	0.239	15
(n)	11%	12%	13%	14%	15%	16%	17%	18%	19%	20%	
1	0.901	0.893	0.885	0.877	0.870	0.862	0.855	0.847	0.840	0.833	1
2	0.812	0.797	0.783	0.769	0.756	0.743	0.731	0.718	0.706	0.694	2
3	0.731	0.712	0.693	0.675	0.658	0.641	0.624	0.609	0.593	0.579	3
4	0.659	0.636	0.613	0.592	0.572	0.552	0.534	0.516	0.499	0.482	4
5	0.593	0.567	0.543	0.519	0.497	0.476	0.456	0.437	0.419	0.402	5
6	0.535	0.507	0.480	0.456	0.432	0.410	0.390	0.370	0.352	0.335	6
7	0.482	0.452	0.425	0.400	0.376	0.354	0.333	0.314	0.296	0.279	7
8	0.434	0.404	0.376	0.351	0.327	0.305	0.285	0.266	0.249	0.233	8
9	0.391	0.361	0.333	0.308	0.284	0.263	0.243	0.225	0.209	0.194	9
10	0.352	0.322	0.295	0.270	0.247	0.227	0.208	0.191	0.176	0.162	10
11	0.317	0.287	0.261	0.237	0.215	0.195	0.178	0.162	0.148	0.135	11
12	0.286	0.257	0.231	0.208	0.187	0.168	0.152	0.137	0.124	0.112	12
13	0.258	0.229	0.204	0.182	0.163	0.145	0.130	0.116	0.104	0.093	13
14	0.232	0.205	0.181	0.160	0.141	0.125	0.111	0.099	0.088	0.078	14
15	0.209	0.183	0.160	0.140	0.123	0.108	0.095	0.084	0.074	0.065	15

Annuity table

Present value of an annuity of 1 i.e. $\dfrac{1-(1+r)^{-n}}{r}$

where r = discount rate

n = number of periods

Periods (n)	1%	2%	3%	4%	5%	6%	7%	8%	9%	10%	
1	0.990	0.980	0.971	0.962	0.952	0.943	0.935	0.926	0.917	0.909	1
2	1.970	1.942	1.913	1.886	1.859	1.833	1.808	1.783	1.759	1.736	2
3	2.941	2.884	20829	2.775	2.723	2.673	2.624	2.577	2.531	2.487	3
4	3.902	3.808	3.717	3.630	3.546	3.465	3.387	3.312	3.240	3.170	4
5	4.853	4.713	4.580	4.452	4.329	4.212	4.100	3.993	3.890	3.791	5
6	5.795	5.601	5.417	5.242	5.076	4.917	4.767	4.623	4.486	4.355	6
7	6.728	6.472	6.230	6.002	5.786	5.582	5.389	5.206	5.033	4.868	7
8	7.652	7.325	7.020	6.733	6.463	6.210	5.971	5.747	5.535	5.335	8
9	8.566	8.162	7.786	7.435	7.108	6.802	6.515	6.247	5.995	5.759	9
10	9.471	8.983	8.530	8.111	7.722	7.360	7.024	6.710	6.418	6.145	10
11	10.37	9.787	9.253	8.760	8.306	7.887	7.499	7.139	6.805	6.495	11
12	11.26	10.58	9.954	9.385	8.863	8.384	7.943	7.536	7.161	6.814	12
13	12.13	11.35	10.63	9.986	9.394	8.853	8.358	7.904	7.487	7.103	13
14	13.00	12.11	11.30	10.56	9.899	9.295	8.745	8.244	7.786	7.367	14
15	13.87	12.85	11.94	11.12	10.38	9.712	9.108	8.559	8.061	7.606	15

(n)	11%	12%	13%	14%	15%	16%	17%	18%	19%	20%	
1	0.901	0.893	0.885	0.877	0.870	0.862	0.855	0.847	0.840	0.833	1
2	1.713	1.690	1.668	1.647	1.626	1.605	1.585	1.566	1.547	1.528	2
3	2.444	2.402	2.361	2.322	2.283	2.246	2.210	2.174	2.140	2.106	3
4	3.102	3.037	2.974	2.914	2.855	2.798	2.743	2.690	2.639	2.589	4
5	3.696	3.605	3.517	3.433	3.352	3.274	3.199	3.127	3.058	2.991	5
6	4.231	4.111	3.998	3.889	3.784	3.685	3.589	3.498	3.410	3.326	6
7	4.712	4.564	4.423	4.288	4.160	4.039	3.922	3.812	3.706	3.605	7
8	5.146	4.968	4.799	4.639	4.487	4.344	4.207	4.078	3.954	3.837	8
9	5.537	5.328	5.132	4.946	4.772	4.607	4.451	4.303	4.163	4.031	9
10	5.889	5.650	5.426	5.216	5.019	4.833	4.659	4.494	4.339	4.192	10
11	6.207	5.938	5.687	5.453	5.234	5.029	4.836	4.656	4.486	4.327	11
12	6.492	6.194	5.918	5.660	5.421	5.197	4.988	4.793	4.611	4.439	12
13	6.750	6.424	6.122	5.842	5.583	5.342	5.118	4.910	4.715	4.533	13
14	6.982	6.628	6.302	6.002	5.724	5.468	5.229	5.008	4.802	4.611	14
15	7.191	6.811	6.462	6.142	5.847	5.575	5.324	5.092	4.876	4.675	15

Normal distribution

This table gives the area under the normal curve between the mean and a point which is Z standard deviations above the mean. The corresponding area for deviations below the mean can be found by symmetry.

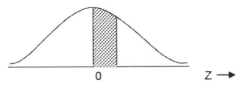

$Z = \dfrac{(x - \mu)}{\sigma}$	0.00	0.01	0.02	0.03	0.04	0.05	0.06	0.07	0.08	0.09
0.0	.0000	.0040	.0080	.0120	.0159	.0199	.0239	.0279	.0319	.0359
0.1	.0398	.0438	.0478	.0517	.0557	.0596	.0636	.0675	.0714	.0753
0.2	.0793	.0832	.0871	.0910	.0948	.0987	.1026	.1064	.1103	.1141
0.3	.1179	.1217	.1255	.1293	.1331	.1368	.1406	.1443	.1408	.1517
0.4	.1554	.1591	.1628	.1664	.1700	.1736	.1772	.1808	.1844	.1879
0.5	.1915	.1950	.1985	.2019	.2054	.2088	.2123	.2157	.2190	.2224
0.6	.2257	.2291	.2324	.2357	.2389	.2422	.2454	.2486	.2518	.2549
0.7	.2580	.2611	.2642	.2673	.2704	.2734	.2764	.2794	.2823	.2852
0.8	.2881	.2910	.2939	.2967	.2995	.3023	.3051	.3078	.3106	.3133
0.9	.3159	.3186	.3212	.3238	.3264	.3289	.3315	.3340	.3365	.3389
1.0	.3413	.3438	.3461	.3485	.3508	.3531	.3554	.3577	.3599	.3621
1.1	.3643	.3665	.3686	.3708	.3729	.3749	.3770	.3790	.3810	.3830
1.2	.3849	.3869	.3888	.3907	.3925	.3944	.3962	.3980	.3997	.4015
1.3	.4032	.4049	.4066	.4082	4099	.4115	.4131	.4147	.4162	.4177
1.4	.4192	.4207	.4222	.4236	.4251	.4265	.4279	.4292	.4306	.4319
1.5	.4332	.4345	.4357	.4370	.4382	.4394	.4406	.4418	.4430	.4441
1.6	.4452	.4463	.4474	.4485	.4495	.4505	.4515	.4525	.4535	.4545
1.7	.4554	.4564	.4573	.4582	.4591	.4599	.4608	.4616	.4625	.4633
1.8	.4641	.4649	.4656	.4664	.4671	.4678	.4686	.4693	.4699	.4706
1.9	.4713	.4719	.4726	.4732	.4738	.4744	.4750	.4756	.4762	.4767
2.0	.4772	.4778	.4783	.4788	.4793	.4798	.4803	.4808	.4812	.4817
2.1	.4821	.4826	.4830	.4834	.4838	.4842	.4846	.4850	.4854	.4857
2.2	.4861	.4865	.4868	.4871	.4875	.4878	.4881	.4884	.4887	.4890
2.3	.4893	.4896	.4898	.4901	.4904	.4906	.4909	.4911	.4913	.4916
2.4	.4918	.4920	.4922	.4925	.4927	.4929	.4931	.4932	.4934	.4936
2.5	.4938	.4940	.4941	.4943	.4945	.4946	.4948	.4949	.4951	.4952
2.6	.4953	.4955	.4956	.4957	.4959	.4960	.4961	.4962	4963	.4964
2.7	.4965	.4966	.4967	.4968	.4969	.4970	.4971	.4972	.4973	.4974
2.8	.4974	.4975	.4976	.4977	.4977	.4978	.4979	.4980	.4980	.4981
2.9	.4981	.4982	.4983	.4983	.4984	.4984	.4985	.4985	.4986	.4986
3.0	.49865	.4987	.4987	.4988	.4988	.4989	.4989	.4989	.4990	.4990
3.1	.49903	.4991	.4991	.4991	.4992	.4992	.4992	.4992	.4993	.4993
3.2	.49931	.4993	.4994	.4994	.4994	.4994	.4994	.4995	.4995	.4995
3.3	.49952	.4995	.4995	.4996	.4996	.4996	.4996	.4996	.4996	.4997
3.4	.49966	.4997	.4997	.4997	.4997	.4997	.4997	.4997	.4997	.4998
3.5	.49977									

Applied Knowledge
Management Accounting (MA)

CHAPTER 1

The nature and purpose of cost and management accounting

Contents
1 Accounting for management
2 Cost and management accounting versus financial accounting
3 Sources of data and information
4 Big data and data analytics
5 Sampling

> **Accounting for management**
>
> - Introduction to cost and management accounting
> - Data and information
> - Types of data
> - Types of analysis
> - Attributes of good information
> - Planning, decision-making and control
> - Strategic, tactical and operational planning

1 Accounting for management

1.1 Introduction to cost and management accounting

Accounting has several purposes, but the main purposes might be stated as follows:

- To provide a record of the financial value of business transactions, and in doing so to establish financial controls and reduce the risks of fraud
- To assist with the management of the financial affairs of an entity
- To provide information – mainly information of a financial nature.

Accounting information is provided for:

- Management, so that managers have the information they need to run the company
- Other users of information, many of them outside the entity. For example, a company produces accounting information for its shareholders in the form of financial statements, and financial statements are also used by tax authorities, investors, trade union representatives and others.

Cost and management accounting is concerned with the provision of information, mainly of a financial nature, for management. A management accounting system is a management information system.

1.2 Data and information

The terms 'data' and 'information' are often used as if they have the same meaning. However, there is a difference between data and information.

- **Data** consists of unprocessed facts and statistics. Data is collected and processed to produce information. Data has no meaning until it has been processed into information.
- **Information** has a meaning and a purpose. It is produced from 'data'. It is processed data that has relevance to a particular useful purpose.

Data may be collected from many different sources, both inside and outside an organisation.

A cost accounting system records data about the costs of operations and activities within the entity. The sources of cost accounting data within an organisation include invoices, receipts, inventory records and time sheets. Many of the documents from which cost data is captured are internally-generated documents, such as time sheets and material requisition notes.

Data is analysed and processed to produce management information, often in the form of:

- routine reports, or
- specially-prepared reports, or
- answers to 'one-off' enquiries that are input to a computer system.

Information produced from cost accounting data is management accounting information. Management accounting systems also obtain information from other sources, including external sources, but the cost accounting system is a major source of management accounting information.

1.3 Types of data

Data consists of a number of observations (measurements) each recording a value or quality of a particular variable.

Categorical data (qualitative data)

Categorical data (qualitative data) is a type of data that allows items/subjects under investigation to be identified into different categories or groups. The categorisation is based on characteristics of items/subjects under investigation and each item can only be identified as belonging to a single category. In other words, each category is mutually exclusive.

Examples of categorical data include gender, quality, colour, model type (e.g. for types of car) etc.

Categorical data can be further classified as:

- **Nominal data:** This refers to data based on a name, label or other such identifier. For example, name (business or person), type of business, gender etc.
- **Ordinal data:** This refers to data that has been ranked in some way. For example, a customer might be asked to give a hotel rating of 1 (poor) to 5 (excellent).

Numerical data (quantitative data)

This is data that is expressed in terms of numbers (as the name suggests) and results from a measurement of some kind. It is data that can only be collected as numbers.

There are two different types of numerical variables:

- discrete variables: and
- continuous variables

Discrete variables are those that can only take on certain and separate values. The measurement of such variables increases in jumps with gaps between possible values. Examples include:

- number of attendees to a web broadcast increases by one person at a time. A fraction of a person cannot attend the broadcast and so cannot be part of the data;
- number of defects in a production batch; or
- number of units produced in a period.

Continuous variables can take any value within a given range. Continuous variables can be measured with any chosen degree of accuracy and not just as discrete numbers. Examples include:

- physical dimensions (height and weight);
- temperature

1.4 Types of analysis

Descriptive analysis

Descriptive analysis of data helps describe or summarise it in a meaningful way (for example, to show patterns that might exist in the data).

Examples of descriptive analysis include:

- The calculation of measures of central tendency (e.g. arithmetic mean) and measures of spread (e.g. the standard deviation) of a series of values. (This is covered in more detail in a later chapter).
- The representation of data on a graph or as a diagram.

Inferential analysis

Descriptive analysis describes data (for example, a chart or graph) but inferential statistics allows predictions (inferences) to be made from that data.

Inferential analysis allows data from samples to be used to make generalisations about a population from which the sample has been taken.

Descriptive analysis is often needed before inferential analysis can be carried out.

An example of inferential analysis is time series analysis (covered in detail in a later chapter) which might show how sales have grown over a defined period and how they varied in each quarter during that period. This can be represented as a table or diagram (descriptive analysis) but can be used to extrapolate forward to predict sales in future quarters (inferential analysis).

1.5 Attributes of good information

Information is only useful to managers if it possesses certain qualities or attributes.

- **Understandable**. Information should be understandable to the individuals who use it. For accountants, this often means having to make sure that the figures provided to managers are set out clearly and are properly explained.

- **Purpose and relevance**. Information should have a purpose and should be needed by management for a particular reason. Unless information has a purpose it has no value at all and it makes no sense to provide it. The information provided should also be relevant to this purpose.

- **Reliable**. Management information must be reliable. This means that the user of the information can rely on the information to make a decision, and should not be worried about whether the information is correct. Information does not have to be 100% accurate. In many cases, information might be provided in the form of an estimate or forecast. However, information should be as accurate or reliable as it needs to be for its purpose. It might also need to be up-to-date.

- **Sufficiently complete**. Information should be as complete as it needs to be. There should be no important omissions. However, information in management reports should not be excessive, because important information may be hidden in the unimportant information, and it will take managers too long to read and understand.

- **Timeliness**. Information must be timely. This means that it must be made available to managers in time to use it for making a decision. If information is provided too late for its purpose, it has no value. With the widespread computerisation of accounting systems, including cost accounting systems, it might be appropriate for up-to-date management accounting information to be available on line and on demand whenever it is needed.

- **Comparability**. In accounting it is often useful to make comparisons, such as comparisons of current year results with previous years, or comparisons of actual results with planned results. To make comparisons possible, information should be prepared on the same basis, using the same methods and the same 'rules'.

- **Communicated to the right person**. Management information should be communicated to the proper person. This is the person with the authority to make a decision on the basis of the information received and who needs the information to make the decision.

- **Its value must exceed its cost**. Management information has a value. If information has no value (= no purpose) there is no point in having it. The value of information comes from improving the quality of management decisions. However providing information involves some expense. More information is worth having only if it helps to improve management decisions, and the benefits from those decisions exceed the cost of providing the additional information. This is why many small business entities do not have a formal cost accounting system – the manager is familiar with the costs and revenues of the business and the cost of operating a cost accounting system might not be worth the expense.

1.6 Planning, decision-making and control

The purpose of management information is to assist management in making decisions. Management decisions can be grouped into three broad categories:

- Planning decisions
- Control decisions
- 'One-off' decisions.

Planning

Planning involves the following:

- setting the objectives for the organisation
- making plans for achieving those objectives.

The planning process is a formal process and the end-result is a formal plan, authorised at an appropriate level in the management hierarchy. Formal plans include long-term business plans, budgets, sales plans, weekly production schedules, capital expenditure plans and so on.

Information is needed in order to make sensible plans – for example in order to prepare an annual budget, it is necessary to provide information about expected sales prices, sales quantities and costs, in the form of forecasts or estimates.

Control

Control of the performance of an organisation is an important management task. Control involves the following:

- monitoring actual performance, and comparing actual performance with the objective or plan
- taking control action where appropriate
- evaluating actual performance.

When operations appear to be getting out of control, management should be alerted so that suitable measures can be taken to deal with the problem. Control information might be provided in the form of routine performance reports or as special warnings or alerts when something unusual has occurred.

'One-off' decision making

Decisions taken by managers include planning decisions and control decisions. In addition, managers might need to make 'one-off' decisions, outside the formal planning and control systems. Management accounting information can be provided to help a manager decide what to do in any situation where a decision is needed.

1.7 Strategic, tactical and operational planning

Managers carry out their responsibilities at different levels in the hierarchy of an organisation, and decisions are made at all levels of management. These may be planning decisions, control decisions or 'one-off' decisions. Decision-making can be categorised into three levels: these different categories are probably most easily understood in relation to planning decisions.

- **Strategic planning.** Strategic planning involves setting overall objectives for the organisation and developing broad plans, mostly over a fairly long-term, about how the objectives should be achieved. An example of a strategic plan is a five-year business plan. Strategic planning is the responsibility of senior management, who plan the strategic direction that the entity should be taking. To make long-term plans, managers need information. Much of this information is not financial in nature, and much of it comes from external sources (from sources outside the organisation). However some accounting and financial information is needed for strategic planning purposes, and 'strategic management accounting' is a term for the provision of information for strategic planning purposes.

- **Tactical planning.** Tactical planning involves developing shorter-term plans to implement longer-term strategic plans. They have a shorter time frame than strategic plans, and many tactical plans cover a period of six months or one year. They might also be sub-divided into shorter control periods, such as monthly periods, for the purpose of routine control reporting. They are also more detailed than strategic plans. In a large organisation, tactical planning involves managers below the most senior level ('middle management'), although tactical plans might require senior management approval. Much of the information for tactical planning comes from sources within the organisation, such as the cost accounting system, and much of it is financial in nature. An example of a tactical plan is an annual budget.

- **Operational planning.** Operational planning is planning the operational activities of an entity in detail. Operational plans include production schedules, work schedules, machine utilisation plans, maintenance schedules, delivery schedules and so on. They are short-term plans such as daily or weekly operating schedules and most are not financial in nature. Operational planning should involve junior management and supervisors, although they might need the approval of middle management.

Management accounting information is provided mainly for strategic planning and tactical planning purposes, and for senior or middle management. However, the use of management accounting for tactical planning and control is probably more widespread than strategic management accounting.

The techniques described in later chapters of this study text relate mainly to the provision of information for planning and control at the tactical level.

> **Cost and management accounting versus financial accounting**
>
> - Purpose and role of cost and management accounting
> - Comparison of financial accounting and cost and management accounting
> - Limitations of management accounting information in providing guidance for supporting decision making

2 Cost and management accounting versus financial accounting

2.1 Purpose and role of cost and management accounting

Cost accounting

Cost accounting is concerned with gathering data about the costs of products or services and the cost of activities. There may be a formal costing system in which data about operational activities is recorded in a 'double entry' system of cost accounts in a 'cost ledger'. The cost accounting data is captured, stored and subsequently analysed to provide management information about costs.

Information provided by cost accounting systems is financial in nature, and analysed in detail. It may be forward-looking, and used to provide information about expected costs and profits in the future. More usually, cost accounting information is historical in nature, and provides information about the actual costs of items and activities that have been incurred.

Management accounting

Management accounting is concerned with providing information to management about costs, sales revenue and profits, so that managers are able to make well-informed decisions. Management accounting information is often prepared from an analysis of cost accounting data, although cost estimates and revenue estimates may be obtained from sources other than the cost accounting system.

The purpose of management accounting is to provide detailed financial information to management, so that they can **plan and control** the activities or operations for which they are responsible. Management accounting information is also provided to help managers make other decisions. In other words, management accounting provides management information to assist with planning, control and 'one-off' decisions.

Management control systems

A management accounting system may be described as a management control system. This is an information system, largely at a **tactical information** level for middle management that helps managers to plan and control the activities of the organisation.

A management control system can be described as a system for:

- identifying the objectives of the organisation: these may be long-term objectives, or may be budget objectives for the next financial year
- setting quantified targets for achieving those objectives
- measuring actual results throughout the planning period, and comparing actual performance with the objectives and targets
- taking control action where necessary when actual results are below target, or taking control action where appropriate to sustain performance when this is better than target.

An example of a management control system is budgeting with standard costs, and measuring actual performance against the standard costs using monthly variance analysis reports.

2.2 Comparison of financial accounting and cost and management accounting

Financial accounting

A financial accounting system is used to record the financial transactions of the entity, such as transactions relating to revenue, expenses, assets and liabilities. The accounting system provides a record of the assets that the company owns, and what it owes. It also provides a record of the income that the entity has earned, and the expenditures it has incurred.

The financial accounting system provides the data that is used to prepare the financial statements of the entity at the end of each financial year (the income statement, balance sheet, cash flow statement, and so on).

The main purpose of the financial statements of companies is to inform the company's shareholders (owners) about the financial performance and financial position of the company. They are also used as a basis for preparing the 'tax accounts' and calculating the tax that the company should pay on its profits. Managers might use the information in the financial statements, but the main purpose of financial reporting is for '**external purposes**' rather than to provide management information.

Financial statements are produced at the end of the financial year. Management need information much more regularly, throughout the year. They also need much more detailed information than is provided by a company's financial statements. They often need forward-looking forecasts, rather than reports of historical performance and what has happened in the past.

There is a statutory requirement for companies to produce annual financial statements, and other business entities need to produce financial statements for the purpose of making tax returns to the tax authorities.

Managers might find financial statements useful, but the main users of the financial statements of a company should be its shareholders. Other external users, such as potential investors, employees, trade unions and banks (lenders to the business) might also use the financial statements of a company to obtain information.

Cost and management accounting

Whereas financial statements from the financial accounting system are intended mainly for external users of financial information, management accounting information (obtained from the cost accounting system) is prepared specifically for internal use by management.

An entity might have a cost accounting system as well as a financial accounting system, so that it has two separate accounting systems in operation. A cost accounting system records the costs and revenues for individual jobs, processes, activities and products or services.

- Like the financial accounting system, a cost accounting system is based on a double entry system of debits and credits.

- However, the accounts in a cost accounting system are different from the accounts in the financial accounting systems. This is because the two accounting systems have different purposes, and so record financial transactions in different ways.

There is no legal requirement for a cost accounting system. Business entities choose to have a cost accounting system, and will only do so if the perceived benefits of the system justify the cost of operating it.

(In business entities where there is no formal cost accounting system, managers still need management accounting information to run their business. Some management accounting information might be extracted from the financial accounting system, but in much less detail than a cost accounting system would provide).

A comparison of financial and cost accounting systems of companies is summarised in the table below:

Financial accounting system	Cost accounting system
Statutory requirement	Not a statutory requirement
Used to prepare financial statements for shareholders and other external users	Used to prepare information for management (internal use only)
Might also provide some information for management	
Records revenues, expenditure, assets and liabilities	Records costs of activities and used to provide detailed information about costs, revenues and profits for specific products, operations and activities
Used mainly to provide a historical record of performance and financial position	Provides historical information, but also used extensively for forecasting (forward-looking)

2.3 Limitations of management accounting information in providing guidance for supporting decision making

Management need complete, relevant and reliable information in order to make decisions. Management accounting may not satisfy these requirements.

Management accounting is based on information from the cost accounting and financial accounting systems. Such information is historic in nature and may not be a reliable indicator of what will happen in the future.

A company may be making a decision outside of its previous experience. Management accounting will provide information about circumstances experienced in the past.

Management accounting cannot provide all information necessary to make a decision. For example, it does not provide information about future demand for a product.

Management accounting provides information but does not make decisions. People make decisions and they must establish decision criteria (i.e. decide on the basis for making a decision).

Note that management information systems evolve to meet the information needs of the company. Companies can set up management information systems to meet many of the shortcomings mentioned above. For example, a company could commission research about future demand for a product.

> **Sources of data and information**
>
> - Three main data sources
> - Information
> - Limitations of external information
> - Impact of the general economic environment on costs and revenues

3 Sources of data and information

3.1 Three main data sources

Machine/sensor data

Machine data is digital information collected or created by machines without human intervention. For example, machine data is automatically generated by the activity of computers, mobile phones, embedded systems and other networked devices.

Machine data input can be used to generate further information and to make decisions, for example:

- As input to an algorithm that calculates risk based on market data
- As inputs to approve or reject an insurance application

Sensor data is a category of machine data. Sensor data is the output of a device that detects and responds to some type of input from the physical environment. The output may be used to provide information or input to another system or to guide a process. For example:

- Sensors may provide information about the function of different aspects of automated production systems allowing direction or adjustment of the operation of parts of that system.
- Sensors on a power grid can provide real time data about grid conditions, allowing for correction to prevent outages, increase capacity etc.

Transactional data

Transactional data is derived as a result of transactions. A transaction describes an internal or external event which takes place as an organisation conducts business.

Typical transactions include:

- Financial transactions (e.g. sales, purchases, payments etc.)
- Operational transactions (e.g. production records, labour timesheets etc.) and
- Logistical transaction (e.g. records of receipts and deliveries of goods etc.).

Transactional data tends to become less relevant with time. For example, data about production costs in previous periods is less useful than data relating to the current period.

Human/social data

Human data is data about individuals and their relationships with other people, businesses, organisations and society as a whole.

Human beings live in a connected world. Human data describes their interaction with the world and its various components.

Human data comprises :

- Personal data. Data specific to an individual and which can be collected from uses of smart phone apps, computer usage, social media use, completion of online surveys, online purchasing history etc.

- Shared data. Data created by a group to which an individual belongs, for example, a household. The increased use of smart devices in the home (e.g. smart meters, smart speakers, voice assistants etc.) allow companies to collect data that sheds insight into patterns of behaviour and preferences.

- Open data. This is data about groups that individuals belong to. This might include data about age group, socio economic group (which could be inferred from a person's address), subscriptions, memberships etc.

- Processed data. This is data derived from information that has already been processed about individuals. A good example of this is a person's credit score.

Social data is about how people interact in social contexts. Social data is information that social media users publicly share, for example, tweets from Twitter, posts on Facebook etc.

It includes data such as the user's location, language, biographical data and shared links. It can be used by businesses to focus marketing and advertising and by political parties to try to win votes.

3.2 Information

Managers need information about customers, competitors and other elements in their business environment. Information might be obtained from internal and external sources. The challenge is to capture and use information that is relevant and reliable.

Sources of internal information

Accounting records are a key source of information. They summarise the historical transactions of the business and this can be used as a basis for predicting the future.

A company will also have records of operational issues like production volumes, material usage, labour usage, sales volumes, sales returns and so on.

Many businesses invest in sophisticated data collection techniques so that they can better understand their business. Supermarkets for instance are able to track the buying patterns of individual customers so that they can be targeted with offers that might be attractive to them.

External information

Examples of the external information needed by companies are set out below:

Information area	Examples of information needed
Customers	What are the needs and expectations of customers in the market?
	Are these needs and expectations changing?
	What is the potential for our products or services to meet these needs, or to meet them better?
Competitors	Who are they?
	What are they doing?
	Can we copy some of their ideas?
	How large are they, and what is their market share?
	How profitable are they?
	What is their pricing policy?
Legal environment	What are the regulations and laws that must be complied with?
Suppliers	What suppliers are there for key products or services?
	What is the quality of their products or services?
	What is the potential of new suppliers?
	What is the financial viability of each supplier?
Political/ environmental issues	Are there any relevant political developments or developments relating to environmental regulation or environmental conditions?
Economic/ financial environment	What is happening to interest rates?
	What is happening to exchange rates?
	What is happening in other financial markets?
	What is the predicted state of the economy

Sources of external information

Sources of external information, some accessible through the Internet, include:

- market research
- supplier price lists and brochures
- trade journals
- newspapers and other media
- government reports and statistics
- reports published by other organisations, such as trade bodies
- general reports in the mass media
- word of mouth communication from suppliers and customers

3.3 Limitations of external information

It is important to recognise the limitations of external information.

- It might not be accurate, and it might be difficult to assess how accurate it is.
- It might be incomplete.
- It might provide either too much or not enough detail.
- It might be difficult to obtain information in the form that is ideally required.
- It might not always be available when required.
- It might be difficult to find.

3.4 Impact of the general economic environment on costs and revenues

The revenue and costs of a business might be affected by the general economic environment.

When an economy is strong, employment levels and consumer confidence are high. Consumers have cash to spend and are willing to do so. Businesses that supply consumers do well and are able to earn in strong revenue streams and generate good profitability. These businesses have money to spend and their suppliers also experience good times.

Conversely, when an economy is weak, unemployment is high and consumer confidence is low. There is less disposable income in the economy and consumers might not be willing to spend what they have. Businesses that supply consumers experience trading conditions resulting in weak revenue streams. These businesses in turn do not have money to spend and that in turn impacts the revenue of their suppliers.

This is of course a great simplification. The actual impact of economic conditions depends on the type of business.

- Some businesses are not really affected by a strengthening or weakening economy. For example, people always need bread. When an economy moves into recession sales of bread do not fall. However, sales of bread do not rise when an economy is booming.
- Other businesses are very sensitive to the strengthening or weakening of the economy. For example, car sales fall as an economy moves into recession but increase as an economy strengthens.

Impact of macroeconomic variables

The impact of macro-economic variables should also be considered.

Interest rates:

High interest rates discourage capital investment by businesses. This reduces the demand for capital goods in the economy.

High interest decreases disposable income of consumers. This reduces demand in the economy causing business revenues to fall.

High interest rates encourage saving. This reduces demand in the economy causing business revenues to fall.

Inflation rates

Understanding the impact of inflation can be quite tricky. An inflation rate announced by a government is an average rate. The inflation rate will be higher for some goods and lower for others.

High inflation rates

High inflation increases costs. Workers may demand higher wages and this in turn increases the costs of a business. A business may or may not be able to increase the prices of the goods they sell. This depends on the type of business and the degree of competition faced.

Exchange rates

If local currency strengthens compared to a foreign currency, goods supplied from overseas become cheaper. This reduces costs of importers. However, goods produced at home become more expensive for foreign customers. This might adversely affect revenues of exporters.

If local currency weakens compared to a foreign currency, goods supplied from overseas become more expensive thus increasing costs of importers. However, goods produced at home become cheaper for foreign customers. This might have a favourable effect on revenues of exporters.

Government policy

Governments pursue macroeconomic objectives for example, controlling inflation, achieving high employment, achieving strong growth etc.

Government policies affect the general economic environment. For example, a government might decide that inflation is too high. The government might increase interest rates to take demand out of the economy and lower inflation. An increase in interest rates makes saving more attractive. Overseas investors might move capital into the country thus increasing the demand for local currency. This strengthens the exchange rate. (Note that this might have an undesired inflationary effect because it makes imports cheaper).

Closing comments

The above example is given to show that the interactions in the economy can be quite complex. This is not an economics exam so do not worry about this. You will only be expected to identify the impact that a simple change in the economic environment might have on costs and revenues.

Big data and data analytics
■ Big data
■ Characteristics of big data
■ Types of of big data
■ Using big data
■ Data analytics

4 Big data and data analytics

4.1 Big data

> **Definition: Big Data**
>
> 'Big Data' is the term used to describe a huge volume of both structured and unstructured data that is so large it is difficult to process using traditional database and software techniques.
>
> McKinsey defines big data as datasets whose size is beyond the ability of typical database software tools to capture, store, manage and analyse.

The definition of big data is relative rather than absolute. This means that the term 'big data' is dynamic and will remain relevant and applicable as improvements continue to be made with processing power, data accessibility and storage capacity.

Big data represents datasets so large that commonly used software and databases are unable to create, manipulate and manage it. Big data is currently measured in petabytes (1,024 terabytes) or exabytes (1,024 petabytes). An example of big data might be the billions (or trillions) of records relating to millions of people from different sources including Web sales, social media and mobile data

4.2 Characteristics of big data

Doug Laney (an American IT analyst) described big data as having the following characteristics (the 3 Vs):

- **Volume:** There is a large volume of data available (more than might be handled by a single computer). For example, Google holds huge amounts of data on the search history of customers and the content of web pages viewed.

- **Velocity:** This refers to the speed at which data becomes available to an organisation. Data streams in at an unprecedented speed and must be dealt with in a timely manner. Data can be collected from a variety of sources including a business's own transactions (e.g. retailer customer loyalty programmes allow retailers to monitor spending patterns of customers), social media, websites etc.

- **Variety:** Data comes in all types of formats – from structured, numeric data in traditional databases to unstructured text documents, email etc..

Some commentators refer to an additional two V's beyond Laney's original three V's. These are:

- **Veracity:** Data needs to be correct and error-free in order to be reliable and relevant.
- **Value:** The huge volume of data is capable of creating huge value for organisations, societies and consumers. Note that value lies in the analysis of big data and converting data into useable information rather than the underlying data itself.

4.3 Types of big data

Big data can be structured, unstructured or semi-structured data:

- **Structured data** describes traditional data that can be processed, stored, and retrieved in a fixed format. It refers to highly organised information that can be easily stored and accessed from a database by simple search engine algorithms. Records of accounting transactions provide a good example of structured data.

- **Unstructured data** describes data that takes many different forms and is generated from many different sources such as industrial sensors, search engines and social media. It can be difficult and time-consuming to process and analyse unstructured data. For example, the content of emails can contain a lot of information but this is in an unstructured form. It would be difficult to search the content of all emails sent and received by employees of a business.

- **Semi-structured data** has features in common with both of the above. It refers to data that contains vital information or tags that segregate individual elements within the data although it has not been classified under a particular database. For example, although email content can be said to be unstructured, emails do have identifying tags (e.g. time, date, title) which allow for certain types of searches.

4.4 Using big data

Big data, when captured, formatted, manipulated, stored and analysed, can help a company to gain useful insight to increase revenues, get or retain customers and improve operations. Analysis of datasets can also help identify new correlations and spot business trends for example to help combat crime and prevent disease.

This can lead to benefits in:

- planning;
- costing;
- decision making; and
- performance management.

Companies who are well placed to benefit from the strategic benefits of big data in particular include those companies positioned in the middle of large information flows where data about products and services, buyers and suppliers, and consumer preferences and intent can be captured and analysed. Such companies might be those which enable global supply chains, those that process millions of transactions, and those that provide platforms for consumer digital experiences.

The use of big data is becoming a key-way for leading companies to outperform their peers. Forward-thinking leaders are able to aggressively build their organisations' big data capabilities, which whilst taking time and costing money, enable them to develop a superior capacity to take advantage of big data and develop competitive advantage over the long term.

4.5 Data analytics

Data analytics is a broad term that encompasses many diverse types of data analysis. Any type of information can be subjected to data analytics techniques to get insight that can be used to improve operations and processes.

The simple existence of big data does not provide value. It must be analysed into useful information. As such it represents a further stage in the evolution of the traditional management accounting function from that of a score keeper to that of a strategic business partner.

Big data has the potential to increase corporate value but first it must be analysed to produce useful insights and those insights must be acted upon. Data analytics is the process of examining data to draw conclusions about the information they contain. Increasingly this involves the use of specialised systems and software. Data analytics technologies and techniques are widely used in commercial industries to enable organizations to make more-informed business decisions.

Many of the techniques and processes of data analytics have been automated into mechanical processes and algorithms that produce information to serve specific needs.

Data analytics techniques can reveal trends and metrics that would otherwise be hidden in the huge volume of information. This information can then be used to optimise processes to increase the overall efficiency of a business or system.

The implementation of data analytics it a business model can lead to cost reductions through the identification of more efficient business methods. Also, it can be used to make better business decisions and help analyse customer trends etc. which could lead to new, improved products and services

> **Sampling**
>
> - Introduction
> - Random sampling
> - Systematic sampling
> - Stratified sampling
> - Other sampling methods

5 Sampling

5.1 Introduction

A population can be defined as including all people or items with a characteristic that a researcher wishes to understand. This means that the term "population" means every single member of a particular group. This could include all kinds of things, for example the residents of Mumbai, all Toyotas sold in the EU or units of production from a specific machine.

In gathering information about a population it is rarely possible or desirable to test (measure an attribute of) each member of that population. Reasons for this include:

- cost
- the population might be dynamic (i.e. individuals making up the population may change over time).
- testing might destroy the item (for example testing a bullet by firing it).

Often a researcher will select a sample of a population and test that with the view to extrapolating the results to the population as a whole for the purposes of making predictions based on statistical inference.

Example

Suppose a clothing retailer wanted to sell garments to male adults in the United Kingdom.

It would not be practical to measure the waist size of all men in the UK. A sample would be selected and the waist size of each member of the sample would be measured. This could then be used as a basis of sizes ordered from the manufacturer for sale throughout the UK.

Note that all efforts should be taken to make sure that the sample fairly represents the population at large.

A clothing manufacturer needs to know about the size of people in its target market.

Example

Returning to the previous example:

Selecting a sample of men based entirely on students at a university would not result in a sample that was representative of the population as a whole. This sample would be from a narrow age group which, by and large would be from the younger and fitter part of the population and would tend to have smaller waist sizes than the population as a whole. If the retailer based its plans on such a sample it would be unable to sell to other age groups.

The three main advantages of sampling are:

- the cost is lower,
- data collection is faster, and
- since the data set is smaller it is possible to ensure homogeneity and to improve the accuracy and quality of the data.

Sampling frame

The sampling frame is a list of all the members of the population used as a basis for sampling. The frame in effect defines the population.

Suppose that an energy company wished to obtain information fuel consumption of cars in the UK. The population would be all cars in the UK. However this is not specific enough for the researcher to draw a sample. The researcher would need a list of those cars. Such a list might be all cars registered with the licensing authority. This then gives a specific population from which a sample can be drawn.

There are different methods by which a sample might be extracted. These include:

- random sampling;
- systematic sampling;
- stratified sampling;
- multi-stage sampling;
- cluster sampling; and
- quota sampling

The objective of any of these techniques is to extract a sample which is representative of the population. This sample is then tested and the results treated as representing the full population.

5.2 Random sampling

A random sample is one where every member of the population has an equal chance of being selected as a member of the sample. A random sample is a bias free sample.

Possible problems with random sampling:

- It can be cumbersome when sampling from an unusually large target population
- It can be prone to sampling error because the randomness of the selection may result in a sample that doesn't reflect the makeup of the population

- It is not suitable for investigators who are interested in issues related to subgroups of a population.

5.3 Systematic sampling

Systematic sampling relies on arranging the target population according to some ordering scheme and then selecting elements at regular intervals through that ordered list. The first item is selected at random and then every n^{th} member of the population is selected. The value for n is the population size divided by the sample size.

A simple example would be to select every 10th name from the telephone directory (an 'every 10th' sample, also referred to as 'sampling with a skip of 10').

One problem with systematic sampling is that it is vulnerable to periodicities in the list and this might result in the sample being unrepresentative of the overall population.

For example suppose a researcher is interested in household income. There might be a street where the odd-numbered houses are all on the north (expensive) side of the road, and the even-numbered houses are all on the south (cheap) side. If the sample started with say number 7 and then every 10th house all houses sampled would be from the expensive side of the street and the data collected would not give a fair reflection of the household incomes of the street.

5.4 Stratified sampling

Where the population is split into relevant strata, the sample may also be split into strata in proportion to the population. Within each stratum, the sample is selected using random sampling methods.

Example

Suppose a clothing retailer wanted to sell garments to male and female adults in the United Kingdom.

As a minimum the population would be split (stratified) into male and female for sampling purposes.

The population could be further stratified by age groups.

Advantages of stratified sampling:

- dividing the population into distinct, independent strata can enable researchers to draw inferences about specific subgroups that may be lost in a random sample.

- stratification can lead to more efficient statistical estimates (provided that strata are selected based upon relevance to the criterion in question, instead of availability of the samples).

- data might be more readily available for individual, pre-existing strata within a population than for the overall population;

- different sampling approaches can be applied to different strata, potentially enabling researchers to use the approach best suited (or most cost-effective) for each identified subgroup within the population.

Note that even if a stratified sampling approach does not lead to increased statistical efficiency, it will not result in less efficiency than simple random sampling, provided that each stratum is proportional to the group's size in the population.

One disadvantage is that the approach can increase the cost and complexity of sample selection, as well as leading to increased complexity of population estimates.

5.5 Other sampling methods

Multi-stage sampling

This technique involves taking random samples of preceding random samples. It is used in nationwide surveys to cut down on travelling.

The approach involves:

- dividing the country into a series of areas (for example counties in the UK);
- picking a random sample of these areas;
- within each of these, picking a random sample of towns;
- within each of these pick a random sample of people.

All people selected at the last stage are then surveyed (interviewed).

It is another way of saving time and money but still having an element of random selection. It is very useful when a complete list of all members of a population does not exist.

Cluster sampling

This is very similar to multi-stage sampling. Interviewers are sent into the areas to interview every person who fits a given definition (for example, mothers with children under 5).

Quota sampling

The population is first segmented into sub-groups (just like stratified sampling). An interviewer is then given a quota of people of different types to interview

For example, an interviewer may be told to sample 200 females and 300 males between the age of 45 and 60.

Practice multiple choice questions

1. Information is processed data.
   Is this statement TRUE or FALSE? *(1 mark)*

2. Which one of the following statements is correct?

   A Management accountants are responsible for planning, decision-making and control.

   B The purpose of a cost accounting system is to collect information about costs.

   C A management accounting system provides all the strategic and tactical information required by management.

   D Management accounting information should be timely and relevant, but does not need to be 100% accurate. *(2 marks)*

3. A company is preparing a budget for an advertising campaign that the sales director has just ordered, subject to approval of the costs. The campaign is expected to last for just over six months. The advertising budget is an example of:

   A Strategic planning

   B Tactical planning

   C Operational planning *(1 mark)*

You will find the answers to the practice multiple choice questions at the end of this book.

Applied Knowledge
Management Accounting (MA)

CHAPTER 2

Cost classification

Contents
1 Production and non-production costs
2 Direct and indirect costs
3 Investment, profit, revenue and cost centres

> **Production and non-production costs**
>
> - The need to know about costs
> - Materials costs, labour costs and expenses
> - Manufacturing: categorising costs as 'production' or 'non-production' costs
> - Elements of non-production costs
> - The importance of separating production and non-production costs

1 Production and non-production costs

1.1 The need to know about costs

An organisation needs to know:

- how much it costs to make the products that it produces, or
- how much it costs to provide its services to customers.

For an organisation that is not required to make a profit (a 'not-for-profit organisation', such as a government department or state-owned agency), it is important to know how much items cost, in order to:

- plan expenditure for the future, and
- compare actual costs with planned costs, and take action to control costs when these seem too high.

For an organisation that is required to make a profit, it is also important to know how much items cost, in order to:

- make sure that the product or service will be sold at a profit
- measure the actual profit that has been made, and
- in the case of some companies, such as manufacturing companies, value inventory at the end of each accounting period.

1.2 Materials costs, labour costs and expenses

Costs can be classified as material costs, labour costs or other expenses.

- **Material costs** are the costs of any material items purchased from suppliers, with the intention of using them or consuming them in the fairly short-term future. In a manufacturing company, material costs include the cost of the raw materials that go into producing the manufactured output. In an office, costs of materials consumed include the costs of stationery and replacement printer cartridges for the office laser printers.

- Material costs do **not** include the cost of longer-term assets (non-current assets) such as plant and equipment, or new trucks for the company's fleet of delivery vehicles.

- **Labour costs** are the remuneration costs of all employees employed and paid by the entity. This includes the wages and salaries of part-time workers and the costs of any bonuses, pension contributions and other items that are paid in addition to basic wages and salaries.

- **Other expenses** include the costs of any items that are not material costs or labour costs. They include the cost of services provided by external suppliers – the charges made by sub-contractors, charges for repairs by external contractors, rental costs, telephone costs, insurance costs, costs of energy (gas, electricity), travelling and subsistence expenses, and depreciation charges for non-current assets.

In a cost accounting system, all these items of cost must be recorded, and there needs to be an organised system for recording them. Cost items need to be grouped into categories of similar costs.

1.3 Manufacturing: categorising costs as 'production' or 'non-production' costs

In a cost accounting system for a manufacturing company, costs will be categorised as either:

- production costs (manufacturing costs) or
- non production costs (non-manufacturing costs).

Production costs, or manufacturing costs, are the costs incurred in manufacturing finished products, up to the time that the manufacture of the goods is completed, and the goods are either transferred to the finished goods inventory or delivered immediately to the customer.

Manufacturing costs include:

- the material cost of the raw materials and components, purchased from suppliers and used in the production of the goods that are manufactured
- the labour cost of all employees working for the manufacturing function, such as machine operators, supervisors, factory supervisors and the factory manager
- other expenses of the factory, such as rental costs for the factory building, energy costs and the cost of depreciation of factory machinery.

Non-production costs are any items of cost that are not manufacturing costs.

1.4 Elements of non-production costs

Non-production costs might be divided into:

- Administration costs
- Sales and distribution costs (also called marketing costs)
- Finance costs

Administration costs

Administration costs are the costs of providing administration services for the entity. They might be called 'head office costs' and usually include the costs of the human relations department and accounting department. They should include:

- the salary costs of all the staff working in the administration departments
- the costs of the office space used by these departments, such as office rental costs
- other administration expenses, such as the costs of heating and lighting for the administration offices, the depreciation costs of equipment used by the administration departments, fees paid to the company's solicitors for legal services, costs of office stationery and so on.

Selling and distribution costs (marketing costs)

Selling and distribution costs are the costs incurred in marketing and selling goods or services to customers, and the costs of delivering the goods to customers. The costs of after-sales services, such as customer support services, are usually included in these costs. Sales and distribution costs include:

- the wages and salary costs of all employees working in the selling and distribution departments, including sales commissions for sales representatives
- advertising costs and other marketing costs
- operating costs for delivery vehicles (for delivering finished goods to customers), such as fuel costs and vehicle repair costs
- other costs, including depreciation costs for the delivery vehicles.

Finance costs

Finance costs include costs that are involved in financing the organisation, for example, loan interest or bank overdraft charges.

Finance costs might be included in general administration costs. Alternatively, finance costs might be excluded from the cost accounting system because they are relevant to financial reporting (and the financial accounting system) but are not relevant to the measurement of costs.

Other non-production costs

Non-production costs are often categorised as administration, sales and distribution or finance costs because these categories of costs are also used in financial statements produced by a financial accounting system.

In a system of cost accounting, it is not essential to use these categories of non-production costs. Sometimes, additional categories of non-production costs might be identified separately, such as costs of research and development.

Separating costs into production, administration, sales and distribution and finance costs is a division of costs according to **function**. Function refers to the nature of the activity.

Example

Functional costs might be used in an income statement to report the profit or loss of a company during a financial period, as follows:

	$000	$000
Sales revenue		600
Manufacturing cost of sales		200
Gross profit		400
Administration costs	120	
Selling and distribution costs	230	
		350
Net profit (or net loss)		50

Separating costs into the costs for each function can provide useful information for management. Functional costs show managers what they are expected to spend on each function (budgeted costs) and how much they are actually spending.

Some costs might be partly manufacturing costs, partly administration costs and partly sales and distribution costs. For example:

- The salary of the managing director, because the managing director spends time on all aspects of the company's operations.

- Building rental costs, when the same building is used by more than one function. For example administration staff and sales staff might share the same offices.

When costs are shared between two or more functions, they are divided between the functions on a fair basis. For example, the salary of the managing director might be divided equally between manufacturing costs, administration costs and sales and distribution costs. Dividing shared costs on a fair basis is called **apportionment** of the cost.

Example

A company uses three categories of functional cost in its cost accounting system. These are manufacturing costs, administration costs and sales and distribution costs.

Identify the functional cost category for each of the following costs:

(1) Salary of the chief accountant

(2) Telephone charges

(3) Cost of office cleaning services

(4) Cost of warehouse staff

Answer

(1) **Chief accountant's salary.** Accounting department costs are an administration cost, and the salary of the chief accountant is treated in full as an administration costs.

(2) **Telephone charges.** These are usually treated as administration costs, unless the charges can be traced directly to telephones in the manufacturing department or the sales and distribution department. When charges can be traced directly to telephones in the manufacturing department, they should be recorded as manufacturing costs.

(3) **Office cleaning services.** These are usually treated as administration costs, unless the charges can be traced directly to offices used by the sales and distribution staff, or the production staff.

(4) **Warehouse staff.** These are manufacturing costs when the warehouse is used to store raw materials and components. They are sales and distribution costs when the warehouse is used to store finished goods. If the warehouse stores raw materials and finished goods, the wages costs should be apportioned between production costs and sales and distribution costs.

1.5 The importance of separating production and non-production costs

Inventory

In a manufacturing business, it is important to separate production costs from non-production costs. This is because at the end of any financial period, there will be some closing inventory of:

- finished goods that have been produced during the financial period but not yet sold (finished goods inventory), and
- partly-finished production, for which production is not yet compete (work-in-progress or WIP, sometimes called work-in-process).

The costs of finished goods inventory and partly-finished production (work-in-progress or WIP) consist of their production costs.

Total production costs during a period must therefore be divided or shared between:

- goods produced and sold in the period
- goods produced but not yet sold (finished goods)
- partly-produced goods in the period (work in progress).

Non-production costs must **never** be included in the cost of inventory.

Reporting profit in the income statement

An income statement reports the profit or loss earned during a financial period. Profit is the revenue for a financial period minus the costs for the period.

Manufacturing costs and non-production costs are shown separately in an income statement in both financial accounting and cost accounting because of inventory costs.

- There is a difference between the **manufacturing costs incurred** during a financial period and the **manufacturing cost of the goods sold** in the period.

- The difference between manufacturing costs incurred and the manufacturing cost of goods sold is the amount of the increase or decrease in inventory values between the beginning and end of the period.

Study the following example carefully. Illustrative numbers are included to demonstrate the calculations required.

	$	$
Opening inventory, work in progress		25,800
Manufacturing costs incurred in the period		156,000
		181,800
Less: Closing inventory, work in progress		(23,600)
Equals: Cost of goods manufactured in the period		158,200
Opening inventory, finished goods	4,000	
Closing inventory, finished goods	(8,500)	
		(4,500)
Equals: Production cost of goods sold in the period		153,700
Non-production costs		
Administration costs	62,000	
Selling and distribution costs	71,000	
		133,000
Total costs for the period in the income statement		286,700

The manufacturing costs incurred during the period were $156,000 but the manufacturing cost of goods sold was $153,700. The difference is attributable to changes in inventory levels between the beginning and the end of the period.

An income statement might be presented as follows, showing inventory changes. Although this is the format of an income statement for financial reporting (financial accounting) it might also be used in a system of cost accounting:

	$000	$000
Sales revenue		600
Opening inventory (raw materials, WIP, finished goods)	15	
Manufacturing costs in the period	210	
	225	
Closing inventory (raw materials, WIP, finished goods)	(25)	
Manufacturing cost of sales		(200)
Gross profit		400
Administration costs	120	
Selling and distribution costs	230	
		(350)
Net profit (or net loss)		50

If you have not yet studied financial accounting or financial reporting, the income statement might not yet be familiar to you. You need to learn how to calculate the cost of sales, gross profit and net profit for a financial period. Try to remember the significance of inventory in this computation, and the need to share costs of production between finished output and closing inventory.

> **Direct and indirect costs**
>
> - Direct costs
> - Indirect costs (overheads)
> - Full cost
> - Cost codes

2 Direct and indirect costs

2.1 Direct costs

In addition to classifying costs as production, administration or sales and distribution costs, costs may also be classified as:

- direct costs, or
- indirect costs, also called **overheads**.

This means that there are direct material costs, indirect material costs, direct labour costs and indirect labour costs, and direct and indirect expenses.

A **direct cost** is a cost that can be attributed **in its entirety** to the cost of an item that is being costed.

For example, in a manufacturing company that produces television sets, the direct cost of making a television consists of direct materials and direct labour costs, and possibly some direct expenses.

- The direct materials cost is the cost of the raw materials and components that have gone into making the television.
- The direct labour cost is the cost of the labour time of the employees who have been directly involved in making the television.

Direct materials

Direct materials are materials that are used directly in the manufacture of a product or the provision of a service. For example:

- the direct materials in the manufacture of a pair of shoes might include leather and rubber heels
- the direct materials in the manufacture of an office chair include wheels, a stand, a seat (with seat cushion), back rest, arm rests and fabric
- the direct materials in a restaurant meal are the major items of food (and drink).

Direct materials may consist of either or both:

- **raw materials**, such as glass, metals and chemicals
- **components** purchased from an external supplier: for example the direct materials of a car manufacturer include components purchased from other suppliers, such as windows, wheels and tyres.

Services might also incur some direct materials costs. For example, with catering and restaurant services the direct materials include the major items of food (and drink).

Direct labour

Direct labour is labour time that can be attributed directly to the item that is being costed. In costing a small item of manufactured output, direct labour time might be quite short, say just a few minutes per unit produced. In costing a large item such as the cost of operating a warehouse, direct labour costs include the labour cost of all employees who spend all their working time on warehouse activities.

As a general rule, labour costs are direct costs for work done by direct labour employees. Direct labour employees are employees whose time is spent directly on the item being costed. For example in a manufacturing company, direct labour employees will include:

- Machinists working in the machining department
- Assembly workers in the assembly department
- Workers in the spray painting shop.

The time of these workers can be attributed directly to the production of the finished output from the manufacturing process. On the other hand some workers in a factory are not direct labour, because they do not work directly in the production of the output from the factory: Inspection staff and supervisors are examples of labour that is not direct labour when costing the output from a factory.

Non-manufacturing businesses also have direct labour employees. These are the employees directly involved in producing the output of the business or providing a service that is sold to customers. For example:

- Bricklayers are direct labour employees of a house-building firm
- Waiters and chefs are direct labour employees of a restaurant
- Miners are direct labour workers in a mining company
- Teachers are direct labour employees in a school.

Direct expenses

Direct expenses are expenses that can be attributed in full to the item being costed. In manufacturing, direct expenses are not common for manufactured units of output, and direct costs normally consist of just direct materials and direct labour costs.

However the cost of large items might include direct expenses. For example, if a construction company is building a new office building, direct expenses of constructing the building will include the rental cost of any cranes or lifting equipment hired to assist with the work. Direct expenses would also include the fees of sub-contractors who are hired to carry out some of the building work. (Work done by external sub-contractors is an expense, not a direct labour cost).

Prime cost

The prime cost of an item is its total direct cost.

	$
Direct material cost	A
Direct labour cost	B
Direct expenses	C
Prime cost	A + B + C

2.2 Indirect costs (overheads)

An **indirect cost** or **overhead cost** is any cost that is not a direct cost, so that its entire cost cannot be attributed in full to the item that is being costed.

- Indirect labour is the cost of labour that cannot be attributed in full to the item being costed. The nature of indirect labour costs is explained in more detail later.

- Indirect expenses are expenses that cannot be attributed in full to an item that is being costed. For example, the rental costs for a factory and the costs of gas and electricity consumption for a factory cannot be attributed in full to any particular units of production. They are indirect production costs (production overheads).

In a manufacturing company, all costs of administration are usually treated as indirect costs (administration overheads) and all or most sales and distribution costs are also usually treated as sales and distribution overheads.

Indirect material costs

Indirect materials are any materials that are used or consumed that cannot be attributed in full to the item being costed. Indirect materials are treated as an overhead cost, and may be classified as production overheads, administration overheads or sales and distribution overheads.

Indirect materials in production include cleaning materials and any materials used by production departments or staff who are not engaged directly in making a product. In a restaurant, indirect materials will include the cost of salt, pepper and spices that are used by the kitchen staff for most meals, but which cannot be attributed to any specific meal.

Indirect production materials may also include some items of materials that are inexpensive and whose cost or value is immaterial. These may include nails, nuts and bolts, buttons and thread, and so on. The effort of measuring a cost for these materials is not worth the value of the cost information that would be produced; therefore these 'direct' materials are often treated as indirect materials.

Example

In which of the following types of company would fuel costs be treated as a direct material cost?

1. Manufacturing company
2. Road haulage (road transport) company
3. Construction company
4. Motorway fuel station

Solution

Manufacturing company. Fuel costs are an indirect expense. Fuel used in the company's vehicles is unlikely to be considered a material cost at all, but would be treated as an overhead expense.

Road haulage company. Since fuel is a major cost of operating a road haulage service, fuel costs are likely to be treated as a direct material cost of operations.

Construction company. Fuel costs are likely to be an indirect expense, for the same reasons that apply to a manufacturing company.

Motorway service station. This sells fuel to customers. In a retail operation, items sold to customers are direct costs of sale. The cost of the fuel sold is therefore a direct material cost (= a cost of sale).

Indirect labour costs

Indirect labour costs consist mainly of the cost of indirect labour employees. Indirect labour employees are individuals who do not work directly on the items that are produced or the services that are provided.

In a manufacturing environment, indirect labour employees include staff in the stores and materials handling department (for example, fork lift truck drivers), supervisors, and repairs and maintenance engineers.

All employees in administration departments and marketing departments (sales and distribution staff) – including management – are normally indirect employees.

2.3 Full cost

The full cost of a unit of product (or the full cost of a unit of service) is a cost that includes both direct costs and some overheads. The full cost of a unit of product might be analysed as follows:

	$	
Direct materials cost	4	
Direct labour cost	5	
Direct expenses	1	
Prime cost	10	
Manufacturing overhead (or production overhead)	8	Production cost
Full production cost	18	
Administration overhead	3	Non-production cost
Selling and distribution overhead	4	
Full cost of sale	25	

Notes:

1 Prime cost plus a share of production overheads are the **full production cost** or 'fully absorbed production cost' of the cost unit.

2 In cost accounting systems, it is common practice to include production overheads in unit costs and measure the full production cost per unit. However, administration and selling and distribution overhead costs are not usually included in the cost of each unit. Instead, they are treated in total as an expense for the period (**'period costs'**).

2.4 Cost codes

Each cost might be given its own code. A code is a collection of symbols used to reference a particular item.

The main purposes of cost codes are to:

- assist the communication of precise information

- reduce clerical work. For example the code 13422 would replace the title 'selling expense - Eastern Division travel', thus simplifying communication and improving accuracy

- facilitate electronic data processing. Computer analysis, summarisation and presentation of data can be performed more easily through the medium of codes

- facilitate a logical and systematic arrangement of costing records i.e. accounts can be arranged in blocks of codes permitting additional codes to be inserted in logical order

- simplify comparison of totals of similar expenses rather than all the individual items. This facilitates control

- incorporate check codes within the main code to check the accuracy of posting

> **Investment, profit, revenue and cost centres**
>
> - Organisational structure and management responsibilities
> - Definitions and explanation
> - Cost objects and cost units
> - Cost centres and cost units
> - Cost centres: direct and indirect costs

3 Investment, profit, revenue and cost centres

3.1 Organisational structure and management responsibilities

Every business organisation has a management structure, and individual managers are given responsibility for a particular aspect of operations or activity. The operations or activity for which they are responsible can be called a **responsibility centre**. Within a large organisation, there is a hierarchy of management, with a hierarchy of delegated responsibilities.

A manager might be in charge of a department, such as a warehouse or the buying department. A part of their responsibility should be to ensure that the department operates efficiently and economically, and that costs (expenditures) are kept under control. A departmental manager is likely to be responsible for preparing the annual cost budget for the departments, subject to approval by his superiors. A manager who is made responsible for costs must have some authority over spending in his department (although a large proportion of departmental costs, such as employees' salaries, might be outside his control).

A manager might be responsible for a department or activity that earns revenue, and for the revenue earned by the department. For example a sales manager might be made responsible for the activities of a sales team and the revenue that the sales team earns. Similarly, the manager of a retail store (in a company that operates a chain of stores) might be responsible for the revenues earned by the store. A manager who is made responsible for revenues might have some authority to adjust or decide selling prices; alternatively a manager might be told what the sales prices will be and is then made responsible for the volume of sales at those prices.

When a manager is responsible for both the costs and the revenues of an operation or department, he (or she) is also responsible for the profits that it earns.

In some cases, a manager might have the responsibility to make decisions about capital investment for an operation, with authority to buy new capital equipment or sell off unwanted assets. For example in a large company or a group of companies, there might be operating divisions where the divisional manager has a large amount of autonomy, with authority over capital spending ('capital budgets') as well as revenues, costs and profits.

3.2 Definitions and explanation

Managers need management accounting information to help them make decisions. For the purpose of cost and management accounting, responsibility centres can be divided into four categories:

- **Investment centres.** An investment centre is a division within an organisation where the management is responsible not only for the costs of the division and the revenues that it earns, but also for decisions relating to the investment in assets for the division. An investment centre manager usually has authority to purchase new assets, such as items of plant or equipment, and so should be responsible for the profit or 'return' that the division makes on the amount that it has invested.

    The performance of an investment centre might be measured by calculating the profit as a percentage of the amount invested (the return on investment or ROI).

    An investment centre might include a number of different profit centres. For example, a company manufacturing cars and trucks might have two investment centres, (1) car-making and (2) truck-making. Within the truck-making division, there might be several profit centres, each of these a separate location or factory at which trucks are manufactured and assembled.

- **Profit centres.** A profit centre is a department or division within the organisation for which revenues as well as costs are established. By measuring the costs of the products or services produced by the centre, and the revenues earned from selling them, it is possible to establish the profit (or loss) that the centre makes.

Example: summarised profit centre report	$000
Revenues of the profit centre	250
Costs of the units sold by the profit centre	(220)
Profit (or loss) of the profit centre	30

    A profit centre might consist of several cost centres. For example, a factory might be treated as a profit centre, and within the factory, the machining department, assembly department and finishing department might be three cost centres.

- **Revenue centres.** A revenue centre is a department or division within the organisation for which revenues are established. In a revenue centre there is no measurement of cost or profit. Revenue centre managers will only need to have information relating to revenues and will be accountable for revenues only. For example, the income accountant in a hospital is only responsible for recording and controlling the different incomes that are received from funding bodies or other sources (for example, private patients, fundraising and so on).

- **Cost centres.** A cost centre is a department or work group for which costs are established, in order to measure the cost of output produced by the centre. For example, in a factory a group of machines might be a cost centre. The costs of operating the machines would be established, and a cost could then be calculated for each unit of product manufactured by the machines.

    In a cost centre, there is no measurement of revenue or profit.

Example

A media company has several divisions. One is a magazine publishing division. This division is divided into three operating units: fashion magazines, sports magazines and business magazines, which operate from different offices. The fashion magazines unit has three main functions: commissioning, editing and printing, and marketing and sales.

The media company might organise its cost and management system as follows:

- Each of the divisions in the media company, including the magazines division, might be an investment centre. The senior manager of the magazines division might have the authority to incur capital expenditure to acquire new assets for the division. The performance of the magazines division might be measured by its annual return on investment (ROI).

- Within the magazines division, the fashion magazines unit, sports magazines unit and business magazines unit might be profit centres. The manager of each unit might be responsible for the revenues and costs of the unit, and the performance of each unit would be measured by the profit that it makes.

- Within the fashions magazine unit, each of the operating functions (commissioning, editing and printing, and marketing and sales) might be a cost centre. The manager in charge of each cost centre is responsible for costs, and the performance of the cost centre might be measured by comparing the actual costs of the cost centre with its budgeted costs.

The differing information needs of cost, revenue, profit and investment centre management

Managers of responsibility centres are responsible for the performance of their part of the organisation and its activities. The performance of an organisation is often measured financially, in terms of:

- keeping expenditure under control
- earning a sufficient amount of revenue
- making a profit
- making a suitable return on investment.

Managers therefore need information about the costs of operations for which they are responsible. They will often also need information about revenues and profit. In some cases, they will also need information about the amount of property, plant and equipment, and other 'assets' for which they are responsible. The information they need to make decisions within their area of responsibility depends on the scope of their management authority and responsibilities.

Managers also need financial information to help them make decisions. For example, they might need information about expected costs to make a decision about how much to charge for a job for a customer. Similarly, they might need information about costs and revenues to decide whether to invest money in a new project.

Management accounting is concerned with providing information to management to help them with planning and control, and for making other decisions.

The accounting information provided to managers should help them to make decisions, and the information provided should be relevant for the decisions they have to make. Clearly, the nature and content of the accounting information required depends on the nature of the manager's responsibilities (i.e. on the type of responsibility centre).

3.3 Cost objects and cost units

A cost accounting system measures the costs of cost objects, and often presents the information as a cost per unit of the cost object.

- A **cost object** is an item whose cost is measured.
- A **cost unit** is a unit of the cost item.

Cost objects and cost units should be selected so as to provide management with the cost information they require.

Here are some examples of cost objects and cost units

Industry/activity	Cost object	Cost unit
Car manufacture	Cars produced	A car
Bakery	Bread produced	A batch of bread items
Steel works	Steel produced	Tonne of steel
Carpet manufacture	Carpets produced	Square metre of carpet
Retail operation	Cost of items sold	Cost per $1 sales
Passenger transport service	Cost of transporting customers	Cost per passenger/mile (i.e. average cost of transporting a passenger one mile)
Road haulage	Cost of transporting items	Cost per tonne/mile (i.e. average cost of carrying one tonne of items for one mile)
University	Cost of teaching	Cost per student

Example 1

A company manufactures tinned foods. It has two products, tinned carrots and tinned beans. In its costing system, it has two cost objects, carrots and beans. The costing system measures the costs and revenues for each cost object.

The costing system will also provide information about the cost per tin of carrots and the cost per tin of beans. These are cost units.

	Cost object	Cost unit
1	Carrots	Production cost per tin of carrots
2	Beans	Production cost per tin of beans

Example 2

Another company manufactures a single product at two factories, one in the North of the country and one in the South of the country. Its costing system might measure:

- the cost of operating the factory in the north and the factory in the south (cost objects), and also

- the total operating cost in each factory per hour of labour worked, or the total operating cost per employee at each factory (these are cost units).

 Example 3

A transport company has a bus depot. The company has a cost accounting system that records and measures the cost of operating the bus depot. The costs of operating the depot are measured in three ways, as follows:

	Cost object	Cost unit
1	Buses	Operating cost per bus per month
2	Bus routes	Operating cost per month for each bus route
3	Bus drivers	Cost of operating the depot per month, per bus driver employed

3.4 Cost centres and cost units

 Example

A group of machines produces units of Product X. During one month, the costs of operating the machines were $36,000. There are 4 machines which were each operated for 150 hours in the month. The machines produced 20,000 units of Product X.

The group of machines might be treated as a cost centre, and the costs of the cost centre in the month were $36,000.

The cost per unit of Product X produced by the cost centre was $1.80.

We can also calculate the cost per machine hour, which is $60 (= $36,000/(4 × 150)).

Both units of Product X and machine hours worked can therefore be costed as cost units: one is a unit of output and the other is a unit of activity.

3.5 Cost centres: direct and indirect costs

Direct costs of a cost centre are costs that are attributable directly to the activity of the cost centre. Direct costs of a cost centre might be indirect costs of the units produced by the cost centre.

Example

The wages of a maintenance and repairs engineer might be a direct cost of the department in which he works. However, his wages are an indirect cost of each individual cost unit produced by the department. This is because the job of the engineer is to fix machines and other equipment when they break down, and he is not involved directly in producing the output of the department.

Management Accounting (MA)

Practice multiple choice questions

1   The cost of a quality inspection checker in a factory is an indirect labour cost of items produced.

    Is this statement TRUE or FALSE? *(1 mark)*

2   Which one of the following would be classified as indirect labour?

    A   Paint sprayers in a car production plant

    B   Accountants in an audit firm

    C   Workers in the stores department of a brick manufacturing company

    D   Roofing workers in a building construction company. *(2 marks)*

3   A publishing company produces books. Which of the following is a direct material cost of production?

    A   printing costs charged by an external printer

    B   a writing fee paid to the author

    C   the cost of copy editing

    D   cost of copies distributed to book reviewers. *(2 marks)*

4   A company owns a factory that produces Component X. All units of Component X are transferred to the company's processing centre where a final product is assembled. Decisions about purchasing equipment for the factory are made at the company's head office. In the company's cost and management accounting system, the factory is likely to be treated as:

    A   A cost centre.

    B   A revenue centre

    C   A profit centre

    D   An investment centre. *(2 marks)*

5   A cost centre manager needs regular information about costs incurred by the centre. In a cost and management accounting system, which of the following is the most likely frequency of regular cost reports for the centre?

    A   Daily

    B   Weekly

    C   Monthly

    D   Annual *(2 marks)*

6 A profit centre manager needs information about which of the following?

    (1)   Costs incurred by the centre

    (2)   Revenues earned by the centre

    (3)   Capital investment in the centre

    A   (1) only

    B   (1) and (2) only

    C   (2) only

    D   (1), (2) and (3)   *(2 marks)*

You will find the answers to the practice multiple choice questions at the end of this book.

Applied Knowledge
Management Accounting (MA)

CHAPTER

3

Cost behaviour

Contents
1 Fixed and variable costs
2 Other cost behaviour patterns

> **Fixed and variable costs**
>
> - Cost behaviour: meaning
> - Variable costs
> - Fixed costs
> - Mixed costs

1 Fixed and variable costs

1.1 Cost behaviour: meaning

Cost behaviour refers to the way in which costs change as the volume of activity changes. The volume of activity may be:

- the volume of sales
- the volume of production
- total labour hours worked or machine hours worked
- the number of production units inspected
- the number of journeys (for buses or trains) or deliveries and so on.

As a general rule, total costs should be expected to increase as the volume of activity rises.

Management might want information about estimated costs, or about what costs should have been. An understanding of cost behaviour is necessary in order to:

- forecast or plan what costs ought to be; and
- compare actual costs that were incurred with what the costs should have been.

The classifications of cost that were described in the previous chapter (functional costs and direct and indirect costs) are used to record and measure costs, and to report profits. However, these classifications of cost do not provide an analysis of how total costs change as more items are produced and sold, or as activity levels increase or fall.

The most important classification of costs for the purpose of cost estimation is the division of costs into fixed costs or variable costs.

1.2 Variable costs

Variable costs are costs that increase, usually by the same amount, for each additional unit of product that is made or each additional unit of service that is provided.

The variable cost of a cost unit is also called the **marginal cost** of the unit.

The variable cost per unit is often the same amount for each additional unit of output or unit of activity. This means that total variable costs increase in direct proportion to the total volume of output or activity. Here are some examples of variable cost items.

- The cost of buying a raw material item might be $5 per litre purchased, regardless of purchase quantity. If so, the variable cost is $5 per litre: the total cost of buying 1,000 litres would be $5,000 and the cost of buying 2,000 litres would be $10,000.
- The rate of pay for hourly-paid workers might be $15 per hour. If so, 400 hours of labour would cost $6,000 and 500 hours would cost $7,500.
- The time needed to produce an item of product is 4 minutes and labour is paid $15 per hour. If so, direct labour is a variable cost and the direct labour cost per unit produced is $1 (= $15 × 4/60).
- The cost of telephone calls might be $0.10 per minute. If so, the cost of telephone calls lasting 6,000 minutes in total would be $600.

1.3 Fixed costs

Fixed costs are items of cost that remain the same in total during a time period, no matter how many units are produced, and regardless of the volume or scale of activity. Fixed costs are also called **period costs**, because they are fixed for a given period of time. Total fixed costs tend therefore to increase with time because of inflation.

Here are some examples of fixed cost items.

- The rental cost of a building, which is $40,000 per month. The rental cost is fixed for a given period: $40,000 per month, or $480,000 per year.
- The salary costs of a worker who is paid $11,000 per month. The fixed cost is $11,000 per month or $132,000 per year.

Cost behaviour graphs: fixed and variable costs

Cost behaviour for items of cost (or for costs in total) can be shown in a graph. Graphs can be drawn for the total cost of an item or for the cost per unit of the item.

Cost behaviour graphs for fixed costs and variable costs are shown in the following diagram.

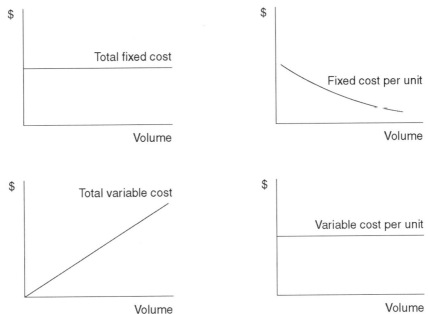

1.4 Mixed costs

A mixed cost, also called a semi-fixed cost or a semi-variable cost, is a cost that is partly fixed and partly variable. A cost behaviour graph showing the total costs for an item of mixed cost is shown below.

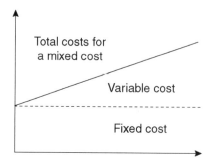

An item of cost that is a mixed cost is an item with a fixed minimum cost per period plus a variable cost for every unit of activity or output.

Example

A company uses a photocopier machine under a rental agreement. The photocopier rental cost is $400 per month plus $0.02 per copy produced.

For example, if the company makes 15,000 copies during a month, the total cost will be $400 fixed costs plus $300 variable costs (= 15,000 × $0.02), making a total cost of $700.

Mixed costs are important in cost and management accounting. It is often assumed that the total costs of an activity are mixed costs, consisting partly of fixed costs and partly of variable costs.

For example, it might be assumed that the total selling and distribution costs for a company each month are mixed costs. If this assumption is used, the total mixed costs can be divided into two separate parts, fixed costs and variable costs.

If costs can be analysed as a fixed amount of cost per period plus a variable cost per unit, estimating what future costs should be, or what actual costs should have been, becomes fairly simple.

Example

The management accountant of a manufacturing company has estimated that production costs in a factory that manufactures Product Y are fixed costs of $250,000 per month plus variable costs of $3 per unit of Product Y output.

The expected output next month is 120,000 units of Product Y. Expected total costs are therefore:

	$
Variable costs (120,000 × $3)	360,000
Fixed costs	250,000
Total costs	610,000

Other cost behaviour patterns

- Stepped fixed cost
- More unusual cost behaviour patterns

2 Other cost behaviour patterns

Some cost items are variable costs, fixed costs or mixed costs. Costs in total might have a cost behaviour pattern that is very close to being a mixed cost. However, there are many cost items that have a more unusual cost behaviour pattern. Unusual cost behaviour patterns can be shown on a cost behaviour graph.

2.1 Stepped fixed cost

A **stepped fixed cost** is a cost which:

- has a fixed cost behaviour pattern within a limited range of activity, and
- goes up or down in steps when the volume of activity rises above or falls below certain levels.

On a cost behaviour graph, step fixed costs look like steps rising from left to right.

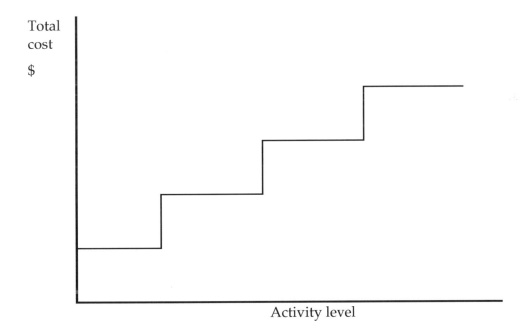

Example

A company might pay its supervisors a salary of $4,000 each month. When production is less than 3,500 hours each month, only one supervisor is needed: when production is between 3,501 and 7,000 hours each month, two supervisors are needed. When output is over 7,000 hours each month, three supervisors are needed.

These supervision costs are therefore fixed costs within a certain range of output, but go up or down in steps as the output level rises above or falls below certain levels.

A cost behaviour graph for the supervision costs can be drawn as follows.

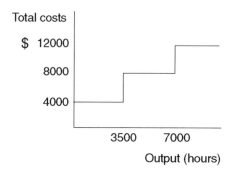

2.2 More unusual cost behaviour patterns

You may be examined on your understanding of more unusual cost behaviour patterns. Several are shown below.

Changes in total variable costs

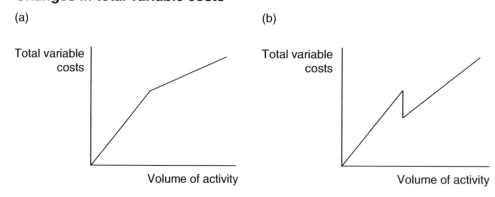

In (a), the variable cost per unit is a particular amount up to a certain level of activity or output, and is a lower amount for all units above that level of activity. For example, the cost might be $2 per unit up to 10,000 units and $1.50 per unit for each unit over 10,000 units.

In (b), the variable cost per unit is a particular amount up to a certain level of activity or output, and above that level of activity the variable cost per unit is a lower amount for all units (not just for the units above that level of activity). For example, a supplier might offer a price of $5 per unit for all units of a raw material, up to 10,000 units per order. If the size of an order is more than 10,000 units, the cost per unit will be $4.75.

Minimum and maximum charges

The cost behaviour pattern in the graph below illustrates a cost during a period when there is a charge per unit, subject to a minimum charge and a maximum charge per period.

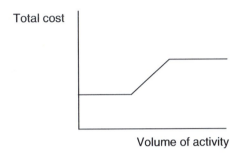

Other patterns

In your examination, you might be given another unusual cost behaviour pattern, and asked to identify the type of cost to which the cost behaviour pattern relates. You will need to study the pattern to identify its fixed and/or variable characteristics, and try to identify what type of cost fits the pattern shown. Here is just one example.

Example

Study the following cost behaviour graph and identify which of the following cost items is shown in the graph.

Total electricity charges for a factory, where the electricity supplier charges:

A   a fixed annual charge plus a constant amount for each unit of electricity consumed, subject to a maximum annual charge

B   a constant amount for each unit of electricity consumed up to a certain amount, and a lower charge per unit for consumption above that amount

C   a constant amount for each unit of electricity consumed but if consumption exceeds a certain amount the charge is reduced to a lower amount for the total amount consumed

D   a fixed charge for the year, then a constant amount for each unit of electricity consumed up to a certain amount, and a lower charge per unit for consumption above that amount

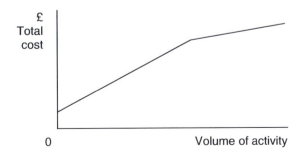

The cost behaviour graph shows that there is some charge even when consumption is zero. This means that there must be a fixed cost element in the annual charge. Total costs then rise in a straight-line fashion up to a certain level of consumption (so variable costs are a constant amount per unit) and above that level total costs continue to rise but the rate of increase is less steep (so variable costs are a new but lower constant amount per unit).

The cost item shown in the graph must therefore be D.

Applied Knowledge
Management Accounting (MA)

CHAPTER 4

Presenting information

Contents
1 Reports
2 Tables, charts and graphs

Reports

1 Reports

A report is a formal communication.

The main features of a report are:

- Title page – This would usually identify the preparer of the report and the parties to whom it is directed and would be dated
- Contents
- Terms of Reference

    The objective of the report

    Who asked for it and why?

    Who supplied the information and whether it has been reviewed/audited
- Executive summary – a summary of the report including conclusions and recommendations
- The body of the report

    This should explain the issue under consideration and provide an analysis and explanation of all relevant information before drawing conclusions and making recommendations.
- Appendices

    Detailed data and calculations are usually set out here.

A good report should:

- be clearly set out and follow a logical structure;
- be easy to follow and interesting to read;
- be as short and simple as possible; and
- contain clear conclusions and recommendations.

> **Tables, charts and graphs**
>
> - Tabulation of data
> - Representing data in charts
> - Plotting data onto graphs

2 Tables, charts and graphs

Reports will often contain analysis of data relevant to an issue under consideration.

Once data is collected, it should be converted into a meaningful form. This can be achieved by:

- Tabulating the data
- Representing the data in charts
- Plotting the data onto graphs

2.1 Tabulation of data

Principles of good tabulation

- Use headings and, if appropriate, state source
- State the unit of measurement
- Secondary statistics, such as percentages, can be incorporated
- Where relevant, insert column and/or row totals.

Example

A company provides online training courses and has collected data on its customers joining a particular online class.

This information might be represented as follows:

CONTINENT	MEN		WOMEN		TOTAL	
	Number	%	Number	%	Number	%
Europe	1	6	2	18	3	11
Asia	9	53	3	27	12	42
Africa	6	35	4	37	10	36
America	1	6	2	18	3	11
TOTAL	17	100	11	100	28	100
	61%		39%		100%	

Interpretation – The following points can be made:

- There are more men than women in the class. The split is 61%/39%.
- There are more people in the class from Asia than from any other continent, with almost as many Africans.
- European and American members of the class make up just one fifth of the total.
- Just over half of the men are Asian, whereas just over a quarter of the women are Asian.
- There are more European and American women than men, but more African and Asian men than women.

Tables make data easier to understand. A further improvement can be made by representing the data in a visual form.

2.2 Representing data in charts

Data might be discrete (also known as discontinuous) or continuous.

Discrete data is data that increases in jumps. For example, the number of attendees to a web broadcast increase by one person at a time. A fraction of a person cannot attend the broadcast and so cannot be part of the data.

Continuous data can increase continuously. Examples of continuous data include 'height' or 'weight'.

Bar charts

Bar charts are usually used for plotting discrete (or 'discontinuous') data i.e. data which has discrete values and is not continuous.

A bar chart or bar graph is a chart with rectangular bars with lengths proportional to the values that they represent. The bars can be plotted vertically or horizontally and can take several forms. These will be illustrated using the data of attendees at the online classes given above.

Simple bar charts

In a simple bar chart the data is represented by a series of bars, the height (or length) of which indicates the size of the number represented.

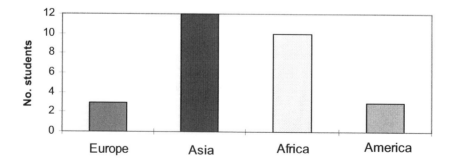

Bar chart showing continent of origin of A class

Simple bar charts are not so useful when the data is made up of several components which might be of interest. For example, it might be of interest to the training company to understand the mix of men and women who attend the online class.

Component bar charts

In this type of bar chart, the bars are divided into component parts. The height (or length) of each component indicates the size of the number represented.

Component bar charts might be plotted to show actual numbers or percentages.

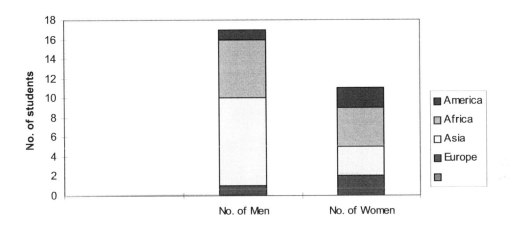

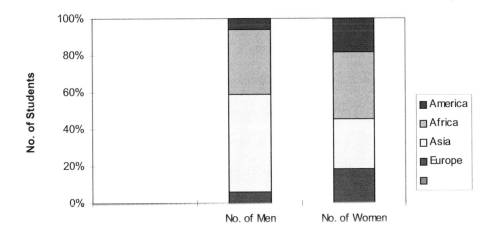

Multiple bar charts

In this type of bar chart, the components are shown as separate bars attached to each other in logical groupings. The height (or length) of which indicates the size of the number represented.

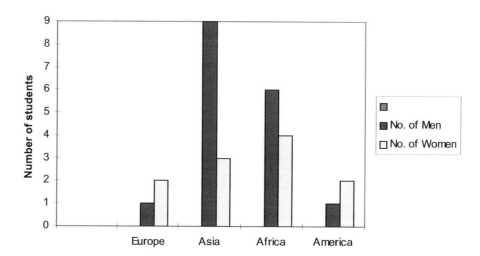

Multiple bar chart showing continent of origin of A class

Pie charts

A pie chart (or a circle graph) is a circular chart divided into sectors. The size of each sector is proportional to the quantity it represents.

Pie charts are very widely used especially to deliver information to an audience with mixed technical knowledge.

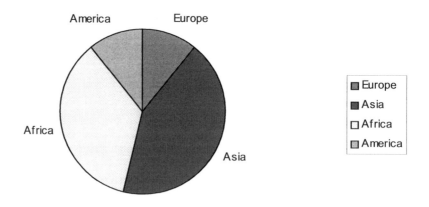

Pie Chart showing continent of origin of A class

Problems with pie charts are that it is difficult to compare different sections of a given pie chart, or to compare data across different pie charts.

2.3 Plotting data onto graphs

A graph is a representation of data by a continuous curve. This is best understood with an example.

Example

The following data is available about the sales of two companies over a 5 year period:

Year	Sales ($000)	
	Company A	Company B
1	2	5
2	4	10
3	8	15
4	16	20
5	32	25

The sales can be represented graphically as follows:

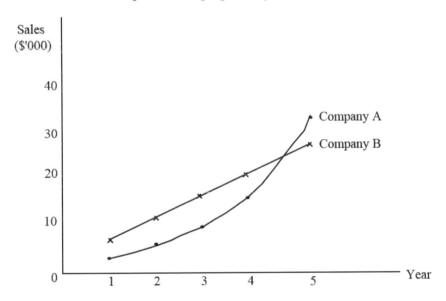

Interpretation – The following points can be made:

- The sales of each company have grown very strongly over the 5 year period.
- Company B's sales have increased at a constant amount (5 in each year) resulting in a straight line graph.
- The rate of increase in Company A's has increased over the 5 year period resulting in a line that is getting steeper in each year.
- In year 1 Company A's sales were less than those of Company B but this is no longer the case in year 5.
- This is because Company A's sales have grown more quickly than those of Company B.

Applied Knowledge
Management Accounting (MA)

CHAPTER

5

Forecasting techniques

Contents
1   Cost estimation: high/low method
2   Linear regression analysis
3   Correlation and the correlation coefficient
4   Time series analysis
5   Spreadsheet models

> **Cost estimation: high/low method**
>
> - Cost estimation
> - A linear function for total costs
> - High/low analysis
> - Advantages and disadvantages of high/low analysis
> - High/low analysis when there is a step change in fixed costs
> - High/low analysis when there is a change in the variable cost per unit

1 Cost estimation: high/low method

1.1 Cost estimation

For the purposes of planning and decision-making, it is often necessary to prepare an estimate of costs. For example, it is often necessary to estimate the total annual costs of an activity or a responsibility centre, or the total annual costs of production overheads or marketing overheads.

Unless there are reasons for a different approach, it is usual to make a cost estimate on the assumption that total costs (for a large number of different cost items together) are a mixture of fixed costs and variable costs. In order to estimate costs, it is therefore necessary to make an estimate of:

- fixed costs for the period, and
- the variable cost per unit of output or sales, or the variable cost per unit of activity (for example, the variable cost per hour worked).

In the same way, individual items of mixed cost can be divided into fixed and variable cost elements. Two cost estimation techniques are:

- high/low analysis
- linear regression analysis.

This chapter explains the high/low method. The linear regression method will be explained in a later chapter.

1.2 A linear function for total costs

If total costs can be divided into fixed costs and variable costs per unit of output or unit of activity, a formula for total costs is:

$y = a + bx$

where

y = total costs in a period

x = the number of units of output or the volume of activity in the period a = the fixed costs in the period

b = the variable cost per unit of output or unit of activity.

Graph of linear cost function

On a cost behaviour graph, total costs would be shown as a straight line, rising with the total volume of activity. (It is a cost behaviour graph for a mixed cost). This rather simple formula is therefore a 'linear function' for total costs.

The linear cost function equation $y = a + bx$ can be drawn as follows.

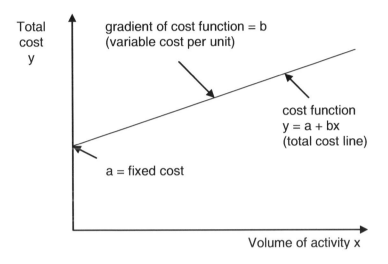

1.3 High/low analysis

High/low analysis can be used to estimate fixed costs and variable costs per unit whenever:

- there are figures available for total costs at two different levels of output or activity
- it can be assumed that fixed costs are the same in total at each level of activity, and
- the variable cost per unit is constant at both levels of activity.

High/low analysis therefore uses two historical figures for cost:

- the highest recorded output level, and its associated total cost
- the lowest recorded output level, and its associated total cost.

It is assumed that these 'high' and 'low' records of output and historical cost are representative of costs at all levels of output or activity.

The **difference** between the total cost at the high level of output and the total cost at the low level of output is **entirely variable cost**. This is because fixed costs are the same in total at both levels of output.

The method

There are just a few simple steps involved in high/low analysis.

Step 1

Take the activity level and cost for:

- the highest activity level
- the lowest activity level.

Step 2

The difference between the total cost of the highest activity level and the total cost of the lowest activity level consists entirely of variable costs. This is because the fixed costs are the same at all levels of activity.

	Activity level	$
High: Total cost of	A =	TCa
Low: Total cost of	B =	TCb
Difference: Variable cost of (A – B) units	(A – B) =	TCa - TCb

From this difference, we can therefore calculate the variable cost per unit of activity.

Variable cost per unit = $(TCa – TCb)/ (A – B) units

Having calculated a variable cost per unit of activity, we can now calculate fixed costs.

Step 3

Having calculated the variable cost per unit, apply this value to the cost of either the highest or the lowest activity level. (It does not matter whether you use the high level or the low level of activity. Your calculation of fixed costs will be the same.)

Calculate the total variable costs at this activity level.

Step 4

The difference between the total cost at this activity level and the total variable cost at this activity level is the fixed cost.

Substitute in the 'low' equation	Cost
	$
Total cost of (low volume of activity)	TCb
Variable cost of (low volume of activity)	V
Therefore fixed costs per period of time	TCb - V

You now have an estimate of the variable cost per unit and the total fixed costs.

The high/low method is a simple but important technique that you need to understand. Study the following example carefully.

Chapter 5: Forecasting techniques

Example

A company has recorded the following costs in the past four months:

Month	Activity	Total cost
	Direct labour hours	$
January	5,800	40,300
February	7,700	47,100
March	8,200	48,700
April	6,100	40,650

Required

Using high/low analysis, prepare an estimate of total costs in May if output is expected to be 7,000 direct labour hours.

Answer

(1) **Steps 1 and 2: Calculate the variable cost per hour**

Take the highest level of activity and the lowest level of activity, and the total costs of each. Ignore the other data for levels of activity in between the highest and the lowest.

	Hours		$
High: Total cost of	8,200 hours	=	48,700
Low: Total cost of	5,800 hours	=	40,300
Difference: Variable cost of	2,400 hours	=	8,400

Therefore variable cost per direct labour hour = $8,400/2,400 hours = $3.50.

(2) **Steps 3 and 4: Calculate fixed costs**

Substitute in the 'high' equation	Cost
	$
Total cost of 8,200 hours	48,700
Variable cost of 8,200 hours (× $3.50 per hour)	(28,700)
Therefore fixed costs per month	20,000

(3) **Using the cost analysis: Prepare a cost estimate**

Cost estimate for May	Cost
	$
Fixed costs	20,000
Variable cost (7,000 hours × $3.50 per hour)	24,500
Estimated total costs	44,500

The technique can be used any time that you are given two figures for total costs, at different levels of activity or volumes of output, and you need to estimate fixed costs and a variable cost per unit.

1.4 Advantages and disadvantages of high/low analysis

Advantages

It is easy to calculate and to understand.

It can provide information using only two sets of data.

The data required to carry out the calculation should be easily accessible from the accounting system.

Disadvantages

It ignores data pairs other than the highest and lowest.

It can be distorted by an unusually high or an unusually low reading.

It assumes that fixed costs are constant over all levels of output. For example, it ignores the possibility of a stepped cost within the observed data and in the use of the information in making projections.

It assumes a straight line relationship between output and costs. Variable costs might change with level of activity.

It assumes that the input data is from normal levels of activity.

Data required to carryout the calculation may be difficult to derive from the accounting systems when a wide variety of products are made in the same factory.

1.5 High/low analysis when there is a step change in fixed costs

High/low analysis can be used even when there is a step increase in fixed costs between the 'low' and the 'high' activity levels, provided that the amount of the step increase in fixed costs is known.

The method of analysis to use depends on whether the step increase in the fixed cost is stated as a money amount of cost, or whether it is stated as a percentage increase.

The step increase in fixed costs is given as a money amount

If the step increase in fixed costs is given as a money amount, the total cost of the 'high' or the 'low' activity level should be adjusted by the amount of the increase, so that total costs for the 'high' and 'low' amounts are comparable.

The high/low method can then be used in the normal way to obtain a fixed cost and a variable cost per unit. The fixed cost will be either the fixed cost at the 'high' level or at the 'low' level, depending on how you made the adjustment to fixed costs before making the high/low analysis. You can then calculate the fixed costs at the other level of activity by adding or subtracting the step change in fixed costs, as appropriate.

Example

A company has the following costs at two activity levels.

Activity	Total cost
units	$
17,000	165,000
22,000	195,000

The variable cost per unit is constant over this range of activity, but there is a step fixed cost and total fixed costs increase by $15,000 when activity level equals or exceeds 19,000 units.

Required

Using high/low analysis, calculate the total cost of 20,000 units.

 Answer

There is an increase in fixed costs above 19,000 units of activity, and to use the high/low method, we need to make an adjustment for the step fixed costs. Since we are required to calculate the total cost for a volume of activity above 19,000 units, the simplest approach is to add $15,000 to the total cost of 17,000 units, so that the fixed costs of 17,000 units and 22,000 units are the same and are also the amount of fixed costs for 20,000 units.

(1) **Steps 1 and 2: Calculate the variable cost per unit**

	Units	$
High: Total cost	22,000 units =	195,000
Low: Adjusted total cost: $(165,000 + 15,000)	17,000 units =	(180,000)
Difference: Variable cost of	5,000 units =	15,000

Therefore variable cost per unit = $15,000/5,000 units = $3 per unit.

(2) **Steps 3 and 4: Calculate fixed costs (above 19,000 units)**

Substitute in the 'high' equation	Cost
	$
Total cost of 22,000 units	195,000
Variable cost of 22,000 units (× $3 per unit)	(66,000)
Therefore fixed costs (above 19,000 units)	129,000

(3) **Using the cost analysis: Prepare a cost estimate**

Cost estimate	Cost
	$
Fixed costs (above 19,000 units)	129,000
Variable cost (20,000 units × $3)	60,000
Estimated total costs	189,000

The step increase in fixed costs is given as a percentage amount

When the step change in fixed costs between two activity levels is given as a percentage amount, the problem is a bit more complex, and to use high/low analysis we need a third figure for total cost, at another level of activity somewhere in between the 'high' and the 'low' amounts.

Total fixed costs will be the same for:

- the 'in between' activity level and
- either the 'high' or the 'low' activity level.

High/low analysis should be applied to the two costs and activity levels for which total fixed costs are the same, to obtain an estimate for the variable cost per unit and the total fixed costs at these activity levels. Total fixed costs at the third activity level (above or below the step change in fixed costs) can then be calculated making a suitable adjustment for the percentage change.

Example

A company has the following costs at three activity levels.

Activity	Total cost
units	$
5,000	180,000
8,000	240,000
11,000	276,000

The variable cost per unit is constant over this range of activity, but there is a step fixed cost and total fixed costs increase by 20% when the activity level exceeds 7,500 units.

Required

Estimate the expected total cost when the activity level is 7,000 units.

Answer

There is an increase in fixed costs above 7,500 units of activity, which means that total fixed costs and the variable cost per unit are the same for 8,000 units and 11,000 units of activity. These activity levels should be used to estimate the variable cost per unit and total fixed costs.

(1) **Steps 1 and 2: Calculate the variable cost per unit**

	Units		$
High: Total cost	11,000 units	=	276,000
'In-between'	8,000 units	=	(240,000)
Difference: Variable cost of	3,000 units	=	36,000

Therefore variable cost per unit = $36,000/3,000 units = $12 per unit.

(2) **Steps 3 and 4: Calculate fixed costs (above 7,500 units)**

Substitute in the 'high' equation	Cost
	$
Total cost of 11,000 units	276,000
Variable cost of 11,000 units (× $12 per unit)	(132,000)
Therefore fixed costs (above 7,500 units)	144,000

(3) **Calculate fixed costs at activity levels below 7,500 units**

Fixed costs increase by 20% above 7,500 units.

Fixed costs above 7,500 units are therefore 120% of fixed costs below 7,500 units.

Fixed costs below 7,500 units are therefore: $144,000 × (100/120) = $120,000.

(Note: Make sure that you understand the adjustment here. We do not subtract 20% from fixed costs above 7,500 units!).

(4) **Using the cost analysis: Prepare a cost estimate**

Cost estimate	Cost
	$
Fixed costs (below 7,500 units)	120,000
Variable cost (7,000 units × $12)	84,000
Estimated total costs	204,000

1.6 High/low analysis when there is a change in the variable cost per unit

High/low analysis can also be used when there is a change in the variable cost per unit between the 'high' and the 'low' levels of activity. The same approach is needed as for a step change in fixed costs, as described above.

The method of analysis to use depends on whether the step increase in the variable cost is stated as a money amount of cost, or whether it is stated as a percentage increase.

The change in unit variable cost is given as a money amount

If the increase or reduction in variable cost per unit is given as a money amount, the total cost of the 'high' activity level should be adjusted by the amount of the increase or reduction, so that total costs for the 'high' and 'low' amounts have the same basis for total variable costs.

The high/low method can then be used in the normal way to obtain a variable cost per unit and a fixed cost at the 'low' activity level.

Example

A company has the following costs at three activity levels.

Activity	Total cost
units	$
21,000	276,000
30,000	327,000

The fixed costs are constant over this range of activity, but variable costs per unit fall by $0.50 above 24,000 units, but only for units above that level (i.e. not for all units).

Required

Using high/low analysis, calculate the total cost of 28,000 units.

Answer

The variable cost per unit falls by $0.50 per unit, but only for units above 24,000. This means that at the 30,000 level of activity, there are 6,000 units costing $0.50 less, which is $3,000 in total.

To carry out high/low analysis, we therefore need to add $3,000 to total costs for the high level of output. The variable cost per unit we calculate will be the variable cost before the $0.50 reduction.

(1) **Steps 1 and 2: Calculate the variable cost per unit**

	Units	$
High: Adjusted total cost $(327,000 + 3,000)	30,000 units =	330,000
Low: Total cost	21,000 units =	(276,000)
Difference: Variable cost of	9,000 units =	54,000

Therefore variable cost per unit (up to 24,000 units) = $54,000/9,000 units = $6 per unit.

The variable cost per unit above 24,000 units is $6 - $0.50 = $5.50.

(2) **Steps 3 and 4: Calculate fixed costs**

Substitute in the 'low' equation	Cost
	$
Total cost of 21,000 units	276,000
Variable cost of 21,000 units (× $6 per unit)	(126,000)
Therefore fixed costs	150,000

(3) **Using the cost analysis: Prepare a cost estimate**

Cost estimate for 28,000 units	Cost
	$
Fixed costs	150,000
Variable cost	
First 24,000 units (× $6)	144,000
Next 4,000 units (× $5.50)	22,000
Estimated total costs	316,000

The change in unit variable cost is given as a percentage amount

When the change in the variable cost per unit is given as a percentage amount, a similar method is needed as for fixed costs. A third 'in between' estimate of costs should be used, and the variable cost per unit will be the same for:

- the 'in between' activity level and
- either the 'high' or the 'low' activity level.

High/low analysis should be applied to the two costs and activity levels for which unit variable costs are the same, to obtain an estimate for the variable cost per unit and the total fixed costs at these activity levels. The variable cost per unit at the third activity level can then be calculated making a suitable adjustment for the percentage change.

Example

A company has the following costs at three activity levels.

Activity	Total cost
units	$
20,000	300,000
25,000	320,000
30,000	356,000

The fixed costs are constant over this range of activity, but there is a 10% reduction in the variable cost per unit above 24,000 units of activity. This reduction applies to all units of activity, not just the additional units above 24,000.

Required

Estimate the expected total cost when the activity level is 22,000 units.

Answer

The variable cost per unit is the same for both 25,000 units and 30,000 units. High/low analysis should therefore be applied to these activity levels.

(1) **Calculate the variable cost per unit above 24,000 units**

	Units	$
High: Total cost	30,000 units =	356,000
'In-between'	25,000 units =	(320,000)
Difference: Variable cost of	5,000 units =	36,000

Therefore variable cost per unit = $36,000/5,000 units = $7.20 per unit.

(2) **Calculate the variable cost per unit below 24,000 units**

The variable cost per unit above 24,000 units is 90% of the cost below 24,000 units.

The variable cost per unit below 24,000 units is therefore (× 100/90) of the cost above 24,000 units.

Variable cost per unit below 24,000 units = $7.20 × 100/90 = $8

(3) **Calculate fixed costs**

Substitute in the 'low' equation	Cost
	$
Total cost of 20,000 units	300,000
Variable cost of 20,000 units (× $8 per unit)	(160,000)
Therefore fixed costs (above 7,500 units)	140,000

(4) **Using the cost analysis: Prepare a cost estimate**

Cost estimate for 22,000 units	Cost
	$
Fixed costs	140,000
Variable cost (22,000 units × $8)	176,000
Estimated total costs	316,000

> **Linear regression analysis**
>
> - The purpose of linear regression analysis
> - The regression analysis formulae
> - Applying the regression analysis formulae
> - Advantages and disadvantages of linear regression analysis

2 Linear regression analysis

2.1 The purpose of linear regression analysis

Linear regression analysis is a statistical technique for calculating a line of best fit from a set of data:

$$y = a + bx$$

The data is in 'pairs', which means that there are a number of different values for x, and for each value of x there is an associated value of y in the data.

Linear regression analysis can be used to estimate the fixed costs and the variable cost per unit from historical data for mixed costs. For example, there might be historical data for the total monthly costs of operating a workshop. It might be assumed that total costs each month vary with the number of direct labour hours worked. Historical data can be collected about total monthly costs in the past (cost in each month = y) and the associated number of direct labour hours worked in that month (hours in each month = x). This data can then be used to estimate fixed costs per month and variable costs per direct labour hour, which can be expressed in a formula $y = a + bx$.

Linear regression analysis can also be used to predict future sales by projecting the historical sales trend into the future (on the assumption that sales growth is rising at a constant rate, in a 'straight line').

Regression analysis is an alternative technique to high-low analysis, which was described in the previous chapter. It can be used for all the same purposes in cost and management accounting that high-low analysis is used for.

Regression analysis and high-low analysis compared

Regression analysis and the high-low analysis are used for the same purposes. Regression analysis is therefore an alternative technique to high-low analysis, which was described in an earlier chapter, but there are important differences between them.

- High-low analysis uses just two sets of data for x and y, the highest value for x and the lowest value for x. Regression analysis uses as many sets of data for x and y as are available.

- Because regression analysis calculates a line of best fit for all the available data, it is likely to provide a more reliable estimate than high-low analysis for the values of a and b.

- In addition, regression analysis can be used to assess the extent to which values of y depend on values of x. For example, if a line of best fit is calculated that estimates total costs for any volume of production, we can also calculate the extent to which total costs do seem to be linked (or 'correlated') to the volume of production. This is done by calculating a **correlation co-efficient**, which is explained later.
- Regression analysis uses more complex arithmetic than high-low analysis, and a calculator or small spreadsheet model is normally needed.

In summary, linear regression analysis is a better technique than high-low analysis because:

- it is more reliable and
- its reliability can be measured.

High-low analysis has the benefit of simplicity and speed/ease of calculation.

2.2 The regression analysis formulae

The formulae for estimating costs using regression analysis are provided in a formulae sheet in your examination. You might be required to apply the formulae to data provided in an examination question.

Linear regression analysis is used to calculate values for a and b in the linear cost equation: y = a + bx.

The linear regression formulae for calculating a and b are shown below. The number of pairs of data that are used in the calculation is n.

The regression analysis formulae are as follows. They will be given to you in your examination:

$$a = \frac{\Sigma y}{n} - \frac{b \Sigma x}{n}$$

$$b = \frac{n \Sigma xy - \Sigma x \Sigma y}{n \Sigma x^2 - (\Sigma x)^2}$$

where:

n = the number of pairs of data used for x and y

x, y represent the values of x (volume of activity or output) and y (total cost)

The value of 'b' is an item in the formula for calculating 'a'. It is therefore necessary to calculate 'b' first before calculating 'a'.

Understanding the formulae

These formulae might seem very complicated, and in your examination you might be given a question that requires you to show your understanding of what the different items in the formulae mean.

- You should think of the pairs of data as a list of values set out in two columns, with one column for the values of x and the second column for the associated values of y.

- You should then prepare two more columns.
- There should be an additional column for x^2. Calculate the square of each value of x in the x column and write the answer in the x^2 column.
- The fourth column is for xy. For each pair of data for x and y, multiply the value of x by the value of y, and enter the answer in the xy column.
- You must then add up the totals for each of the four columns. Σx is the total of all the values in the x column. Σy is the total of all the values in the y column. Σx^2 is the total of all the values in the x^2 column and Σxy is the total of all the values in the xy column.
- You now have all the values you need to calculate a value for b in the formula y = a + bx.
- The only other item you might not be sure about is $(\Sigma x)^2$. This is not the same as Σx^2. It is the square of the value for Σx.
- Having calculated a value for b, you can then use the formula for calculating the value of a: this includes the value for b, which is why you need to calculate b first.

2.3 Applying the regression analysis formulae

The formulae might seem complicated, but they are actually fairly straightforward provided that you understand the meaning of the Σ items in the formulae, and remember that n is the number of pairs of data used to make the estimate. Study the following example carefully.

Example

The total costs and output volumes of a manufacturing company in the first six months of the year have been as follows.

Month	Output	Total cost
	'000 units	$000
January	5	146
February	7	152
March	6	148
April	5	142
May	8	164
June	6	151

Required

Using regression analysis:

- estimate a value for fixed costs each month and a variable cost per unit
- estimate the expected costs in September if output volume is expected to be 8,000 units.

Answer

The starting point is to draw a table showing the values of x (output) and y (total cost). For each value of x and y, you should calculate the value of:

- x^2 and
- xy.

For reasons to be explained later, the value of y^2 will also be calculated here.

There are six pairs of data, so there should be six different values for x, y, x^2, xy and y^2.

Add the figures in each column to obtain totals for:

- Σx (= the sum of the values of x)
- Σy (= the sum of the values of y)
- Σx^2
- Σxy
- Σy^2. (The reason for calculating Σy^2 will be explained later.)

Month	Output	Total cost			
	000 units	$000			
	x	y	x^2	xy	y^2
January	5	146	25	730	21,316
February	7	152	49	1,064	23,104
March	6	148	36	888	21,904
April	5	142	25	710	20,164
May	8	164	64	1,312	26,896
June	6	151	36	906	22,801
	37	903	235	5,610	136,185
	$= \Sigma x$	$= \Sigma y$	$= \Sigma x^2$	$= \Sigma xy$	$= \Sigma y^2$

There are six pairs of data, so n = 6.

We now have all the figures we need to calculate values for 'a' and 'b, starting with 'b'.

$$b = \frac{n\Sigma xy - \Sigma x \Sigma y}{n\Sigma x^2 - (\Sigma x)^2}$$

$$b = \frac{6(5,610) - (37)(903)}{6(235) - (37^2)} = \frac{33,660 - 33,411}{1,410 - 1,369} = \frac{249}{41} = 6.07$$

This is the estimate of the variable cost per unit.

The value of 'b' is used to calculate a value for 'a', as follows.

$$a = \frac{\sum y}{n} - \frac{b \sum x}{n}$$

$$a = \frac{903}{6} - \frac{6.07(37)}{6} = 150.5 - 37.4$$

$$a \text{ (in \$000)} = 113.1$$

Answer (a)

Estimated fixed costs each month = a = $113,100

Estimated variable cost per unit = b = $6.07

Therefore, linear cost function, y, is estimated to be:

y = 113,100 + 6.07x

For simplicity, this could be rounded to:

y = 113,000 + 6x.

Answer (b)

Using y = 113,100 + 6.07x, when monthly output is expected to be 8,000 units, the expected total costs will be:

	$
Fixed	113,100
Variable (8,000 × $6.07)	48,560
	161,660

Linear regression analysis and your examination

As you might appreciate, calculating a linear equation using linear regression analysis is a time-consuming process, unless you have a programmed calculator or spreadsheet. You will therefore not be required to use the full technique in your examination. However, you might be required to:

- comment on the meaning of items in the formulae, such as $\sum x^2$, $\sum xy$ and $(\sum x)^2$, or

- calculate a value for a or b, given values in the question for $\sum x$, $\sum y$, $\sum x^2$ and $\sum xy$.

2.4 Advantages and disadvantages of linear regression analysis

Advantages

It uses all available data and is not greatly influenced by unusual sets of data.

It is based on a rigorous mathematical model.

The data required to carry out the calculation should be easily accessible from the accounting system.

Disadvantages

It is more difficult to calculate and understand than the high/low method (though it is relatively easy to set up a spreadsheet model to carry out the calculation).

It assumes that fixed costs are constant over all levels of output. For example, it ignores the possibility of a stepped cost within the observed data and in the use of the information in making projections.

It assumes a straight line relationship between output and costs. In fact, it imposes a straight line on any type of data. Variable costs might change with level of activity.

It assumes that the input data is based on normal levels of activity.

Data required to carry out the calculation may be difficult to derive from the accounting systems when a wide variety of products are made in the same factory.

> **Correlation and the correlation coefficient**
>
> - Correlation
> - Degrees of correlation
> - Correlation coefficient, r
> - Coefficient of determination, r^2

3 Correlation and the correlation coefficient

3.1 Correlation

Linear regression analysis can be applied to any sets of data where the data is in pairs (x and y). It could be used, for example, to calculate a line of best fit for total weekly costs of an activity by taking pairs of data for total weekly costs (= y) and the associated values for the activity. However, the activity level might be any of the following:

- units of output each week, if it is assumed that weekly costs vary with the volume of output produced
- direct labour hours each week, if it is assumed that weekly costs vary with the number of direct labour hours worked
- machine hours operated each week, if it is assumed that weekly costs vary with the number of machine hours.

Which activity is the best one to choose as 'x'?

You could even use linear regression analysis to calculate a line of best fit between total weekly costs and the air temperature on the factory floor at midday, if you decided that total costs vary with the air temperature. (This might seem a ridiculous idea, but the point that you should try to understand is that linear regression analysis can be used to calculate a line of best fit for any two variables, given pairs of data, even when there is no actual connection between them).

Since a line of best fit can be calculated between any two variables using regression analysis, important questions are:

- How can we assess the reliability of the line of best fit?'
- How do we know whether our choice of activity as 'x' is a good one?

The answer to both questions is that the reliability of the regression formula can be assessed using a statistic called the coefficient of correlation.

Correlation is a measure of the strength of the relationship between two variables. Variables are said to be correlated if a change in one variable results in a change in the other variable.

If you plot a graph of the data relating to two variables, you should be able to see if any visible relationship exists between them (such a graph is known as a scattergraph or scatterchart). If a visible relationship is seen to exist, the data on the graph can be plotted to show the 'line of best fit'. The 'line of best fit' is of the form y = a + bx (linear cost function) and indicates that a 'possible' linear relationship exists between two variables.

3.2 Degrees of correlation

The following scattergraphs show the different degrees of correlation that may be seen to exist between two variables.

Perfect positive correlation

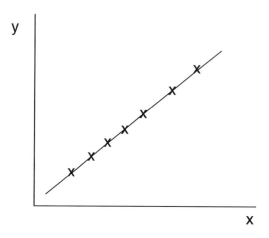

Perfect correlation is seen to exist when all the data points plotted lie in an exact straight line and a linear relationship exists between the two variables.

Perfect positive correlation means that high values of are variable are associated with high values of another variable. Alternatively, low values of one variable may be associated with low values of another variable.

Perfect negative correlation

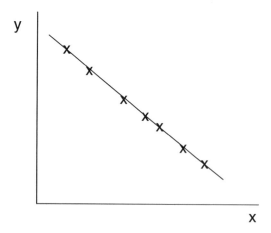

Perfect negative correlation is seen to exist when all the data points plotted lie in an exact straight line and that high values of one variable are associated with low values of another variable. Alternatively, low values of one variable may be associated with high value of another variable.

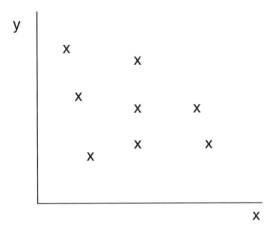

No correlation (uncorrelated)

'Uncorrelated' means that no correlation is seen to exist between the variables.

Positive correlation (but not perfect correlation)

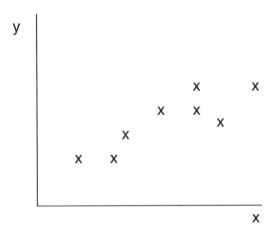

Positive correlation means that there appears to be some correlation between the values of y and x, and in general the value of y increases as the value of x increases. However, the correlation is not perfect because all the data does not lie exactly on a straight line on the scattergraph.

Negative correlation

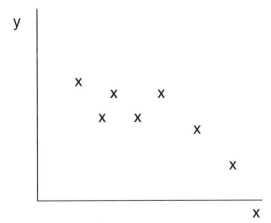

Management Accounting (MA)

Negative correlation means that a relationship exists between two variables, and the value of y declines as the value of x increases. However, the correlation is not perfect.

As an alternative to drawing a scattergraph to see whether a visible relationship exists between the two variables x and y, the correlation between them can be measured by calculating a **correlation coefficient**.

3.3 Correlation coefficient r

An advantage of using the regression analysis method is that the reliability of the estimates can be assessed statistically, by calculating a correlation coefficient.

The formula for the correlation coefficient (r) will be given to you in the examination.

$$r = \frac{n\sum xy - \sum x \sum y}{\sqrt{(n\sum x^2 - (\sum x)^2)(n\sum y^2 - (\sum y)^2)}}$$

This formula might seem difficult, but it is fairly similar to the formula for calculating 'b' in the linear cost equation. The only additional value that we need to calculate the correlation coefficient is a value for $[n\sum y^2 - (\sum y)^2]$.

- If you look back at the previous example, you will see that the value for $\sum y^2$ has already been calculated. In the example, there is a separate column for y^2. Calculate the square of each value of y in the y column and enter it in the same row in the y^2 column. Then add up all the values of y^2 in the y^2 column to get $\sum y^2$.

- $(\sum y)^2$ is a different value. It is the square of the value for $\sum y$.

The value of the correlation coefficient, r, in the example in paragraph 2.3 is therefore calculated as follows. Remember that most of the values for the formula have been calculated in paragraph 1.3 as parts of the formula for calculating the value of b.

$$r = \frac{249}{\sqrt{(41[6(136{,}1850) - (903^2)]}} = \frac{249}{\sqrt{(41(1{,}701)}} = \frac{249}{264} = +.94$$

The correlation coefficient is + 0.94.

Significance of the correlation coefficient

The value of the correlation coefficient must always be in the range – 1 to + 1.

- A value of – 1 indicates that there is perfect negative correlation between the values for y and the values for x that have been used in the regression analysis estimates. Perfect negative correlation means that all the values for x and y, plotted on a graph, would lie on a straight downward-sloping line.

- A value of + 1 indicates that there is perfect positive correlation between the values for y and the values for x that have been used in the regression analysis estimates. Perfect positive correlation means that all the values for x and y, plotted on a graph, would lie on a straight upward-sloping line.

- A value of r = 0 indicates no correlation at all between the values of x and y.

For cost estimation, a value for r close to + 1 would indicate that the cost estimates are likely to be very reliable.

As a general guide, a value for r between + 0.90 and + 1 indicates good correlation between the values of x and y, suggesting that the formula for costs can be used with reasonable confidence for cost estimation.

If you calculate a value for r that is more than +1 or is a greater negative value than − 1, your calculation will be wrong.

3.4 Coefficient of determination r^2

The square of the correlation coefficient, r^2, is called the coefficient of determination. The value of r^2 shows how much the variations in the value of y, in the data used to calculate the regression analysis formula, can be explained by variations in the value of x.

Significance of coefficient of determination

The value of the coefficient of determination must always be in the range 0 to +1.

- If the value of r is + 0.70, this means that on the basis of the data used in the regression analysis formula, 0.49 or 49% (= 0.70^2) of variations in the value of y can be explained by variations in the value of x.

- Similarly, if the value of r is − 0.80, this means that on the basis of the data used in the regression analysis formula, 0.64 or 64% (= 0.80^2) of variations in the value of y can be explained by variations in the value of x. Since r is negative, this means that y falls in value as the value of x increases.

In the example above, where r = + 0.94, we can say that from the data used to produce a formula for total costs, 88.36% (0.94 × 0.94 = 0.8836) of the variations in total cost can be explained by variations in the volume of output. This would suggest that the formula obtained for total costs is likely to be fairly reliable for estimating future costs for any given (budgeted) volume of production.

The coefficient of correlation and the coefficient of determination can therefore be used to give a statistical measurement to the reliability of estimates of y from a given value for x, using a line of best fit that has been calculated by linear regression analysis. As you might imagine, this can be a very useful item of management information for the purpose of forecasting or planning.

> **Time series analysis**
>
> - The nature of a time series
> - Linear regression analysis and forecasting a trend line
> - Moving averages
> - Calculating seasonal variations
> - Using the trend line and seasonal variations to make forecasts
> - Advantages and disadvantages of time series analysis
> - Impact of the product lifecycle on forecasting

4 Time series analysis

4.1 The nature of a time series

A time series is a record of data over a period of time. In budgeting, an important time series is the amount of annual sales revenue (or sales revenue per month or revenue per quarter) over time. Historical data about sales might be used to predict what sales will be in the future, in the budget period, when it is assumed that there is an upward or downward trend over time.

Trends might be identified over time for other aspects of a business, such as the number of people employed by the entity or the number of customer orders handled.

There are several techniques that may be used to predict a future amount from historical data for a time series. With these techniques, it is assumed that:

- There is an underlying trend, which is either an upward trend or downward trend.
- There may be seasonal variations (or monthly variation or daily variations) around the trend line.

The diagram below shows a trend line with seasonal variations above and below the trend line. The general trend in this diagram is up and the trend can be shown as a straight line. However the actual value in each time period is above or below the trend, because of the seasonal variations.

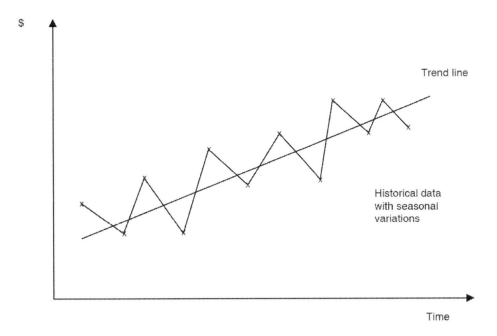

Analysing a time series

There are two aspects to analysing a time series from historical data:

- Estimating the trend line
- Calculating the amount of the seasonal variations (or monthly variations or daily variations).

The time series can then be used to make estimates for a future time period, by calculating a trend line value and then either adding or subtracting the appropriate seasonal variation for that time period.

Two methods of calculating a trend line are:

- Linear regression analysis
- Moving averages.

Methods of calculating seasonal variations are explained later.

4.2 Linear regression analysis and forecasting a trend line

Linear regression analysis can be used in forecasting, if it can be assumed that there has been a linear trend in the past, and this same linear trend will continue into the future. For example, if sales revenue has grown at a fairly constant rate in the past, it might be assumed that sales will continue to grow at the same rate in the future. Linear regression analysis can be used to establish a time series and forecast future sales.

Exactly the same method is used in forecasting as for estimating fixed and variable costs. The trend line is a formula $y = a + bx$, where x is the year or month.

To simplify the arithmetic for analysing the historical data, you should number the years 1, 2, 3, 4 and so on (or even start at year 0, and number the years 0, 1, 2, 3 and so on). This is much easier than using the actual numbers for the years 2010, 2011, 2012, 2013, 2014, 2015 and so on.

Linear regression analysis is a useful method for analysing a time series, but only if:

- a straight line trend can be assumed, and
- there are no seasonal variations in the historical data..

4.3 Moving averages

Moving averages are an alternative method to linear regression analysis for estimating a trend line, particularly when there are seasonal variations in the data. Moving averages are calculated as follows:

- **Step 1**. Decide the length of the cycle. The cycle is a number of days or weeks, or seasons or years. For example, the cycle will be seven days when historical data is collected daily for each day of the week. The cycle will be one year when data is collected monthly for each month of the year, or quarterly for each season.

- **Step 2**. Use the historical data to calculate a series of moving averages. A moving average is the average of all the historical data in one cycle. For example, suppose that historical data is available for daily sales over a period Day 1 – Day 21, and there are seven days of selling each week. A moving average can be calculated for Day 1 – Day 7. Another moving average can be calculated for Day 2 – Day 8. Another moving average can be calculated for Day 3 – Day 9, and so on up to a moving average for Day 15 – Day 21.

- **Step 3**. Match each moving average with an actual time period. The moving average should be matched with the middle time period of the cycle. For example a moving average for Day 1 – Day 7 is matched with Day 4, which is the middle of the period. Similarly, a moving average for Day 2 – Day 8 is matched with Day 5, and a moving average for Day 15 – Day 21 is matched with Day 18.

- **Step 4**. Use the moving averages (and their associated time periods) to calculate a trend line, using simple averaging, the high low method or linear regression analysis. It is also often useful to plot the data on a graph and extend a line of best fit.

Example

A company operates for five days each week. Sales data for the most recent three weeks are as follows:

Sales	Monday units	Tuesday units	Wednesday units	Thursday units	Friday units
Week 1	78	83	89	85	85
Week 2	88	93	99	95	95
Week 3	98	103	109	105	105

For convenience, it is assumed that Week 1 consists of Days 1 – 5, Week 2 consists of Days 6 – 10, and Week 3 consists of Days 11 – 15.

This sales data can be used to estimate a trend line. A weekly cycle in this example is 5 days, so we must calculate moving averages for five day periods, as follows:

Period	Middle day		Moving average
Days 1 – 5	Day 3	[78 + 83 + 89 + 85 + 85] /5	84
Days 2 – 6	Day 4	[83 + 89 + 85 + 85 + 88] /5	86
Days 3 – 7	Day 5	[89 + 85 + 85 + 88 + 93] /5	88
Days 4 – 8	Day 6	[85 + 85 + 88 + 93 + 99] /5	90
Days 5 – 9	Day 7	[85 + 88 + 93 + 99 + 95] /5	92
Days 6 – 10	Day 8	[88 + 93 + 99 + 95 + 95] /5	94
Days 7 – 11	Day 9	[93 + 99 + 95 + 95 + 98] /5	96
Days 8 – 12	Day 10	[99 + 95 + 95 + 98 + 103] /5	98
Days 9 – 13	Day 11	[95 + 95 + 98 + 103 + 109] /5	100
Days 10 – 14	Day 12	[95 + 98 + 103 + 109 + 105] /5	102
Days 11 – 15	Day 13	[98 + 103 + 109 + 105 + 105]/5	104

In this example, all the moving average figures lie on a perfect straight line. It can be seen that each day the trend increases by 2. If x = the day number, the formula for the trend can be calculated by taking any day, say day 12

a + 2 × 12 = 102 so a = 78.

The formula is daily sales = 78 + 2x.

This trend line can be used to calculate the 'seasonal variations' (in this example the daily variations in sales above or below the trend).

Moving averages and trend line when there is an even number of seasons

When there is an even number of seasons in a cycle, the moving averages will not correspond to an actual season. When this happens it is necessary to take moving averages of the moving averages, which will correspond to an actual season of the year.

Example

The following sales figures have been recorded for a company, where sales are known to fluctuate with the season of the year. There are four seasons (four quarters) in the year. Historical data for quarterly sales is shown in the table below.

Sales	Quarter 1 $000	Quarter 2 $000	Quarter 3 $000	Quarter 4 $000
Year 1	20	24	27	31
Year 2	35	39	44	47
Year 3	49	56	60	64

These quarters for the three years will be called Quarter 1 – Quarter 12. There are four seasons in the annual cycle, so moving average values for each quarter are calculated as follows:

Period	Middle quarter	Moving average	Moving average of moving average (average of 2)
Quarters 1 – 4	Quarter 2.5	25.50	
	Quarter 3		27.375
Quarters 2 – 5	Quarter 3.5	29.25	
	Quarter 4		31.125
Quarters 3 – 6	Quarter 4.5	33.00	
	Quarter 5		35.125
Quarters 4 – 7	Quarter 5.5	37.25	
	Quarter 6		39.250
Quarters 5 – 8	Quarter 6.5	41.25	
	Quarter 7		43.000
Quarters 6 – 9	Quarter 7.5	44.75	
	Quarter 8		46.875
Quarters 7 – 10	Quarter 8.5	49.00	
	Quarter 9		51.000
Quarters 8 – 11	Quarter 9.5	53.00	
	Quarter 10		55.125
Quarters 9 – 12	Quarter 10.5	57.25	

The moving averages in the right hand column correspond with an actual season. These moving averages are used to estimate the trend line and the seasonal variations.

4.4 Calculating seasonal variations

The trend line on its own is not sufficient to make forecasts for the future. We also need estimates of the size of the 'seasonal' variation for each of the different seasons. In the two examples above:

- In the first example we need an estimate of the amount of the expected daily variation in sales, for each day of the week.

- In the second example we need to calculate the variation above or below the trend line for each season or quarter of the year.

A 'seasonal variation' can be measured from historical data as the difference between the actual historical value for the time period, and:

- the corresponding moving average value, where moving averages are used, or

- the corresponding straight line value for the trend line, where linear regression analysis is used.

Either of two assumptions might be made about seasonal variations.

- The **additive assumption**. This assumption is that the sum of seasonal variations above and below the trend line in each cycle adds up to zero. Seasonal variations below the trend line have a negative value and variations above the trend line have a positive value. Taking all the seasonal variations together in one cycle, they will add up to 0.

- The **proportional assumption**. This assumption is that the actual value in each season can be expressed as a proportion of the trend line value. For example, sales in Quarter 1 might be 120% of the trend line value, sales in Quarter 2 95% of the trend line value, sales in Quarter 3 103% of the trend line value and sales in Quarter 4 85% of the trend line value. When the proportional assumption is used for seasonal variations, the seasonal variations in the cycle multiplied together must = 1. In the example above, $1.20 \times 0.95 \times 1.03 \times 0.85 = 1.0$ (allowing for a small rounding error).

Estimating seasonal variations: the additive model

The seasonal variation for each season (or daily variation for each day) is estimated as follows, when the additive assumption is used:

- Use the moving average values that have been calculated from the historical data, and the corresponding historical data. ('actual' data) for the same time period.

- Calculate the difference between the moving average value and the actual historical figure for each time period. This is a seasonal variation. You will now have a number of seasonal variations, covering several weekly or annual cycles.

- Group these seasonal variations into the different seasons of the year (or days of the week). You will now have several seasonal variations for each day of the week or season of the year.

- For each season (or day), calculate the average of these seasonal variations.

- This average seasonal variation for each day of the week or season of the year is used as the seasonal variation for the purpose of forecasting. However, if the seasonal variations for the cycle do not add up to zero, adjust the seasonal variations so that they do add up to zero.

The seasonal variations can then be used, with the estimated trend line, to make forecasts for the future.

Example

Using the example above of the trend line for daily sales, the seasonal variations are calculated as follows:

Middle day	Day of the week	Moving average value	Actual sales	Variation (Actual – Moving average)
Day 3	Wednesday	84	89	+ 5
Day 4	Thursday	86	85	- 1
Day 5	Friday	88	85	- 3
Day 6	Monday	90	88	- 2
Day 7	Tuesday	92	93	+ 1
Day 8	Wednesday	94	99	+ 5
Day 9	Thursday	96	95	- 1
Day 10	Friday	98	95	- 3
Day 11	Monday	100	98	- 2
Day 12	Tuesday	102	103	+ 1
Day 13	Wednesday	104	109	+ 5

The seasonal variation (daily variation) is now calculated as the average seasonal variation for each day, as follows:

Variation	Monday units	Tuesday units	Wednesday units	Thursday units	Friday units
Week 1			+ 5	- 1	- 3
Week 2	- 2	+ 1	+ 5	- 1	- 3
Week 3	- 2	+ 1	+ 5		
Average	- 2	+ 1	+ 5	- 1	- 3

Points to note

(1) In this example, the average seasonal variation for each day of the week is exactly the same as the actual seasonal variations. This is because the historical data in this example produces a perfect trend line.

(2) The total of the seasonal variations for each day of the week is 0. (- 2 + 1 + 5 – 1 – 3 = 0). When seasonal variations are applied to a straight-line trend line, they must always add up to zero. If the seasonal variations did not add up to 0, the trend line would not be straight. It would 'curve' up or down, depending on whether the sum of the seasonal variations is positive or negative.

(3) If the total of the seasonal variations over a cycle do not add up to 0, the variations should be adjusted so that they do add up to 0 – for example by adding 1 or subtracting 1 from the variation for the seasons with the largest variations.

Estimating seasonal variations with the proportional model

When a proportional model is used to calculate seasonal variations, rather than the additive model, the seasonal variations for each time period are calculated by dividing the actual data by corresponding moving average or trend line value.

Example

Using the previous example for quarterly sales, actual sales and the corresponding moving average value were as follows:

Quarter	Actual sales in the quarter	Moving average value of sales	Seasonal variation: actual sales as a proportion of the moving average
Year 1, Quarter 3	27	27.375	0.986
Year 1, Quarter 4	31	31.125	0.996
Year 2, Quarter 1	35	35.125	0.996
Year 2, Quarter 2	39	39.250	0.994
Year 2, Quarter 3	44	43.000	1.023
Year 2, Quarter 4	47	46.875	1.003
Year 3, Quarter 1	49	51.000	0.961
Year 3, Quarter 2	56	55.125	1.016

Variation	Quarter 1	Quarter 2	Quarter 3	Quarter 4
Year 1			0.986	0.996
Year 2	0.996	0.994	1.023	1.003
Year 3	0.961	1.016		
Average	0.978	1.004	1.004	0.999
Adjust to	0.98	1.01	1.01	1.00

In this example, the seasonal variations are very small. The average variation for each quarter is found by multiplying the values for the variations, and taking the nth root. In quarter 1 for example, the average variation is calculated as $\sqrt{(0.996 \times 0.961)} = 0.978$.

The adjustment is made so that the seasonal variations, when multiplied together, come to 1.0.

In this example, the seasonal variations are very small.

4.5 Using the trend line and seasonal variations to make forecasts

When the trend line and seasonal variations have been estimated, we can make forecasts for the future. In the example above of daily sales, suppose that we wanted to forecast sales in units each day during Week 4 (days 16 – 20) and the trend line is 78 + 2x.

The 'seasonal variations' (daily variations) are as calculated above: - 2, + 1, + 5, - 1 and - 3.

The daily sales forecasts are calculated as follows:

Day		Trend line value (78 + 2x)	Seasonal variation	Forecast sales (units)
16	Monday	110	- 2	108
17	Tuesday	112	+ 1	113
18	Wednesday	114	+ 5	119
19	Thursday	116	- 1	115
20	Friday	118	- 3	115

4.6 Advantages and disadvantages of time series analysis

Advantages

The input data should be readily available from the accounting system.

The technique is easy to use and understand.

It is easy to check the output of the model against actual data at an early stage and make corrections to a forecast where necessary.

Disadvantages

The assumption of the existence of a straight-line trend may not be true. For example, the process ignores where a product might be in its lifecycle.

Forecasts using estimated trends and seasonal variations are based on the assumptions that the past is a reliable guide to the future. This assumption may be incorrect.

The historical data does not provide a perfect trend line. The trend line that is estimated with the historical data is a 'best estimate', not a perfect estimate.

It is assumed that seasonal variations are a constant value, whereas they might be changing over time.

Estimates based on judgement and experience

There is an argument that instead of using models to forecast future sales (or make any other time series forecast), it might be better to rely on the judgement and experience of management.

Management will be aware of changes in the business environment or in the market that might affect results in the future, and time series analysis based on moving averages and seasonal variations would not make any allowance for these expected changes.

However, the drawback to relying on management judgement is that managers can make incorrect guesses.

4.7 Impact of the product lifecycle on forecasting

The product life cycle was explained in an earlier chapter (Chapter 12: Alternative accounting systems).

The stage that a product is at in its product lifecycle has a big effect on future plans in respect of that product.

Stage	Budgeting impact
Product development	No sales. Further investment required. Net cash outflows for this product.
Introduction to the market	Production costs incurred. Marketing and advertising to raise product awareness (strong focus on market share). Costs of setting up distribution channels. Sales growth will be forecast.
Growth	Increase in production costs as sales volume grows. Increased costs of working capital. Further sales growth will be forecast.
Maturity	Incur costs to maintain manufacturing capacity. Marketing and product enhancement costs may extend maturity phase. Positive cash inflows. No further growth in sales expected.
Decline	Close attention to costs needed as withdrawal decision might be expensive.
Withdrawal	Asset decommissioning costs Possible restructuring costs Remaining warranties to be supported

Knowledge of where a product is at in its lifecycle will impact budgeting in respect of that product. There are problems associated with this including:

- It is difficult to know where a product is in its lifecycle
- It is difficult to estimate the duration of each phase.

> **Spreadsheet models**
>
> - Features of a spreadsheet
> - Using spreadsheets
> - Applications of spreadsheets in cost and management accounting
> - 'What if' analysis: sensitivity analysis

5 Spreadsheet models

5.1 Features of a spreadsheet

Spreadsheets are used extensively in management accounting, because they enable accountants to make long and detailed calculations very quickly.

A spreadsheet program is a type of computer software. A spreadsheet is a table of rows and columns. Like any table, the rows and columns can contain words, figures or other symbols. A spreadsheet program is used to create spreadsheets.

A spreadsheet created by a spreadsheet program enables the user to prepare one or more tables of figures. Any table of figures, no matter how complex, can be prepared in a spreadsheet.

A blank spreadsheet is simply a huge table of rows and columns, with each row and having a unique identity number and each column having a unique letter code (A, B, C …AA, AB, etc). The table therefore consists of boxes or cells, and each cell can be identified by a unique combination of column letters and row number, such as B5, T28, AA4 and so on.

5.2 Using spreadsheets

A blank spreadsheet can be used to create a table of figures by entering words, figures and formulae. Figures are entered in the appropriate cells if their values are known. Otherwise a formula can be entered into a cell, and the spreadsheet model will convert the formula into a numerical value. The use of formulae in spreadsheets is the reason why they can be used to produce tables of figures so quickly. Formulae avoid the need to make calculations 'by hand' with a calculator.

Example

The example below is a very simple illustration of how spreadsheets are used to construct accounting calculations.

Column	All text in this column F	Entered in the spreadsheet file as text of formulae G	Shown in the spreadsheet on screen or printout G
Row			
6	**Year**	**Sales**	**Sales**
7		$	$
8	1	100,000	100,000
9	2	=G8*1.05	105,000
10	3	=G9*1.05	110,250
11	Total sales Years 1 - 3	=G8+G9+G10	315,250
12	Average annual sales	=G11/3	105,083

Column G is shown twice here. The left hand column for G shows the data as it has been entered into the spreadsheet as formulae. The right hand column for G shows the data that is displayed on the screen and in printouts.

The figures in the spreadsheet can be changed quickly simply by amending some of the data in the cells. For example, if the accountant wants to change the figures so that sales in Year 1 are $110,000 and annual sales growth in Years 2 and 3 is 4%, he can do this by amending the number in cell G8 to 110,000 and amending cells G9 and G10 to change 1.05 to 1.04.

Example

Here is another example of a simple accounting calculation entered as text, numbers and formulae in a spreadsheet.

Column	C	D	E	F
Row		1st 6 months	2nd 6 months	Year
4	Output (units)	10,000	15,000	= D4+E4
5		$	$	$
6	Variable costs	=D4*F11	=E*F11	=D6+E6
7	Fixed costs	40,000	=D7	=D7+E7
8	Total costs	=D6+D7	=E6+E7	=D8+E8
9				
10	Average cost/unit	=D8/D4	=E8/E4	=F8/F4
11	Variable cost/unit			3.00

This would appear on screen as follows:

Column	C	D	E	F
Row		1st 6 months	2nd 6 months	Year
4	Output (units)	10,000	15,000	25,000
5		$	$	$
6	Variable costs	30,000	45,000	75,000
7	Fixed costs	40,000	40,000	80,000
8	Total costs	70,000	85,000	155,000
9				
10	Average cost/unit	7.00	5.67	6.20
11	Variable cost/unit			3.00

The figures can be re-calculated using different figures for output in each half of the year, or different figures for fixed costs or the unit variable costs. All that is required is an alteration to the number in cells D4, E4, D7 or F11.

5.3 Applications of spreadsheets in cost and management accounting

Spreadsheets can be used for many tasks in cost and management accounting, where a large number of calculations are required. They are used to construct mathematical 'models' and to carry out a large number of calculations quickly and accurately.

Examples of applications of spreadsheets in management accounting include:

- Preparing forecasts of sales, and forecasts of profit or loss
- Cost estimation using linear regression analysis and the calculation of a correlation coefficient and coefficient of determination
- Preparing financial plans, such as budgets
- Comparing actual results with a plan or budget (control reporting).

Each table or set of related tables in a spreadsheet is held in a single file and accountants often carry a number of spreadsheet files on their laptop computer.

There are cost and management applications for which spreadsheets are not suitable. These include any application involving the recording and filing of large amounts of data. For these applications, involving the maintenance of records and large files, other types of software are more suitable, such as:

- A cost accounting software package for keeping cost accounting records (in a double entry 'book-keeping' system)
- An inventory control software package for maintaining records of inventory
- A database for maintaining and accessing other large files of data.

Graphical reproduction of spreadsheet data

Spreadsheets can be printed out and included in management reports. It is very common in practice to find tables of figures produced in a spreadsheet to be included as appendices in management reports.

In addition, the figures in a spreadsheet can be converted by the spreadsheet program into graphical display format, and shown as graphs, bar charts or pie charts. This facility can also be very useful for the preparation of management reports.

For example, if a spreadsheet is used for linear regression analysis, it can be used to show the line of best fit as a graph. Similarly, if a spreadsheet is used to prepare an estimate of costs, the percentage of total costs made up by different items of cost (direct materials, direct labour, production overheads etc) can be shown as a pie chart or a bar chart.

Applications of spreadsheets in management accounting include:

- Making forecasts, such as sales forecasts
- Preparing budgets and other financial plans
- Preparing flexible budgets for comparing actual and expected costs
- Preparing a complex income statement.

Some examples of spreadsheets are illustrated below. Don't worry about the detail in these examples. Cost-volume-profit analysis will be explained in a later chapter.

Example

Cost-volume-profit analysis is a technique in cost accounting that might be used to prepare profit forecasts or to estimate what the profit might be at different selling prices per unit or at different sales volumes. In this example, numbers might have been entered in cells C7, D7, F7 and G7. All the other cells, except for the text cells, will contain formulae.

The estimates for selling price, variable costs, budgeted sales units and fixed costs can be amended simply by changing the numbers in C7, D7, F7 and G7.
(However, in this example, the text cells A8 – A12 might also need changing).

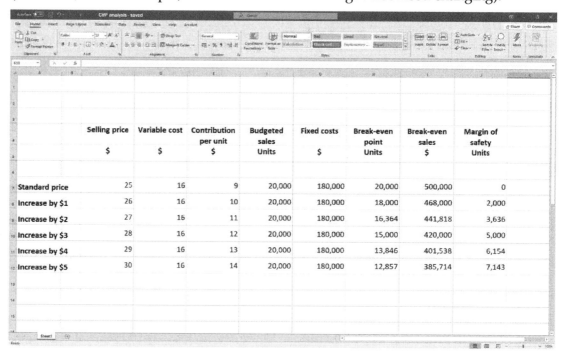

Graphical reproduction of spreadsheet data

In the Microsoft Excel spreadsheet program, the facility to produce graphical displays is provided by the Charts facility.

A 'Recommended Charts' icon is on the menu bar and appears as follows:

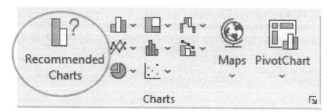

The example below shows how the profits for six different companies can be shown in the form of a graph using 'Recommended Charts'.

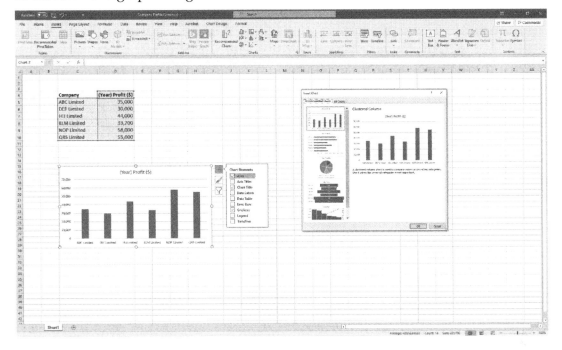

5.4 'What if' analysis: sensitivity analysis

An important feature of spreadsheets is the ability to re-calculate figures very quickly simply by changing the number or formula in one cell, or several cells.

For example if a spreadsheet is used to prepare a budget, the budget can be re-calculated changing the assumption about sales volume from, say, '50,000 units in month 1 and rising by 1,000 units each month' to '48,000 units in month 1 and rising by 800 units in each month' This would need amendments to just two cells in the spreadsheet.

Sensitivity analysis is a method of risk and uncertainty analysis. It analyses what the outcome will be if some factors are more favourable or more adverse than expected. For example, if a budget is prepared on the assumption that raw materials prices will increase by 3% compared with the previous year, sensitivity analysis could be used to estimate what the profit would be if raw material costs were higher, say 5% higher than the previous year.

By changing some key assumptions and seeing what happens to the profit, sensitivity analysis provides management with information about the sensitivity of the budget to changes in different assumptions about unit costs, sales volumes or selling prices.

The ability to carry out sensitivity analysis is improved enormously by using spreadsheets. Each analysis of the sensitivity of the outcome to changes in a key variable can be made quickly, by amending one or two items in the spreadsheet. A task that could take hours if done by hand can be finished in seconds (or possibly as much as a few minutes) using a spreadsheet.

Exercise

A company has recorded the following costs in the past six months:

Month	Activity	Total cost
	Units of output	$
January	14,000	98,700
February	12,600	91,700
March	15,300	103,350
April	14,900	101,000
May	16,100	107,450
June	16,000	107,080

Required

Using high/low analysis, prepare an estimate of total costs in August if output is expected to be 15,000 units.

You will find the answer to the Exercises and practice multiple choice questions at the end of this book.

Practice multiple choice questions

1 A company has the following costs at two activity levels.

Activity	Total cost
units	$
60,000	960,000
72,000	1,104,000

The variable cost per unit is constant over this range of activity, but there is a step fixed cost and total fixed costs increase by $36,000 when the activity level exceeds 64,000 units.

What is the expected total cost when the activity level is 70,000 units?

- A $1,050,000
- B $1,080,000
- C $1,086,000
- D $1,116,000

(2 marks)

2 A company has the following costs at three activity levels.

Activity	Total cost
units	$
60,000	960,000
72,000	1,104,000

The fixed cost is constant over this range of activity, but there is a reduction in the variable cost per unit by 10% when the activity level exceeds 15,000 units. This reduction applies to all units.

What is the expected total cost when the activity level is 14,000 units?

- A $224,000
- B $408,000
- C $424,800
- D $426,667

(2 marks)

3 The following statements relate to the calculation of a line of best fit for y = a + bx using the formulae in the formula sheet for your examination.

(i)   n represents the number of pairs of data used

(ii) $\sum x^2$ is calculated as the square of $\sum x$

(iii) $\sum xy$ is calculated by multiplying $\sum x$ by $\sum y$.

Which of the statements is/are correct?

- A (i) only
- B (i) and (ii) only
- C (ii) and (iii) only
- D (i) and (iii) only

(2 marks)

4 Regression analysis is being used to estimate a line of best fit from five pairs of data. The following values have been calculated from the data.

$\sum x = 258$, $\sum y = 2,670$, $\sum xy = 138,546$, $\sum x^2 = 13,732$, $\sum y^2 = 269,361$.

What is the value of 'a' (to the nearest whole number) in the line of best fit calculated from this data?

- A 439
- B 457
- C 629
- D 734

(2 marks)

5 Which one of the following is a feasible value for a correlation coefficient?

- A + 1.05
- B - 0.78
- C - 1.25
- D + 2.0

(1 mark)

6 The following statements relate to the use of spreadsheets in cost and management accounting.

(i) a spreadsheet is suitable for storing large quantities of data as cost records

(ii) a spreadsheet can be used to calculate a line of best fit using linear regression analysis

(iii) figures in a spreadsheet table can be converted by a spreadsheet program into a bar chart form

Which of the statements are correct?

- A (i) and (ii) only
- B (i) and (iii) only
- C (ii) and (iii) only
- D (i), (ii) and (iii)

(2 marks)

You will find the answers to the practice multiple choice questions at the end of this book.

Applied Knowledge
Management Accounting (MA)

CHAPTER

6

Simple and weighted index numbers

Contents
1 Index numbers
2 Weighted index numbers

> **Index numbers**
>
> - The purpose of index numbers
> - The base of 100 or 1,000
> - Price indices and quantity indices
> - Constructing index numbers

1 Index numbers

1.1 The purpose of index numbers

Index numbers are used to measure changes over time. Common examples of index numbers and indices are:

- a consumer price index or retail prices index, which measures changes in price levels over time; and

- a stock market index, which measures changes in a group of share prices over time (for example, changes in the prices of the top 500 shares traded in the USA – the S&P 500 Index).

Index numbers might be constructed in a relatively straightforward way by taking a list of values and choosing one as a base against which other values are compared. Alternatively index numbers might be constructed in a complex way, combining the price and quantity of many items. The retail price index is constructed in this way.

Index numbers can be used to judge the effects of changes, such as price changes, in the past. They can also be used to predict the future, by forecasting what the index number will be at a future date.

1.2 The base of 100 or 1,000

Most indices have a base number, which is usually given a value of 100 or 1,000. This makes it easy to monitor changes.

Example: Use of a base

In January Year 1 a base of 100 was set for a price index. This represents price levels at this time.

The price index at January Year 3 is 112.5 and at January Year 4 it is 118.1.

Price increase between:

January Year 1 and January Year 3 $= \left(\dfrac{112.5}{100.0}\right) - 1 = 0.125$ or 12.5%

January Year 1 and January Year 4 $= \left(\dfrac{118.1}{100.0}\right) - 1 = 0.181$ or 18.1%

January Year 3 and January Year 4 $= \left(\dfrac{118.1}{112.5}\right) - 1 = 0.05$ or 5.0%

Chapter 6: Simple and weighted index numbers

1.3 Price indices and quantity indices

A **price index** measures changes in the prices of a group of items over time. New prices are applied to a basket comprising the same amounts of the same items so that the index measures price changes only.

The group of items is often described as a basket of goods (and services). Government might choose the contents of the basket to reflect typical purchases in a society in order for the price index to provide a measure of inflation of relevance to government planning.

A **quantity index** measures changes over time in the quantities of items in a 'basket'. The price levels applied to the baskets at different points in time are kept constant so that the index only reflects movements in the quantity of goods and services purchased.

This chapter will first explain how index numbers might be constructed for a single item and then move on to talk about how they might be constructed for a group of items.

1.4 Constructing index numbers

By far the most common application of index numbers is to compare a series of annual figures. In order to do this a base year must be selected. This is the year against which all other years are compared.

Simple index numbers

Where we are interested in information about a single item the calculation of the index numbers is straightforward.

Formulae Simple index numbers

Simple price index (known as the price relative)	Simple quantity index (known as the quantity relative)
$$\text{Price index} = \frac{p_1}{p_0} \times 100$$ **Where:** p_0 = prices in the base period p_1 = prices in the current period	$$\text{Quantity index} = \frac{q_1}{q_0} \times 100$$ q_0 = quantities in the base period q_1 = quantities in the current period

Example: Simple index numbers

The following information relates to the price and quantity of coffee machines sold over a five year period.

	Price ($)	Quantity
20x1	65	12,178
20x2	68	13,493
20x3	69	15,149
20x4	72	16,287
20x5	75	17,101

Index numbers are to be constructed using 20x3 as a base year.
These would be as follows:

Simple price (price relative)		$\frac{p_1}{p_0} \times 100$	Index number
20x1	65	$\frac{65}{69} \times 100 =$	94
20x2	68	$\frac{68}{69} \times 100 =$	99
20x3	69	$\frac{69}{69} \times 100 =$	100
20x4	72	$\frac{72}{69} \times 100 =$	104
20x5	75	$\frac{75}{69} \times 100 =$	109

Simple quantity (quantity relative)		$\frac{q_1}{q_0} \times 100$	
20x1	12,178	$\frac{12,178}{15,149} \times 100 =$	80
20x2	13,493	$\frac{13,493}{15,149} \times 100 =$	89
20x3	15,149	$\frac{15,149}{15,149} \times 100 =$	100
20x4	16,287	$\frac{16,287}{15,149} \times 100 =$	108
20x5	17,101	$\frac{17,101}{15,149} \times 100 =$	113

Rebasing an index

Sometimes an index is adjusted to change its base year. This is a straightforward exercise.

The new index numbers are constructed by dividing the existing index number in each year by the existing index number for new base year and multiplying the result by 100.

Example: Simple index numbers

The following information relates to the price of a product sold over a seven year period.

The figures are to be rebased to 20x7.

	Simple price index		New simple price index
20x1	94	$\frac{94}{128} \times 100 =$	73
20x2	99	$\frac{99}{128} \times 100 =$	77
20x3	**100**	$\frac{100}{128} \times 100 =$	78
20x4	104	$\frac{104}{128} \times 100 =$	81
20x5	109	$\frac{109}{128} \times 100 =$	85
20x6	115	$\frac{115}{128} \times 100 =$	90
20x7	128	$\frac{128}{128} \times 100 =$	100

Note that this does not change the story told by the index numbers. It simply tells it in a different way.

 Example: Percentage change 20x1 to 20x7

	Old index	New index
20x1	94	73
20x7	128	100
Change	$\frac{128}{94} \times 100 = 136$	$\frac{100}{73} \times 100 = 136$
Percentage change	36%	36%

This information might be of interest to makers of the product but usually index numbers are required in circumstances where there is more than one item.

1.5 Index number with more than one item

Consider price index numbers where there is more than one item.

The aim is to construct a figure (index number) to compare costs (or quantities) in a year under consideration to a base year.

One way of doing this would be to calculate the simple aggregate price index.

Formula: Simple aggregate price index

$$\text{Simple aggregate price index} = \frac{\Sigma p_1}{\Sigma p_0} \times 100$$

Where:

Σp_0 = sum of prices in the base period

Σp_1 = sum of prices in the current period

Example: Index numbers with more than one item

A manufacturing company makes an item which contains four materials.

The prices of each material were as follows in the base period, January Year 1, and the most recent period, December Year 2

Material	January Year 1 (base period) Price per kilo p_0	December Year 2 (Current period) Price per kilo p_1
A	0.5	0.75
B	2.0	2.1
C	4.0	4.5
D	1.0	1.1
	7.5	8.45

$$\text{Simple aggregate price index} = \frac{\Sigma p_1}{\Sigma p_0} \times 100 = \frac{8.45}{7.5} \times 100 = 1.13$$

The index indicates that prices have increased from a base of 100 to 113, an increase of 13%.

This approach has a problem which might be obvious to you. It gives no indication of the relative importance of each material. The price of material A has increased from 0.5 to 0.75. This is an increase of 50%.

If each unit of production used 1 kg of B, C and D but 100kg of A, the simple aggregate price index would not capture the serious impact that the price increase has had on the cost base.

A more sophisticated method is needed to take the relative importance of items into account.

This is very important to governments who need to collect information about inflation. To do this they must construct a price index to measure changes in the prices of a group of items over time. As mentioned earlier, the group of items is often described as a basket of goods (and services).

A government must decide what goods and services to include in the group how much of these goods and services to reflect typical purchases in a society in order for the price index to provide a measure of inflation of relevance to government planning.

The next section explains the construction of indices based on baskets of goods (and services) in more detail.

> **Weighted index numbers**
> - Introduction
> - Price indices
> - Laspeyre and Paasche - comments
> - Quantity indices

2 Weighted index numbers

2.1 Introduction

An index is usually calculated as a weighted index. This means that the index is weighted to allow for the relative significance of each item in the 'basket'.

There are different ways of weighting an index. The two most common types of indices are:

- Laspeyre indices; and
- Paasche indices.

2.2 Price indices

A weighted price index can be calculated as either a Laspeyre price index or as a Paasche price index. A price index can be based either on the original quantities or on the current quantities of items in the 'basket'.

Laspeyre price index

The Laspeyre price index measures price changes with reference to the quantities of goods in the basket at the date that the index was first established.

This is the usual form of a weighted price index.

Formula: Laspeyre price index

$$\frac{\Sigma(p_1 \times q_0)}{\Sigma(p_0 \times q_0)} \times 100$$

Where:

$p_0 =$ prices in the base period for the index

$p_1 =$ prices in the current period for which an index value is being calculated

$q_0 =$ the original quantities in the base index.

Example: Laspeyre price index

A manufacturing company makes an item which contains four materials.

The price of each material, and the quantities required to make one unit of finished product, were as follows in the base period, January Year 1, and the most recent period, December Year 2

Material	January Year 1 (Base period)		December Year 2 (Current period)	
	Price per kilo	Kilos per unit	Price per kilo	Kilos per unit
	p_0	q_0	p_1	q_1
A	0.5	10	0.75	11.0
B	2.0	3	2.1	2.5
C	4.0	2	4.5	3.0
D	1.0	2	1.1	5.0

	p_0	q_0	p_1	q_1	$p_0 q_0$	$p_1 q_0$
A	0.5	10	0.75	11.0	5.0	7.5
B	2.0	3	2.1	2.5	6.0	6.3
C	4.0	2	4.5	3.0	8.0	9.0
D	1.0	2	1.1	5.0	2.0	2.2
					21.0	25.0

Laspeyre price index as at December Year 2:

$$\frac{\Sigma(p_1 \times q_0)}{\Sigma(p_0 \times q_0)} \times 100$$

$$\frac{25.0}{21.0} \times 100 = 119.0$$

The Laspeyre index shows that prices have risen by 19% between January Year 1 and December Year 2.

Paasche price index

The Paasche price index measures price changes with reference to current quantities of goods in the basket.

Formula: Paasche price index

$$\frac{\Sigma(p_1 \times q_1)}{\Sigma(p_0 \times q_1)} \times 100$$

Where:

p_0 = prices in the base period for the index

p_1 = prices in the current period for which an index value is being calculated

q_1 = are the quantities in the current period for which an index value is being calculated.

Example: Paasche price index

A manufacturing company makes an item which contains four materials.

The price of each material, and the quantities required to make one unit of finished product, were as follows in the base period, January Year 1, and the most recent period, December Year 2

Material	January Year 1 (Base period)		December Year 2 (Current period)	
	Price per kilo	Kilos per unit	Price per kilo	Kilos per unit
	p_0	q_0	p_1	q_1
A	0.5	10	0.75	11.0
B	2.0	3	2.1	2.5
C	4.0	2	4.5	3.0
D	1.0	2	1.1	5.0

	p_0	q_0	p_1	q_1	$p_0 q_1$	$p_1 q_1$
A	0.5	10	0.75	11.0	5.50	8.25
B	2.0	3	2.1	2.5	5.00	5.25
C	4.0	2	4.5	3.0	12.00	13.50
D	1.0	2	1.1	5.0	5.00	5.50
					27.50	32.50

Laspeyre price index as at December Year 2:

$$\frac{\Sigma(p_1 \times q_1)}{\Sigma(p_0 \times q_1)} \times 100$$

$$\frac{32.5}{27.5} \times 100 = 118.2$$

The Paasche index shows that prices have risen by 18.2% between January Year 1 and December Year 2.

2.3 Laspeyre and Paasche - comments

There might be little difference between the two indices unless there is a change in the pattern of consumption.

Difficulty in preparation

The denominator in the calculation of the Laspeyre price index (p_0q_0) does not change from year to year. The only new information that has to be collected each year is the prices of items in the index.

The denominator in the Paasche price index (p_0q_1) has to be recalculated every year to take account of the most recent quantities consumed. This information might be difficult to collect.

In summary, more information has to be collected to construct the Paasche price index than to construct the Laspeyre price index. This helps to explain why the Laspeyre price index is used more than the Paasche price index in practice.

Over/understatement of inflation

Laspeyre price index tends to overstate inflation whereas the Paasche price index tends to understate it. This is because consumers react to price increases buy changing what they buy.

The Laspeyre index which is based on quantities bought in the base year fails to account for the fact that people will buy less of those items which have risen in price more than others. These are retained in the index with the same weighting even though the volume of consumption has fallen.

The Paasche index is based on the most recent quantities purchased. This means that it has a focus which is biased to the cheaper items bought by consumers as a result of inflation.

2.4 Quantity indices

A quantity index can be calculated as either a Laspeyre index or a Paasche index. In the previous example, the quantities of each material in the product changed between January Year 1 and December Year 2, and there has been a change in the overall quantities of materials in the product.

A weighted quantity index can be calculated, but we need to decide whether to calculate the index using the prices in the base period for the index, or whether to use the price levels in the current period.

Laspeyre quantity index

Laspeyre index uses the price levels at the base period date.

Formula: Laspeyre quantity index

$$\frac{\Sigma(p_0 \times q_1)}{\Sigma(p_0 \times q_0)} \times 100$$

Where:

p_0 = prices in the base period for the index

q_0 = the original quantities in the base index.

q_1 = quantities used currently.

Example: Laspeyre quantity index

Using the data from the previous example.

	p_0	q_0	p_1	q_1	$p_0 q_0$	$p_0 q_1$
A	0.5	10	0.75	11.0	5.0	5.50
B	2.0	3	2.1	2.5	6.0	5.00
C	4.0	2	4.5	3.0	8.0	12.00
D	1.0	2	1.1	5.0	2.0	5.00
					21.0	27.50

Laspeyre quantity index as at December Year 2:

$$\frac{\Sigma(p_0 \times q_1)}{\Sigma(p_0 \times q_0)} \times 100$$

$$\frac{27.5}{21.0} \times 100 = 131.0$$

The Laspeyre index shows that there has been an increase of 31% in the quantities used between January Year 1 and December Year 2.

Paasche quantity index

A Paasche index uses the current price levels.

Formula: Paasche quantity index

$$\frac{\Sigma(p_1 \times q_1)}{\Sigma(p_1 \times q_0)} \times 100$$

Where:

$p_1 =$ prices in the current period for which an index value is being calculated

$q_0 =$ the original quantities in the base index.

$q_1 =$ are the quantities in the current period for which an index value is being calculated.

Example: Paasche quantity index

Using the data from the previous example.

	p_0	q_0	p_1	q_1	$p_1 q_0$	$p_1 q_1$
A	0.5	10	0.75	11.0	7.5	8.25
B	2.0	3	2.1	2.5	6.3	5.25
C	4.0	2	4.5	3.0	9.0	13.50
D	1.0	2	1.1	5.0	2.2	5.50
					25.0	32.50

Paasche quantity index as at December Year 2:

$$\frac{\Sigma(p_1 \times q_1)}{\Sigma(p_1 \times q_0)} \times 100 = \frac{32.5}{25.0} \times 100 = 130.0$$

The Paasche index shows that there has been an increase of 30% in the quantities used between January Year 1 and December Year 2.

Applied Knowledge
Management Accounting (MA)

CHAPTER 7

Summarising and analysing data

Contents
1   Collection and tabulation of data
2   Mean, mode and median
3   Measures of dispersion
4   Expected values
5   Normal distribution

> **Collection and tabulation of data**
>
> - Introduction
> - Different types of data
> - Organising and summarising data
> - Frequency distributions
> - Class boundaries

1 Collection and tabulation of data

1.1 Introduction

Statistics is a branch of mathematics that is concerned with the collection and analysis of data with the aim of improving understanding of the real world.

Statistics can be divided into two very broad categories:

- Descriptive statistics is concerned with describing numbers about situations in the present or the past; and

- Inferential statistics is concerned with drawing conclusions from observed numbers to make inferences about the population from which the data is collected and about future trends.

Inferential statistics is built on the foundation of descriptive statistics. This chapter is about descriptive statistics.

Data and information

Data is a term that refers to facts. It must be turned into information in order for it to become useful. Information is derived from facts that have been processed, structured and analysed.

1.2 Different types of data

A lot of the work in statistics involves collecting and analysing data.

Data consists of a number of observations (measurements) each recording a value of a particular variable.

- Variable: A characteristic that assumes different values for different entities (where an entity is an observation made about persons, places and things).

- Observations: The different values of a variable observed (measured).

Different types of variable

Quantitative and qualitative variables:

- Quantitative variables are those that take numerical values. Examples include:
  - time taken to complete a journey;
  - heights of adult students in a school;
  - number of customers entering a store each day;
  - number of rejects in a production run etc.
- Qualitative variables (also called attributes) are those that take non-numerical values (i.e. they are not numbers). Examples include:
  - eye colour;
  - favourite foods.

There are two different types of quantitative variables

- Discrete variables are those that can only take on certain and separate values. The measurement of such variables increases in jumps with gaps between possible values. Examples include:
  - number of attendees to a web broadcast increases by one person at a time. A fraction of a person cannot attend the broadcast and so cannot be part of the data;
  - number of defects in a production batch;
  - number of units produced.
- Continuous variables can take any value within a given range. Examples include:
  - physical dimensions like height and weight;
  - temperature

1.3 Organising and summarising data

Raw data is often collected in large volumes. In order to make it useful it must be analysed and rearranged into a format that is easier to understand.

Consider the following data.

Example: Raw data

The following list of figures is the distance travelled by 100 salesmen in one week (kilometres).

561	581	545	487	565
549	526	492	530	489
548	517	531	538	534
502	515	491	482	572
550	577	529	500	561
521	553	486	527	564
584	594	579	541	539
551	530	517	536	533
532	554	587	532	497
529	526	556	515	543
494	590	509	536	569
512	495	498	539	513
499	481	535	511	504
538	528	518	576	588
503	500	502	520	537
523	524	514	547	509
534	531	558	560	547
541	557	542	577	573
574	486	541	511	503
505	512	553	510	550

The human mind cannot assimilate data in this form. It must be rearranged in order to make it easier to understand.

Array

The obvious first step is to arrange the data into ascending or descending order. This is called an array.

 Example: Data in an array

481	505	526	539	558
482	509	527	539	560
486	509	528	541	561
486	510	529	541	561
487	511	529	541	564
489	511	530	542	565
491	512	530	543	569
492	512	531	545	572
494	513	531	547	573
495	514	532	547	574
497	515	532	548	576
498	515	533	549	577
499	517	534	550	577
500	517	534	550	579
500	518	535	551	581
502	520	536	553	584
502	521	536	553	587
503	523	537	554	588
503	524	538	556	590
504	526	538	557	594

1.4 Frequency distributions

A frequency distribution shows the various values which a group of items may take, and the frequency with which each value arises within the group.

Many values in the above list occur more than once. The next step might be to simplify the array by writing the number of times each value appears. This is called the frequency and is denoted with the letter f.

The data in this form is known as an ungrouped frequency distribution.

 Example: Ungrouped frequency distribution

	f		f		f		f		f
481	1	504	1	526	2	542	1	564	1
482	1	505	1	527	1	543	1	565	1
486	2	509	2	528	1	545	1	569	1
487	1	510	1	529	2	547	2	572	1
489	1	511	2	530	2	548	1	573	1
491	1	512	2	531	2	549	1	574	1
492	1	513	1	532	2	550	2	576	1
494	1	514	1	533	1	551	1	577	2
495	1	515	2	534	2	553	2	579	1
497	1	517	2	535	1	554	1	581	1
498	1	518	1	536	2	556	1	584	1
499	1	520	1	537	1	557	1	587	1
500	2	521	1	538	2	558	1	588	1
502	2	523	1	539	2	560	1	590	1
503	2	524	1	541	3	561	2	594	1

There are still too many figures for most minds to grasp. The distribution can be simplified further by grouping the figures. For example, instead of showing the frequency of each individual distance we could show the frequency of weekly distances of 480 and above but less than 500 and 500 and above but less than 520. Such groupings are known as classes. The size of the class is known as the class interval.

Points to be noted in the construction of a grouped frequency distribution are:

- The number of classes should be kept relatively small (say 6 or 7).

- In general, classes should be of the same width (of equal class interval) for easier comparison. (However, opening and closing classes might be wider to cater for extreme values and central classes may be narrower to afford greater detail).

- Open-ended classes ('over 50', 'under 10') are assumed to have the same width as adjacent classes for the purposes of drawing charts and performing statistical calculations.

- The end limits of the classes must be unambiguous. For example, '0 to 10' and '10 to 20' leaves it unclear in which 10 would appear. '0 to less than 10' and '10 to less than 20' is clear.

Example: Grouped frequency distribution

Distance travelled by salesmen in week xx.

Distance in km	Frequency (f)
480 to under 500	13
500 to under 520	22
520 to under 540	27
540 to under 560	19
560 to under 580	13
580 to under 600	6

1.5 Class boundaries

Each class has an upper and a lower limit. These limits are called class limits.

Data must be divided into groups or classes with no gaps between them.

Continuous data is already arranged into classes without any gaps. The upper limit of one class is the lower limit of the next so there are no gaps (as can be seen above).

Discrete data

A grouped frequency distribution of discrete data has gaps between the classes. It must be treated as continuous when used in further analysis (for example in constructing cumulative frequency graphs and histograms which will be covered in the next section).

Discrete data is converted into continuous data by identifying class boundaries.

Class boundary: The midpoint of the upper class limit of one class and the lower class limit of the subsequent class.

Each class thus has an upper and a lower class boundary. The upper class boundary of one class and the lower class boundary of the subsequent class are the same.

This is often necessary for the further analysis of data in grouped frequency distributions.

Assume that the following grouped frequency distribution is data relating to a discrete variable.

Example

Grouped frequency distribution (number of sale visits per annum made by members of sales force).

Number of visits	Frequency	Class boundaries
41 to 50	6	40.5 to 50.5
51 to 60	8	50.5 to 60.5
61 to 70	10	60.5 to 70.5
71 to 80	12	70.5 to 80.5
81 to 90	9	80.5 to 90.5
91 to 100	5	90.5 to 100.5

The lower class boundary of the first class is identified by deducting the same amount as is added to the upper limit 0.5 in this case).

Similarly, the upper class boundary of the last class is identified by adding the same amount as is deducted from the lower limit (0.5 in this case).

The class boundaries identified above are not part of the data set. In other words, they do not form part of the collected data but are rather, a tool needed to allow for certain further analysis.

Also note the following:

Formula: Class width

$$\text{class width} = \text{upper class boundary} - \text{lower class boundary}$$

Formula: Mid-point of a class

$$\text{mid-point} = \frac{\text{lower class boundary} + \text{upper class boundary}}{2}$$

Example

Grouped frequency distribution (number of sale visits per annum made by members of sales force).

Number of visits	Frequency	Class boundaries	Class width	Mid-point of class
41 to 50	6	40.5 to 50.5	10	45.5
51 to 60	8	50.5 to 60.5	10	55.5
61 to 70	10	60.5 to 70.5	10	65.5
71 to 80	12	70.5 to 80.5	10	75.5
81 to 90	9	80.5 to 90.5	10	85.5
91 to 100	5	90.5 to 100.5	10	95.5

> **Mean, mode and median**
>
> - Introduction
> - Mean, median and mode – ungrouped data
> - Mean – grouped data (frequency distributions)
> - Measures of central tendency compared

2 Mean, mode and median

2.1 Introduction

Data is usually clustered around some central value. The first step in analysing data is perhaps to understand the location of this central value and then to understand how other observations are dispersed around it. In other words we need:

- measures of central tendency;
- measures of spread or dispersion from the centre; and
- whether the dispersion around the mean is symmetrical or skewed to one side.

This section explains the measures of central tendency and the next section go on to explain measures of dispersion and skew.

Averages

An average is a measure of central tendency. There are three types of average that might be used:

- mean;
- median; and
- mode.

You must be able to calculate these measures for ungrouped data and the mean for grouped data

Note that the word average is used as a general term above but is also used as an alternative word for the mean. Also note that the term mean is usually used to describe the arithmetic mean but there are other kinds.

2.2 Mean, median and mode – ungrouped data

Mean

The arithmetic mean is a mathematical representation of the typical value of a series of numbers. It is computed as the sum of the numbers in the series divided by the number of numbers in that series.

Formula: Mean of ungrouped data

$$\bar{x} = \frac{\sum x}{n}$$

Where:

$\bar{x}$ = mean

n = number of items

$\sum x$ = the sum of all values of x

The mean need not be one of the values found in the series. In fact, it might not even be a round number.

The mean is usually taken as the best single figure to represent all the data.

Median

The median is the middle value when the data is arranged in ascending or descending order. Consequently, we must first arrange the data in order.

In cases where there is a large number of values the position of the median can be found by using the following expression:

Formula: Position of the median

$$\text{Position of the median} = \frac{n+1}{2}$$

Where:

n = number of items in the distribution

Mode

This is the most frequently occurring value. There may be more than one mode, or there may be no mode at all.

Example: Mean, median and mode

Find the mean, median and mode of the following numbers:

22, 18, 19, 24, 19, 21, 20

Mean

	x
	22
	18
	19
	24
	19
	21
	20
Sum of x	143

$$\bar{x} = \frac{\sum x}{n} = \frac{143}{7} = 20.4$$

Median

The items must be converted into an array:

18, 19, 19, 20, 21, 22, 24,

$$\text{Position of the median} = \frac{n+1}{2} = \frac{7+1}{2} = \text{4th item}$$

The 4th item in the array is 20

Mode = 19

If there is an even number of items, then there is no middle item. For example, if there had been 8 values in the data above (say an extra value of 25) the position of the median would be item 4.5.

In that case the median would be calculated as the mean of the 4th and 5th items. (Note that for large samples this would not be necessary).

2.3 Mean – grouped data (frequency distributions)

Formula: Mean of grouped frequency distribution

$$\bar{x} = \frac{\sum fx}{\sum f}$$

Where:

x = mid-point of the class

f = number of incidences in a class

Example: Grouped frequency distribution

Annual salary ($000)	Number of employees
5 and under 10	2
10 and under 15	15
15 and under 20	18
20 and under 25	12
25 and under 30	2
30 and over	1

The mean is found as follows:

Annual salary ($000)	Mid-point of class (x) x	Number of people (f) f	fx
5 and under 10	7.5	2	15
10 and under 15	12.5	15	187.5
15 and under 20	17.5	18	315
20 and under 25	22.5	12	270
25 and under 30	27.5	2	55
30 and over (closed at 35)	32.5	1	32.5
		50	875

Mean:

$$\bar{x} = \frac{\sum fx}{\sum f} = \frac{875}{50} = 17.5$$

2.4 Measures of central tendency compared

Measure	Advantages	Disadvantages
Mean	Uses every value in the distribution.	Can be distorted by extreme values when samples are small.
	Used extensively in other statistical applications.	The mean of discrete data will usually result in a figure not in the data set.
Median	Not influenced by extreme values	Little use in other applications.
	Is an actual value (as long as there is an odd number of observations).	
Mode	Is an actual value.	Little use in other applications.

> **Measures of dispersion**
> - Introduction
> - Standard deviation and variance
> - Measures of dispersion compared

3 Measures of dispersion

3.1 Introduction

Knowledge of the average provides information about the "typical value" of an array of data but gives no indication of the degree of clustering around that value. There are a number of measures that might be used to provide such information including:

- Standard deviation
- Variance

3.2 Standard deviation and variance

Standard deviation is a measure of variation around the mean and is used with the arithmetic mean as a pair of summary measures to describe a distribution of data.

Standard deviation of ungrouped data

Formula: Standard deviation of ungrouped data

$$s = \sqrt{\frac{\Sigma(x - \bar{x})^2}{n}}$$

Where:

s = standard deviation

n = number of items in the sample

Example: Standard deviation of ungrouped data

Standard deviation of six numbers: 50, 51, 48, 51, 49, 51

x	$(x - \bar{x})$	$(x - \bar{x})^2$
50	0	0
51	1	1
48	-2	4
51	1	1
49	-1	1
51	1	1
300	0	8

n = 6

$$\bar{x} = \frac{\sum x}{n} = \frac{300}{6} = 50$$

$$s = \sqrt{\frac{\sum(x - \bar{x})^2}{n}} = \sqrt{\frac{8}{6}} = 1.154$$

Standard deviation of grouped data

Formula: Standard deviation of a grouped frequency distribution

$$s = \sqrt{\frac{\sum fx^2}{\sum f} - \left(\frac{\sum fx}{\sum f}\right)^2}$$

Where:

x = mid-point of a class

f = frequency of a class

Example: Standard deviation of a simple frequency distribution

Find the mean and standard deviation of the following distribution:

Number of goals scored per soccer match (x)	Number of matches (f)	fx	fx²
0	8	0	0
1	7	7	7
2	3	6	12
3	1	3	9
4	1	4	16
	20	20	44

$$\bar{x} = \frac{\sum fx}{\sum f} = \frac{20}{20} = 1$$

$$s = \sqrt{\frac{\sum fx^2}{\sum f} - \left(\frac{\sum fx}{\sum f}\right)^2} = \sqrt{\frac{44}{20} - \left(\frac{20}{20}\right)^2} = 1.095 \text{ goals}$$

Variance

The variance is the standard deviation squared.

Formula: Variance

	Standard deviation (s)	Variance (s²)
Ungrouped data	$s = \sqrt{\dfrac{\sum(x - \bar{x})^2}{n}}$	$s^2 = \dfrac{\sum(x - \bar{x})^2}{n}$
Grouped data	$s = \sqrt{\dfrac{\sum fx^2}{\sum f} - \left(\dfrac{\sum fx}{\sum f}\right)^2}$	$s^2 = \dfrac{\sum fx^2}{\sum f} - \left(\dfrac{\sum fx}{\sum f}\right)^2$

When two distributions are combined, the arithmetic mean of the combination is simply the arithmetic mean of the two separate means.

This is not the case for the standard deviation as they cannot be added. However, variances can be added. Therefore, in order to find the standard deviation of a combined distribution, the following steps must be followed:

Step 1: Compute the variances of the individual distributions by squaring the standard deviation.

Step 2: Sum the two variances. The result is the variance of the combined distribution.

Step 3: Take the square root of the variance of the combined distribution. The result is the standard deviation of the combined distribution.

Example: Combining distributions

	Distribution A	Distribution B
Mean ($\bar{x}$)	40	50
Standard deviation (s)	10	12
Variance (s^2)	100	144

Combining the distributions:

Mean of the combination
$$\bar{x} = \frac{40 + 50}{2} = 45$$

Variance of the combination
$$s^2 = 100 + 144 = 244$$

Therefore, the standard deviation of the combination is:
$$s = \sqrt{244} = 15.6$$

Coefficient of variation

The coefficient of variation is a measure of relative dispersion that expresses the standard deviation in terms of the mean. The aim of this measure is to allow comparison of the variability of two sets of figures.

Formula: Coefficient of variation

$$\text{Coefficient of variation} = \frac{s}{\bar{x}} \times 100$$

 Example: Coefficient of variation

A class of children sat 2 exams (one marked out of 20 and one marked out of 100). The results were as follows:

	Distribution A	Distribution B
Maximum possible mark	20	100
Mean ($\bar{x}$)	12	64
Standard deviation (s)	3	10

Coefficient of variation

Test 1
$$= \frac{s}{\bar{x}} \times 100 = \frac{3}{12} \times 100 = 25\%$$

Test 2
$$= \frac{s}{\bar{x}} \times 100 = \frac{10}{64} \times 100 = 15.625\%$$

Test 1 results have the higher relative dispersion.

3.3 Measures of dispersion compared

Measure	Advantages	Disadvantages
Standard deviation	Uses all values Very useful in further applications	Difficult to understand Difficult to calculate (but perhaps this is no longer true due to programmes like excel).
Variance	Can be used to find the standard deviation of a distribution Useful in further applications	

> **Expected values**
>
> - Expected values
> - Expected values and decsion making

4 Expected values

4.1 Expected values

One technique for comparing risk and return of different decision options is the use of expected values.

Expected values can be used to analyse information where risk can be assessed in terms of probabilities of different outcomes. Where probabilities are assigned to different outcomes, we can evaluate the worth of a decision as the expected value or weighted average of these outcomes.

Expected value (EV) = weighted average of possible outcomes.

The weighted average value is calculated by multiplying the probability of each possible outcome by the value of the outcome.

Formula: Expected value

$$Expected\ value = \sum px$$

Where:

p = the probability of each outcome

x = the value of each outcome

An EV is a measurement of weighted average value.

A decision might be based on selecting the course of action that offers the highest EV of profit, or the lowest EV of cost. In other words, the 'decision rule' is to select the course of action with the highest EV of profit or the lowest EV of cost.

The main advantage of using EVs to make a decision is that it takes into consideration the probability or likelihood of each different possible outcome, as well as its value (profit or cost).

Example: Expected value

A business entity is selecting one of three projects for investment. The three projects are mutually exclusive.

The projects do not involve any initial capital expenditures.

The expected annual profits from investing in each of the projects depend on the state of the market. The following estimates of annual profits (operational cash flows) have been prepared:

State of market	Declining	Static	Expanding
Probability	0.4	0.3	0.3
Project 1	100	200	900
Project 2	0	500	600
Project 3	180	190	200

> This type of table is called a 'pay-off table' or a 'pay-off matrix'. It shows all the possible 'pay-offs' or results from different possible decisions or strategies.

Project 1	Profit	Probability (p)	Profit × (p)
Declining	100	0.4	40
Static	200	0.3	60
Expanding	900	0.3	270
			370

Project 2	Profit	Probability (p)	Profit × (p)
Declining	0	0.4	0
Static	500	0.3	150
Expanding	600	0.3	180
			330

Project 3	Profit	Probability (p)	Profit × (p)
Declining	180	0.4	72
Static	190	0.3	57
Expanding	200	0.3	60
			189

Based on expected values, project 1 should be selected because it has the highest EV of annual profit.

Advantages of using expected values

An EV is a weighted average value, that is based on all the different possible outcomes and the probability that each will occur.

It recognises the risk in decisions, based on the probabilities of different possible results or outcomes.

It expresses risk in a single figure, which makes it easy to compare different options and reach a decision.

Disadvantages of using expected values

The probabilities of the different possible outcomes may be difficult to estimate. If the probabilities are unreliable, expected values will also be unreliable.

The EV is unlikely to be an actual outcome that could occur. In the example above, the EVs for projects 1, 2 and 3 ($370,000, $330,000 and $189,000 respectively) are not expected to occur. They are simply weighted average values.

Unless the same decision has to be made many times, the average will not be achieved. It is therefore not a valid way of making a decision about the future when the outcome will happen only once.

An EV is an average value. It gives no indication of the range or spread of possible outcomes. It is therefore an inadequate measurement of risk.

4.2 Expected values and decision making

Expected values should be reliable for decision-making when:

- Probabilities can be estimated with reasonable accuracy, and
- The outcome from the decision will happen many times, and will not be a 'one-off' event.

In the following example, the estimate of monthly repair costs using expected value is likely to be very reliable, since the probabilities are based on historical records and the outcome happens many times over (10,000 times each month).

Example: Expected value

A company makes and sells 10,000 units of Product K each month.

Currently, when customers complain that there are or more defects in a product, the company repairs the product at its own cost.

Management is now considering selling the product for $6 less but no longer accepting liability for any defects.

The decision as to whether to change the policy is to be made by comparing the expected monthly cost of the new policy to the expected monthly cost of the current policy.

Expected monthly cost of new policy: 10,000 units × $6 = $60,000

Expected cost of existing policy:

The estimates of defects in each product with a calculation of expected defects are given as follows:

Number of defects per product	Probability (p)	Number of defects × (p)
0	0.99	0
1	0.07	0.07
2	0.02	0.04
3	0.01	0.03
		0.14
Number of products sold per month		10,000
Expected number of defects per month		1,400

The estimate of the cost of repairing a defect with a calculation of expected cost is given as follows:

Cost of repairing one defect ($)	Probability (p)	Cost of repairing one defect ($) × (p)
20	0.2	4
30	0.5	15
40	0.3	12
Expected cost of each repair		31
Expected number of defects per month		1,400
Expected cost of all repairs		$43,400

The policy should not be changed.

> **Normal distribution**
>
> - The features of a normal distribution
> - A standard normal distribution table
> - Using a standard normal distribution table
> - Normal distribution tables and confidence levels

5 Normal distribution

When a measurement is taken of a population or a sample of items, we can calculate an average value for the population or sample.

For example, a business can calculate its average daily sales from a sample of daily sales figures. The actual sales on any day will usually be above or below the average, so there is a range of daily sales figures that the average sales figure represents. Actual daily sales are therefore 'distributed' around the average or mean value. So daily sales might average $2,400, but actual daily sales might be anywhere in a range of, say, $1,200 to $3,700.

It has been found from experience that the distribution of actual values around the average is often very close to a normal distribution. A normal distribution is a distribution that can be defined mathematically, and whose properties are measurable. If a population of items has a distribution that is similar to a normal distribution, the distribution can be analysed statistically using normal distribution tables.

5.1 The features of a normal distribution

A normal distribution is a symmetrical distribution of values around an average ('mean'). The distribution of values below the average is mirrored exactly by the distribution of values above the average.

This symmetrical distribution can be drawn as a bell-shaped curve as follows:

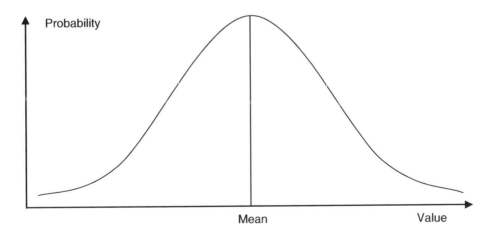

This is a graph where the y axis represents probability and the x axis represents the value of the item being measured (such as daily sales). The total area under the curve represents 100% of total values.

A normal distribution therefore shows that the most likely actual value is the mean value, but the actual value can be above or below the mean. Values close to the mean are more probable (more likely to happen) than values a long way above or below the mean.

Because of the mathematical properties of a normal distribution, it is possible to measure the probability of a value being:

- above a specified amount
- below a specified amount, or
- within a specified range of values.

A key statistical feature of a normal distribution is that the probability of a value being more or less than a specified amount can be measured in terms of standard deviations above or below the average/mean.

- The normal distribution is symmetrical. Because the distribution is symmetrical, there is a 50% probability that a value will be higher than the average ('above the mean' and a 50% probability that a value will be less than the average ('below the mean').

- Because of the mathematical properties of the normal distribution, it is also possible to predict the probability that a value will be within a given number of standard deviations above or below the mean. For example:
    - there is a probability of 34.13% that a value will be within a range of one standard deviation below the mean and the mean
    - there is a probability of 34.13% that a value will be within a range of the mean and one standard deviation above the mean
    - there is therefore a probability of 68.26% (2 × 34.13%) that a value will be in a range of one standard deviation below the mean to one standard deviation above the mean.

- For similar reasons we can predict that there is a probability of 15.87% (50% - 34.13%) that a value will be more than one standard deviation below the mean and there is also a probability of 15.87% that a value will be more than one standard deviation above the mean.

These probabilities can be obtained from normal distribution tables. A normal distribution table is provided in the formula sheet in your examination.

5.2 A standard normal distribution table

A standard normal distribution table is shown in the introductory pages to this text, in the pages for the formulae and tables.

The table represents the probabilities in one half of a normal distribution. Since the normal distribution is symmetrical, the table represents either the half of the distribution below the mean or the half that is above the mean.

- The rows and columns represent the number of standard deviations above or below the mean.
- The figures in the table are the probabilities that a value will be within that number of standard deviations of the mean.

For example:

- The value for 1 standard deviation is in the row 1.0 and the column 0.00. The value here is 0.3413. This shows that in a normal distribution, there is a probability of 0.3413 or 34.13% of a value between the mean and 1 standard deviation below the mean. There is a similar probability of 0.3413 or 34.13% of a value between the mean and 1 standard deviation above the mean.
- The value for 1.25 standard deviations is in the row 1.2 and the column 0.05. The value in the table is 0.3944. This shows that in a normal distribution, there is a probability of 0.3944 or 39.44% of a value between the mean and 1 standard deviation below the mean. There is a similar probability of 0.3944 or 39.44% of a value between the mean and 1 standard deviation above the mean. This also means that the probability that a value will be somewhere between 1.25 standard deviations below the mean and 1.25 standard deviations above the mean is 78.88%.

5.3 Using a standard normal distribution table

For any value whose variability can be approximated by a normal distribution, normal distribution tables can be used for probability analysis and so for risk analysis. The following examples show how this can be done:

Example

A simulation model has been used to calculate the expected value of the NPV of a project. This is + $31,950. The standard deviation of the project is $18,000.

The variability in the NPV approximates to a normal distribution. (This is usual for the output results from a simulation model).

(a) What is the probability that the NPV will be greater than $0?
(b) What is the probability that the NPV will be greater than $40,000?

Answer

(a) An NPV of $0 is below the mean value of $31,950, by $31,950. We need to convert this into a number of standard deviations, or 'Z score'.

Z = 31,950/18,000 = 1.775 standard deviations.

The probability that the NPV will be between the mean (the EV of the NPV) and a value that is 1.775 standard deviations below the mean is between 0.4616 (1.77 standard deviations) and 0.4625 (1.78 standard deviations). Since 1.775 is exactly half-way between 1.77 and 1.78, we can estimate by interpolation that the probability for 1.775 standard deviations is 0.46205 (0.4616 + (0.4625 − 0.4616) × 50%).

This can be rounded to 0.4620.

The probability that the NPV will be between the mean (the EV of the NPV) and a value that is 1.775 standard deviations below the mean is therefore 0.4620. The probability that the NPV will be above the mean (the EV of the NPV) is 0.5000 (50%). The probability that the NPV will be higher than $0 is therefore 0.9620 or 96.20%.

	Probability
NPV between $0 and the EV(mean)	0.4620
Above the mean	0.5000
Above $0	0.9620

(b) An NPV of $40,000 is $8,050 above the mean value of $31,950.

The Z score is 8,050/18,000 = 0.447.

The probability that the NPV will be between the mean value (EV) and 0.447 standard deviations above the mean is somewhere between 0.1700 (0.44 standard deviations) and 0.1736 (0.45 standard deviations). We can estimate by interpolation that the probability for 0.447 standard deviations is 0.1726 (0.1700 + (0.1736 − 0.1700) × 70%).

The probability that the NPV will be more than 0.447 standard deviations above the mean is therefore 0.5000 − 0.1726 = 0.3274 or 32.74%.

5.4 Normal distribution tables and confidence levels

A normal distribution table can also be used to establish confidence levels. In risk analysis, it is usual to assess risk at the 95% confidence level or the 99% confidence level.

- A 95% confidence level means that there is a 95% probability.
- A 99% confidence level means that there is a 99% probability.

Confidence levels for values within a range

We can use normal distribution tables to calculate, at a given confidence level, that the value of an item will be within a specified range of values above and below the mean.

For example, suppose that a simulation model produces results showing that the EV of the NPV for a project is $125,000 and the standard deviation (project volatility) is $40,000. We can predict at the 95% confidence level that the NPV of the project will be within a specified range around the EV.

To establish a 95% confidence level for the range around the NPV, we need to identify the range of values below the mean that represent 47.5% of total probabilities and the range of values above the mean that represent 47.5% of total probabilities (since 2 × 47.5% = 95%).

We therefore need to identify the number of standard deviations from the mean that cover 47.5% of all probabilities. From the normal distribution table, we can identify that this is 1.96 standard deviations.

At a 95% confidence level, we can therefore predict that the NPV will be somewhere in the range between 1.96 standard deviations below the mean and 1.96 standard deviations above the mean.

Similarly, at a 99% confidence level, we can predict that the NPV will be somewhere in the range between 2.575 standard deviations below the mean and 2.575 standard deviations above the mean. (This is because there is a probability of 0.4950 that the value will be 2.575 standard deviations below the mean and a probability of 0.4950 that the value will be 2.575 standard deviations above the mean.)

Example

A simulation model has been used to calculate the expected value of the NPV of a project. This is + $150,000. The standard deviation of the project is $55,000.

The variability in the NPV approximates to a normal distribution. (This is usual for the output results from a simulation model).

At the 95% confidence level, we can predict that the NPV of the project will be in the range of 1.96 standard deviations above and below the mean. 1.96 × $55,000 = $107,800. At the 95% confidence level, we can therefore predict that the NPV will be somewhere in the range $42,800 to $257,800.

At the 99% confidence level, we can predict that the NPV of the project will be in the range of 2.57 standard deviations above and below the mean. 2.57 × $55,000 – $141,350. At the 99% confidence level, we can therefore predict that the NPV will be somewhere in the range + $8,650 to $291,350.

Confidence levels for values above or below a specified amount

Confidence levels can also be established to identify the probability that the actual value will be above or below a specified amount. For example, we can establish at the 95% or 99% level of confidence that a value will be more than $X or less than $X (or not more than $X or not less than $X).

With this type of calculation we are looking at only one side of the normal distribution table (and carrying out a 'one-tailed test'). This differs from confidence levels for a range above and below the mean, where we are looking at both sides of the normal distribution, above and below the mean.

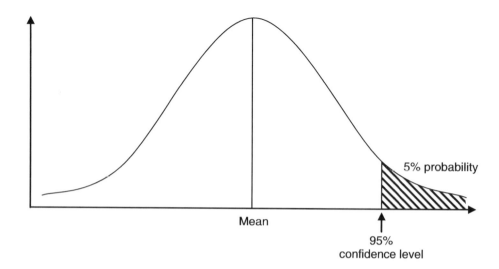

The diagram shows that if we want to establish a 95% confidence level for a value that is above the mean, we need to calculate the number of standard deviations above the mean for which there is a 45% probability. There is a 50% probability that the value will be less than the mean, so taken together we have a 95% probability level.

From the normal distribution table, we can find that 0.4500 of probabilities are within 1.645 standard deviations of the mean, on one side of the normal distribution table.

At the 95% level of confidence we can therefore state that the value will be less than an amount equal to 1.645 standard deviations below the mean. We can also state that at the 95% confidence level, the value will not exceed an amount that is more than 1.645 standard deviations above the mean.

 Example

A simulation model has been used to calculate the expected value of the NPV of a project. This is + $70,000. The standard deviation of the project is $28,000.

The variability in the NPV approximates to a normal distribution.

At the 95% confidence level, we can therefore predict that the NPV will be not less than $46,060 (1.645 × $28,000) below the EV of $70,000. This means that at the 95% confidence level the NPV will be not less than $23,940.

To establish the 99% confidence level, we can establish that 0.4900 of probabilities are between the men and about 2.33 standard deviations of the mean. At the 99% confidence level, we can therefore predict that the NPV will be not less than $65,240 (2.33 × $28,000) below the EV of $70,000. This means that at the 99% confidence level the NPV will be not less than + $4,760.

Applied Knowledge
Management Accounting (MA)

CHAPTER

8

Accounting for materials

Contents
1 Materials: procedures and documentation
2 Costing of issues from inventory
3 Material purchase quantities: Economic Order Quantity
4 Material purchase quantities: purchase discounts and gradual replenishment
5 Inventory reorder level and other warning levels

> **Materials: procedures and documentation**
>
> - The need for procedures and documentation of materials
> - The procedures and documents
> - Monitoring physical inventory: comparison with the inventory records
> - Entries and balances in a materials inventory account

1 Materials: procedures and documentation

1.1 The need for procedures and documentation of materials

When an entity purchases materials from a supplier, the purchasing process should be properly documented. There are several reasons for this.

Any purchase of materials from a supplier should be properly authorised and approved at the appropriate management level. Documentation of the purchasing process provides evidence that approval has been obtained.

The receipt of materials from a supplier should also be documented, to make sure that the goods that were ordered have actually been delivered.

There should be an invoice from the supplier for the goods that have been delivered. (In rare cases when goods are bought for cash, there should be a receipt from the supplier). The amount payable for the materials provides documentary evidence about their cost.

When materials are received from a supplier, they might be held in a store or warehouse until needed. When they are issued from the store, there should be a documentary record of who has taken the materials and how many were taken. This is needed to provide a record of the cost of materials used by different departments or cost centres.

Documentation of materials is therefore needed:

- to ensure that the procedures for ordering, receiving and paying for materials has been conducted properly, and there is no error or fraud;
- to provide a record of materials purchases for the financial accounts; and
- to provide a record of materials costs for the cost and management accounts.

1.2 The procedures and documents

The detailed procedures for purchasing materials and the documents used might differ according to the size and nature of the business. However, the basic requirements should be the same for all types of business where material purchases are made.

Purchasing procedures and documents

In a large company with a purchasing department (a buying department) and a stores department, the procedures for purchasing materials might be as follows.

- The stores department identifies the need to re-order an item of raw materials for inventory. It produces a request to the purchasing department to buy a quantity of the materials. This request is called a **purchase requisition.** It should be properly authorised by a manager with the authority to approve any such requisition.

- A buyer in the purchasing department selects a supplier and provides the supplier with **a purchase order,** stating the identity of the item to be purchased, the quantity required and possibly also the price that the supplier has agreed.

- When the supplier delivers the goods, the goods are accompanied by a **delivery note** from the supplier. The delivery note is a statement of the identity and quantity of the items delivered, and it provides confirmation that the items have been delivered. One copy is kept with the stores department, and another copy is retained by the supplier (the driver of the delivery vehicle), as evidence of the delivery.

- The stores department prepares a **goods received note,** recording the details of the materials received. This should include the inventory identity code for the item, as well as the quantity received.

- Copies of the delivery note and goods received note are sent to the accounts department, where they are matched with a copy of the purchase order.

- A **purchase invoice** is received from the supplier, asking for payment. The accounts department checks the invoice details with the details on the purchase order and goods received note, to confirm that the correct items have been delivered in the correct quantities.

- The purchase invoice is used to record the purchase in the **accounting records**.

- In the cost accounting system, there should be **inventory records** to record the quantities and costs of materials received. Data for recording costs of purchases for each item of inventory is obtained from the goods received note (quantity and inventory code) and purchase invoice (cost).

The purchase process

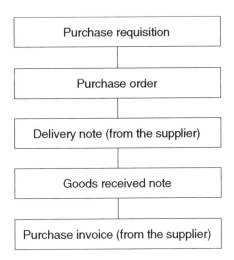

Inventory records

An entity should keep an up-to-date record of the materials that it is holding in inventory.

- **In the stores department**, the materials should be kept secure, and there should be systems, processes and controls to prevent loss, theft or damage. The stores department should keep a record of the quantity of each item of material currently held in inventory. For each item of material, there might therefore be an inventory record card, or 'bin card'. This card is used to keep an up-to-date record of the number of units of the material currently in the stores department, with records of each receipt and issue of the inventory item. This process of continuous record-keeping is known as **perpetual inventory**. The inventory record should be updated every time materials are delivered into store from a supplier, and every time that materials are issued to an operating department. Instead of having a 'physical' card for each stores item, there may be a computerised record containing similar information.

- **In the cost accounting department**, another separate record of inventory might be kept, with an **inventory ledger record** for each item of material. The inventory ledger record is a record of the quantity of the materials currently held in inventory, the quantities received into store from suppliers and the quantities issued to operational departments. In addition the inventory ledger record also records the **cost** of the materials currently held in inventory, the cost of new materials purchased and the cost of the materials issued to each operating department (cost centre).

- **In a computerised inventory control system**, the stores department and the cost accounting department should use the same computerised records for inventory.

Issues and returns of materials

A cost accounting system also needs to record the quantities and cost of items of materials that are issued to the user departments, and the quantities and cost of any items that are subsequently returned to store unused.

The documentation for the issue and returns of materials are:

- A **materials requisition note**: this is a formal request from a user department to the stores department for a quantity of an item of materials

- A materials return note: when items are returned to store unused, the stores department should record the return on a **materials returns note**.

A materials requisition note is used to record:

- the details of the quantity of materials issued
- the department (cost centre) that receives them, and
- (in a cost accounting system) their cost.

The inventory records are updated from the requisitions notes and returns notes to record all issues and returns of materials.

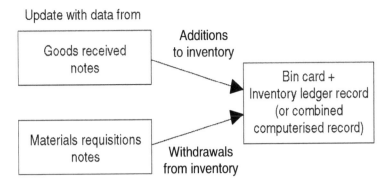

A simplified version of an inventory record for a perpetual inventory system is shown below, to demonstrate that inventory records can be used to record receipts and issues (and returns) of materials, and their cost or value. The record needs to identify the cost centres that have issued or returned materials, and will probably also record the number of the materials requisition note or materials returns note (although this data is not shown in the example below).

Inventory item   **Code number** 1234
                     Description

		Issues		Returns		Purchases		Balance	
		Quantity	Cost	Quantity	Cost	Quantity	Cost	Quantity	Cost
			$		$		$		$
Date	Department (code)								
March									
1								200	400
3						300	630	500	1,030
7	23	250	505					250	525
9	23			30	63			220	462
12	18	100	210					120	252

1.3 Monitoring physical inventory: comparison with the inventory records

For various reasons, the inventory records in the cost accounts might not agree with the physical quantities of materials actually held in store. There are several reasons for this.

- **Errors in recording receipts, issues and returns.** Mistakes might be made in recording transactions for materials received from the supplier, materials issued from store and returns to store. For example, an issue of material item 1234 from inventory might be recorded as an issue of item 1243. This would result in inaccurate inventory records for both item 1234 and item 1243.

- **Omissions.** Similarly, some purchases, issues and returns to store might not be recorded, due to mistakes.

- **Theft or physical loss.** Some inventory might be stolen or might get lost, and the theft or loss might not be noticed or recorded.

- **Damage to stores items** or **deterioration of items.** Stores items might deteriorate in quality when they are stored, particularly if they are stored in poor conditions. Damaged items might be thrown away, but the write-off might not be recorded.

Management should try to minimise these discrepancies between inventory records (in a perpetual inventory system) and physical inventory in the store.

- It is the responsibility of the stores manager to minimise losses due to theft, loss or deterioration and damage.
- Documentation and record keeping should be accurate and mistakes should be minimised. All movements of materials should be properly recorded in a document, and the data from the document should be transferred accurately into the inventory records.

Even so, good record keeping and goods stores management will not prevent some discrepancies between inventory records and physical inventory in store. This discrepancy should be checked from time to time. The stores department staff can do this by carrying out a **physical count** of the quantity of each material item currently held, and comparing this 'physical count' with the figures in the stores records. The records should then be adjusted to the correct quantities. (Quantities that are 'missing' will be recorded as a write-off of materials in the accounts).

Minimising discrepancies and losses

When physical inventory is checked against the inventory records, there will often be some differences. When the differences are big, there could be a serious problem with either:

- Poor control over inventory. Some losses through theft, deterioration and breakages should be expected, but the losses should not be large.
- Poor inventory records. If the inventory records are inaccurate, the information prepared for management from inventory records will be unreliable.

Whichever failing is the reason for big discrepancies between physical inventory and inventory records, management should take measures to deal with the problem.

- Theft can be reduced by keeping inventory locked in a safe place. TV cameras can be used to monitor activity in the warehouse.
- Deterioration of inventory can be reduced by keeping the inventory in better storage condition.
- Poor procedures for recording inventory movements in and out of the store can be improved through better procedures and suitable controls, such as better supervision of the recording process and better staff training.

1.4 Entries and balances in a materials inventory account

In a system of cost accounting, a separate record is kept for each inventory item. This record – an inventory account – is used to maintain a record of all movements in the materials, in terms of both quantities and cost.

The main contents of an inventory record are shown in the previous example. An inventory record in the cost accounts provides a continual record of the following:

- Purchases/deliveries from suppliers: quantity and cost
- Returns to suppliers: quantity and cost
- Issues of the item to user departments: quantity, cost and department identity

- Returns from user departments to the stores: quantity, cost and department identity
- The balance held in inventory (quantity and cost or value).

The inventory records are combined into a total record for all inventory, which is used for reporting purposes such as the preparation of a costing statement or an income statement of the profit or loss made in a period. The system for recording inventory and materials costs might also be a part of a bigger cost accounting system.

A cost accounting system is a system for recording all costs and in large organisations it is maintained in the form of a double entry accounting system of cost records in a 'cost ledger'.

> **Costing of issues from inventory**
>
> - The reason for inventory valuation methods
> - Opening inventory, purchases, closing inventory and cost of materials used
> - First-in, first-out (FIFO) method
> - Last-in, first-out (LIFO) method
> - Weighted average cost (AVCO) methods
> - Summary

2 Costing of issues from inventory

2.1 The reason for inventory valuation methods

A record can be kept of all materials purchased and all materials that are used, and their cost. It is necessary to calculate the cost of materials in order to calculate the cost of the cost units and cost centres that use the materials.

- If materials are purchased for a specific item of work, the actual cost of the materials can be charged directly to the item.

- However, it is usually too difficult and impractical to associate each unit of materials issued from stores with its actual original purchase cost. Materials are purchased and stored in large quantities, and are issued to user departments in no particular order.

- A system is therefore needed for deciding the cost of each quantity of materials issued from store. This is called 'pricing the material issues'. There are several material pricing methods, including:
    - first-in first-out (FIFO)
    - last-in first-out (LIFO)
    - weighted average cost (AVCO)
    - standard cost.

2.2 Opening inventory, purchases, closing inventory and cost of materials used

It is also important to know the connection between the cost of materials purchased in a financial period and the cost of materials used in the period. These two costs differ by the amount of the increase or decrease in inventory between the beginning and the end of a period.

Example

	$
Value of opening inventory, 1 January	3,000
Purchases in the period	7,000
	10,000
Value of closing inventory, 31 December	(2,000)
Cost of materials issued and used in the year	8,000

Choice of inventory valuation method

The value of inventory and the cost of materials issued and used in the period are determined by a selected inventory valuation method, such as FIFO, LIFO, weighted average cost or standard cost.

The choice of valuation method – FIFO, weighted average cost, LIFO – therefore affects the reported profit for each period.

LIFO is not allowed as a valuation method in financial reporting, but it may be used in cost accounting systems, which are not governed by the rules of accounting standards and external financial reporting.

2.3 First-in, first-out (FIFO) method

With the first-in, first-out (FIFO) method of inventory valuation, it is assumed that:

- the earliest units received into store are the first materials issued, and are priced accordingly, and so
- at any time, the remaining units in store are the most recently purchased.

 Example

On 1 October, a company had 100 units in store of a material whose item code is 2345. These units have a cost of $5 each. During October, it made the following purchases, totalling $6,900:

- 4 October: 300 units at $6 each
- 12 October: 500 units at $7 each
- 22 October: 200 units at $8 each.

During the month, there were four issues of materials, each of 200 units, on 7 October, 16 October, 23 October and 30 October.

Required

(a) What was the cost of the material issued from store in October, using the FIFO valuation method?

(b) What was the value of the closing inventory on 31 October?

Answer

Date	Quantity	Inventory value	Issued	Comments
	Units	$	$	
1 Oct	100	500		Opening inventory, 100 at $5
4 Oct purchase	300	1,800		300 at $6
	400	2,300		100 at $5, 300 at $6
7 Oct issue	(200)	(1,100)	1,100	100 at $5, 100 at $6
	200	1,200		200 at $6
12 Oct purchase	500	3,500		500 at $7
	700	4,700		200 at $6, 500 at $7
16 Oct issue	(200)	(1,200)	1,200	200 at $6
	500	3,500		500 at $7
22 Oct purchase	200	1,600		200 at $8
	700	5,100		500 at $7, 200 at $8
23 Oct issue	(200)	(1,400)	1,400	200 at $7
	500	3,700		300 at $7, 200 at $8
30 Oct issue	(200)	(1,400)	1,400	200 at $7
31 Oct: Closing inventory	300	2,300		100 at $7, 200 at $8
Total cost of issues in October			5,100	

2.4 Last-in, first-out (LIFO) method

With the last-in, first-out (LIFO) method of inventory valuation it is assumed that:

- the most recent units received into store are the first materials issued, and are priced accordingly

- at any time, the remaining units in store are likely to have been purchased some time ago.

Example

On 1 October, a company had 100 units in store of a material whose code item is 2345. These units have a cost of $5 each. During October, it made the following purchases, totalling $6,900:

- 4 October: 300 units at $6 each

- 12 October: 500 units at $7 each

- 22 October: 200 units at $8 each.

During the month, there were four issues of materials, each of 200 units, on 7 October, 16 October, 23 October and 30 October.

Required

(a) What was the cost of the material issued from store in October, using the LIFO valuation method?

(b) What was the value of the closing inventory on 31 October?

Answer

Date	Quantity	Inventory value	Issued	Comments
	Units	$	$	
1 Oct	100	500		Opening inventory, 100 at $5
4 Oct purchase	300	1,800		300 at $6
	400	2,300		100 at $5, 300 at $6
7 Oct issue	(200)	(1,200)	1,200	200 at $6
	200	1,100		100 at $5, 100 at $6
12 Oct purchase	500	3,500		500 at $7
	700	4,600		100 at $5, 100 at $6, 500 at $7
16 Oct issue	(200)	(1,400)	1,400	200 at $7
	500	3,200		100 at $5, 100 at $6, 300 at $7
22 Oct purchase	200	1,600		200 at $8
	700	4,800		100 at $5, 100 at $6, 300 at $7, 200 at $8
23 Oct issue	(200)	(1,600)	1,600	200 at $8
	500	3,200		100 at $5, 100 at $6, 300 at $7
30 Oct issue	(200)	(1,400)	1,400	200 at $7
31 Oct closing inventory	300	**1,800**		100 at $5, 100 at $6, 100 at $7
Total cost of issues in October			5,600	

2.5 Weighted average cost (AVCO) methods

With the weighted average cost (AVCO) method of inventory valuation it is assumed that all units are issued at the current weighted average cost per unit.

Continuous weighted average method

The normal method of measuring average cost is the **continuous basis method**. With the continuous basis AVCO method, a new average cost is calculated whenever more items are purchased and received into store. The weighted average cost is calculated as follows:

$$\frac{\text{Cost of inventory currently in store} + \text{Cost of new items received}}{\text{Number of units currently in store} + \text{Number of new units received}}$$

Items 'currently in store' are the items in store immediately before the new delivery is received.

Example

On 1 October, a company had 100 units in store of a material whose item code is 2345. These units have a cost of $5 each. During October, it made the following purchases, totalling $6,900:

- 4 October: 300 units at $6 each
- 12 October: 500 units at $7 each
- 22 October: 200 units at $8 each.

During the month, there were four issues of materials, each of 200 units, on 7 October, 16 October, 23 October and 30 October.

Required

(a) What was the cost of the material issued from store in October, using the continuous weighted average cost (AVCO) valuation method?

(b) What was the value of the closing inventory on 31 October?

Remember that with the continuous AVCO method, a new weighted average cost is calculated whenever there is a new receipt of inventory items into store.

Answer

Date	Quantity	Inventory value	Issued	Comments
	Units	$	$	
1 Oct	100	500		Opening inventory = 100 at $5
4 Oct purchase	300	1,800		
	400	2,300		New average cost = $2,300/400 = $5.75
7 Oct issue	(200)	(1,150)	1,150	200 at $5.75
	200	1,150		200 at $5.75
12 Oct purchase	500	3,500		
	700	4,650		New average cost = $4,650/700 = $6.64
16 Oct issue	(200)	(1,328)	1,328	200 at $6.64
	500	3,322		500 at $6.64
22 Oct purchase	200	1,600		
	700	4,922		New average cost 700 at $7.03
23 Oct issue	(200)	(1,406)	1,406	200 at $7.03
	500	3,516		500 at $7.03
30 Oct issue	(200)	(1,406)	1,406	200 at $7.03
31 Oct (closing inventory)	300	2,110		300 at $7.03
Total **cost of issues** in October			5,290	

Periodic weighted average cost method

Instead of calculating average cost using the continuous basis method, it is possible to calculate a periodic weighted average cost. This might be used when the business entity has a period-end inventory system. It cannot be used for continuous inventory systems, because it relies on calculating just one weighted average cost for each financial period, at the end of the period.

A single weighted average cost is calculated at the period end and used to cost all issues (i.e. the cost of sales) and all units of closing inventory.

The periodic weighted average is calculated as follows:

$$\frac{\text{Cost of opening inventory + Cost of all purchases in the period}}{\text{Units of opening inventory + Units purchased in the period}}$$

Example

On 1 October, a company had 100 units in store of a material whose item code is 2345. These units have a cost of $5 each. During October, it made the following purchases, totalling $6,900:

- 4 October: 300 units at $6 each
- 12 October: 500 units at $7 each
- 22 October: 200 units at $8 each.

During the month, there were four issues of materials, each of 200 units, on 7 October, 16 October, 23 October and 30 October.

Required

(a) What was the cost of the material issued from store in October, using the periodic weighted average cost valuation method?

(b) What was the value of the closing inventory on 31 October?

Using the periodic AVCO method, a new weighted average cost is calculated at the end of each period (where the period is chosen by the management).

Answer

Date	Quantity	Inventory value	Comments
	Units	$	
1 Oct	100	500	
4 Oct purchase	300	1,800	
12 Oct purchase	500	3,500	
22 Oct purchase	200	1,600	
	1,100	7,400	Average cost = 7,400/1,100 = $6.73
Issues:			
7 Oct issue	200		
16 Oct issue	200		
23 Oct issue	200		
30 Oct issue	200		
	(800)	(5,384)	800 units at $6.73
31 Oct (closing)	300	2,016	

2.6 Summary

The following table summarises the results from the above example showing the inventory movement under each method for the month of October

	FIFO	LIFO	Continuous WA	Periodic WA
	$	$	$	$
Opening inventory	500	500	500	500
Purchases	6,900	6,900	6,900	6,900
	7,400	7,400	7,400	7,400
Closing inventory	(2,300)	(1,800)	(2,110)	(2,016)
Cost of materials issued	5,100	5,600	5,290	5,384

> **Material purchase quantities: Economic Order Quantity**
>
> - Minimising materials costs
> - Holding costs and ordering costs
> - Economic order quantity (EOQ)
> - EOQ: changes in the variables in the formula

3 Material purchase quantities: Economic Order Quantity

3.1 Minimising materials costs

Organisations that purchase and consume large quantities of materials should try to minimise the total costs. Total materials costs, for any item of materials, consist of:

- the cost of materials purchased (the purchase price)
- the costs of making purchase orders to buy the material (ordering costs)
- the costs of holding inventory (this is often a cost of interest on the investment in inventory).

In most cases, the most significant cost is the purchase cost of the materials. However, ordering costs and holding costs might also be substantial.

3.2 Holding costs and ordering costs

It is useful to be aware of what holding costs and ordering costs consist of.

Holding costs for inventory include costs such as:

- the interest cost of the investment in inventory
- the costs of losses through holding inventory, due to obsolescence, deterioration in the condition of the inventory and theft of inventory items
- the costs of insurance of inventory.

Inventory has to be paid for, and when an organisation holds a quantity of inventory it must therefore obtain finance to pay for it. For example suppose that a company holds between 0 units and 1,000 unit of an item of material that costs $10 per unit to purchase. The cost of the materials held in store therefore varies between $0 and $10,000. On average the cost of the inventory in store is likely to be about $5,000. This inventory must be financed, and it is usual to assume (for simplicity) that it is financed by borrowing that has an interest cost. In this example, if the interest cost of holding inventory is 5% per year, the cost per year of holding the inventory would be $250 (= $5,000 × 5%).

There are other inventory holding costs too, such as the costs of operating a stores department – the rental cost of the stores, the wages or salaries of stores staff and other running costs.

Ordering costs are the costs of making an order to purchase a quantity of a material item from a supplier. They include costs such as:

- the cost of delivery of the purchased items, if these are paid for by the buyer
- the costs associated with placing an order, such as the costs of telephone calls
- costs associated with checking the inventory after delivery from the supplier.

3.3 Economic order quantity (EOQ)

If the price of materials is the same no matter what the size of the purchase order, the purchase order quantity that minimises total costs is the quantity at which ordering costs plus the costs of holding inventory are minimised.

This order quantity or purchase quantity that minimises the total annual cost of ordering the item plus holding it in store is called the economic order quantity or EOQ.

- EOQ minimises Ordering costs + Holding costs
- Ordering costs each year = $\left(\dfrac{C_o \times D}{Q}\right)$
- Inventory holding costs each year = $\left(\dfrac{Q}{2}\right) \times C_H$

Where:

- Q = the quantity of materials purchased in each order (EOQ)
- D = the annual demand for the materials
- C_o = the cost of making an order for materials
- C_H = the cost of holding one unit of material in store for one year

Assumptions:

- There is a constant demand for the materials throughout the year. For example, if annual demand is 4,000 units of the item each year, the item is consumed at a constant rate throughout the year.
- There will be an immediate supply of new materials (Q units) as soon as existing quantities in store run down to 0. The minimum quantity held in store is therefore 0 units and this always occurs just before a new purchase order quantity is received. The maximum quantity is Q units. The average amount of inventory held is therefore Q/2 and total holding costs each year are (Q/2) × C_H.
- The number of orders each year is D/Q. Total ordering costs each year are therefore (D/Q) × C_O.

The economic order quantity (EOQ) is the order size that will minimise the total of these costs during a period (normally one year), given the assumptions stated above.

The formula for the EOQ is as follows:

Economic order quantity (EOQ) = $\sqrt{\dfrac{2C_o D}{C_H}}$

This formula is given to you in the examination (on the formulae sheet), although you should be able to learn it.

A note on ordering costs and inventory holding costs. For the purpose of the EOQ formula, the costs that should be used in the formula are only those costs that are incurred as a **direct consequence** of ordering inventory or holding inventory. Costs that would be incurred anyway – such as the salary costs of the buyer or the costs of renting warehouse space – should not be used in the formula because they are not relevant costs for deciding the EOQ size. Relevant costs are explained in more detail in a later chapter.

Examination hint: annual demand and annual holding cost per unit

It is important to make sure that all the items in the EOQ formula are based on the same time period. The demand should be annual demand and the holding cost should be an annual holding cost per unit. You might be given an examination in which demand is stated as a quantity for each three-month period but the holding cost is given as an annual cost. You would therefore need to convert the three-monthly demand into an annual demand for using in the EOQ formula.

Example

A company uses 14,450 units of Material X each year, which costs $2 for each unit. The cost of placing an order is $125 for each order. The cost of holding inventory each year is 10% of the purchase cost.

What is the order quantity for Material X that will minimise annual costs?

Answer

$$EOQ = \sqrt{\frac{2C_oD}{C_H}}$$

Where:

$C_o = 125$

$D = 14{,}450$

$C_H = 10\% \times 2 = 0.2$

$$= \sqrt{\left(\frac{2 \times 14{,}450 \times 125}{0.2}\right)} = \sqrt{18{,}062{,}500} = 4{,}250 \text{ units}$$

The economic order quantity is 4,250 units, which means that the average number of orders placed with suppliers will be 3.4 orders each year (= 14,450/4,250).

EOQ: Annual holding costs = Annual ordering costs

It might be useful to know that the EOQ is also an order quantity where the total annual costs of ordering and the total annual holding costs are exactly the same. In the example above:

- EOQ = 4,250 units
- Annual ordering costs = $(C_O \times D)/Q$ = ($125 × 14,450)/4,250 = $425
- Annual holding costs = $(Q/2) \times C_H$ = (4,250/2) × $0.20 = $425.
- Ordering costs and holding costs each year are both $425.

Total annual ordering costs and annual holding costs are always the same whenever the purchase quantity for materials is the EOQ and the assumptions on which the EOQ is based (described earlier) apply.

Exercise 1

The purchase cost of an item of inventory is $60 per unit. In each three-month period, 5,000 units of the item are used. Annual holding costs for this item are 8% of its cost. The cost of placing an order is $250.

What is the economic order quantity for this item, to the nearest whole unit?

3.4 EOQ: changes in the variables in the formula

You need to develop a good understanding of the EOQ formula. An examination question might test your ability to assess the consequences of a change in the value of any variable in the formula. For example, what would be the consequences of:

- an increase in the annual holding cost per unit
- a reduction in the annual holding cost per unit
- an increase or a reduction in the order cost
- an increase or a reduction in the annual order quantity.

A change in any of these variables will affect:

- the size of the EOQ, and because the EOQ changes
- total annual ordering costs, and
- total annual holding costs.

Example

A company uses the economic order quantity formula to decide the purchase quantities for its major items of material purchases. The holding cost of inventory is currently 6% of the purchase cost.

Required

What will be the effect of a reduction in the interest rate to 5% on:

(a) the EOQ

(b) total annual ordering costs

(c) total annual holding costs?

Answer

$$EOQ = \sqrt{\frac{2C_oD}{C_H}}$$

A fall in interest rates will reduce the value of C_H.

(a) C_H is below the line in the EOQ formula and if it falls in value, the EOQ will increase.

(b) An increase in the EOQ will result in a reduction in ordering costs. Since the EOQ is higher, the number of orders each year (= D/Q) will fall, and given no change in the cost of each order, total ordering costs must therefore fall.

(c) If the order quantity is EOQ, total annual ordering costs and total annual holding costs are the same. If total annual ordering costs fall, it follows that total annual holding costs will fall too.

Example

A company uses the economic order quantity formula to decide the purchase quantities for its major items of material purchases. The cost of an order increases by 10%.

Required

What will be the effect of the increase in order cost on:

(a) the EOQ

(b) total annual ordering costs

(c) total annual holding costs?

Answer

$$EOQ = \sqrt{\frac{2C_oD}{C_H}}$$

The approach to a solution is similar to the previous example.

An increase in the order cost means an increase in C_O.

(a) C_O is above the line in the EOQ formula and if it increases in value, the EOQ will increase.

(b) An increase in the EOQ will result in a higher average inventory quantity (Q/2 will be higher). Given no change in the annual holding cost per unit, total holding costs must therefore increase.

(c) If the order quantity is EOQ, total annual ordering costs and total annual holding costs are the same. If total annual holding costs increase, it follows that total annual ordering costs will also rise.

> **Material purchase quantities: purchase discounts and gradual replenishment**
>
> - Order quantity with price discounts for large orders
> - Economic batch quantity (EBQ): gradual replenishment of inventory

4 Material purchase quantities: purchase discounts and gradual replenishment

4.1 Order quantity with price discounts for large orders

The optimum purchase quantity is the order size that minimises the total costs of:

- Annual purchase costs = (D × price per unit)

- Ordering costs each year = $\dfrac{(C_o \times D)}{Q}$

- Inventory holding costs each year = $\left(\dfrac{Q}{2}\right) \times C_H$

When the EOQ formula is used to calculate the purchase quantity, it is assumed that the purchase cost per unit of material is a constant amount, regardless of the order quantity.

In some cases, however, a supplier might offer a discount on the purchase price for orders above a certain quantity. When this situation arises, the order quantity that minimises total costs will be either:

- the economic order quantity, or
- the **minimum** order quantity necessary to obtain the price discount.

To identify the order quantity that minimises costs, you need to calculate the total costs each year of purchases, ordering costs and holding costs, for both order quantities (the EOQ and the minimum order quantity to obtain the discount).

(If a supplier offers a discount for order quantities above a certain amount and a larger discount for orders above an even larger quantity, you need to compare total costs for the EOQ and for each minimum quantity at which a different purchase discount applies).

Example

A company uses 14,450 units of Material X each year, which costs $2 for each unit before discount. The costs of making an order are $125 for each order. The annual cost of holding inventory is 10% of the purchase cost. The supplier will offer a price discount of $0.10 per unit for orders of 6,000 up to 10,000 units, and a discount of $0.20 per unit for orders of 10,000 units or more.

What is the order quantity that will minimise total costs?

Answer

The economic order quantity, ignoring discounts, is 4,250 units (see earlier example). The order quantity that will minimise costs is therefore one of the following:

4,250 units, the economic order quantity

6,000 units, the smallest quantity required above the EOQ to get a discount of $0.10 per unit

10,000 units, the smallest quantity required above the EOQ to get a discount of $0.20 per unit.

	Order quantity		
	4,250 units $	6,000 units $	10,000 units $
Annual purchase costs (14,450 units) (W1)	28,900	27,455	26,010
Annual ordering costs $\frac{(C_o \times D)}{Q}$ (W2)	425	301	181
Holding costs $\left(\frac{Q}{2}\right) \times C_H$ (W3)	425	570	900
Total costs	29,750	28,326	27,091

Conclusion

The order quantity that minimises total costs is 10,000 units.

Workings

(W1) Annual purchase costs

Order quantity Units		Annual purchase cost $
4,250 (= EOQ)	14,450 × $2	28,900
6,000	14,450 × $(2 – 0.10)	27,455
10,000	14,450 × $(2 – 0.20)	26,010

(W2) Annual ordering costs

Order quantity Units		Annual ordering costs $
4,250 (= EOQ)	(14,450/4,250) × $125	425
6,000	(14,450/6,000) × $125	301
10,000	(14,450/10,000) × $125	181

(W3) Annual holding costs

Order quantity		Annual holding costs
Units		$
4,250 (= EOQ)	(4,250/2) × $2	425
6,000	(6,000/2) × $1.90	570
10,000	(10,000/2) × $1.80	900

4.2 Economic batch quantity (EBQ): gradual replenishment of inventory

Batch production

The EOQ formula is based on the assumption that when inventory is replenished with a new delivery, the full order quantity is received into store immediately. The inventory level therefore ranges between 0 units and Q units. The economic order quantity is used when materials are purchased from external suppliers.

A similar situation arises when an entity manufactures items itself in batches and holds them as inventory until they are sold or used for further processing. For example, a company might produce finished goods in batches, and on completion of production, the materials are transferred to finished goods inventory until they are sold.

However, when it takes some time to produce a batch of items the items might be delivered into store gradually, whilst production is still in progress. The first units are therefore received into store before production of the batch is complete.

If we assume that the first items from a new production batch are received into store when the inventory level falls to 0 units, and if we assume that the order quantity (or 'batch quantity') is Q units, the maximum inventory level will be less than Q. This is because by the time that the full batch has been delivered into store, some of the units have already been used.

Economic batch quantity (EBQ)

The economic batch quantity (EBQ) is similar to the economic order quantity. It is used to calculate the order quantity that minimises total annual costs. If it is assumed that the cost per unit produced is the same regardless of the batch size, the economic batch size is the quantity that minimises the total annual costs of:

- getting each batch production run ready ('set-up costs') and
- inventory holding costs for the finished goods inventory.

Set-up costs. Set-up costs occur in production when items are manufactured in batches. These are the costs incurred in cleaning up the machinery and equipment from the previous batch and getting the machinery ready for making the new batch. (In the context of the EBQ formula, they are similar to order costs in the EOQ formula).

Set-up costs each year $= \dfrac{(C_o \times D)}{Q}$

Inventory holding costs. As stated earlier, it is assumed that inventory is replenished as soon as it reaches 0. However, the replenishment of inventory continues throughout the time that the batch of units is still being manufactured. New units are produced continually throughout the batch production process.

For example, suppose that a factory has the capacity to make 8,000 units of an item each year, but it only needs 4,000 units a year. It therefore produces the units in batches. Suppose the batch size is 2,000 units. This is a quarter of the factory capacity, so it would take at least three months to complete one batch. As the units are produced, they are transferred to inventory. There is no need to wait until the end of the batch production run before transferring any of the units to inventory.

This means that the maximum inventory level is not Q. It is a smaller amount:

$Q(1 - D/R)$

where:

Q = the quantity of materials produced in each batch

D = the annual demand for the material item

R = the annual rate at which the materials can be produced

In the example above, the maximum inventory level will be $2,000(1 - 4,000/8,000) = 2,000 \times 0.5 = 1,000$ units. If this is the maximum inventory level, average inventory is 500 units.

Give an annual holding cost per unit of C_H:

$$\text{Inventory holding costs each year} = \frac{Q\left(1 - \frac{D}{R}\right)}{2} \times C_H$$

This is similar to the economic order quantity formula, with the exception that average inventory is not $\frac{Q}{2}$ units, but $\frac{Q\left(1 - \frac{D}{R}\right)}{2}$ units.

Economic batch production quantity: formula

The formula for the economic batch quantity is

$$\text{Economic batch quantity (EBQ)} = \sqrt{\frac{2C_oD}{C_H\left(1 - \frac{D}{R}\right)}}$$

This formula is also given to you in the examination, in the formulae sheet. It is identical to the EOQ formula, except for the assumption about the maximum inventory quantity – due to the gradual replenishment of inventory during the batch production process.

Example

A company uses 9,000 units of product A23 each year, in batches. The annual production rate at which Product A23 could be made is 30,000 units each year. The cost of preparing for the production of a new batch is $405. The annual cost of holding inventory of finished goods is $5.71 per unit.

What is the batch quantity size for Product A23 that will minimise annual costs?

Answer

$$\text{Economic batch quantity} = \sqrt{\frac{2 \times 405 \times 9{,}000}{5.71\left(1 - \frac{9{,}000}{30{,}000}\right)}} = \sqrt{\left(\frac{7{,}290{,}000}{4}\right)}$$

$$= \sqrt{1{,}822{,}500}$$

$$= 1{,}350 \text{ units}$$

EBQ: total holding costs and total set-up costs

When the batch production quantity is the EBQ and the assumptions of the EBQ model apply, total annual holding costs and total annual set-up costs will be the same. This is the same situation that applies to the EOQ for total holding costs and total ordering costs.

In the example above:

- If the EBQ is 1,350 units:
- Average inventory will be 1,350(1 – 9,000/30,000) = 945 units
- Total annual holding costs will be (945/2) × $5.71 = $2,698 – say $2,700
- Total set-up costs per year will be (9,000/1,350) × $405 = $2,700

Allowing for a small rounding error of $2, it can be seen that total annual holding costs and total annual set-up costs are the same when the batch production quantity is calculated by the EBQ formula.

You might be tested in your examination on the effect on the EBQ, annual holding costs and annual set-up costs of a change in any variable in the EBQ formula. The approach to analysis should be the same as for changes invariables in the EOQ formula (explained earlier), but the EBQ formula is bit more complex and you should be careful when analysing the effect of any change.

Example

A company uses the economic batch quantity formula to decide the batch production quantities for an item of material. Due to improvements in efficiency in the factory, the production capacity (speed of production) is increased.

Required

What will be the effect of the increase in production speed on:

(a) the economic batch quantity (EBQ)

(b) total annual set-up costs

(c) total annual holding costs?

 Answer

Economic batch quantity (EBQ) = $\sqrt{\dfrac{2C_oD}{C_H\left(1-\dfrac{D}{R}\right)}}$

An increase in output capacity means an increase in the value of R.

An increase in the value of R increases the value of (1 – D/R).

An increase in the value of (1 – D/R) increases the value below the line in the EBQ formula

The EBQ will therefore become smaller.

(a) A reduction in the EBQ will result in an increase in set-up costs, because there will be more batches each year. Given no change in the set-up cost per batch, total set-up costs must therefore be higher.

(b) If the order quantity is the EBQ, total annual set-up costs and total annual holding costs are the same. If total annual set-up costs increase, it follows that total annual holding costs will also rise. Although the batch quantity is lower, the maximum inventory level (Q (1 – D/R) is higher.

> **Inventory reorder level and other warning levels**
>
> - Introduction
> - Reorder level
> - Maximum inventory level
> - Minimum inventory level

5 Inventory reorder level and other warning levels

5.1 Introduction

So far, it has been assumed that when an item of materials is purchased from a supplier, the delivery from the supplier will happen immediately. In practice, however, there is likely to be some uncertainty about when to make a new order for materials in order to avoid the risk of running out of inventory before the new order arrives from the supplier. There are two reasons for this.

- There is **a supply 'lead time'**. This is the period of time between placing a new order with a supplier and receiving the delivery of the purchased items. The length of this supply lead time might be uncertain and might be several days, weeks or even months.

- The daily or weekly usage of the material may not be a constant amount, even if constant as an annual amount, D. During the supply lead time, the actual usage of the material may be more than or less than the average usage.

However, the examination syllabus specifies that you will only be examined about situations where the demand during the lead time is constant; therefore only the length of the supply lead time might be uncertain.

Running out of an item of inventory (or stock) is called a **stock-out**. (However, you might come across the unusual term 'inventory-out' in your examination).

When there is a stock-out of a key item of materials, there might be a hold-up in production and a disruption to the production schedules. This in turn may lead to a loss of sales and profits.

Management responsible for inventory control might want to know:

- when a new order for each item of materials should be made, in order to avoid any stock-out.

- whether the inventory level for each item of materials appears to be too high or too low.

In an inventory control system, there may be warning levels for inventory, warning management that:

- the materials item should now be reordered (the reorder level)

- the inventory level is too high (a maximum inventory level) or

- the inventory level is getting dangerously low (a minimum inventory level).

It is assumed that it is management policy to avoid running out of any item of inventory. In other words, it is assumed that there will be no stock-out of any material item.

- The material item must be re-ordered when the inventory level falls to the reorder quantity: If the item is not reordered at this point there will be some risk of a stock-out during the supply lead time, before the new purchase quantity is received.

- If the inventory level is higher than the maximum inventory level, something unusual must have happened. For example the supplier might have delivered a new order quantity much sooner than usual (and much sooner than expected) or demand for the item must be below even the expected minimum.

- If the inventory level falls below the minimum level, this should act as a warning to the stores manager that there might be a stock-out. The stores manager might need to check with the supplier about why there is a delay in the delivery, and how soon a new delivery of the material item can be expected.

5.2 Reorder level

A new quantity of materials should be ordered when current inventory reaches the reorder level for that material.

- If the supply lead time (time between placing an order and receiving delivery) is constant or certain, the reorder level is:

    [Demand for the material item per day/week] × [Lead time in days/weeks]

- If the supply lead time is uncertain or not constant, but demand during the lead time is constant, there should be a safety level of inventory. The **reorder level should be**:

    [Demand for the material item per day/week] × [Maximum supply lead time in days/weeks]

Buffer (safety) inventory buffer

The reorder level is therefore set at the maximum expected consumption of the material item during the supply lead time. This is more than the average usage during the supply lead time. As a result, more inventory is held than is needed on average.

If the order quantity is Q, the average inventory level is Q/2 + 'buffer inventory'.

Buffer inventory is the average amount of inventory held in excess of average requirements in order to remove the risk of a stock-out (or 'inventory out'). The size of the buffer inventory is calculated as follows:

		Units
Reorder level	(Demand per day × Maximum lead time)	X
Average usage in the lead time period	(Demand per day × Average lead time)	X
Buffer inventory		X

The cost of holding buffer inventory is the size of the buffer inventory multiplied by the holding cost per unit.

5.3 Maximum inventory level

The inventory level should never exceed a maximum level. If it does, something unusual has happened to either the supply lead time or demand during the supply lead time.

When demand during the supply lead time is constant, the maximum inventory level is:

Reorder level + Reorder quantity – [Demand for the material item per day/week × Minimum supply lead time in days/weeks]

This maximum level should occur at the time that a new delivery of the item has been received from the supplier. If the supply lead time is shorter there are still some units of inventory when the new delivery is received.

5.4 Minimum inventory level

The inventory level could be dangerously low if it falls below a minimum warning level. When inventory falls below this amount, management should check that a new supply will be delivered before all the inventory is used up, so that there will be no stock-out.

When demand during the supply lead time is constant, the minimum (warning) level for inventory is:

Reorder level – [Demand for the material item per day/week × Average lead time in days/weeks]

Example

A company uses material item BC56. The reorder quantity for this material is 12,000 units. Weekly usage of the item is 1,500 units per week, but there is some uncertainty about the length of the lead time between ordering more materials and receiving delivery from the supplier.

	Supply lead time (weeks)
Average	2.5
Maximum	3
Minimum	1

Required

Calculate the reorder level, the maximum inventory level and the minimum inventory level for material item BC56.

Answer

Re-order level = [Demand for the material item per day/week] × [Maximum lead time in days/weeks]

Demand per week	1,500 units
Maximum lead time (weeks)	3 weeks
Re-order level	**4,500 units**

Maximum inventory level = Reorder level + Reorder quantity - [Demand for the material item per day/week × Minimum lead time in days/weeks]

		Units
Re-order level		4,500
Reorder quantity		12,000
Demand per week	1,500 units	
Minimum lead time (weeks)	× 1 week	
		(1,500)
Maximum inventory level		**15,000**

Minimum inventory level = Reorder level - [Demand for the material item per day/week × Average lead time in days/weeks]

		Units
Re-order level		4,500
Demand per week	1,500 units	
Average lead time (weeks)	× 2.5 weeks	
Subtract:		(3,750)
Minimum inventory level		**750**

Management Accounting (MA)

Practice multiple choice questions

1   The demand for an item of material is 8,000 units each year. The cost of making an order is $240. The purchase cost per unit is $9 and the holding cost of inventory is 6% per annum of the purchase cost. Using the economic order quantity formula, what quantity of the item should be purchased in each order (to the nearest unit)?

    A   800

    B   843

    C   1,886

    D   2,667 *(1 mark)*

2   A manufacturing company uses the economic order quantity (EOQ) formula to decide the purchase quantities for its main items of raw materials. Due to an increase in interest rates, the cost of holding inventory has increased. What will be the effect of this cost increase on the EOQ for each raw material item and on annual ordering costs?

    A   The EOQ will be lower and annual ordering costs higher.

    B   The EOQ will be lower and annual ordering costs will not be affected.

    C   The EOQ will be higher and annual ordering costs lower.

    D   The EOQ will be higher and annual ordering costs higher. *(2 marks)*

3   A company uses the economic order quantity formula to decide the purchase quantity for materials. The purchase cost of item 1234 is $25 per unit. Annual demand is 10,000 units. The annual holding cost is $2.50 per unit and ordering costs are $500 per order. The supplier is offering a reduction in the purchase price to $23 per unit on all orders of 5,000 units or more.

Which one of the following statements is correct?

    A   The company will minimise its total annual costs if it continues to purchase in the economic order quantity of 1,000 units per order.

    B   The company will minimise its total annual costs if it continues to purchase in the economic order quantity of 2,000 units per order.

    C   The company will minimise its total annual costs if it takes the large order discount and purchases in quantities of 5,000 units per order.

    D   The company will minimise its total annual costs if it takes the large order discount and purchases in quantities of 10,000 units per order. *(2 marks)*

4 A company manufactures Product Z in batches. Output capacity is 1,000 units of Product Z per week but demand is only 200 units per week. There are 50 weeks in each year. The annual cost of holding finished units o Product Z in store is $2 per unit per year. Set-up costs for a batch of Product Z are $800 per batch.

What batch production quantity for Product Z will minimise total annual costs, to the nearest 100 units?

 A 400 units

 B 2,800 units

 C 3,200 units

 D 7,100 units *(2 marks)*

5 A production department uses Component P to manufacture a product. This component is purchased from an external supplier in quantities of 3,000 units per order. Daily usage is 150 units of the component each day. The supply lead time is normally 6 days, but might be as little as 4 days or as much as 10 days.

To avoid the risk of running out of inventory of Component P, what should be the reorder level for this item?

 A 3,900 units

 B 1,500 units

 C 900 units

 D 600 units *(2 marks)*

You will find the answers to the practice multiple choice questions at the end of this book.

Applied Knowledge
Management Accounting (MA)

CHAPTER

9

Accounting for labour

Contents
1 Labour costs: direct and indirect labour costs
2 Labour costs: remuneration methods
3 Labour efficiency and labour turnover

> **Labour costs: direct and indirect labour costs**
>
> - Elements of labour costs
> - Direct and indirect labour costs
> - Recording labour costs

1 Labour costs: direct and indirect labour costs

1.1 Elements of labour costs

Labour costs consist of:

- the basic wages and salaries of employees
- additional payments for overtime working
- bonuses and other payments on top of basic pay and overtime (such as contributions paid by the employer into a pension scheme for its employees).

1.2 Direct and indirect labour costs

In an earlier chapter, it was explained that a distinction is made in cost accounting between direct labour employees and indirect labour employees. Direct labour employees are those who work directly on the goods or services produced by the entity.

The general rule is that direct labour costs are the costs of direct labour employees and indirect labour costs are the costs of indirect labour employees. However, there are some exceptions to this general rule, and some costs of direct labour employees are treated as indirect labour costs. Two exceptions are:

- the cost of idle time
- the cost of overtime premium.

Idle time

Idle time is time when employees are paid and are available to work but are not doing any active work. The cause of idle time could be a breakdown in production equipment or a delay in the delivery of materials from a supplier. Idle time might also occur when there are no orders from customers, and there will be no more work until the next order arrives.

Idle time should be treated as an indirect labour cost. However, in order to treat idle time as an indirect cost, the cost accounting system must be able to identify the amount of time that is lost as idle time. To do this, idle time must be recorded on labour time sheets (which are often used to document the use of labour time, for the purpose of cost accounting).

Overtime premium

When hourly-paid employees work hours in excess of their normal working hours, they are usually paid 'overtime' at a higher rate of pay per hour than the basic rate.

- The total rate of pay per hour is the basic rate per hour plus an overtime 'premium'.
- Total overtime hourly rate = Basic hourly rate + Overtime premium.

For example, if the basic rate of pay is $20 per hour and overtime is paid at time and a half (100% + 50% = 150% of the basic rate), the overtime premium is $10 per hour and the total overtime pay is $30 per hour.

In costing systems, it is usual to separate the labour cost at the basic rate per hour from the cost of the overtime premium. This is because overtime premium costs are usually treated as an indirect labour cost (an overhead cost) and should be measured separately.

Example

During one week, Masha works 46 hours. This includes 8 hours of overtime working. Her basic rate of pay is $10 per hour and overtime is paid at time and a half. The overtime rate per hour is $10 × 150% = $15, consisting of the $10 basic rate plus a premium of $5 per hour.

Her weekly cost is calculated as follows, keeping the overtime premium separate from the basic pay for the hours worked.

	$
Basic pay – 46 hours × $10	460
Overtime premium (8 hours × $10 × 50%)	40
Total weekly pay	500

The reason why overtime premium is usually treated as an indirect labour cost is that when employees are paid for working hours of overtime, it is a matter of chance what work they are doing in normal hours and what work they do in overtime. It is therefore 'unfair' to charge the work done in overtime directly with the overtime premium.

The main rules about whether production labour costs should be treated as a direct labour cost or as an indirect labour cost can be summarised as follows.

	Direct labour costs	**Indirect labour costs**
Direct labour employees	Basic wage or salary for hours worked	
	Overtime premium only if the overtime hours are worked specifically at a customer's request	In most cases, the overtime premium cost of hours worked in overtime
		In most cases, all other costs of direct labour employees. This includes: • the cost of all hours recorded as 'idle time' – time spent doing nothing

	Direct labour costs	Indirect labour costs
		• the cost of other hours spent away from direct production work, such as time spent on training courses.
Indirect labour employees		All labour costs of indirect labour employees

1.3 Recording labour costs

In a cost accounting system, there must be a system for relating the cost of labour to work that is done. There are various ways in which labour time might be recorded, but the main methods are:

- payroll records
- time sheets or similar time records.

Payroll records can be used to:

- identify employees as direct labour or indirect labour employees
- charge the labour costs of each employee to the department (cost centre) where he or she is employed.

Time sheets or similar time recording systems can be used within a cost centre to record the time spent by each employee on different activities or tasks (or as idle time). Time sheets are not necessary if an employee does the same work all the time. For example, it is not necessary to prepare time sheets for a machine worker if the employee spends all his time working at the same machine producing the same items of output.

However, time sheets are needed if employees spend time on more than one cost item, so that their labour cost has to be allocated to the different cost items. For example, a manufacturing centre might product two products, Product A and Product B, and a direct labour employee might spend time working on both products. Time sheets can be used to record the time spent on each product, so that the labour cost can be allocated to each product according to the amount of time spent on each. Similarly time sheets are needed to work out the labour cost of specific jobs or contracts: the time spent by employees on each job or contract should be recorded, so that the cost of the time can be allocated and the labour cost for each job or contract can be calculated.

Accounting for labour costs

Within a cost accounting system, indirect and direct labour costs are recorded and charged to the appropriate cost centres and cost units. The records of labour costs are included within the double-entry cost accounting system (where such a costing system is used).

Accounting for labour costs with 'ledger entries' in a cost accounting system is explained in a later chapter.

> **Labour costs: remuneration methods**
>
> - Calculating the cost of labour
> - Time-based systems
> - Piecework systems
> - Incentive schemes

2 Labour costs: remuneration methods

2.1 Calculating the cost of labour

The labour cost of a product, service, job or activity is calculated as the cost of paying the employees to do the work. Labour costs are allocated between different jobs or activities on the basis of the time spent working on each job or activity.

Many employees are paid a fixed salary each month. Their costs are allocated to the departments they work in and to the activities they perform on a time basis. For example, if an employee spends half his time on one type of activity and half of his time on another activity, the cost of his labour will be divided 50:50 between the two activities.

Some employees are paid by the hour, and a few are paid a piecework rate. The labour costs of these employees can be measured and charged to the units of work they produce.

2.2 Time-based systems

When employees are paid an hourly rate, their basic pay (per week or month) is calculated as follows:

Basic pay = Hours worked × Rate of pay per hour

Production records should kept of the time spent by these employees on specific jobs or batches of production, so that the labour cost for this work can be measured accurately.

As explained earlier, any overtime premium for overtime working is usually treated as an indirect labour cost. (Overtime premium is charged as a direct cost only when the overtime is worked for a specific purpose, for example to meet specific demands by a customer for meeting a delivery date).

2.3 Piecework systems

In piecework systems, employees are usually paid a certain amount for the number of units of output produced:

Basic pay = Units produced × Rate paid per unit produced

Example

A worker in a textile company sews buttons on shirts. She is paid $0.20 for each shirt that she completes. During one week, she completes 800 shirts.

Her pay for the week, and the labour cost of sewing buttons on the 800 shirts, is:

800 × $0.20 = $160.

Differential piecework systems

Differential piecework systems encourage employees to increase the number of units they produce by paying higher rates per unit when more units are produced.

It is quite common for employees involved in piecework schemes to be paid a guaranteed minimum wage so that their earnings do not suffer too much when production levels are low because of circumstances outside of their control.

For example, an employee is paid the following rates of pay:

Production	Rate of pay per unit
Units	$
0 – 100	1.50
101 – 200	1.75
201 – 300	2.00

The company pays a guaranteed minimum wage of $300 per week. In a week, the employee produces 220 units. How much are his earnings for the week?

Production	Rate of pay per unit	Earnings
Units	$	$
0 – 100	1.50	150
101 – 200	1.75	175
201 – 300	2.00	40
		365

Don't forget that if the employee had earned less than $300, he still would have been paid the guaranteed minimum wage of $300 per week.

2.4 Incentive schemes

Employees might be offered an incentive or bonus payment for improving their productivity, or for achieving certain production targets during a period. The purpose of an incentive scheme for greater productivity should be to:

- increase total production output with the same number of employees, or
- achieve the same total output volume, but in fewer hours of work.

Some of the benefits of the productivity improvement are given to the employees, in the form of a bonus. This should give them an incentive to achieve the productivity improvement. Incentive schemes may be based on:

- an individual's performance or
- the performance of a work group as a whole.

Individual incentive schemes and group incentive schemes are similar for the purpose of cost accounting.

(If the cost of a bonus payment can be traced directly to a cost unit it should be treated as a direct labour cost. If it is difficult to trace the cost of a bonus payment to a specific cost unit, for example because it is paid at a much later date, it will be recorded as an indirect labour cost).

The employer (company) also benefits from the productivity improvements, because the unit cost of production should be reduced. If the total reduction in costs is greater than the additional amount paid to employees, the company will benefit.

Example

A manufacturing company produces 1,000 units of a product each week. This requires 900 direct labour hours. Direct labour employees are paid $12 per hour.

The company introduces an incentive scheme, in which it will pay a bonus of 5% of the basic rate per hour worked if productivity can be improved by 10%, and either:

- the employees can make 10% more units each week in 900 hours, or
- the employees can produce 1,000 units each week in 10% fewer hours.

Does this bonus scheme benefit the company? If so, by how much?

Answer

At the moment the weekly cost of direct labour is 900 hours × $12 = $10,800, and the direct labour cost per unit is $10,800/1,000 = $10.80.

(a) If 10% more units are made each week in the same number of hours (900 hours), the labour cost will be (including the bonus of 5%):
- 900 hours × $12 × 1.05 = $11,340.
- The cost per unit will be $11,340/1,100 = $10.31.
- The cost per unit will fall by $0.49 or 4.5%.

(b) If 1,000 units are made each week in only 810 hours (90% × 900), the direct labour cost will be (including the bonus of 5%):
- 810 hours × $12 × 1.05 = $10,206.
- The cost per unit will be $10,206/1,000 = $10.21.
- The cost per unit will fall by $0.59 or 5.5%.

> **Labour efficiency and labour turnover**
>
> - Labour performance
> - Labour efficiency ratio (productivity ratio)
> - Capacity utilisation ratio
> - Production volume ratio (activity ratio)
> - Labour turnover rate

3 Labour efficiency and labour turnover

3.1 Labour performance

Non-financial information about labour performance might be provided to management. Performance measures are based on comparisons of the actual hours used to make the actual production, the number of hours that were expected to be used to make the actual production and the total number of hours that were expected to be used in the period.

Example

During July, a factory planned to make 4,000 units of a product. The expected production time is 3 direct labour hours for each unit.

The factory actually produced 3,600 units of the product.

The actual number of direct labour hours worked in the month was 10,000 hours.

Therefore:

	Hours
Actual hours to make actual production	10,000
Expected time to make the actual production (3,600 units should have used 3 hours per unit)	10,800
Total number of hours expected to be used (4,000 units should have used 3 hours per unit)	12,000

In the above example, the factory expected each unit to be made in 3 hours. Three hours is described as the standard time per unit. Therefore, the expected time to make the actual production could also be called the standard hours for actual production. Standard costing is an important part of the syllabus and is explained in detail in later chapter. It is mentioned here so that you will be able to see the connection when you come to study standard costing.

Three ratios are relevant:

- The labour efficiency ratio (the productivity ratio)
- The capacity utilisation ratio
- The production volume ratio (the activity ratio)

3.2 Labour efficiency ratio (productivity ratio)

$$\text{Labour efficiency ratio} = \frac{\text{Expected hours to produce the actual output}}{\text{Actual hours to produce the actual output}} \times 100$$

or (restated in terms of standard hours)

$$\text{Labour efficiency ratio} = \frac{\text{Standard hours to produce the actual output}}{\text{Actual hours to produce the actual output}} \times 100$$

When output is produced in exactly the time expected, the efficiency ratio is 100%. When output is produced more quickly than expected, the efficiency ratio is above 100%.

Example

During July, a factory planned to make 4,000 units of a product. The expected production time is 3 direct labour hours for each unit.

The factory actually produced 3,600 units of the product.

The actual number of direct labour hours worked in the month was 10,000 hours.

Therefore:

$$\text{Labour efficiency ratio} = \frac{(3,600 \times 3 \text{ hours}) = 10,800 \text{ hours}}{10,000 \text{ hours}} \times 100 = 108\%$$

Efficiency ratio and idle time

Employees are not always engaged in active work during the time they attend the work place. Employees might be 'idle' for several reasons, such as waiting for the next work to come along, or because of a halt in production due to a machine breakdown.

When a labour efficiency ratio is calculated, the actual hours worked should **exclude** any hours recorded as idle time.

3.3 Capacity utilisation ratio

A capacity utilisation ratio is a ratio that measures the actual hours actively working as a percentage of the total hours available for work.

The total number of hours available for work is known as capacity. Capacity might be expressed in terms of actual hours that were available for working but is more usually expressed as total number of hours that were expected to be available. This is known as the budgeted number of hours.

$$\text{Capacity utilisation ratio} = \frac{\text{Actual hours worked}}{\text{Total hours available for work}} \times 100$$

Example (capacity utilisation based on expected hours)

During July, a factory planned to make 4,000 units of a product. The expected production time is 3 direct labour hours for each unit.

The factory actually produced 3,600 units of the product.

The actual number of direct labour hours worked in the month was 10,000 hours.

Therefore:

$$\text{Capacity utilisation ratio} = \frac{10,000 \text{ hours}}{(4,000 \times 3 \text{ hours}) = 12,000 \text{ hours}} \times 100 = 83.33\%$$

Example (capacity utilisation based on actual hours)

A production department has 6 employees who each work 40 hours a week. In a particular week, the recorded idle time was 25 hours.

Total hours available for work = 6 employees × 40 hours = 240 hours.

$$\text{Capacity utilisation ratio} = \frac{240 - 25 = 215 \text{ hours}}{(6 \times 40 \text{ hours}) = 240 \text{ hours}} \times 100 = 89.6\%$$

3.4 Production volume ratio (activity ratio)

Labour activity can also be measured by a production volume ratio which is calculated as follows:

$$\text{Production volume ratio} = \frac{\text{Expected hours to produce the actual output}}{\text{Total hours available for work}} \times 100$$

Example

During July, a factory planned to make 4,000 units of a product. The expected production time is 3 direct labour hours for each unit.

The factory actually produced 3,600 units of the product.

The actual number of direct labour hours worked in the month was 10,000 hours.

Therefore:

$$\text{Production volume ratio} = \frac{(3{,}600 \times 3 \text{ hours}) = 10{,}800 \text{ hours}}{12{,}000 \text{ hours}} \times 100 = 90\%$$

The production volume ratio can be calculated as follows:

Production volume ratio = Labour efficiency ratio × Capacity utilisation ratio

Example

During July, a factory planned to make 4,000 units of a product. The expected production time is 3 direct labour hours for each unit.

The factory actually produced 3,600 units of the product.

The actual number of direct labour hours worked in the month was 10,000 hours.

Using answers obtained previously:

Labour efficiency ratio	108%
Capacity utilisation ratio	× 83.33%
Production volume ratio	90%

Example

During May there were 21 working days of 8 hours per day. The workforce consists of 10 employees, who all do the same work.

Due to problems in the production system and a machine breakdown, 240 hours were recorded as idle time during the month.

During May, the workforce produced 5,400 units of output. The expected time per unit of output is 15 minutes (= 0.25 hours).

Required

Calculate, for May:

(a) the efficiency ratio

(b) the capacity utilisation ratio

(c) the production volume ratio

Answer

To calculate the efficiency ratio, the hours worked should exclude idle time. Hours worked = (21 days × 8 hours × 10 employees) − 240 hours idle time = 1,680 − 240 = 1,440 hours.

(a) **Efficiency ratio**

Expected time to produce 5,400 units = 5,400 × 0.25 hours = 1,350 hours.

Efficiency ratio = (1,350/1,440) × 100% = 93.75%

(b) **Capacity utilisation ratio**

Active hours worked/Hours available

= (1,440 hours/1,680 hours) × 100% = 85.71%

(c) **Production volume ratio**

Expected time to produce 5,400 units/Total hours available

= (1,350 hours/1,680 hours) × 100% = 80.35%.

Efficiency ratio × Capacity utilisation ratio = Production volume ratio

93.75% × 85.71% = 80.35%.

3.5 Labour turnover rate

Labour turnover occurs when employees leave their job and have to be replaced. The labour turnover rate is a measure of the rate at which employees are leaving and have to be replaced.

$$\frac{\text{Number of employees leaving/being replaced each year}}{\text{Average number of employee positions in the year}} \times 100\%$$

Example

A company employs 4,800 employees. During the past 12 months, 660 employees left the company and had to be replaced.

Labour turnover rate = $100\% \times \left(\frac{660}{4,800}\right) = 13.75\%$

Example

A company employed 2,800 people at the beginning of the year. During the year 420 people left and 450 were recruited. There were 2,830 employees at the end of the year.

Average number of employees = (2,800 + 2,830)/2 = 2,815

Labour turnover rate = (420/2,815) × 100% = 14.9%.

Exercise

A company employed 600 employees at the beginning of the year and 630 employees at the end of the year. During the past 12 months, 35 employees left the company and had to be replaced.

What was the labour turnover rate?

You will find the answer to the Exercises and practice multiple choice questions at the end of this book.

Costs and causes of labour turnover

The main cause of labour turnover is when employees leave one company to go and work for another.

Labour turnover can be very costly for an employer, and result in higher costs.

- When employees leave, their experience is lost. New employees taking their place are less experienced, and will be less efficient until they learn how to do the job. A high labour turnover, by reducing efficiency, increases costs.

- New employees might make many more mistakes, and so there will be additional costs of correcting faulty work.

- New employees might have to be trained, and there will be additional training costs.

- A very high labour turnover rate could have an adverse effect on the morale and efficiency of the employees who remain in their jobs.

Management Accounting (MA)

Practice multiple choice questions

1 A production department consists of 15 direct labour employees who each work 36 hours per week. Output from the department is expected to be 4 units of product per direct labour hour worked. During a particular week, the department recorded 500 hours of time spent working on production and actual output was 2,100 units of the product.

What was the production volume ratio for the department for the week?

A 92.5%

B 97.2%

C 102.9%

D 105.0% *(2 marks)*

2 A company employed 5,700 employees at the end of a financial year. During the year 600 employees left the company and 360 were recruited.

What was the rate of labour turnover in the year?

A 10.3%

B 10.5%

C 10.8%

D 16.5% *(2 marks)*

You will find the answers to the practice multiple choice questions at the end of this book.

Applied Knowledge
Management Accounting (MA)

CHAPTER 10

Accounting for overheads

Contents
1 Definition and purpose of absorption costing
2 Stages in absorption costing
3 Overhead apportionment
4 Apportionment of service department costs
5 Overhead absorption
6 Under-absorbed and over-absorbed overheads
7 Fixed and variable overheads

> **Definition and purpose of absorption costing**
>
> - Introduction to absorption costing
> - The treatment of direct and indirect expenses
> - Definition of absorption costing
> - The purpose of absorption costing

1 Definition and purpose of absorption costing

1.1 Introduction to absorption costing

This chapter describes the basic principles and methods of absorption costing. Absorption costing is a method of costing in which overhead costs are added to the cost of cost units, and a 'full cost' is calculated. The full cost of an item is the prime cost plus a share of overhead costs.

The absorption costing method can be used in either manufacturing industries or service industries, but it is more commonly associated with costing for manufacturing. This is because in manufacturing there are usually large quantities of inventory, and work-in-progress and finished goods are normally valued (or 'costed') to include some production overhead costs.

The absorption costing method therefore focuses mainly on production costs and the treatment of production overheads.

1.2 The treatment of direct and indirect expenses

In cost accounting, direct and indirect costs are treated differently.

- Direct costs are charged directly to the cost of production. They are directly identified with cost units, batches of production, a production process or a job or a contract.

- **Overheads are indirect costs**, and cannot be identified directly with specific cost units, jobs or processes etc. They are therefore recorded as overhead costs, and a distinction is made between production overheads, administration overheads and sales and distribution (marketing) overheads.

Overhead costs can then be treated in either of two ways.

- **Method 1 – Marginal costing.** They might be treated as period costs, and charged as an expense against the period in which they are incurred, without any attempt to add a share of the overhead costs to the cost of units of production.

- **Method 2 – Absorption costing.** They might be shared out between cost units or processes. Overhead costs might be charged to cost units in addition to direct costs, so that the cost of goods sold (the cost of cost units) includes a fair share of overhead costs.

	$ per unit
Direct material costs	X
Direct production labour cost	X
Production overheads	X
Full production cost	X
Administration overhead	X
Sales and distribution overhead	X
Full cost of sale	X

This chapter deals with absorption costing. In absorption costing, a share of overhead costs is added to direct costs, to obtain a 'full cost' or a 'fully absorbed cost' for cost units. This chapter explains the methods that are used to calculate the amount of overhead costs to add to unit costs in order to obtain a full cost per unit. Marginal costing is explained in a later chapter.

1.3 Definition of absorption costing

Absorption costing is based on the idea that the cost of a product or a service should be:

- its direct costs (direct materials, direct labour and sometimes direct expenses)
- plus a share of overhead costs.

Absorption costing is therefore a system of costing in which a share of overhead costs is added to direct costs, to obtain a full cost. This might be:

- a full production cost, or
- a full cost of sale.

An absorption costing system might be used to decide the **full production cost** of the product, so that only a share of production overheads is added to product costs. Administration overheads and selling and distribution overheads are simply charged as an expense to the period in which they occur.

Inventory valuation is an important feature of absorption costing, because the cost of production in any period depends partly on the valuation of opening and closing inventory, including work-in-progress and finished goods inventory.

In some costing systems, a share of administration overhead and selling and distribution overhead might be added to the full production cost, to obtain a **full cost of sale**. However, it is not common practice to calculate a full cost of sale, because it has only limited value as management information.

Income statement: absorption costing	$000	$000	$000
Sales			950
Cost of inventory at the beginning of the period		80	
Production cost of items manufactured in the period:			
Direct materials	280		
Direct labour	120		
Direct expenses (if any)	0		
Production overhead added to cost ('absorbed')	240		
		640	
		720	
Less: Cost of inventory at the end of the period		(120)	
Production cost of items sold			(600)
Gross profit			350
Administration overhead		100	
Selling and distribution overhead		200	
			(300)
Net operating profit			50

1.4 The purpose of absorption costing

There are several reasons why absorption costing is sometimes used, and production overhead costs are added to direct costs to calculate the full production cost of products (or services).

- There is a view that inventory should include a fair share of production overhead cost. This view is applied in financial accounting and financial reporting. It can therefore be argued that inventory should be valued in a similar way in the cost accounting system. (However, inventory valuations may differ between the cost accounts and the financial accounts).

- There is also a view that in order to assess the profitability of products or services, it is appropriate to charge products and services with a fair share of overhead costs. Unless products contribute sufficiently to covering indirect costs, its 'profitability' might be too low, and the business as a whole might not be profitable.

Criticisms of absorption costing

There are criticisms of absorption costing. The main criticisms are as follows:

- Absorption costing does not provide reliable information about profitability. Methods of charging overhead costs to products, as we shall see, are not 'scientific', and rely on fairly arbitrary assumptions.

- There are better methods of measuring profitability, such as marginal costing. There are also better ways of providing cost information to help managers make decisions (relevant costs). Marginal costing and relevant costs are explained in later chapters.

When absorption costing was first used in manufacturing, well over 100 years ago, total overhead costs were fairly small compared with direct costs. Manufacturing was labour-intensive, and direct labour costs were a significant proportion of total costs. Adding a share of overheads to product costs, usually in proportion to the cost of direct labour or direct labour time, was therefore a reasonable method of dealing with overhead costs.

In a modern manufacturing environment, however, direct labour is a fairly small proportion of total costs. Most work in production now consists of the 'support' activities of indirect labour employees, and the cost of this labour is an overhead cost. Overhead costs are high compared to direct labour costs. As a consequence, it is often argued that a costing system should use a different approach to overhead costing, and try to present overhead costs in a way that is more useful to management for information purposes. One such technique, activity based costing, is outside the scope of the syllabus.

> **Stages in absorption costing**
>
> - Cost centres and general expenses
> - Allocation, apportionment and absorption (recovery)
> - Overhead cost allocation

2 Stages in absorption costing

2.1 Cost centres and general expenses

In a system of absorption costing, each item of overhead cost is charged either:

- to a cost centre, or
- as a general expense.

The cost centres might be:

- a cost centre in the production function (production overhead)
- a cost centre in administration (= administration overhead)
- a cost centre in sales and distribution (= sales and distribution overhead).

The cost centres in the production function might be:

- a department engaged directly in production work (a production department), or
- a department or service section engaged in support activities, such as inventory management, production planning and control, quality control, repairs and maintenance, and so on (= '**service departments**').

In a system of absorption costing, overheads are charged to products or services on the basis of this structure of cost centres and general expenses.

2.2 Allocation, apportionment and absorption (recovery)

There are three main stages in absorption costing for charging overhead costs to the cost of production and cost units:

- **Allocation.** Overheads are allocated to cost centres. If a cost centre is responsible for the entire cost of an item of expenditure, the entire cost is charged directly to the cost centre.

- **Apportionment.** Many overhead costs are costs that cannot be allocated directly to one cost centre, because they are shared by two or more cost centres. These costs are apportioned between the cost centres. 'Apportionment' means sharing on a fair basis.

- **Absorption** (also called overhead **'recovery'**). When overheads have been allocated and apportioned to production cost centres, they are charged to the cost of products manufactured in the cost centre. The method of charging overheads to cost units is to establish a charging rate (an absorption rate or recovery rate) and to apply this rate to all items of production.

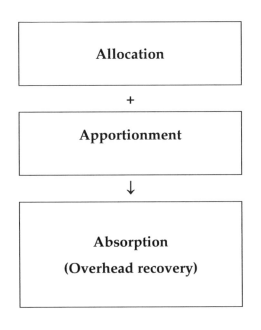

Allocation	Overhead costs are recorded. Initially they are allocated to a cost centre or recorded as a general expense
Apportionment	Overhead costs are shared between the departments or activities that benefit from them
Absorption (Overhead recovery)	Overheads are added to the cost of cost units, using a fair basis for charging (absorption costing only)

2.3 Overhead cost allocation

Many items of indirect cost cannot be charged directly to a cost unit (a unit of product or service), but they can be charged directly to a cost centre (for example, a department or work group). Items of expense that can be identified with a specific cost centre should be charged in full as a cost to the cost centre. The process of charging costs directly to cost centres is called cost **allocation.**

In absorption costing for a manufacturing company, overhead costs may be allocated to:

- **production departments** or production centres: these are cost centres that are directly engaged in manufacturing the products

- **service departments** or service centres: these are cost centres that provide support to the production departments, but are not directly engaged in production, such as engineering, repairs and maintenance, the production stores and materials handling department (raw materials inventory), production planning and control, and so on

- administration departments

- selling departments and distribution departments.

Production overheads are the overhead costs of both the production departments and the service departments.

Overhead costs that cannot be directly allocated to a cost centre must be shared (apportioned) between two or more cost centres.

For example:

- The salary of the manager of the production planning department can be allocated directly as a cost of the production planning cost centre, which is a service department cost centre within production.

- Similarly, the rental cost of equipment used by engineers in the maintenance department can be allocated directly as a cost of the maintenance department, which is also a service department cost centre within production.

- If the machining department has its own electricity power supply, electricity charges for the machining department can be allocated directly to the department, which is a production department cost centre.
- The salary of a supervisor in the finishing department can be allocated directly to the finishing department, which is also a production department cost centre.
- The cost of security guards for the manufacturing site cannot be allocated to any specific department or cost centre; therefore, security guard services are likely to be recorded as a general production overhead expense, and the cost is allocated to 'security services'.

> **Overhead apportionment**
>
> - The apportionment of shared costs between cost centres
> - The basis of apportionment
> - Double entry

3 Overhead apportionment

3.1 The apportionment of shared costs between cost centres

Some costs cannot be allocated in full to a cost centre, because they are shared by two or more cost centres. These are divided between the cost centres on a fair basis. The process of dividing the shared costs is called **apportionment.**

Shared costs may be divided between administration cost centres and selling and distribution cost centres, as well as production centres and service centres. However, examination questions on absorption costing will usually concentrate on production overhead costs.

The apportionment of production overhead costs might be in two stages:

- sharing (or dividing) general costs between production centres and service centres
- then sharing the costs of the service centres between the production centres.

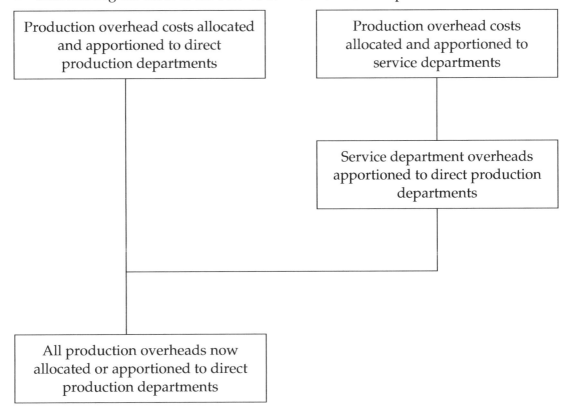

After this has been done, all the production overhead costs have been allocated or apportioned to the production centres. The total overhead costs of each production centre should be:

(1) costs allocated directly to the production centre, plus

(2) shared costs apportioned to the production centre, plus

(3) a share of the costs of each service department, apportioned to the production centre.

3.2 The basis of apportionment

Shared overhead costs should be apportioned on a fair basis between cost centres. For each item of shared expense, a 'fair' basis for apportionment must be selected.

Choosing the basis of apportionment for each cost is a matter of judgement, but there is often an 'obvious' basis to choose. For example, the rental cost of a building and the insurance costs for the building will be apportioned between the cost centres that use the building. The basis of apportionment will probably be to share the costs in relation to the floor space used by each cost centre.

In some cases, however, it might not be clear what the most suitable basis of apportionment should be, and the choice is then simply a matter of judgement and preference.

At the end of the apportionment process, all overhead costs should be allocated or apportioned to a cost centre.

Example: apportionment of shared costs

A manufacturing company has two production departments, Machining and Assembly, and two service departments, Repairs and Quality Control. The following information is available about production overhead costs.

	Total	Machining	Assembly	Repairs	Quality control
	$	$	$	$	$
Indirect labour cost	15,500	5,000	5,000	3,500	2,000
Indirect materials	5,300	1,500	2,400	1,000	400
Factory rental	14,400				
Power costs	4,800				
Depreciation (note 1)	14,000				
Building insurance	1,800				
Equipment insurance	4,200				
	60,000				

Note: Depreciation is a charge for the use of items of plant and equipment, such as machinery.

Indirect labour and indirect material costs have been allocated directly to these four cost centres. This allocation will utilise the information available from time sheets (indirect labour) and materials requisition notes (indirect materials). The other overhead costs are shared between the cost centres and so cannot be allocated directly.

Other information

	Total	Machining	Assembly	Repairs	Quality control
Cost of plant/equipment ($)	70,000	40,000	15,000	5,000	10,000
Floor area (square metres)	1,800	500	900	100	300
Kilowatt hours (000s)	800	600	100	50	50

Required

How should overheads be allocated and apportioned between the four cost centres?

Answer

The indirect labour costs and indirect materials costs are allocated directly to the cost centres. The basis of apportionment chosen for each of the other shared costs will be as follows:

Item of cost	Basis of apportionment	Rate of apportionment	
Factory rental	Floor area	$14,400/1,800 =	$8 per square metre
Power costs	Kilowatt hours	$4,800/800 =	$6 per kilowatt hour
Depreciation	Cost of plant and equipment	$14,000/$70,000 =	20% of cost
Building insurance	Floor area	$1,800/1,800 =	$1 per square metre
Equipment insurance	Cost of plant and equipment	$4,200/70,000 =	6% of cost

Make sure that you understand how the apportionment of costs is calculated. The rate of apportionment ensures that the total cost can be shared out in full between the cost centres.

These apportionment rates can be used to establish the amount of overheads to apportion to each of the four departments.

	Total	Machining	Assembly	Repairs	Quality control
	$	$	$	$	$
Indirect labour cost	15,500	5,000	5,000	3,500	2,000
Indirect materials	5,300	1,500	2,400	1,000	400
Factory rental	14,400	4,000	7,200	800	2,400
Power costs	4,800	3,600	600	300	300
Depreciation (note 1)	14,000	8,000	3,000	1,000	2,000
Building insurance	1,800	500	900	100	300
Equipment insurance	4,200	2,400	900	300	600
	60,000	25,000	20,000	7,000	8,000

If you are not sure how these figures are obtained, the workings for the machining department are shown below.

	Absorption rate		Machining
	$		$
Indirect labour cost: allocated	–		5,000
Indirect materials: allocated	–		1,500
Factory rental	$8 per square metre	× 500	4,000
Power costs	$6 per kilowatt hour	× 600	3,600
Depreciation (note 1)	20% of cost	× 40,000	8,000
Building insurance	$1 per square metre	× 500	500
Equipment insurance	6% of cost	× 40,000	2,400
Totasa overheads			25,000

3.3 Double entry

The accounting objective is to identify the cost of units of production. Costs are initially recorded in individual cost accounts. The process of apportionment results in the transfer of these costs into departments.

Example: apportionment of shared costs

The following double entry would be necessary to reflect the above apportionment to the two production departments (machining and assembly) to the two service departments (repairs and quality control).

	Dr	Cr
	$	$
Machining	25,000	
Assembly	20,000	
Repairs	7,000	
Quality control	8,000	
Indirect labour cost		15,500
Indirect materials		5,300
Factory rental		14,400
Power costs		4,800
Depreciation (note 1)		14,000
Building insurance		1,800
Equipment insurance		4,200
	60,000	60,000

> **Apportionment of service department costs**
>
> - The reciprocal method of apportioning service department costs
> - Simple application of the reciprocal method
> - Reciprocal method: repeated distribution technique
> - Reciprocal method: simultaneous equations technique

4 Apportionment of service department costs

After production overheads have been allocated and apportioned to production departments and service departments, the costs of the service departments must then be apportioned to the production departments. When this has been done, all production overhead costs will have been allocated or apportioned to the production departments.

The purpose of doing this is to calculate an absorption rate for each production department. Absorption rates are used to add overhead costs to the prime costs of production (the cost of the cost units produced in the production department).

4.1 The reciprocal method of apportioning service department costs

There are several methods of apportionment of service department costs. Each method uses an **estimate of the proportion of its work** that each service department does for the other departments.

The only method of apportionment of service department costs that you need to know for your examination is called the **reciprocal method** of cost apportionment.

A feature of the reciprocal method is that when service department overheads are apportioned, the apportionment method allows for the work that each service department does for other service departments, as well as production departments. An example might help to illustrate this point.

Example

A manufacturing company has two production departments, Department 1 and Department 2. It also has two service departments, the factory canteen and the repairs department.

Allocated overhead costs and apportioned general overhead costs for each cost centre are as follows:

Department 1:	$100,000
Department 2:	$200,000
Canteen:	$150,000
Repairs:	$220,000

The repairs department does no work for the canteen: 75% of its time is spent on repair work for Department 1 and 25% of its time is spent on repair work for Department 2. There are 10 employees in Department 1, 20 employees in Department 2 and 20 employees in the repairs department.

How should the service department costs be apportioned between the production departments?

The costs of the canteen are $150,000 and a fair basis for apportioning these costs is the number of employees in each department. If we ignored the repairs department, the costs of the canteen would be divided between Department 1 and Department 2 in the ratio 10:20 respectively. However, the repairs department has 20 employees (who presumably eat in the canteen!), and it would be more fair to recognise the use that the repairs department makes of the factory canteen. The canteen costs should therefore be divided between Departments 1 and 2 and also the repairs department in the ratio 10:20:20.

The repairs department costs can be apportioned between Department 1 and Department 2 (since it does no work for the canteen) in the ratio 75:25 respectively. You might recognise that as a consequence of charging some canteen costs to the repairs department, Department 1 will end up with a larger share of total production overhead costs than if the canteen costs had been charged directly to Departments 1 and 2.

The apportionment of overheads using the reciprocal method will therefore be as follows:

	Basis of apportionment	Dept. 1 $	Dept. 2 $	Canteen $	Repairs $
Initial costs		100,000	200,000	150,000	220,000
Apportion. canteen	(10:20:20)	30,000	60,000	(150,000)	60,000
					280,000
Apportion. repairs	(75:25)	210,000	70,000	–	(280,000)
		340,000	330,000	nil	nil

After the apportionment of the service department costs, Department 1 has overhead costs of $340,000 and Department 2 has overhead costs of $330,000. These add up to the total of all production overhead costs.

Double entry

The costs which had been initially apportioned to the service departments are transferred to the production departments.

	Dr $	Cr $
Department 1 ($30,000 + $240,000)	240,000	
Department 2 ($60,000 + $70,000)	130,000	
Canteen		150,000
Repairs		220,000
	370,000	370,000

4.2 Simple application of the reciprocal method

In your examination, you are unlikely to be given a question with more than two service departments. This is because with three or more service departments, the computations to apportion the service centre costs can become lengthy – and too long for a 1 mark or 2 mark question.

The simplest application of the reciprocal method is in a situation where:

- there are two service centres
- one service centre does work for the production departments and also the other service centre
- the second service centre does work for the production departments, but not for the other service centre.

In this situation, the reciprocal method of service centre overhead apportionment is as follows:

- Begin by apportioning the overhead costs of the service centre that does work for the other service centre as well as the production departments, using a basis for apportionment that seems appropriate.
- Next, apportion the overheads of the service centre that does work only for the production departments. The overheads of this service centre will now include the overheads apportioned from the other service centre.
- Having done this, all overhead costs will be apportioned to the production departments.

The sequence in which the service centre costs are apportioned is important. With the reciprocal method, the costs of the service centre that does work for the other service centre must be apportioned first.

Example

A manufacturing company has two production departments, P1 and P2 and two service departments, S1 and S2. The following information is available.

	P1	P2	S1	S2
Allocated and apportioned production overheads	$200,000	$250,000	$195,000	$180,000
Work done by service department for other departments				
S1	40%	60%	-	-
S2	50%	25%	25%	-

The service centre costs should be apportioned using the reciprocal method, because this method fully recognises any work done by one service centre for another.

The service centre costs should be apportioned by apportioning the costs of S2 first. This is because S2 does work for S1 as well as the production departments

	Basis of apportionment	P1	P2	S1	S2
		$	$	$	$
Initial costs		200,000	250,000	195,000	180,000
Apportion S2	(50:25:25)	90,000	45,000	45,000	(180,000)
				240,000	
Apportion S1	(40:60)	96,000	144,000	(240,000)	
		386,000	439,000	nil	nil

Double entry

	Dr	Cr
	$	$
P1 ($90,000 + $96,000)	186,000	
P2 ($45,000 + $144,000)	189,000	
S1		195,000
S2		180,000
	375,000	375,000

4.3 Reciprocal method: repeated distribution technique

It is quite possible that if you are given a question in your examination on service centre overhead cost apportionment, the situation will be as described in the previous examples, where only one service department does work for the other service department.

A situation may arise where both service departments do work for the other service department, as well as the production departments. When this happens, the process of apportioning service centre costs is more lengthy – possibly too lengthy for an examination question. Even so, it is useful to be aware of how to deal with a situation where each of two service departments does some work for the other service department.

In this type of situation, reciprocal apportionment can be done in either of two ways. Both give the same result:

- repeated distribution method
- simultaneous equations method.

The repeated distribution method is probably easier, but takes a bit longer. The simultaneous equations method is quicker, but it is important to get the arithmetic correct.

With the repeated distribution method, you should take each service department in turn. It does not matter which service department you take first. (However, you will probably complete the calculations more quickly if you start by selecting the service department that does the least amount of its work for the other service department).

Taking each service department in turn, you should apportion all the allocated and apportioned overheads of the service department. The overheads should be apportioned to the other service department as well as to the production departments.

When you apportion the costs of each service department you will be apportioning some of the overhead costs apportioned from other service department(s).

When you have apportioned the costs of each service department once, repeat the process again. Keep on repeating the process until all the overheads have been apportioned to the production departments only, and the overheads of each service department are 0.

The repetitive nature of the overhead apportionment process explains the name of the technique – 'repeated distribution'.

Example

A manufacturing company has two production departments, Machining and Assembly, and two service departments, Repairs and Quality Control. The following information is available.

	Total	Machining	Assembly	Repairs	Quality control
Allocated/apportioned overhead costs	$60,000	$25,000	$20,000	$7,000	$8,000
Work done by the service departments:					
Repairs	100%	60%	10%	–	30%
Quality Control	100%	30%	50%	20%	–

Required

The costs of the two service departments should be apportioned to the production departments, to establish the total overhead costs for each production department.

Answer

	Total	Machining	Assembly	Repairs	Quality control
	$	$	$	$	$
Allocated/apportioned overhead costs	60,000	25,000	20,000	7,000	8,000
Apportion costs of service departments:					
Repairs (60:10:30)		4,200	700	(7,000)	2,100
				0	10,100
Quality Control (30:50:20)		3,030	5,050	2,020	(10,100)
Now repeat:					
Repairs (60:10:30)		1,212	202	(2,020)	606
Quality Control (30:50:20)		182	303	121	(606)
Repeat again					
Repairs (60:10:30)		73	12	(121)	36
Quality Control (30:50:20)		11	18	7	(36)
Repeat again					
Repairs (60:10:30)		4	1	(7)	2
Quality Control (30:50:20)		1	1	0	(2)
	60,000	33,713	26,287	nil	nil

Comment

The total overhead costs of $60,000 have been apportioned. ($33,713 + $26,287 = $60,000).

Double entry

	Dr	Cr
	$	$
Repairs	7,000	
Quality control	8,000	
Machining		
(4,200 + 3,030 + 1,212 + 182 + 73 + 11 + 4 + 1)		8,713
Assembly		
(700 + 5,050 + 202 + 303 + 12 + 18 + 1 + 1)		6,287
	15,000	15,000

Chapter 10: Accounting for overheads

4.4 Reciprocal method: simultaneous equations technique

This technique is an alternative to the repeated distribution technique, and should produce exactly the same final apportionment of overhead costs between the production departments.

The method is to create two equations for the apportionment of service department overheads. These are simultaneous equations, which must then be solved. The solutions to the simultaneous equations can then be used to calculate the overhead apportionment to each production department.

The technique will be illustrated using the previous example.

Example

The information is as follows:

	Total	Machining	Assembly	Repairs	Quality control
Allocated/apportioned overhead costs	$60,000	$25,000	$20,000	$7,000	$8,000
Work done by the service departments:					
Repairs	100%	60%	10%	–	30%
Quality Control	100%	30%	50%	20%	–

Step 1: formulate the simultaneous equations

The first step is to establish two simultaneous equations. There should be one equation for each service department.

Each equation should state the total amount of overheads that will be apportioned from the service department. This total overhead is the original overhead cost allocation/apportionment for the service department, plus the proportion of the costs of the other service department that will be apportioned to it.

Using the example, the two equations are formulated as follows.

- Let the total overheads apportioned from the Repairs department be X.
- Let the total overheads apportioned from the Quality Control department be Y.

X = Original overheads of Repairs department + 20% of Quality Control costs.

Y = Original overheads of Quality Control department + 30% of Repair costs.

This gives us:

- $X = 7{,}000 + 0.20Y$
- $Y = 8{,}000 + 0.30X$

Make sure that you understand these formulae. It is easy to get them wrong and confuse the percentage figure that goes into each equation. Here, the first equation (for overheads apportioned from the Repairs department) includes 20% of Quality Control costs because 20% of the costs of this service department are apportioned to Repairs.

Step 2

The next step is to solve these simultaneous equations.

Re-arrange the two equations:

$$X - 0.2Y = 7,000 \quad \ldots\ldots(1)$$
$$-0.3X + Y = 8,000 \quad \ldots\ldots(2)$$

Solve to find values for X and Y.

(You need to know how to solve simultaneous equations. The aim should be to multiply one of the equations – or both equations if necessary – so that the coefficient for either X or Y is the same in both equations. Then add the equations, or subtract one from the other, in order to get a value for either X or Y. Having obtained a value for X or Y, substitute this value in one of the simultaneous equations, in order to obtain the remaining unknown value, for Y or X).

In this example, the easiest method of solution is to multiply equation (1) by 5, so that the coefficient for Y is -1. This matches the coefficient of +1 in equation (2). Add the two equations to obtain a value for X.

$$5X - Y = 35,000 \quad \ldots\ldots(1) \times 5 = (3)$$
$$-0.3X + Y = 8,000 \quad \ldots\ldots(2)$$
$$4.7X = 43,000 \quad \ldots\ldots(2) + (3)$$

$$X = 9,149 \quad (= 43,000/4.7)$$

Now substitute this value for X in equation (2)

$$-0.3X + Y = 8,000$$
$$Y = 8,000 + 0.3(9,149)$$
$$Y = 10,745$$

Step 3

Use the values for X and Y that you have calculated to establish the total costs to apportion from the service department to each production department.

In this example:

- Of the total value of X, 60% is apportioned to Machining and 10% to Assembly
- Of the total value of Y, 30% is apportioned to Machining and 50% to Assembly.

	Machining	Assembly
	$	$
Allocated/apportioned overhead costs	25,000	20,000
Apportion costs of service departments:		
Repairs (60% and 10% of X = 9,149)	5,489	915
Quality Control (30% and 50% of Y =10,745)	3,224	5,372
Final apportionment	33,713	26,287

This is the same as with the repeated distribution method.

Exercise 1: reciprocal method of cost apportionment of service department costs

A manufacturing company has two production departments P1 and P2, and two service departments S1 and S2. The allocated and apportioned production overheads for each of the four departments are shown below, together with the proportion of the work of each service department that is done for the other departments.

	Total	P1	P2	S1	S2
Allocated/apportioned overhead costs	$92,000	$32,520	$22,000	$15,000	$22,480
Work done by the service departments:					
S1	100%	20%	60%	-	20%
S2	100%	70%	20%	10%	-

Required

Using the reciprocal method of cost apportionment for service department overheads:

- apportion the service department costs to production departments P1 and P2 and
- calculate the total allocated and apportioned overheads for each production department.

Management Accounting (MA)

> **Overhead absorption**
>
> - Full production cost
> - Overhead absorption rate (recovery rate)
> - Departmental absorption rates or a factory-wide absorption rate?
> - The treatment of non-production overheads

5 Overhead absorption

5.1 Full production cost

When all production overheads have been allocated or apportioned to the production departments, a rate can be calculated for absorbing the overheads into the cost of the cost units manufactured in each department. This is the **overhead absorption rate** or **overhead recovery rate**.

Cost unit	$
Direct materials cost	X
Direct labour cost	X
Production overheads absorbed	X
Full production cost	X

5.2 Overhead absorption rate (recovery rate)

The overhead absorption rate for a production department is calculated as follows:

$$\frac{\text{Total allocated and apportioned overheads}}{\text{Volume of activity in the period}}$$

The volume of activity can be any of the following:

Activity basis (volume of activity)	Absorption rate
Units produced in the period, but only if all units are identical	Absorption rate per unit. Not practical where units are not identical. However, used in standard costing.
Direct labour hours worked in the period	Absorption rate per direct labour hour. Commonly-used method.
Direct labour cost in the period	Overhead absorbed as a percentage of direct labour cost. Could be used when there are no records for direct labour hours worked.

Activity basis (volume of activity)	Absorption rate
Machine hours operated in the period	Absorption rate per machine hour. Commonly-used method in *machine-intensive* production departments.
Prime costs of production in the period (direct materials plus direct labour costs)	Overhead absorbed as a percentage of prime cost. This is uncommon.

The basis of activity selected for an absorption rate should be one that charges overhead costs to cost units on a fair basis. A rate per direct labour hour and a rate per machine hour are the most common methods, although a rate per unit is used in standard costing or where a single identical unit of product is manufactured.

Example: absorption rate

The allocated and apportioned overhead costs of Production Department X are $24,000 during a period when the department produces the following units of product:

	Product A	Product B	Product C
Units produced (quantity)	3,000	4,000	1,000
Prime cost per unit	$3	$4	$5
Direct labour hours per unit	0.1	0.2	0.4
Direct labour cost	$3,500	$8,000	$4,500
Machine hours per unit	0.2	0.1	0.2

It has been decided that production overheads will be absorbed on a direct labour hour basis.

The overhead absorption rate is calculated as follows.

Step 1: Calculate the total number of direct labour hours

	Direct labour hours
Product A: (3,000 units × 0.1 hours)	300
Product B: (4,000 units × 0.2 hours)	800
Product C: (1,000 units × 0.4 hours)	400
Total direct labour hours	1,500

Step 2: Calculate an absorption rate per direct labour hour

Production overhead expenditure	$24,000
Number of labour hours	1,500
Absorption rate per direct labour hour	$16

Step 3: Use this absorption rate to charge overhead costs to products

This could be done in a variety of ways.

Using the total number of hours used making each product:

	$
Overheads absorbed by each product:	
Product A: (3,000 × 0.1 hrs) = 300 hours × $16	4,800
Product B: (4,000 × 0.2 hrs) = 800 hours × $16	12,800
Product C: (1,000 × 0.4 hrs) = 400 hours × $16	6,400
Total	24,000

Using the overhead absorbed per product:

	$
Overheads absorbed by each product:	
Product A: (0.1 hrs × $16 per hour) × 3,000 units	4,800
Product B: (0.2 hrs × $16 per hour) × 4,000 units	12,800
Product C: (0.4 hrs × $16 per hour) × 1,000 units	6,400
Total	24,000

The unit cost can also be constructed as follows:

	Product A	Product B	Product C
	$	$	$
Prime cost per unit	3.00	4.00	5.00
Overhead at $16/direct labour hour	1.60	3.20	6.40
Full production cost/unit	4.60	7.20	11.40

The choice of the basis for absorbing overheads can have a significant effect on the overheads charged to each product or cost unit.

Double entry

	Dr	Cr
	$	$
Product A	4,800	
Product B	12,800	
Product C	6,400	
Overhead		24,000
	24,000	24,000

Exercise 2

(a) Calculate the overhead absorption rate and the full production cost per unit in the example above, if overheads are absorbed on a machine hour basis.

(b) Calculate the overhead absorption rate in the example above, if overheads are absorbed as a percentage of direct labour costs, and show how much overhead would be absorbed into the cost of each of the three products A, B and C.

5.3 Departmental absorption rates or a factory-wide absorption rate?

An overhead absorption rate can be calculated for each production department separately.

Alternatively, a single overhead absorption rate might be used for all the production departments in the factory. Calculating a single factory-wide rate involves less time and effort than calculating separate absorption rates for each production department within the factory. However, it might be argued that a single-factory wide absorption rate is less 'exact' or less 'fair' in sharing overhead costs between products or cost units.

Example: absorption rate

A manufacturing company has two production departments. Each department is involved in making two products, X and Y. Information about costs and production volume in the year is shown below:

	Production departments		Products	
	Department P1	Department P2	Product X	Product Y
Overhead costs	$60,000	$90,000		
Direct labour hours/unit:				
Product X	0.5 hours	2 hours		
Product Y	3.5 hours	1.5 hours		
Units produced			2,000	4,000

Required

Calculate the total production overhead cost/unit for Product X and Product Y using:

(1) separate departmental overhead rates for departments P1 and P2

(2) a single absorption rate for the entire factory.

Answer

Separate departmental rates

	Department P1		Department P2	
Direct labour hours		hours		hours
Product X	(2,000 × 0.5)	1,000	(2,000 × 2)	4,000
Product Y	(4,000 × 3.5)	14,000	(4,000 × 1.5)	6,000
		15,000		10,000
Overhead expenditure		$60,000		$90,000
Absorption rate/direct labour hour		$4		$9

Production overhead cost/unit	Product X	Product Y
	$	$
Department P1 (at $4/hour)	2	14.00
Department P2 (at $9/hour)	18	13.50
Total production overhead cost/unit	20	27.50

Single factory rate

$$\frac{(\$60,000 + \$90,000)}{(15,000 + 10,000) \text{ hours}} = \$6 \text{ per direct labour hour}$$

Production overhead costs

- Product X: (0.5 hours + 2 hours) × $6 = $15 per unit of Product X.
- Product Y: (3.5 hours + 1.5 hours) × $6 = $30 per unit of Product Y.

In your examination, if you are given a question about overhead absorption rates, with two production departments, you should normally assume that you are required to calculate separate overhead absorption rates for each department.

5.4 The treatment of non-production overheads

In many costing systems, administration overheads and sales and distribution overheads are not absorbed into product costs. Instead, they are treated in full as an expense in the financial period to which they relate.

Non-production overhead costs are never added to the value of inventory. The main reason for absorbing production overheads is normally to calculate a value for inventory, for the purpose of measuring profit.

However, it is possible to add non-production overheads to the full production cost of units produced, to obtain a full cost of sale. When this happens, the basis for absorbing the overhead costs should be 'fair'.

- Administration overheads might be added as a percentage of production costs.
- Sales and distribution overheads might also be added as a percentage of production costs. Alternatively, they might be added as a percentage of the value of sales.

Example: non-production overheads

A company has budgeted to make and sell 100,000 units of Product X and 50,000 units of Product Y. Product X will sell for $5 per unit and Product Y will sell for $6 per unit.

The following costs have been budgeted.

	$
Full production cost, Product X	200,000
Full production cost, Product Y	100,000
Administration overheads	120,000
Sales and distribution overheads	200,000

Administration overheads will be absorbed into product costs as a percentage of full production costs. Selling and distribution overheads will be absorbed as a percentage of sales revenue.

Required

Calculate the cost of sales for each product and the budgeted profit for each product.

Answer

Budgeted administration overheads = $120,000

Budgeted production costs ($200,000 + $100,000) = $300,000.

Absorption rate for administration overheads = (120,000/300,000) × 100% = 40% of production cost.

	$
Budgeted sales revenue, Product X (100,000 × $5)	500,000
Budgeted sales revenue, Product Y: (50,000 × $6)	300,000
Total budgeted sales revenue	800,000
Budgeted sales and distribution costs	200,000

Absorption rate for sales and distribution overheads = (200,000/800,000) × 100%

= 25% of budgeted sales revenue.

	Product X		Product Y	
	$	$	$	$
Sales		500,000		300,000
Production costs	200,000		100,000	
Administration costs				
(40% of production cost)	80,000		40,000	
Sales and distribution costs				
(25% of sales revenue)	125,000		75,000	
Full cost of sale		405,000		215,000
Profit		95,000		85,000

> **Under-absorbed and over-absorbed overheads**
>
> - Problem with calculating actual overhead costs
> - Calculating a pre-determined overhead rate
> - Under-absorption or over-absorption of overheads
> - The reasons for under- or over-absorption: expenditure and volume variances

6 Under-absorbed and over-absorbed overheads

6.1 Problem with calculating actual overhead costs

Overhead rates are normally calculated for the entire financial year, and the same absorption rate is used throughout the year. If overhead rates are based on actual overhead expenditure and actual direct labour hours or machine hours, it would be necessary to wait until the end of the financial year to calculate any overhead absorption rates and product costs. This is unacceptable, because of the delay in providing management information about costs and profitability.

The cost accountant needs to know what the overhead absorption rate is in order to calculate product costs as soon as the products are manufactured. For this to be possible, the absorption rate must be decided in advance, for the entire financial year.

Pre-determined absorption rates are therefore calculated and used. The absorption rates are calculated in advance using estimates for cost and production volume in the annual financial plan or **budget.**

6.2 Calculating a pre-determined overhead rate

The pre-determined overhead absorption rates are calculated from:

- budgeted (planned) overhead expenditure, and
- the budgeted volume or activity levels (planned labour hours or machine hours).

The method of calculating a pre-determined overhead rate, either for separate production departments or as a factory-wide rate, are the processes of allocation, apportionment and absorption that have already been described. Budgeted data is used, rather than data about actual costs and output.

6.3 Under-absorption or over-absorption of overheads

Actual overhead expenditure and actual production volume will almost certainly be different from the planned expenditure and production volume. This means that the production overheads absorbed into product costs will be higher or lower than the actual production overhead expenditure.

- **Over-absorption.** If the amount of production overheads absorbed into product costs is more than the actual production overhead expenditure, there **is over-absorbed overhead.** Too much overhead cost has been charged to production costs, because actual costs were lower. The over-absorbed overhead is accounted for as an adjustment to the profit in the period, and is added to profit in the cost accounting income statement.

- **Under-absorption.** If the amount of production overheads absorbed into product costs is less than the actual production overhead expenditure, there is **under-absorbed overhead.** Not enough overhead cost has been charged to production costs, because actual costs were higher. Under-absorbed overhead is accounted for as an adjustment to the profit in the period, and is deducted from profit.

There is no adjustment to the value of closing inventory to allow for any over-absorption or under-absorption of overhead in the cost accounting income statement.

Example

A company manufactures and sells a range of products in a single factory. Its budgeted production overheads for Year 6 were $150,000, and budgeted direct labour hours were 50,000 hours.

Actual results in Year 6 were as follows:

	$	
Sales	630,000	
Direct materials costs	130,000	
Direct labour costs	160,000	
Production overhead	140,000	(40,000 hours)
Administration overhead	70,000	
Selling and distribution overhead	90,000	

There was no opening or closing inventory at the beginning or end of Year 6.

The company uses an absorption costing system, and production overhead is absorbed using a direct labour hour rate.

Required

(a) Calculate the production overhead absorption rate.

(b) Calculate the cost per unit produced

(c) Show how the profit or loss for the year will be reported.

Answer

The pre-determined absorption rate is $150,000/50,000 hours = $3 per direct labour hour.

The full production cost per unit produced is:

	$
Direct materials costs	130,000
Direct labour costs	160,000
Production overhead absorbed (40,000 hours × $3)	120,000
Full production cost (= cost of sales in this example)	410,000

Double entry

	Dr $	Cr $
Absorption of production overhead		
Inventory (then cost of sale)	120,000	
Production overheads		120,000
Under absorption		
Cost of sales	20,000	
Overhead		20,000
	140,000	140,000

The double entries clear the production account as follows:

Production overhead

	$		$
Cash	140,000	Inventory	120,000
		Cost of sales	20,000
	140,000		140,000

The profit for the year is reported as follows. Notice that under-absorbed overhead is an adjustment that reduces the reported profit. Over-absorbed overhead would be an adjustment that increases profit.

	$	$
Sales		630,000
Full production cost of sales		(410,000)
		220,000
Overhead absorbed	120,000	
Actual overhead expenditure	140,000	
Under-absorbed overhead		(20,000)
		200,000
Administration overhead	70,000	
Selling and distribution overhead	90,000	
		(160,000)
Profit for Year 6		40,000

Exercise 3

A manufacturing company uses absorption costing and absorbs overhead costs on a direct labour hour basis.

For Year 7, budgeted production overheads were $240,000, and 30,000 direct labour hours were budgeted.

Actual production overhead costs in Year 7 were $258,000 and 33,000 direct labour hours were worked.

Required

(a) How much production overhead was charged to the cost of production in year 7?

(b) What was the under- or over-absorbed overhead in Year 7?

6.4 The reasons for under- or over-absorption: expenditure and volume variances

There are two reasons for over-absorbed or under-absorbed overheads. These can be measured as:

- an overhead expenditure variance, and
- an overhead volume variance.

The pre-determined overhead absorption rate is based on budgeted overhead expenditure and budgeted production volume. What was expected in the budget might not actually happen. When there are differences between actual and budget fixed overhead expenditure, and actual and budgeted activity volume, an under- or over-absorption of overheads occurs.

An overhead variance is reported as either favourable (F) or adverse (A).

- When an overhead variance causes **over-absorption of overhead**, it is a **favourable variance**. The over-absorption is an adjustment that increases profit.
- When an overhead variance causes **under-absorption of overhead**, it is an **adverse variance**. The under-absorption is an adjustment that reduces profit.

Expenditure variance

Actual overhead expenditure might be different from the budgeted expenditure. Therefore, there will be some under-absorbed or over-absorbed overheads because actual overhead expenditure differs from the budgeted expenditure.

	$	
Expected overhead expenditure	X	
Actual overhead expenditure	X	
Expenditure variance	X	(favourable or adverse)

When actual fixed overhead expenditure exceeds the budget, there is an 'adverse' variance, and this will result in some under-absorption of fixed overheads. When actual fixed overhead expenditure is less than budget, there is a 'favourable' variance and this will result in over-absorption of fixed overhead.

The reasons for an expenditure variance might be either:

- excessive spending on overhead items, or
- under-estimating fixed overhead expenditure in the budget.

Volume variance

The second reason for under- or over-absorption of fixed overhead is a difference between the actual and budgeted volume of activity (= the volume of activity on which the pre-determined overhead absorption rate was calculated).

	Units or hours	
Expected production volume	X	
Actual production volume	X	
Volume variance (in units or hours)	X	(favourable or adverse)
× Absorption rate per unit/hour	$X	
Volume variance (in $)	$X	

When actual activity volume exceeds the budget, there will be over-absorption of fixed overheads, which is a 'favourable' variance. When actual activity volume is less than budget, there will be under-absorption of fixed overhead, which is an 'adverse' variance.

When overheads are absorbed on the basis of direct labour hours or machine hours, the actual hours worked might be higher or lower than budgeted. The reasons for a favourable or an adverse volume variance might therefore be any of the following.

- Working more hours than budgeted might be caused by working overtime, or taking on additional direct labour employees.

- Working fewer hours than budgeted might be caused by staff shortages (due to employees leaving or absence from work), hold-ups in production or lack of customer orders.

Example

In its annual financial plan for Year 1, a manufacturing company budgets that production overhead expenditure will be $800,000 and that there will be 100,000 direct labour hours of work. It uses a single absorption rate, which is a rate per direct labour hour.

Actual production overhead during Year 1 was $805,000 and 105,000 direct labour hours were worked.

Answer

The total under- or over-absorbed overhead

The production overhead absorption rate for the year is $800,000/100,000 = $8 per direct labour hour. All cost units produced during the year are charged with production overheads at the rate of $8 for each direct labour hour.

	$
Overheads absorbed (105,000 hours × $8)	840,000
(Overheads included in product costs)	
Actual overhead expenditure	805,000
Over-absorbed overheads	35,000

This is added to profit when calculating the actual profit for Year 1.

Explaining the over-absorbed overhead

The over-absorbed overhead of $35,000 can be explained by a combination of an expenditure variance and a volume variance.

	$	
Budgeted overhead expenditure	800,000	
Actual overhead expenditure	805,000	
Expenditure variance	5,000	Adverse

The expenditure **variance is adverse** because actual expenditure was more than planned expenditure, and this has resulted in some **under-absorption** of overhead.

	Hours	
Budgeted volume (direct labour hours)	100,000	
Actual volume (direct labour hours)	105,000	
Volume variance (direct labour hours)	5,000	Favourable
Absorption rate/direct labour hour	$8	
Volume variance in $	$40,000	Favourable

The volume **variance is favourable** because actual hours worked exceeded the planned hours, and this has resulted in some **over-absorption** of overhead.

Summary	$	
Expenditure variance	5,000	Adverse
Volume variance	40,000	Favourable
Total over-absorbed overhead	35,000	Favourable

Exercise 4

In its annual financial plan for Year 2, a manufacturing company budgets that production overhead expenditure will be $720,000 and that there will be 120,000 direct labour hours of work. It uses a single absorption rate, which is a direct labour hour rate.

Actual production overhead during Year 2 was $704,000 and 106,000 direct labour hours were worked. The company worked on two jobs during the year, Job 123 and Job 124. 50,000 hours were worked on Job number 123, which had a prime cost in total of $270,000 and 56,000 hours were worked on Job number 124, which had prime costs in total of $360,000. Job 123 and Job 124 were both started at the beginning of Year 2 and were completed on the final day of Year 2.

Required

(a) Calculate the under- or over-absorbed overhead in Year 2, and analyse this into an expenditure variance and a volume variance.

(b) Calculate the full production cost of Job 123 and Job 124.

> **Fixed and variable overheads**
>
> - Definition of fixed and variable overheads
> - Absorption rates for fixed and variable production overheads
> - Calculating under- or over-absorbed overhead with fixed and variable overheads

7 Fixed and variable overheads

7.1 Definition of fixed and variable overheads

Most overhead is usually fixed, but some overhead might be a variable cost.

- **Fixed overhead** is overhead expenditure that should be a fixed amount in total during a given period of time, and will not change if more or less production work is done.

- **Variable overhead** is overhead that increases as more production work is done. Total variable overhead expenditure therefore depends on the volume of production. Variable overhead is usually calculated as an amount for each direct labour hour worked.

7.2 Absorption rates for fixed and variable production overheads

When an absorption costing system identifies fixed and variable overhead costs separately, there will be separate absorption rates for fixed overheads and variable overheads.

Example

The budgeted production overhead expenditure for Year 1 is $2,400,000 of fixed overheads plus variable overheads of $3 per direct labour hour. The budgeted direct labour hours are 100,000 for the year.

	$
Budgeted fixed overhead	2,400,000
Budgeted variable overhead (100,000 × $3)	300,000
Total budgeted overhead expenditure	2,700,000

The overhead absorption rate per direct labour hour is calculated as a separate rate for fixed and variable overheads:

	$
Fixed overhead absorption rate ($2,400,000/100,000)	24
Variable overhead absorption rate	3
Total absorption rate per direct labour hour	27

Total overhead expenditure

The total fixed overhead **expenditure** is unaffected by changes in production volume. However, total variable overhead expenditure increases or falls with increases or falls in production volume.

Unit overhead cost and overhead absorption rate

The budgeted fixed overhead cost per unit or per direct labour hour decreases as the planned production volume increases. The variable overhead absorption rate and spending rate is the same, regardless of the volume of production.

Example

Suppose that in the previous example, the budget is amended, and the new plan is to work 120,000 direct labour hours, rather than 100,000 hours. The new budget for overhead expenditure will be as follows:

	$
Budgeted fixed overhead	2,400,000
Budgeted variable overhead (120,000 × $3)	360,000
Total budgeted overhead expenditure	2,760,000

The overhead absorption rate per direct labour hour would be calculated as follows, with the fixed overhead absorption rate lower due to the higher budgeted direct labour hours, but the variable overhead absorption rate unchanged.

	$
Fixed overhead absorption rate ($2,400,000/120,000)	20
Variable overhead absorption rate	3
Total absorption rate/direct labour hour	23

7.3 Calculating under- or over-absorbed overhead with fixed and variable overheads

When there is some variable overhead, the method of calculating under- or over-absorbed overhead is slightly different from the calculation when all overheads are fixed. This is because variable overhead expenditure is expected to vary with the actual volume of activity.

Example

A company has budgeted fixed production overheads of $600,000 for Year 3, and a variable overhead cost of $2 per direct labour hour. The budgeted production volume is 60,000 direct labour hours of work. Actual production in Year 3 was 62,000 direct labour hours, and actual overhead expenditure (fixed and variable) was $790,000 in total.

Required

Calculate the under- or over-absorbed overhead in the year, and analyse this into an expenditure and a volume variance.

Answer

The fixed overhead absorption rate is $600,000/60,000 hours = $10 per direct labour hour.

Absorbed overheads	$
Fixed overheads (62,000 hours × $10)	620,000
Variable overheads (62,000 hours × $2)	124,000
Total absorbed overheads	744,000
Actual overhead expenditure	790,000
Under-absorbed overheads	46,000

Explaining the under-absorbed overhead

This under-absorbed overhead of $46,000 can be analysed into an expenditure and a volume variance. There are two important points to note.

- The expected overhead expenditure is the budgeted fixed overhead expenditure plus the expected variable overhead expenditure for the hours actually worked.
- The volume variance affects fixed overheads only, not variable overheads.

Expected overhead expenditure	$	
Expected fixed overheads (= Budgeted fixed overhead)	600,000	
Expected variable overheads (62,000 × $2)	124,000	
Total expected overhead expenditure	724,000	
Actual overhead expenditure	790,000	
Expenditure variance	66,000	Adverse

	Hours	
Budgeted volume (direct labour hours)	60,000	
Actual volume (direct labour hours)	62,000	
Volume variance (direct labour hours)	2,000	Favourable
Fixed overhead absorption rate/direct labour hour	× $10	
Volume variance in $ (fixed overhead only)	$20,000	Favourable

Summary	$	
Expenditure variance	66,000	Adverse
Volume variance	20,000	Favourable
Total under-absorbed overhead	46,000	Adverse

Exercise 5

A company has budgeted fixed production overheads of $800,000 for Year 4, and a variable overhead cost of $4 per direct labour hour. The budgeted production volume is 100,000 direct labour hours of work. Actual production in Year 4 was 97,000 direct labour hours, and actual overhead expenditure (fixed and variable) was $1,120,000 in total.

Required

Calculate the under- or over-absorbed overhead in the year, and analyse this into an expenditure and a volume variance.

Management Accounting (MA)

Practice multiple choice questions

1 A factory consists of two production centres P1 and P2, and two service centres S1 and S2. The total overheads allocated and apportioned to each of these cost centres is as follows.

	P1	P2	S1	S2
Total overheads	$300,000	$450,000	$320,000	$350,000

The work done by the service centres for each of the other centres has been estimated as follows:

	P1	P2	S1	S2
% of service centre S1 to:	30%	70%	-	-
% of service centre S2 to:	30%	40%	30%	-

The costs of the service centres are apportioned to production cost centres using a method that fully recognises any work done by one service cost centre for another.

What are the total overheads for production cost centre P2 after the re-apportionment of all service centre costs?

- **A** $814,000
- **B** $874,000
- **C** $887,500
- **D** $947,500

(2 marks)

2 A company manufactures two products Y and Z in a factory that has two production cost centres, CC1 and CC2. The following budgeted data are available.

Cost centre	Product Y hours per unit	Product Z hours per unit	Allocated and apportioned fixed overheads
CC1	4	2	$660,000
CC2	5	4	$540,000

Budgeted output is 20,000 units of each product. Fixed overhead costs are absorbed on a direct labour hour basis.

What is the budgeted fixed overhead cost per unit for Product Z?

- **A** $23.00
- **B** $24.00
- **C** $37.00
- **D** $39.50

(2 marks)

3   A company manufactures two products P and Q in a factory that has two production cost centres, C1 and C2. The following budgeted data are available.

	Cost centre	
	C1	C2
Allocated and apportioned fixed overheads	$324,000	$583,200
Direct labour hours per unit:		
Product P	2	5
Product Q	4	3

Budgeted output is 15,000 units of each product. Fixed overhead costs are absorbed on a direct labour hour basis.

What is the budgeted fixed overhead cost per unit for Product Q?

A $28.98

B $30.24

C $31.50

D $32.58 *(2 marks)*

4   A manufacturing company uses absorption costing with a pre-determined fixed overhead absorption rate based on direct labour hours worked. The following situations occurred in the previous three months.

(i)   Budgeted direct labour hours were more than the actual direct labour hours worked.

(ii) Actual fixed overhead expenditure was higher than the planned expenditure.

Which one of the following statements is correct?

A   Situation (i) would cause overheads to be over-absorbed and situation (ii) would cause overheads to be under-absorbed.

B   Situation (i) would cause overheads to be under-absorbed and situation (ii) would cause overheads to be over-absorbed.

C   Both situations would cause overheads to be over-absorbed.

D   Both situations would cause overheads to be under-absorbed. *(2 marks)*

5   A manufacturing company budgeted 36,000 direct labour hours of work and overhead spending of $144,000. It uses absorption costing, and absorbs overhead costs on the basis of direct labour hours. During the period, overhead spending was $157,500 and 37,500 direct labour hours were worked.

What was the amount of overheads under- or over-absorbed?

A   Under-absorbed $13,500

B   Over-absorbed $13,500

C   Over-absorbed $6,000

D   Under-absorbed $7,500 *(2 marks)*

6 A manufacturing company budgeted 24,000 direct labour hours of work and production overhead spending of $300,000. It uses absorption costing, and absorbs overhead costs on the basis of direct labour hours. During the period, overhead spending was $318,500 and 26,000 direct labour hours were worked.

What was the amount of overheads under- or over-absorbed?

- **A** Over-absorbed $6,500
- **B** Over-absorbed $24,500
- **C** Over-absorbed $25,000
- **D** Under-absorbed $18,500

(2 marks)

Applied Knowledge
Management Accounting (MA)

CHAPTER 11

Accounting for costs: ledger entries

Contents

1. The cost ledger
2. Double entry accounting for costs: basic rules
3. Double entry accounting for costs: overheads
4. Completing the cost accounting income statement

> **The cost ledger**
>
> - The nature and purpose of the cost ledger
> - Accounts in the cost ledger
> - Double entry cost accounting system

1 The cost ledger

1.1 The nature and purpose of the cost ledger

An accounting system is needed to record costs of production and sales. One way of doing this is to record transactions relating to costs in a set of cost accounts. Cost accounts are held in the cost ledger. (A ledger is a word meaning 'a collection of related accounts').

If you already know about double entry ledger accounting, you will find this chapter easier to follow than if you are reading about double entry accounting systems for the first time. If you do not know anything about double entry accounting systems (debits and credits) you should be able to learn what you need to know by reading this chapter carefully.

1.2 Accounts in the cost ledger

The accounts in the cost ledger are used to record transactions relating to:

- the costs of materials, labour and expenses
- overhead costs
- the costs of production
- sales and the cost of sales
- profit or loss.

There are other accounts in the cost ledger, such as an account for recording the under-absorbed or over-absorbed production overhead within a system of absorption costing.

There might also be accounts for recording the cost of abnormal losses (process costing) or variances (standard costing). These accounts will be explained in later chapters dealing with process costing and standard costing.

The inventory accounts

There are accounts in the cost ledger for recording work as it progresses through the production process. In a simple cost accounting system, there are accounts for raw materials, work-in-progress and finished goods:

- **Raw materials.** A costing system keeps a continuous record of transactions involving receipts into stores and issues from stores. The raw materials inventory account, or stores account, is used to record the cost of materials purchased, and the cost of materials issued from the stores department to other departments. The balance on the raw materials inventory account shows the cost of the raw materials currently held as inventory.

- **Work-in-progress (WIP).** A costing system keeps a continuous record of costs of production. In an absorption costing system, the WIP account records the costs of direct materials, direct labour and direct expenses (if any), and absorbed production overhead costs. It also records the cost of finished production. (Finished production is either transferred to a finished goods store or sold directly to the customer.) The balance on the WIP inventory account shows the cost of production still in progress and not yet completed. This inventory of unfinished production is called 'work–in-progress'.

- **Finished goods.** The finished goods account is a stores account for completed production that has not yet been sold. It records the production cost of completed units transferred from production into the finished goods store, and the production cost of goods that are then transferred from the store and sold to customers. The balance on the finished goods inventory account shows the production cost of finished output held in store.

1.3 Double entry cost accounting system

A cost accounting system, like the financial accounting book-keeping system, uses a double entry system for recording transactions. With double entry, every transaction is recorded twice in the accounts:

- as a debit entry in one account, and
- as a credit entry in a different account.

The total of debit entries and the total of credit entries must always be equal. It is useful to think of an account as having a T shape, with a debit side and a credit side, as follows:

Name of the account

Debit side	$	Credit side	$

The **balance on an account** is the difference between the total value of entries on the debit side and the total value of entries on the credit side.

- When the total value of debit entries is higher than the total value of credit entries, there is a debit balance.
- When the total value of credit entries is higher than the total value of debit entries, there is a credit balance.

The **balance on the three inventory accounts** should always be either zero (= no inventory) or a debit balance (= the cost of the inventory that is currently held).

> **Double entry accounting for costs: basic rules**
>
> - Recording costs incurred
> - Costs of production and the WIP account
> - From raw materials to cost of sales
> - Non-production overheads
> - Opening and closing inventory
> - The costing system income statement
> - The financial ledger control account

2 Double entry accounting for costs: basic rules

There are some basic rules that need to be remembered when recording costs in the cost accounting system.

2.1 Recording costs incurred

Some accounts are used to record costs that are incurred.

- The **raw materials account** records the cost of materials purchased.

- The **wages and salaries cost account** records the cost of labour. (Sometimes, you might come across a direct labour cost account, which records the wages and salary costs of direct labour only).

- **Overhead cost accounts** record the overhead costs incurred.

- The **work-in-progress account** records the production costs of items produced. It records the cost of direct materials, direct labour and production overheads absorbed. These costs are transferred to work in progress from the raw materials account, wages and salaries cost account and production overheads account.

- The **finished goods account** records the production cost of completed production that is transferred from work in progress to the store of finished goods inventory.

- The **cost of sales account** records the total cost of sales, which consists of production costs, administration costs and sales and distribution costs.

Costs incurred are recorded as debit entries in these accounts.

2.2 Costs of production and the WIP account

The WIP account is used to record the costs of production – direct materials, direct labour and production overheads absorbed. These costs are recorded in a double entry cost accounting system as follows:

		Debit	Credit
1)	Direct materials issued from stores to production	WIP account	Raw materials account (stores account)
2)	Direct labour costs in production	WIP account	Wages and salaries account
3)	Production overheads absorbed into production costs	WIP account	Production overheads account

Example

Raw materials costing $6,000 are transferred from the stores account into production. Direct labour costs of $12,500 were incurred and overheads of $25,000 were absorbed into production costs

In a cost ledger system these items would be accounted for as follows.

Work in Progress

(Debit side)	$	(Credit side)	$
Raw materials (stores) account	6,000		
Wages account	12,500		
Production overhead account	25,000		

The balance on this account is now a debit balance of $43,500.

Stores account

(Debit side)	$	(Credit side)	$
		Work in progress	6,000

Wages account

(Debit side)	$	(Credit side)	$
		Work in Progress	12,500

Production overhead account

(Debit side)	$	(Credit side)	$
		Work in Progress	25,000

2.3 From raw materials to cost of sales

Materials progress through the production system, from raw materials to work in progress, from work in progress to finished goods, and from finished goods to cost of sales. This is recorded in the double entry system as follows:

		Debit	Credit
1)	Direct materials issued from stores to production (work in progress)	WIP account	Raw materials account (stores account)
2)	Completed production transferred from WIP to finished goods (at production cost)	Finished goods account	WIP account
3)	Finished goods sold to customers	Cost of sales account	Finished goods account (production cost of sales)

Example

Continuing the previous example, the cost of finished output is $40,000. This is transferred to the finished goods warehouse, and finished goods costing $35,000 are sold.

In a cost ledger system these items would be accounted for as follows.

Work in Progress

(Debit side)	$	(Credit side)	$
Raw materials (stores) account	6,000	Finished goods account	40,000
Wages account	12,500		
Production overhead account	25,000		

The balance on this account is now a debit balance of $3,500. This means that unfinished work-in-progress has a cost of $3,500.

Finished goods account

(Debit side)	$	(Credit side)	$
Work in progress	40,000	Cost of sales account	35,000

The balance on this account is now a debit balance of $5,000. This means that finished goods held in the finished goods warehouse has a cost of $5,000.

Cost of sales account

(Debit side)	$	(Credit side)	$
Finished goods account	35,000		

2.4 Non-production overheads

Non-production overheads are recorded initially in an administration overheads account and a sales and distribution overheads account. They are transferred from these accounts to the cost of sales account. The cost of sales account therefore records the production cost of finished goods sold, administration overheads costs and sales and distribution overheads costs.

		Debit	Credit
1)	Administration overheads	Cost of sales account	Administration overheads account (administration overheads for the period)
2)	Sales and distribution overheads	Cost of sales account	Sales and distribution overheads account (sales and distribution overheads for the period)

Example

Continuing the previous example, finished goods with a production cost of $35,000 are sold. Administration overhead costs are $15,000 and sales and distribution overheads are $20,000.

In a cost ledger system these items would be accounted for as follows.

Cost of sales account

(Debit side)	$	(Credit side)	$
Finished goods account	35,000		
Administration overhead	15,000		
Sales and distribution overhead	20,000		

The total cost of sales is $70,000.

Administration overhead account

(Debit side)	$	(Credit side)	$
		Cost of sales	15,000

Sales and distribution overhead account

(Debit side)	$	(Credit side)	$
		Cost of sales	20,000

2.5 Opening and closing inventory

The raw materials account, work-in-progress account (incomplete production) and finished goods account provide a record of the cost of opening and closing inventory at the beginning and end of each accounting period.

The value of the inventory is the current balance on the inventory account. This is always either 0 or a debit balance.

However, at the end of an accounting period, an account is 'closed off' for the period, and the balance on the account is:

- carried forward as a closing balance for the period that has just ended, and
- an opening balance at the beginning of the new period.

An example of a materials account is shown below, to illustrate how the opening and closing inventory are recorded:

Materials account

	$		$
Period 1		*Period 1*	
Opening inventory b/f	5,000	Work in progress (direct materials)	35,000
Purchases	46,000	Production overheads (indirect materials)	9,000
		Closing inventory c/f	7,000
	51,000		51,000
Period 2			
Opening inventory b/f	7,000		

The closing inventory at the end of a period is entered on the credit side 'above the line' and the corresponding double entry is a debit entry 'below the line' as opening inventory at the beginning of the next period.

'b/f' means 'brought forward'. You might also see the letters 'b/fwd' or 'b/d' (meaning 'brought down'). Similarly, 'c/f' means carried forward. You might also see the letters 'c/fwd' or c/d (for 'carried down').

The opening inventory brought forward is called the 'balance' on the account at the beginning of the period. In the example above, the opening balance of $7,000 at the beginning of period 2 could be calculated as (Opening inventory + Purchases) – Materials issued. Here this is $5,000 + 46,000 - $(35,000 + 9,000) = $7,000.

2.6 The costing system income statement

There is an income statement in the cost ledger, for recording the profit or loss in each accounting period. This is a part of the double entry cost accounting system.

The credit side of the income statement records sales. The debit side of the income statement records the cost of sales.

There might also be other items in this account, such as under- or over-absorbed overheads (in an absorption costing system) or variances (in a standard costing system) or abnormal loss or abnormal gain (in a process costing system). The basic rules of double entry, however, are as follows:

	Debit	Credit
Sales	Sales account	Income statement account
Cost of sales	Income statement account	Cost of sales account

The balance on this income statement account is:

- a credit balance when sales are higher than the cost of sales, and there is a profit.
- a debit balance when sales are less than the cost of sales, and there is a loss.

The profit or loss for the period is then transferred to a retained profits account, so that the balance on the income statement becomes 0.

Example

Continuing the previous example, finished goods with a production cost of $35,000 are sold. Administration overhead costs are $15,000 and sales and distribution overheads are $20,000. Sales in the period are $82,000.

In a cost ledger system these items would be accounted for as follows.

Cost of sales account

(Debit side)	$	(Credit side)	$
Finished goods account	35,000	Income statement	70,000
Administration overhead	15,000		
Sales and distribution overhead	20,000		
	70,000		70,000

Cost accounting income statement

(Debit side)	$	(Credit side)	$
Cost of sales account	70,000	Sales account	82,000

The profit of $12,000 is shown by the credit balance on the costing income statement account.

	Debit	Credit
Profit	Income statement account	Accumulated profit account, or financial ledger control account
Loss	Accumulated profit account, or financial ledger control account	Income statement account

2.7 The financial ledger control account

The cost ledger includes accounts relating to costs. There are many other accounts that are not specifically related to costs, such as the bank account, the account for trade receivables, the account for trade payables, an account for accumulated profits, and so on. In the cost ledger, a special account called the financial ledger control account (or the cost ledger control account) may be used to record one of the double entry transactions required when the appropriate account does not exist in the cost ledger.

Examples

- A company buys raw materials on credit from a supplier, at a cost of $2,000. It has an addition to its materials, and owes the supplier. The double entry is:

    Debit: Materials account $2,000

    Credit: Financial ledger control account $2,000.

- A company pays wages of $3,000 to its work force. It has incurred labour costs, and paid for them out of its bank account. The double entry is:

    Debit: Wages and salaries cost account $3,000

    Credit: Financial ledger control account $3,000.

- A company incurs production overhead expenses, such as factory rental costs, and either pays for them out of its bank account or obtains the items on credit from a supplier. The double entry is:

    Debit: Production overheads account

    Credit: Financial ledger control account.

Exercise 1

A company incurs the following costs:

(a) Purchases of raw materials $20,000

(b) Costs of wages and salaries $25,000

(c) Cost of production overhead expenses $4,000

(d) Cost of other overhead expenses (administration overheads and selling and distribution overheads) $7,000

(e) The opening inventory in the materials account is a balance of $1,000 and in the work-in-progress account the opening balance is $4,000. The opening balance on the financial ledger control account is $5,000.

(f) The company also had sales of $90,000.

Required

Record these transactions in the following cost accounts:

- Materials account
- Wages and salaries account
- Production overheads account
- Other overheads account

- Sales account
- Financial ledger control account.

(You are not required to show the WIP account, although you can do so if you want to see that all the debit entries and all the credit entries add up to the same total amount).

You will find the answer to the Exercises and practice multiple choice questions at the end of this book.

> **Double entry accounting for costs: overheads**
>
> - Accounting for direct and indirect materials and labour costs
> - Absorbed production overheads

3 Double entry accounting for costs: overheads

3.1 Accounting for direct and indirect materials and labour costs

Direct materials costs and direct labour costs are direct costs of production and are charged to the work-in-progress account.

Indirect materials costs and indirect labour costs are overhead costs of production and are charged to the production overhead account, administration overhead account or selling and distribution overheads account, as appropriate.

	Debit	Credit
Direct materials issued from stores to production	WIP account	Raw materials account (inventory account)
Direct labour costs in production	WIP account	Wages and salaries account
Indirect materials		
Indirect materials issued from stores to production cost centres	Production overheads account	Raw materials account (inventory account)
Indirect materials issued from stores to administration cost centres	Administration overheads account	Raw materials account (inventory account)
Indirect materials issued from stores to sales and distribution cost centres	Sales and distribution overheads account	Raw materials account (inventory account)
Indirect labour		
Indirect labour production cost	Production overheads account	Wages and salaries account
Administration costs of labour	Administration overheads account	Wages and salaries account
Sales and distribution labour costs	Sales and distribution overheads account	Wages and salaries account

3.2 Absorbed production overheads

Production overheads are absorbed into the cost of production. This is accounted for as follows:

	Debit	Credit
Production overheads absorbed	WIP account (Absorbed overheads are added to the cost of production)	Production overheads account

The balance on the production overhead account is the under-absorbed overhead or over-absorbed overhead. At the end of each accounting period, this balance is transferred to an under- or over-absorbed overhead account.

Example

During an accounting period, a company recorded the following transactions:

(a) Opening inventory: raw materials $5,000; WIP $3,000

(b) Purchased raw materials costing $23,000

(c) Used $14,000 of direct materials in production and $5,000 of indirect production materials.

(d) Incurred total labour costs of $25,000. Of this total, $12,000 were direct labour costs, $6,000 were indirect production labour costs and $7,000 were other overhead labour costs.

(e) Production overhead expenses were $18,000.

(f) Absorbed $27,000 of production overheads into the cost of production.

These transactions are accounted for as follows. Work through the accounting entries carefully, and make sure that you can see how each item is accounted for. 'Balance' in some of the accounts here means 'balancing item': this is the entry required to complete the account, which is calculated from the other figures in the account.

Raw materials

	$		$
Opening inventory b/f	5,000	Work-in-progress	14,000
Purchases (financial ledger control account)	23,000	Production overheads	5,000
		Closing inventory c/f (balance)	9,000
	28,000		28,000
Opening inventory b/f	9,000		

Wages and salaries

	$		$
Costs incurred	25,000	Work-in-progress	12,000
(financial ledger control		Production overheads	6,000
account)			
		Other overhead	7,000
	25,000		25,000

Production overheads

	$		$
Expenses (fin. ledger control)	18,000	Work-in-progress (absorbed)	27,000
Raw materials	5,000	Under-absorbed o'head (balance)	2,000
Wages and salaries	6,000		
	29,000		29,000

Work-in-progress

	$		$
Opening inventory b/f	3,000		
Materials	14,000		
Wages and salaries	12,000		
Production overhead	27,000		

Other overheads

	$		$
Wages and salaries	7,000		

Under-absorbed overhead account

	$		$
Production overhead	2,000		

> **Completing the cost accounting income statement**
>
> - The finished goods account
> - The cost of sales account and the sales account
> - The cost accounting income statement

4 Completing the cost accounting income statement

The cost ledger includes an income statement where sales are matched with the cost of sales. Other adjustments, such as an adjustment for under- or over-absorbed overheads, are also recorded in the income statement, and the balance on the account is the profit or loss for the period.

4.1 The finished goods account

The finished goods account records the production cost of finished goods completed in the period, and the production cost of goods sold in the period.

Finished goods account

	$		$
Opening inventory b/f	18,000	Cost of sales	95,000
Work-in-progress (= cost of completed production)	87,000	Closing inventory c/f	10,000
	105,000		105,000
Opening inventory b/f	10,000		

4.2 The cost of sales account and the sales account

The cost of sales account records the total cost of sales in the period – the production cost of sales and administration and sales and distribution overheads.

Cost of sales account

	$		$
Finished goods (= production cost of goods sold)	95,000	Income statement (= cost of sales)	155,000
Administration overheads	20,000		
Sales and distribution overheads	40,000		
	155,000		155,000

Sales are recorded in a sales account, and then transferred to the income statement at the end of each costing period.

Sales account

	$		$
Income statement	200,000	Financial ledger control account (= sales in the period)	200,000
	200,000		200,000

4.3 The cost accounting income statement

The profit or loss is recorded in a cost accounting income statement. The income statement also includes any other adjustments to profit, such as under- or over-absorbed overhead, abnormal loss or gain, or standard cost variances.

The balance on the income statement is the profit or loss for the period. The matching double entry is in the financial ledger control account (accumulated profits).

Cost accounting income statement

	$		$
Cost of sales	155,000	Sales	200,000
Under-absorbed overheads	3,000		
Profit	42,000		
	200,000		200,000

Exercise 2

Record the following transactions in the cost ledger accounts.

Prepare a statement of the closing balances.

	$
Opening balances:	
Materials	7,000
Work-in-progress	3,000
Finished goods	4,000
Financial ledger control account	14,000
Transactions in the period	
Material purchases	50,000
Direct materials used in production	33,000
Indirect production materials	17,000
Indirect materials: other overheads	2,000
Wages and salaries costs	45,000
Direct labour costs	28,000
Indirect production labour	7,000
Indirect labour: other overheads	10,000
Expenses: production overheads	24,000
Expenses: other overheads	15,000
Production overheads absorbed	50,000
Closing inventory, work-in-progress	8,000
Production cost of goods sold	109,000
Sales	160,000

You will find the answer to the Exercises and practice multiple choice questions at the end of this book.

Applied Knowledge
Management Accounting (MA)

CHAPTER

12

Marginal costing and absorption costing

Contents
1 Marginal cost and marginal costing
2 Reporting profit with marginal costing
3 Marginal costing and absorption costing compared
4 Advantages and disadvantages of absorption and marginal costing

> **Marginal cost and marginal costing**
>
> - Marginal cost
> - Marginal costing and its uses
> - Assumptions in marginal costing
> - Contribution

1 Marginal cost and marginal costing

1.1 Marginal cost

The marginal cost of an item is its variable cost.

- **Marginal production cost** =
  Direct materials + Direct labour + Variable production overhead.

- **Marginal cost of sale** for a **product** =
  Direct materials + Direct labour + Variable production overhead + Other variable overhead (for example, variable selling and distribution overhead).

- **Marginal cost of sale** for a **service** =
  Direct materials + Direct labour + Variable overhead.

It is usually assumed that **direct labour costs** are variable (marginal) costs, but in some situations, direct labour costs might be fixed costs, and so would not be included in marginal cost.

Variable overhead costs might be difficult to identify. In practice, variable overheads might be measured using a technique such as high/low analysis or linear regression analysis, to separate total overhead costs into fixed costs and a variable cost per unit of activity.

For variable production overheads, the unit of activity is often either direct labour hours or machine hours, although another measure of activity might be used.

- For variable selling and distribution costs, the unit of activity might be sales volume or sales revenue.

- Administration overheads are usually considered to be fixed costs, and it is very unusual to come across variable administration overheads.

Marginal costs and total costs

When marginal costing is used, total costs are the sum of variable costs (marginal costs) and fixed costs. It is important in marginal costing that you should separate variable costs from fixed costs, and identify them separately. Remember that there might be some variable selling and distribution costs. The table below shows how variable and fixed costs might be separated in a marginal costing analysis.

	$	$
Direct materials		60,000
Direct labour		40,000
Direct expenses		5,000
Prime cost		105,000
Variable production overheads		15,000
Variable selling and distribution overheads		10,000
Total variable costs (marginal cost)		**130,000**
Fixed costs		
Fixed production overheads	60,000	
Fixed administration overheads	40,000	
Fixed selling and distribution overheads	50,000	
Fixed costs		150,000
Total costs		280,000

1.2 Marginal costing and its uses

Marginal costing is a method of costing with marginal costs. It is an alternative to absorption costing as a method of costing. In marginal costing, fixed production overheads are not absorbed into product costs.

There are several reasons for using marginal costing:

- To measure profit (or loss), as an alternative to absorption costing
- To forecast what future profits will be
- To calculate what the minimum sales volume must be in order to make a profit

It can also be used to provide management with information for decision making.

This chapter looks at using marginal costing to measure profit, as an alternative to absorption costing.

Its main uses, however, are for planning (for example, budgeting), forecasting and decision making.

1.3 Assumptions in marginal costing

For the purpose of marginal costing, the following assumptions are normally made:

- Every additional unit of output or sale, or every additional unit of activity, has the same variable cost as every other unit. In other words, the variable cost per unit is a constant value.
- Fixed costs are costs that remain the same in total in each period, regardless of how many units are produced and sold.

- Costs are either fixed or variable, or a mixture of fixed and variable costs. Mixed costs can be separated into a variable cost per unit and a fixed cost per period. Techniques such as high/low analysis or linear regression analysis should be used to do this.
- The marginal cost of an item is therefore the extra cost that would be incurred by making and selling one extra unit of the item.

1.4 Contribution

Contribution is a key concept in marginal costing.

Contribution = Sales – Variable costs

Fixed costs are a constant total amount in each period. To make a profit, an entity must first make enough contribution to cover its fixed costs. Contribution therefore means: 'contribution towards covering fixed costs and making a profit'.

Total contribution – Fixed costs = Profit

- When fixed costs have been covered, any additional contribution adds directly to profit.
- If total contribution fails to cover fixed costs, there is a loss.

2 Reporting profit with marginal costing

> **Reporting profit with marginal costing**
>
> - Total contribution minus fixed costs
> - A marginal costing income statement with opening and closing inventory

2.1 Total contribution minus fixed costs

With marginal costing, profit is measured as follows (illustrative figures are shown):

When you are measuring profits using marginal costing, it is usual to identify contribution, and then to subtract fixed costs from the total contribution in order to get to the profit figure. A simplified example of a marginal costing income statement is shown below.

	$	$
Sales		360,000
Direct costs	105,000	
Variable production costs	15,000	
Variable sales and distribution costs	10,000	
Total marginal costs		130,000
Total contribution		230,000
Total fixed costs		150,000
Profit		80,000

Total contribution and contribution per unit

In marginal costing, it is assumed that the variable cost per unit of product (or per unit of service) is constant. If the selling price per unit is also constant, this means that the contribution earned from selling each unit of product is the same.

Total contribution can therefore be calculated as: Units of sale × Contribution per unit.

Example

A company manufactures and sells two products, A and B. Product A has a variable cost of $6 and sells for $10, and product B has a variable cost of $8 and sells for $15. During the period, 20,000 units of Product A and 30,000 units of Product B were sold. Fixed costs were $260,000. What was the profit or loss for the period?

Answer

Contribution per unit:

- Product A: $10 − $6 = $4
- Product B: $15 − $8 = $7

	$
Contribution from Product A: (20,000 × $4)	80,000
Contribution from Product B: (30,000 × $7)	210,000
Total contribution for the period	290,000
Fixed costs for the period	(260,000)
Profit for the period	30,000

Exercise 1

An entity sells two products, X and Y. Product X sells for $8 per unit and has a variable cost of $3. Product Y sells for $6 per unit and has a variable cost of $2. Fixed costs each month are $250,000.

Monthly sales are 40,000 units of Product X and 30,000 units of Product Y. There is no inventory of either product.

Required

Using marginal costing, calculate the profit for the month.

You will find the answer to the Exercises and practice multiple choice questions at the end of this book.

2.2 A marginal costing income statement with opening and closing inventory

The explanation of marginal costing has so far ignored opening and closing inventory.

In absorption costing, the production cost of sales is calculated as 'opening inventory value + production costs incurred in the period – closing inventory value'.

The same principle applies in marginal costing. The variable production cost of sales is calculated as 'opening inventory value + variable production costs incurred in the period – closing inventory value'.

When marginal costing is used, inventory is valued at its marginal cost of production (= variable production cost), without any absorbed fixed production overheads.

If an income statement is prepared using marginal costing, the opening and closing inventory might be shown, as follows:

Income statement for the period ended [date]	$	$
Sales		440,000
Opening inventory at variable production cost	5,000	
Variable production costs		
Direct materials	60,000	
Direct labour	30,000	
Variable production overheads	15,000	
	110,000	
Less: Closing inventory at variable production cost	(8,000)	
Variable production cost of sales	102,000	
Variable selling and distribution costs	18,000	
Variable cost of sales		(120,000)
Contribution		320,000
Fixed costs:		
Production fixed costs	120,000	
Administration costs (usually 100% fixed costs)	70,000	
Selling and distribution fixed costs	90,000	
Total fixed costs		(280,000)
Profit		40,000

However, when the variable production cost per unit is a constant amount, there is no need to show the opening and closing inventory valuations, and the income statement could be presented more simply as follows:

Income statement for the period ended [date]	$	$
Sales		440,000
Variable production cost of sales	102,000	
Variable selling and distribution costs	18,000	
Variable cost of sales		120,000
Total contribution		320,000
Fixed costs:		
Production fixed costs	120,000	
Administration costs	70,000	
Selling and distribution fixed costs	90,000	
Total fixed costs		280,000
Profit		40,000

> **Marginal costing and absorption costing compared**
>
> - Reporting profit with absorption costing
> - The difference in profit between marginal costing and absorption costing
> - Calculating the difference in profit: increase in inventory during a period
> - Calculating the difference in profit: reduction in inventory during a period
> - Summary: comparing marginal and absorption costing profit

3 Marginal costing and absorption costing compared

3.1 Reporting profit with absorption costing

Absorption costing is the 'traditional' way of measuring profit in a manufacturing company. Inventory is valued at the full cost of production, which consists of direct materials and direct labour cost plus absorbed production overheads (fixed and variable production overheads).

The absorption rate for variable production overheads should be the same as the variable overhead rate of expenditure. However in absorption costing variable and fixed production overheads might not be separated.

In absorption costing, there is some under- or over-absorbed overhead, which occurs because the absorption rate is a pre-determined rate.

The full presentation of an absorption costing income statement might therefore be as follows (illustrative figures included):

Income statement for the period ended [date]	$	$
Sales		430,000
Opening inventory at full production cost	8,000	
Production costs		
Direct materials	60,000	
Direct labour	30,000	
Production overheads absorbed	100,000	
	198,000	
Less: Closing inventory at full production cost	(14,000)	
Full production cost of sales		(184,000)
		246,000
Production overheads absorbed	100,000	
Production overheads incurred	(95,000)	
Over-absorbed overheads		5,000
		251,000
Administration costs	70,000	
Selling and distribution costs (fixed + variable)	108,000	
		(178,000)
Profit		73,000

3.2 The difference in profit between marginal costing and absorption costing

The profit for an accounting period calculated with marginal costing is different from the profit calculated with absorption costing. The difference in profit is due **entirely** to the differences in inventory valuation.

When there is no opening or closing inventory, exactly the same profit will be reported using marginal costing and absorption costing.

The main difference between absorption costing and marginal costing is that:

- in absorption costing, inventory cost includes a share of fixed production overhead costs
- in marginal costing, inventory cost contains no fixed production overhead costs.

The following rules may be applied to calculate the difference in the profit for a period calculated with marginal costing and with absorption costing.

3.3 Calculating the difference in profit: increase in inventory during a period

Look at the difference between the quantity of opening inventory and closing inventory. Establish whether:

- closing inventory is larger than opening inventory, or
- closing inventory is less than opening inventory.

Closing inventory is higher than opening inventory when the quantity produced in the period is more than the quantity sold. If the cost per unit is a constant amount, using marginal costing or absorption costing, when the production quantity exceeds the sales quantity:

- There is an increase in inventory during a period
- Closing inventory is therefore higher in value than opening inventory
- The increase in inventory will be greater with absorption costing, by the amount of the increase in fixed production costs in the inventory value
- The production cost of sales is therefore lower with absorption costing than with marginal costing, and the difference is this increase in fixed costs in the inventory value
- Therefore the profit is higher with absorption costing than with marginal costing, by the amount of the increase in fixed costs in the inventory value.

Basic rule: comparing marginal costing and absorption costing profit

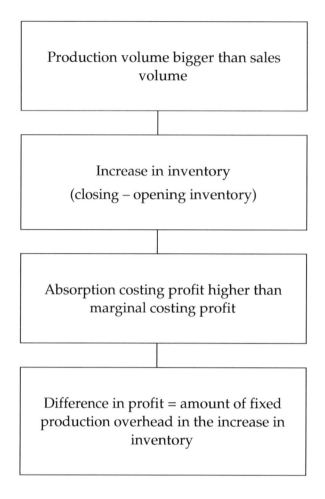

 Example

A company uses marginal costing. In the financial period that has just ended, opening inventory was $8,000 and closing inventory was $15,000. The reported profit for the year was $96,000.

If the company had used absorption costing, opening inventory would have been $16,000 and closing inventory would have been $35,000.

Required

What would have been the profit for the year if absorption costing had been used?

Answer

There was an increase in inventory. It was $7,000 using marginal costing (= $15,000 − $8,000). It would have been $19,000 using absorption costing.

	$
Increase in inventory, marginal costing	7,000
Increase in inventory, absorption costing	19,000
Difference (profit higher with absorption costing)	12,000
Profit with marginal costing	96,000
Profit with absorption costing	108,000

The profit is higher with absorption costing because there has been an increase in inventory (production volume has been more than sales volume).

3.4 Calculating the difference in profit: reduction in inventory during a period

When there is a reduction in inventory during a period, and closing inventory is lower in value than opening inventory, the reverse situation applies.

Closing inventory is lower than opening inventory when the quantity sold exceeds the quantity produced in the period. If the cost per unit is a constant amount, using marginal costing or absorption costing, when the sales quantity exceeds the production quantity:

- There is a reduction in inventory during a period

- Closing inventory is therefore lower in value than opening inventory

- The reduction in inventory will be greater with absorption costing, by the fixed production costs in the amount by which inventory has been reduced.

- The production cost of sales is therefore higher with absorption costing than with marginal costing, and the difference is the amount of fixed production costs in the reduction in inventory value

- Therefore the profit is lower with absorption costing than with marginal costing, by the amount of the fixed costs in the fall in inventory value.

Basic rule: comparing marginal costing and absorption costing profit

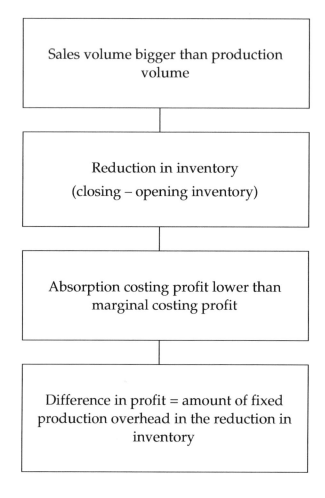

Example

A company uses absorption costing. In the financial period that has just ended, opening inventory was $76,000 and closing inventory was $49,000. The reported profit for the year was $183,000.

If the company had used marginal costing, opening inventory would have been $40,000 and closing inventory would have been $28,000.

Required

What would have been the profit for the year if marginal costing had been used?

Answer

There was a reduction in inventory. It was $27,000 using absorption costing (= $76,000 − $49,000). It would have been $12,000 using marginal costing.

	$
Reduction in inventory, absorption costing	27,000
Reduction in inventory, marginal costing	12,000
Difference (profit higher with marginal costing)	15,000
Profit with absorption costing	183,000
Profit with marginal costing	198,000

Profit is higher with marginal costing because there has been a reduction in inventory during the period.

3.5 Summary: comparing marginal and absorption costing profit

An examination might test your ability to calculate the difference between the reported profit using marginal costing and the reported profit using absorption costing. To calculate the difference, you might need to make the following simple calculations.

- Calculate the increase or decrease in inventory during the period, in units.
- Calculate the fixed production overhead cost per unit.
- The difference in profit is the increase or decrease in inventory quantity multiplied by the fixed production overhead cost per unit.
- If there has been an increase in inventory, the absorption costing profit is higher. If there has been a reduction in inventory, the absorption costing profit is lower.
- You should **ignore fixed selling overhead or fixed administration overhead**. These are written off in full as a period cost in both absorption costing and marginal costing, and only fixed production overheads are included in inventory values.

Example

The following information relates to a manufacturing company for the next costing period.

Production	16,000 units	Fixed production costs	$80,000
Sales	14,000 units	Fixed selling costs	$28,000

Using absorption costing, the profit for this period would be $60,000

Required

What would have been the profit for the year if marginal costing had been used?

Answer

Ignore the fixed selling overheads. These are irrelevant since they do not affect the difference in profit between marginal and absorption costing.

- There is an increase in inventory by 2,000 units, since production volume (16,000 units) is higher than sales volume (14,000 units).
- If absorption costing is used, the fixed production overhead cost per unit is $5 (= $80,000/16,000 units).
- The difference between the absorption costing profit and marginal costing profit is therefore $10,000 (= 2,000 units × $5).
- Absorption costing profit is higher, because there has been an increase in inventory.
- Marginal costing profit would therefore be $60,000 – $10,000 = $50,000.

Exercise 2

A company budgets to make 37,000 units of a product and fixed production costs are expected to be $111,000.

The budgeted direct costs of production are $5 per unit, and there are no variable overhead costs. Budgeted sales are 40,000 units and the sales price is $11 per unit.

Budgeted administration overheads and selling and distribution overheads are $80,000 (all fixed costs).

Required

(a) Calculate the expected profit for the period using marginal costing.

(b) Having calculated the marginal costing profit, calculate what the absorption costing profit would be for the period. (Assume that the cost per unit of opening inventory is the same as the cost per unit of closing inventory.)

You will find the answer to the Exercises and practice multiple choice questions at the end of this book.

Chapter 12: Marginal costing and absorption costing

> **Advantages and disadvantages of absorption and marginal costing**
>
> - Advantages and disadvantages of absorption costing
> - Advantages and disadvantages of marginal costing

4 Advantages and disadvantages of absorption and marginal costing

The previous sections of this chapter have explained the differences between marginal costing and absorption costing as methods of measuring profit in a period. Some conclusions can be made from these differences.

- The amount of profit reported in the cost accounts for a financial period will depend on the method of costing used.

- Since the reported profit differs according to the method of costing used, there are presumably reasons why one method of costing might be used in preference to the other. In other words, there must be some advantages (and disadvantages) of using either method.

4.1 Advantages and disadvantages of absorption costing

Absorption costing has a number of advantages and disadvantages.

Advantages of absorption costing

- Inventory values include an element of fixed production overheads. This is consistent with the requirement in financial accounting that (for the purpose of financial reporting) inventory should include production overhead costs.

- Calculating under/over absorption of overheads may be useful in controlling fixed overhead expenditure.

- By calculating the full cost of sale for a product and comparing it with the selling price, it should be possible to identify which products are profitable and which are being sold at a loss.

Disadvantages of absorption costing

- Absorption costing is a more complex costing system than marginal costing.

- Absorption costing does not provide information that is useful for decision making (like marginal costing does).

4.2 Advantages and disadvantages of marginal costing

Marginal costing has a number of advantages and disadvantages.

Advantages of marginal costing

- It is easy to account for fixed overheads using marginal costing. Instead of being apportioned they are treated as period costs and written off in full as an expense in the income statement for the period when they occur.
- There is no under/over-absorption of overheads with marginal costing, and therefore no adjustment necessary in the income statement at the end of an accounting period.
- Marginal costing provides useful information for decision making.
- Contribution per unit is constant, unlike profit per unit which varies as the volume of activity varies.

Disadvantages of marginal costing

- Marginal costing does not value inventory in accordance with the requirements of financial reporting. (However, for the purpose of cost accounting and providing management information, there is no reason why inventory values should include fixed production overhead, other than consistency with the financial accounts).
- Marginal costing can be used to measure the contribution per unit of product, or the total contribution earned by a product, but this is not sufficient to decide whether the product is profitable enough. Total contribution has to be big enough to cover fixed costs and make a profit.

Practice multiple choice questions

1 The costs and sales revenue in a period are as follows.

	$000
Direct materials	24
Direct labour	36
Direct expenses	5
Variable production overheads	6
Fixed production overheads	70
Administration overheads	30
Variable selling overheads	8
Fixed selling overheads	35
Sales	250

What is the total contribution for the period?

A $171,000
B $176,000
C $179,000
D $184,000

(2 marks)

2 The following information relates to a manufacturing company for the next costing period.

Production	24,000 units	Fixed production costs	$96,000
Sales	25,000 units	Fixed selling costs	$75,000

Using marginal costing, the profit for this period would be $65,000

Required

What would have been the profit for the year if absorption costing had been used?

A $58,000
B $61,000
C $69,000
D $72,000

(2 marks)

3 The following information relates to a manufacturing company for the next costing period.

Production 32,000 units   Fixed production costs $160,000

Sales   30,000 units   Fixed selling costs $30,000

Using absorption costing, the profit for this period would be $101,000

Required

What would have been the profit for the year if marginal costing had been used?

- A $89,000
- B $91,000
- C $111,000
- D $113,000

(2 marks)

4 The following information relates to a manufacturing company for the next costing period.

Fixed production costs $125,000

Fixed selling costs $25,000

Production   25,000 units

The profit for the period using absorption costing would be $15,000 less than if marginal costing were used.

Required

What is the expected sales volume in the period?

- A   22,000 units
- B   23,000 units
- C   27,000 units
- D   28,000 units

(2 marks)

You will find the answers to the practice multiple choice questions at the end of this book.

Applied Knowledge
Management Accounting (MA)

CHAPTER 13

Job costing, batch costing and service costing

Contents
1   Job costing
2   Batch costing
3   Service costing

> **Job costing**
>
> - The nature of job costing
> - The cost of a job
> - Cost records and accounts for job costing

1 Job costing

Costing systems are used to record total costs. They are also used to record the costs of individual cost units. The method used to measure the cost of cost units depends on the production system and how the products are made.

1.1 The nature of job costing

Job costing is used when a business entity carries out tasks or jobs to meet specific customer orders. Although each job might involve similar work, they are all different and are carried out to the customer's specific instructions or requirements.

Examples of 'jobs' include work done for customers by builders or electricians, audit work done for clients by a firm of auditors, and repair work on motor vehicles by a repair firm.

Job costing is similar to contract costing, in the sense that each job is usually different and carried out to the customer's specification or particular requirements. However, jobs are short-term and the work is usually carried out in a fairly short period of time. Contracts are usually long-term and might take several months or even years to complete.

1.2 The cost of a job

A cost is calculated for each individual job, and this cost can be used to establish the profit or loss from doing the job.

Job costing differs from most other types of costing system because each cost unit is a job, and no two jobs are exactly the same. Each job is costed separately.

- The expected cost of a job has to be estimated so that a price for the job can be quoted to a customer.

- A costing system should also calculate the actual cost of each job that has been carried out.

A job costing system is usually based on absorption costing principles, and in addition a cost is included for non-production overheads, as follows.

Job cost

	$
Direct materials	500
Direct labour	300
Direct expenses	200
Prime cost	1,000
Production overhead absorbed	750
Production cost of the job	1,750
Non-production overheads	400
Total job cost	2,150

In many cases, job costs include not just direct materials costs and direct labour costs, but also **direct expenses**, such as:

- the rental cost of equipment hired for the job
- the cost of work done for the job by sub-contractors
- the depreciation cost of equipment used exclusively on the job.

Production overheads might be absorbed on a direct labour hour basis, or on any other suitable basis.

Non-production overheads might be added to the cost of the job:

- as a percentage of the prime cost of the job, or
- as a percentage of the production cost of the job.

Example

The following cost information has been gathered about Job number 453.

The direct materials cost is $100, the direct labour cost is $60 and direct expenses are $40. Direct labour costs $20 per hour. Production overheads are charged at the rate of $30 per direct labour hour and non-production overheads are charged at the rate of 40% of prime cost.

The job cost for Job 453 is calculated as follows:

Job cost: Job 453

	$
Direct materials	100
Direct labour (3 hours at $20)	60
Direct expenses	40
Prime cost	200
Production overhead (3 hours at $30)	90
Production cost of the job	290
Non-production overheads (40% of prime cost)	80
Total job cost	370

1.3 Cost records and accounts for job costing

In order to establish the cost of each individual job in a costing system, it is necessary to have procedures for recording direct costs in such a way that they can be allocated to specific jobs. Production overheads and non-production overheads can be charged using overhead absorption rates within a system of absorption costing.

Each job is given a unique identity number, or job number. The costs for individual jobs are recorded as follows.

- The direct materials costs for a job are issued directly from stores to the job. The materials requisition note should specify the job number and the costs of the materials that are charged to the job.

- The labour time spent on a job is recorded on time sheets or job sheets. The time sheets for each individual employee identify the jobs he has worked on and the time that he spent on each job. These can be converted into a cost for the job at the employee's hourly rate.

- A system is needed for recording direct expenses to specific jobs. Costs might be obtained from purchase invoices from suppliers, and recorded in the job cost record (the 'job sheet') for the job.

- Production overheads are charged to the job (absorbed, in an absorption costing system) at the appropriate absorption rate, when the job has been completed.

- Similarly, non-production overheads can be charged when the job has been finished by charging them at the appropriate absorption rate.

Direct costs and overheads are recorded on a job sheet or job card for the job. At one time, a job card used to be an actual card or sheet of paper, although job costing systems are now likely to be computerised.

In a costing system, a job account is similar to a work in progress account, except that it is for one job only. In a company that specialises in jobbing work, the work in progress account is the total of all the individual job accounts.

Job account: Job 12345

	$		$
Direct materials	1,800	Cost of sales	7,300
Direct wages	2,500		
Direct expenses			
Production overhead	3,000		
	7,300		7,300

When the job is finished, the total cost of the job is transferred to the cost of sales.

> **Batch costing**
>
> - The nature of batch production
> - The nature of batch costing
> - Cost records and accounts for batch costing

2 Batch costing

2.1 The nature of batch production

As the name might suggest, batch costing is a system of costing for items that are produced in batches rather than individually. A batch might also be called a 'production run'.

Batch costing is used when production units are manufactured in batches or production runs.

Batch production is used in manufacturing in the following circumstances:

- The capacity of a factory to make a product exceeds the sales demand for the product. The factory is therefore not required to make the product continuously. Instead it makes the product in occasional 'production runs' or batches.

- The factory makes several different products using the same equipment or machinery. The machinery must therefore switch between making the different products, which means that the products will not be manufactured continuously. Instead the products are made in occasional 'production runs' or batches. For example, a company might manufacture a range of wooden furniture items on the same machinery. It might manufacture a batch of 100 tables, followed by a batch of 400 chairs, followed by a batch of 200 bookshelves, and so on.

- In some industries, it might be impractical to manufacture items except by making them several units at a time, in batches. An example is the manufacture of bread rolls and other products in a bakery. Several bread rolls are put into the baking oven on the same tray and they are made at the same time, all in the same batch.

The products are therefore made in batches, several units at a time. The finished units are transferred to finished goods inventory. The product is not manufactured again until the finished goods inventory is sold and more units are required. Another batch of the product is then manufactured.

2.2 The nature of batch costing

In **batch costing**, the total cost is established for each individual batch, where each batch consists of a large number of similar units or items.

Unlike job costing, however, it is less common to include non-production overhead costs within the total batch cost, although it is certainly possible to do so.

To establish the cost per unit, the total batch cost is divided by the number of units produced in the batch.

In all other respects, batch costing is very similar to job costing.

Batch number 123	$
Direct materials	550
Direct labour	300
Production overhead absorbed	750
Total production cost, batch 123	1,600
Number of units made in the batch	2,000
Production cost per unit	$0.80

To prepare for the next batch production run, there might be set-up costs. If so, set-up costs can be charged directly to the cost of the batch.

2.3 Cost records and accounts for batch costing

In job costing, it is necessary to record the direct costs of each job. In the same way, in a system of batch costing there must be a system for charging costs directly to individual batches or production runs.

- Each batch or production run should be given a unique identity code.

- When direct materials are issued from store, the materials requisition note should specify the batch for which the materials will be used.

- Direct labour time spent on each production run or batch can be recorded on time sheets within each production cost centre.

> **Service costing**
>
> - The nature of services and operations
> - Service costing, product costing and job costing compared
> - Cost units in service costing: composite cost units
> - Calculating the cost per unit of service (or operation)

3 Service costing

3.1 The nature of services and operations

It is usual to explain costing in terms of how to calculate and record the costs of manufactured products. However, many business entities do not make and sell products: they provide services. Hotel services, consultancy services, legal and accounting services, providers of telephone services (telecommunications companies), providers of television and radio channels, entertainment services, postal services, medical services, and so on.

Operations are activities. Like services, they do not result in a finished product to sell to customers. Examples of operations include a customer service centre taking telephone calls and e-mails from customers, and the staff canteen providing meals to employees.

Costs can be established for services, such as hotel accommodation, telephone calls, auditing work, holidays and travel, and so on. The costs of a service are the sum of direct materials, direct labour, direct expenses (if any) and a share of operational overheads.

Costs can also be established for operations, in a similar way.

3.2 Service costing, product costing and job costing compared

Service costing differs from costing in manufacturing industries in several ways.

- There is no production system; therefore there are no production overheads.
- Direct materials costs are often a fairly small proportion of total costs (for example, the direct materials costs to a telecommunications company of providing telephone services are very small).
- In some service industries, direct labour costs are high (for example, in the film-making industry, accountancy and investment banking).
- General overhead costs can be a very high proportion of total costs.
- Inventory is usually very small, or zero; therefore absorption costing is usually of little or no value for management information purposes.

Not all entities that provide services will use service costing. The purpose of service costing is to provide information to management about the costs of different services that the entity provides, and the profitability of each of the different services. Each service should be fairly standard. If they are not standard services, it is more sensible to use job costing to calculate the cost of each 'job' of service. For example:

- Service costing might be used by a hospital to record or calculate the cost of each of the different services provided by the hospital, such as the cost of treating a patient for a particular condition.

- Job costing might be used by a professional firm such as a firm of accountants or solicitors, where the cost of each job depends largely on the amount of time spent on each job by the professional staff.

3.3 Cost units in service costing: composite cost units

One of the main problems with service costing is that it can be difficult to identify a suitable cost unit for the service. It is often appropriate to use a composite cost unit in service costing. This is a cost that is made up from two variables, such as a cost per man per day (a cost per 'man/day'). Here, the two variables are 'men' (the number of employees) and 'days'.

Examples of composite **cost units used in service costing** are as follows:

- The cost per room per day. This is a useful unit cost in the hotel services industry.

- The cost per passenger mile or the cost per passenger kilometre (= the average cost of transporting a passenger for one mile or one kilometre). This unit measure of cost is used by transport companies that provide bus or train services.

- The cost per tonne mile delivered (= the average cost of transporting one tonne of goods for one mile). This unit cost is commonly used for costing freight services and delivery operations.

- The cost per patient/day (= the average cost of treating one patient for one day) or the cost per hospital bed/day (= the cost of maintaining one hospital bed in a hospital for one day). These costs are used by health service providers.

- The cost per man day. This unit cost is widely used in professional services, such as auditing, legal services and consultancy services.

Composite cost units can be used in addition to a 'job costing' type of service costing system. For example, a firm of accountants might calculate the cost of each job performed for a client. In addition, it might calculate the average cost per man day for the professional services that it provides.

- The cost of each service 'job' enables management to monitor costs and profits on individual jobs for a customer.

- The composite cost, which is an average cost for all 'jobs' allows management to monitor the general level of costs.

3.4 Calculating the cost per unit of service (or operation)

The cost of a service unit (or composite cost unit) is calculated as follows.

Cost per unit of service = $\dfrac{\text{Total costs of the service}}{\text{Number of units of service}}$

Total costs are the costs of direct materials, direct labour and direct expenses, plus a charge for overheads (unless marginal costing is used to cost the services).

The total number of service units might be a bit more difficult to calculate. Here are a few examples.

Example

A hotel has 80 standard twin-bedded rooms. The hotel is fully-occupied for each of the 350 days in each year that it is open. The total costs of running the hotel each year are $3,360,000.

What would be a useful measure of the cost of providing the hotel services?

Answer

A useful unit cost is the cost per room/day. This is the average cost of maintaining one room in the hotel for one day.

Room days per year = 80 rooms × 350 days = 28,000

Cost per room/day = $3,360,000/28,000 = $120.

Example

A train company operates a service between two cities, Southtown and Northtown. The distance between the cities is 400 miles. During the previous year, the company transported 200,000 passengers from Southtown to Northtown and 175,000 passengers from Northtown to Southtown. The total costs of operating the service were $60 million.

What would be a useful measure of the cost of providing the train service between the two cities?

Answer

A useful unit cost is the cost per passenger/mile. This is the average cost of transporting one passenger for one mile.

Passenger/miles per year = (200,000 × 400) + (175,000 × 400) = 150 million.

Cost per passenger/mile = $60,000,000/150,000,000 = $0.40

Management Accounting (MA)

Practice multiple choice questions

1 A company does jobbing work for customers. Job 947 has direct materials costs of $125, direct labour costs of $80 and direct expenses of $25. Direct labour is paid $20 per hour. Production overheads are charged at the rate of $35 per hour and non-production overheads are charged as 60% of prime cost.

What is the cost for Job 947?

   A $493
   B $508
   C $514
   D $592

(2 marks)

2 Which one of the following firms is most likely to use a system of job costing?

   A   A company that manufactures motor cars on a production line
   B   A telephone company that provides mobile telecommunications services
   C   A chemical manufacturer that produces processed chemicals
   D   A company that installs elevators in office buildings

(2 marks)

3 A road haulage company transports goods. It operates two trucks. During a particular period, the two trucks travelled a total of 80,000 kilometres carrying goods. The average load was 3 tonnes per journey. In total they made 200 journeys. Total costs were $720,000.

What is the average cost per tonne-kilometre transported?

   A $3
   B $4.50
   C $6
   D $12

(2 marks)

You will find the answers to the practice multiple choice questions at the end of this book.

Applied Knowledge
Management Accounting (MA)

CHAPTER

14

Process costing

Contents
1   Introduction to process costing
2   Process costing: losses
3   Process costing: abnormal gain
4   Process costing: inventory valuation and equivalent units
5   Equivalent units: weighted average cost method
6   Equivalent units: FIFO method
7   Losses and gains at different stages in the process
8   Process costing: joint products and by-products

> **Introduction to process costing**
>
> - The characteristics of process costing
> - Situations where process costing might be appropriate

1 Introduction to process costing

1.1 The characteristics of process costing

Process costing is a system of costing output from a production process. There are several characteristics that make process costing different from other types of costing, such as unit costing, job costing and batch costing. (Process costing provides a system of costing where any or all of these characteristics occur).

- There is a manufacturing process in which output is continually produced from the process and output is normally measured in total quantities, such as tonnes or litres produced, or in very large quantities of small units (such as the number of cans or tins).

- In the production process, materials might be added in full at the start of a process, or might be added gradually throughout the process. The materials are processed to produce the final output. In a process costing system, it is usual to distinguish between:
    - direct materials and
    - conversion costs, which are direct labour costs and production overheads.

- There might be losses in the process, due to evaporation or chemical reaction and the quantity of output might therefore be less than the quantity of materials input. Process costing provides a system of costing that allows for expected losses in the manufacturing process.

- When there is a continuous production process, it is difficult to measure the quantity of work-in-process (incomplete production) at the end of a financial period. Process costing provides a method of measuring and costing incomplete WIP.

- In some processes, more than one product might be output from the same process. When more than one product is output, they might be called joint products or a by-product. Process costing offers methods of costing each of the different products.

- In some process manufacturing systems, there is a series of sequential processes. For example a manufacturing system might consist of three consecutive processes: raw materials are input to Process 1, then the output from Process 1 goes onto the next process (Process 2) and the output from Process 2 then goes into a final process, Process 3. The output from Process 3 is the final product.

Processes are different, and all these characteristics do not occur in all processes. For the purpose of your examination, processes will not include all these characteristics. For example, you might be given a question in which there are losses in process but no opening or closing WIP; or you might be given a question in which there is opening or closing WIP but no losses in process.

Even so, process costing can be fairly complex, and you need to study this chapter carefully.

1.2 Situations where process costing might be appropriate

Process costing is used when output is produced in a continuous process system, and it is difficult to separate individual units of output. Examples of manufacturing where process costing is used are:

- chemicals manufacture
- the manufacture of liquids
- the continuous manufacture of high volumes of low-cost food items such as tins of peas or beans, or bottles of tomato ketchup.

In these types of production process, losses in process might occur and there are often problems in measuring exactly the amount of unfinished work-in-process at the end of a period.

The basic principle of costing is the same as for other types of costing. The cost of output from a process is measured as:

$$\frac{\text{Total costs of the process}}{\text{Total units produced}}$$

However, in process costing there are special methods for costing loss in process and for dealing with process costs when there is opening and closing WIP.

> **Process costing: losses**
>
> - Process costing and normal loss
> - Accounting for normal loss
> - Process costing: accounting for normal loss when loss has a scrap value
> - Introduction to abnormal loss
> - Accounting for abnormal loss
> - Process costing: abnormal loss and loss with a scrap value

2 Process costing: losses

2.1 Process costing and normal loss

A feature of process manufacturing is that there is often some loss or wastage in production, and output quantities are less than input quantities of materials.

- **Normal loss** is the expected loss in processing. Normal loss is usually expressed as a percentage of the input units of materials.

- **Expected output** = Input materials quantities − Normal loss

2.2 Accounting for normal loss

Normal loss is not given a value if it does not have a scrap value. This is logical, because if there will always be some loss in a process, it makes no sense to give a cost to the expected loss. It makes more sense to calculate the cost of the expected output by making an allowance for the expected loss.

The cost per unit of output =

$$\frac{\text{Total costs of the process}}{\text{Expected units of output}}$$

For example, suppose that input to a process is 100 units and expected loss is 10% of the input quantity. The process costs are $4,500. Expected output is 90 units.

- We could calculate the cost of production as $45 per unit of input, so that the cost of output is $4,050 (= 90 units × $45) and the expected loss has a cost of $450 (= 10 units × $45). This is not appropriate, however, because the loss is expected to happen and giving it a cost serves no useful purpose and certainly does not provide useful management information.

- We could calculate the cost of output as $50 per unit, which is the cost of the process divided by the expected output (= $4,500/90 units). This is the method of costing used when there is normal loss. Output is costed in a way that recognises the loss that should be expected to occur.

Example

The following information relates to a production process:

Input quantities of materials: 2,000 litres

Direct materials cost: $3,600

Direct labour cost: $300

Production overhead absorbed: $600

Normal loss as % of input: 10%

Actual output is 1,800 litres, and actual loss = expected loss (normal loss)

The cost per unit produced can be calculated as follows:

	$
Direct materials	3,600
Direct labour	300
Production overheads	600
Total production cost	4,500
Expected output (90% of 2,000)	1,800 litres
Cost per litre (= production cost/expected output)	$2.50

Accounting for normal loss: cost ledger

These costs could be set out in a process cost account. This is a work-in-progress account for the process. The debit side of the account records direct materials and direct labour costs, and production overheads absorbed (= a work-in-progress account for the process) as follows. The credit side of the WIP account records the cost of the finished output.

The account also includes memorandum columns for the quantities of direct materials input and the quantities of output and loss. Normal loss is shown so that the quantities columns add up to the same amount on the debit or credit sides, but the normal loss has no cost.

Process account

	litres	$		litres	$
Direct materials	2,000	3,600	Cost of sales	1,800	4,500
Direct labour	-	300	(at $2.50 each)		
Overhead	-	600	Normal loss	200	-
	2,000	4,500		2,000	4,500

2.3 Process costing: accounting for normal loss when loss has a scrap value

In some cases, losses in a process have a scrap value. When loss has a scrap value, the **scrap value of the normal loss** is deducted from the cost of the process. A cost per unit of output is calculated as:

$$\frac{\text{Total costs of the process minus the scrap value of normal loss}}{\text{Expected units of output}}$$

Example: scrap value of normal loss

The following information relates to a production process:

Input quantities of materials: 2,000 litres

Direct materials cost: $3,600

Direct labour cost: $300

Production overhead absorbed: $600

Normal loss as % of input: 10%

Actual output is 1,800 units, and actual loss = expected loss (normal loss)

Loss has a scrap value of $0.90 per litre.

The cost per unit produced can be calculated as follows:

	$
Direct materials	3,600
Direct labour	300
Production overheads	600
	4,500
Less: scrap value of normal loss (200 x $0.90)	(180)
	4,320
Expected output (90% of 2,000)	1,800 litres
Cost per litre	$2.40

These costs could be set out in a process cost account as follows.

Process account

	litres	$		litres	$
Direct materials	2,000	3,600	Cost of sales	1,800	4,320
Direct labour	-	300	(at $2.40 each)		
Overhead	-	600	Normal loss (at	200	180
			$0.90): scrap account		
	2,000	4,500		2,000	4,500

This is exactly the same as the previous process account showing normal loss, with the exception that the scrap value of the normal loss is shown as a value for the normal loss in the credit side of the account.

2.4 Introduction to abnormal loss

Normal loss is the expected amount of loss in a process. Actual loss might be more than the expected or normal loss. When actual loss exceeds normal loss, there is abnormal loss. The difference between total actual loss and normal loss is abnormal loss.

Abnormal loss = Actual loss − Expected (normal) loss, when actual loss is higher than expected loss.

Alternatively:

Total loss = Normal loss + Abnormal loss.

Abnormal loss is not expected and should not happen. It therefore makes sense to give it a cost. By giving a cost to abnormal loss, management information about the loss can be provided, and management can be made aware of the extent of any problem that might exist with excessive losses in process.

2.5 Accounting for abnormal loss

Units of abnormal loss are given a cost. If it is assumed that all losses in process occur at the end of the process, units of abnormal loss are costed in exactly the same way as units of finished output.

The cost of actual output units and the cost of abnormal loss units = the cost of an expected unit of output. The cost per unit of abnormal loss is therefore:

$$\frac{\text{Total costs of the process}}{\text{Expected units of output}}$$

The cost of units of abnormal loss is treated as an expense for the period, and charged as an expense in the income statement for the period.

Example: abnormal loss

The following information relates to a production process:

Input quantities of materials: 2,000 litres

Direct materials cost: $3,600

Direct labour cost: $300

Production overhead absorbed: $600

Normal loss as % of input: 10%

Actual output is 1,700 units.

Actual loss is 300 units in total (= 2,000 – 1,700). Normal loss = 200 litres (= 10% of 2,000); therefore abnormal loss = 100 litres.

The cost per unit produced can be calculated as follows:

	$
Direct materials	3,600
Direct labour	300
Production overheads	600
	4,500
Expected output (90% of 2,000 = actual output + abnormal loss)	1,800 litres
Cost per litre	$2.50

Cost of finished output = 1,700 units × $2.50 = $4,250.

Cost of abnormal loss = 100 units × $2.50 = $250.

Accounting for abnormal loss: ledger entries

These costs could be set out in a process cost account as follows.

Process account

	litres	$		litres	$
Direct materials	2,000	3,600	Cost of sales (at $2.50)	1,700	4,250
Direct labour	-	300	Normal loss	200	0
Overhead	-	600	Abnormal loss (at $2.50)	100	250
	2,000	4,500		2,000	4,500

Notice that abnormal loss is included in the credit side of the account, in the same way that normal loss is shown on the credit side. However whereas normal loss has no value/cost, abnormal loss has a cost. The appropriate double entry in the cost ledger is:

Debit: Abnormal loss account

Credit: Process account

Abnormal loss account

	litres	$		$
WIP account	100	250		

At the end of the financial period, the balance on the abnormal loss account is written off as a cost in the costing income statement.

2.6 Process costing: abnormal loss and loss with a scrap value

When loss has a scrap value, the scrap value of **normal loss** is deducted from the process cost, as explained earlier.

Any abnormal loss will also have a scrap value. However, the scrap value of abnormal loss is treated differently from the scrap value of normal loss.

- The cost of expected units of output is calculated in the usual way.
- In the process account the cost of abnormal loss = units of abnormal loss × cost per expected unit of output.
- The scrap value of abnormal loss is set off against the cost of abnormal loss in the abnormal loss account, not the process account (WIP).
  - Debit: Cash (= scrap value: money from sale of the scrapped units)
  - Credit: Abnormal loss account (abnormal loss units × scrap value per unit)
- The net cost of abnormal loss (= cost of abnormal loss minus its scrap value) is then transferred as a cost to the cost accounting income statement at the end of the accounting period.

Example: abnormal loss when loss has a scrap value

The following information relates to a production process:

Input quantities of materials: 2,000 litres

Direct materials cost: $3,600

Direct labour cost: $300

Production overhead absorbed: $600

Normal loss as % of input: 10%

Loss has a scrap value of $0.90 per litre.

Actual output is 1,700 litres, and actual loss is 300 litres. Normal loss = 200 litres; therefore abnormal loss = 100 litres.

	$
Direct materials	3,600
Direct labour	300
Production overheads	600
	4,500
Scrap value of **normal loss** (200 × $0.90)	(180)
	4,320
Expected output (1,700 litres + 100 litres)	1,800 litres
Cost per litre	$2.40

These costs would be set out in a process cost account as follows:

Process account

	litres	$		litres	$
Direct materials	2,000	3,600	Cost of sales (at $2.40)	1,700	4,080
Direct labour	-	300	Normal loss (at $0.90)	200	180
Overhead	-	600	Abnormal loss (at $2.40)	100	240
	2,000	4,500		2,000	4,500

Abnormal loss account

	litres	$		litres	$
Process a/c	100	240	Scrap (at $0.90)	100	90

At the end of the financial period, the balance on this account should be written off in the costing income statement as a cost for the period.

Abnormal loss account

	litres	$		litres	$
Process a/c	100	240	Scrap (at $0.90)	100	90
			Costing P&L		150
		240			240

Scrap account

	litres	$		litres	$
WIP: normal loss	200	180	Bank (or financial ledger control account)	300	270
Abnormal loss	100	90			
		270			270

> **Process costing: abnormal gain**
>
> - Definition of abnormal gain
> - Accounting for abnormal gain: no scrap value for loss
> - Accounting for abnormal gain: where loss has a scrap value

3 Process costing: abnormal gain

3.1 Definition of abnormal gain

Abnormal loss occurs when actual loss is more than the expected (normal) loss. **Abnormal gain** occurs when the actual loss is less than normal loss. Abnormal gain is the difference between the normal loss (expected loss) and the actual loss.

Abnormal gain = Expected (normal) loss − Actual loss, when actual loss is less than expected loss.

Alternatively:

Actual loss = Normal loss − Abnormal gain

3.2 Accounting for abnormal gain: no scrap value for loss

The method of costing for abnormal gain is the same in principle as for abnormal loss. If it is assumed that all losses occur at the end of the process, the cost per unit of finished output and the value/cost of abnormal gain are calculated as the cost per expected unit of output.

When loss has no scrap value, the cost/value per unit of abnormal loss is therefore:

$$\frac{\text{Total costs of the process}}{\text{Expected units of output}}$$

The differences between costing for abnormal loss and costing for abnormal gain are that:

- Abnormal gain is a benefit rather than a cost: whereas abnormal loss is written off as a cost at the end of the financial period, abnormal gain is an adjustment that increases the profit for the period.

- Abnormal gain is recorded as a debit entry in the process account, because it is a benefit.

- The other half of the double entry is recorded in an abnormal gain account. At the end of the period, the balance on the abnormal gain account is then transferred to the income statement as a benefit for the period, adding to profit.

Example: abnormal gain

The following information relates to a production process:

Input quantities of materials: 2,000 litres

Direct materials cost: $3,600

Conversion costs (= direct labour + production overheads): $900

Normal loss as % of input: 10%

Actual output is 1,850 litres, and actual loss is 150 litres.

Normal loss = 200 litres (= 10% of 2,000) and actual loss is 150 units. There is abnormal gain of 50 litres.

The cost per unit produced can be calculated as follows:

	$
Direct materials	3,600
Conversion costs	900
	4,500
Expected output	1,800 litres
Cost per litre	$2.50

Cost of actual finished output = 1,850 units × $2.50 = $4,625

Value of abnormal gain = 50 units × $2.50 = $125.

Accounting for abnormal gain: ledger entries

These costs could be set out in a process cost account as follows:

Process account

	litres	$		litres	$
Direct materials	2,000	3,600	Cost of sales (at $2.50)	1,850	4,625
Conversion costs	–	900	Normal loss	200	0
Abnormal gain (at $2.50)	50	125			
	2,050	4,625		2,050	4,625

Notice that the abnormal gain is shown on the debit side of the account, and the total number of units in the memorandum column for quantities (2,050) is larger than the actual quantity of units input to the process (2,000).

Abnormal gain account

	litres	$		litres	$
			WIP	50	125

The balance on this account should be taken to the costing income statement at the end of the period, and will add to the reported profit.

3.3 Accounting for abnormal gain: where loss has a scrap value

When loss has a scrap value, the value of abnormal gain is actually less than the amount shown in the WIP account. This is because actual revenue from scrap will be less than the expected revenue, due to the fact that actual loss is less than the expected loss.

Accounting for the scrap value of abnormal gain is similar to accounting for the scrap value of abnormal loss.

- In the process account (WIP), abnormal gain is valued at the cost per expected unit of output.

- The scrap value of normal loss is normal loss units × scrap value per unit.

- The scrap value of abnormal gain is the scrap revenue that has been 'lost' because actual loss is less than expected loss. This is abnormal gain units × scrap value per unit.

- The scrap value of abnormal gain is recorded as a debit entry in the abnormal gain account (in a similar way to recording the scrap value of abnormal loss as a credit entry in the abnormal loss account).

- The scrap value of the abnormal gain is set off against the value of the abnormal gain in the abnormal gain account, not the process account.

- The balance on the abnormal gain account is the net value of abnormal gain (= value of abnormal gain minus the scrap value not earned). This balance is transferred as a net benefit to the cost accounting income statement at the end of the accounting period.

Example

The following information relates to a production process:

Input quantities of materials: 2,000 litres

Direct materials cost: $3,600

Conversion costs (= direct labour + production overhead): $900

Normal loss as % of input: 10%

Loss has a scrap value of $0.90 per litre.

Actual output is 1,850 litres, and actual loss is 150 litres. Normal loss = 200 litres; therefore abnormal gain = 50 litres.

	$
Direct materials	3,600
Conversion costs	900
	4,500
Scrap value of normal loss (200 × $0.90)	(180)
	4,320
Expected output	1,800 litres
Cost per litre	$2.40

Cost of actual finished output = 1,850 units × $2.40 = $4,440

Value of abnormal gain = 50 units × $2.40 = $120.

These costs could be set out in a process cost account as follows:

Process (WIP) account

	litres	$		litres	$
Direct materials	2,000	3,600	Cost of sales (at $2.40)	1,850	4,440
Conversion costs	–	900	Normal loss (at $0.90 scrap value)	200	180
Abnormal gain (at $2.40)	50	120			
	2,050	4,620		2,050	4,620

Abnormal gain account

	litres	$		litres	$
Scrap (at $0.90)	50	45	WIP	50	120
					120

The balance on this account is $75. This is treated as an addition to profit in the cost accounting income statement for the period.

Exercise 1: process costing and losses

From the following information, prepare:

- the process account,
- the abnormal loss or abnormal gain account.

Process: Input 6,000 units

Normal loss: 5% of input

Direct materials: $21,600

Direct labour: $8,000

Production overhead: $16,000

Actual output: 5,500 units

Loss has a scrap value per unit of $3.80.

Exercise 2: process costing and losses

- From the following information, prepare the process account.

Process: Input 10,000 units

Normal loss: 4% of input

Direct materials: $35,200

Conversion costs: $29,600

Actual output: 9,750 units

Loss has no scrap value.

You will find the answer to the Exercises and practice multiple choice questions at the end of this book.

Chapter 14: Process costing

> **Process costing: inventory valuation and equivalent units**
>
> - Sharing out process costs between finished units and unfinished inventory
> - Equivalent units
> - A three-stage calculation
> - Weighted average cost and FIFO valuation methods

4 Process costing: inventory valuation and equivalent units

4.1 Sharing out process costs between finished units and unfinished inventory

When manufacturing is a continuous process, there may be unfinished work-in-progress ('work-in-process') at the beginning of an accounting period and at the end of the period. Since inventory is unfinished, its cost or value is less than the cost of a unit of completed output. The common costs of the process must be shared between finished output and unfinished work-in-process on a fair basis. The basis of apportionment used in process costing is equivalent units.

4.2 Equivalent units

An equivalent unit means 'equal to one finished unit of output'.

- One fully-finished unit of production = 1 equivalent unit
- One unit 50% complete = 0.50 equivalent units. 400 units 50% complete = 200 equivalent units.
- One unit 20% complete = 0.20 equivalent units. 400 units 20% complete = 80 equivalent units.

Costs are shared between finished units and inventory by calculating a cost per equivalent unit:

$$\text{Cost per equivalent unit} = \frac{\text{Costs of the process}}{\text{Number of equivalent units produced}}$$

Equivalent units of closing inventory

It is normally assumed that direct materials are added to the production process at the beginning of the process and that direct labour operations are carried out throughout the process. When this assumption is used, units of closing inventory are:

- 100% complete for direct material costs added at the beginning of the process, but
- only partly-complete for direct labour and production overhead costs, and only partly complete for additional materials that are added throughout the process.

The number of equivalent units of direct materials cost in a period will therefore differ from the number of equivalent units of conversion costs (direct labour and production overhead).

A cost per equivalent unit is therefore calculated separately for:

- direct materials
- conversion costs.

Costs for finished output and closing inventory can be calculated from the number of equivalent units and the cost per equivalent unit.

4.3 A three-stage calculation

We recommend a three-stage calculation:

- Prepare a **statement of equivalent units**. This should calculate the equivalent units (direct materials and conversion costs) for output from the process and for closing WIP.

- Next, prepare a **statement of cost per equivalent unit**. There should be a separate cost per equivalent unit of direct materials and a cost per cost per equivalent unit of conversion costs.

- Third, prepare a **statement of evaluation**. This is a statement of the cost of finished output and closing WIP, which is prepared from your statement of equivalent units and statement of cost per equivalent unit.

Example

At the beginning of a financial period, there were no units of opening work-in-process. During the period, input to the process was 4,000 units. During the period 3,500 units were output from the process and closing WIP was 500 units.

All the direct materials are added to production at the beginning of the process.

Closing inventory of 500 units was therefore 100% complete for materials, and production was 40% complete.

Costs incurred during the period were:

Direct materials: $24,000

Conversion costs: $7,400

Required: calculate the cost of the finished output and the value of closing WIP.

Answer

Statement of equivalent units

Output	Total units	Direct materials		Conversion costs	
		Degree of completion	Equivalent units	Degree of completion	Equivalent units
Finished output	3,500	100%	3,500	100%	3,500
Closing WIP	500	100%	500	40%	200
	4,000		4,000		3,700

Statement of cost per equivalent unit

	Direct materials	Conversion costs
Total costs	$24,000	$7,400
Equivalent units	4,000	3,700
Cost per equivalent unit	$6	$2

Statement of evaluation

		Finished output		Closing WIP
		$		$
Direct materials	(3,500 × $6)	21,000	(500 × $6)	3,000
Conversion costs	(3,500 × $2)	7,000	(200 × $2)	400
Total cost		28,000		3,400

These costs would be recorded in the process account as follows.

Process (WIP) account

	units	$		units	$
Direct materials	4,000	24,000	Finished goods	3,500	28,000
Conversion costs	-	7,400	Closing WIP	500	3,400
	4,000	31,400		4,000	31,400

4.4 Weighted average cost and FIFO valuation methods

Another problem with establishing the cost of finished output and inventory in process costing is the problem of how to work out costs when there is opening inventory at the beginning of the period. When there is opening WIP, output from a process (and closing WIP) can be valued on either of the following bases:

- weighted average cost method
- first-in, first-out (FIFO) method

You need to know how to apply each of these different valuation methods.

> **Equivalent units: weighted average cost method**
>
> - The underlying principle
> - The three-stage calculation
> - Weighted average cost method: summary

5 Equivalent units: weighted average cost method

5.1 The underlying principle

When the weighted average cost method is used, the assumption is that all units produced during the period and all units of closing inventory are indistinguishable, and so should be valued at the same cost per equivalent unit for materials and the same cost per equivalent unit for conversion costs.

An average cost per equivalent unit is therefore calculated for all units of output and closing inventory. This includes the units that were partly-completed at the beginning of the period (and which were therefore valued as closing WIP at the end of the previous period).

5.2 The three-stage calculation

The costs are worked out in a similar way to the previous example (where there was no opening WIP).

- **Statement of equivalent units.** Prepare a statement of equivalent units for finished output (1 equivalent unit of direct materials and 1 equivalent unit of conversion costs each) and for closing WIP.

- **Statement of cost per equivalent unit.** Calculate the cost per equivalent unit for direct materials and the cost per equivalent unit for conversion costs. However, remember to include the cost of the opening WIP. The materials cost of the opening WIP should be included in the total direct materials cost, and the conversion costs in the opening WIP should be added to the conversion costs for the current period.

    $$\text{Cost per equivalent unit} = \frac{\text{Cost of opening inventory} + \text{Costs incurred in the period}}{\text{Equivalent units of output and closing inventory}}$$

    Remember that you will normally have to calculate a separate cost per equivalent units for materials and for conversion costs. This is because the equivalent units of closing inventory will be different for materials and conversion costs.

- **Statement of evaluation.** Having calculated the equivalent units and a cost per equivalent unit, prepare a statement of evaluation.

Chapter 14: Process costing

Example

From the following information relating to a production process in March, calculate the cost of finished output in the month and the value of the closing inventory, using the weighted average cost valuation method:

Opening inventory on 1 March: 3,000 units

  100% complete for direct materials

  30% complete for conversion costs

  Cost = $13,570 (= direct materials $12,600 + conversion costs $970)

Costs incurred during March:

  Direct materials: 7,000 units input, cost $28,000

  Conversion costs: $17,430

  Units completed in the month (finished goods): 8,000 units

Closing inventory:

2,000 units: 100% complete for direct materials and 60% complete for conversion costs.

Answer

Equivalent units	Total	Direct materials		Conversion costs
	Total units	Equivalent units		Equivalent units
Completed units	8,000	8,000		8,000
Closing inventory	2,000	2,000	(2,000 x 60%)	1,200
Total equivalent units	10,000	10,000		9,200

Statement of cost per equivalent unit

Costs	Direct materials	Conversion costs
	$	$
Opening inventory	12,600	970
Costs incurred in the period	28,000	17,430
Total costs	40,600	18,400
Equivalent units	10,000	9,200
Cost per equivalent unit	$4.06	$2

Statement of evaluation

		Finished output		Closing WIP	
		$			$
Direct materials	(8,000 × $4.06)	32,480	(2,000 × $4.06)		8,120
Conversion costs	(8,000 × $2)	16,000	(1,200 × $2)		2,400
Total cost		48,480			10,520

These costs would be recorded in the process account as follows.

Process (WIP) account

	units	$		units	$
Opening WIP	3,000	13,570	Finished goods	8,000	48,480
Direct materials	7,000	28,000			
Conversion costs	-	17,430	Closing WIP	2,000	10,520
	10,000	59,000		10,000	59,000

5.3 Weighted average cost method: summary

The weighted average cost method for process costing with opening WIP can be summarised as follows.

- All output and closing inventory is valued at the same cost per equivalent unit
- Cost of opening inventory + Costs in the period = Total costs
- Units of closing inventory + Units of output in the period = Total equivalent units
- Cost per equivalent unit = Total costs/Total equivalent units

	Direct materials	Conversion costs
Cost of opening inventory	M_1	C_1
Costs incurred in the period	M_2	C_2
Total costs	$M_1 + M_2$	$C_1 + C_2$
Number of units output	P	P
Equivalent units of closing inventory	I_m	I_c
Total equivalent units	$P + I_m$	$P + I_c$
Cost per equivalent unit	$(M_1 + M_2) \div (P + I_m)$	$(C_1 + C_2) \div (P + I_c)$

Exercise 3: weighted average cost method

From the following information relating to Process 2 in April:

(a) calculate the cost of finished output in the month and the value of the closing inventory, using the weighted average cost valuation method

(b) prepare the process account for the period.

Opening inventory on 1 April: 2,000 units:

100% complete for direct materials

80% complete for conversion costs

Cost $20,900 (= direct materials $14,800 + conversion costs $6,100)

Costs incurred during April:

Direct materials: 14,000 units input, cost $70,000

Conversion costs: $34,200

Completed units in the month: 11,000 units

Closing inventory on 30 April:

5,000 units: 100% complete for direct materials and 40% complete for conversion costs.

You will find the answer to the Exercises and practice multiple choice questions at the end of this book.

> **Equivalent units: FIFO method**
>
> - Assumption with the FIFO method of process costing
> - Equivalent units of work done in the current period
> - The three-stage calculation
> - FIFO method: summary

6 Equivalent units: FIFO method

6.1 Assumption with the FIFO method of process costing

With the weighted average cost method of costing, it is assumed that all units of output in a period have the same cost per unit.

With the first-in, first-out (FIFO) method of process costing, it is assumed that the opening units of work-in-process at the beginning of the month will be the first units completed. The cost of these units is their value at the beginning of the period plus the cost to complete them in the current period.

6.2 Equivalent units of work done in the current period

It is necessary to calculate the number of equivalent units of work done in the period. This consists of:

- The equivalent units of direct materials and conversion costs required to complete the opening WIP. These are the first units completed in the period.
- The equivalent units of finished output in the period that was started as well as finished in the period. These have one equivalent unit of direct materials and one equivalent unit of conversion costs. The total number of these units is:
   - the total finished output in the period
   - **minus** the quantity of opening WIP (which are completed first)
- The equivalent units of closing WIP (calculated in the normal way).

A cost per equivalent unit, for direct materials and conversion costs, is now calculated as:

$$\frac{\text{Costs of the process in the current period (exclude opening WIP value)}}{\text{Number of equivalent units of work done in the period}}$$

The equivalent units in the current period to complete the opening WIP are calculated using the following percentage value:

- 100%
- minus the degree of completion at the beginning of the period.

For example, suppose that opening WIP is 1,000 units which is 100% complete for direct materials and 70% complete for conversion costs. The number of equivalent units in the current period to complete the opening WIP is 0 for direct materials (= 1,000 × (100 − 100)%) and 300 for conversion costs (= 1,000 × (100 − 70)%).

6.3 The three-stage calculation

The three-stage calculation with the FIFO method is similar to the calculation method previously described, with the exception that in the statement of evaluation, the cost of finished output consists of:

- the finished cost of opening WIP (completed first) plus
- the cost of finished output started as well as finished in the period.

The finished cost of opening WIP is the sum of:

- the costs in the opening WIP value at the start of the period
- the costs in the current period to complete these units.

Study the following example carefully.

Example
FIFO method of process costing

From the following information relating to Process 1 in March, calculate the cost of finished output in the month and the value of the closing inventory, using the FIFO cost valuation method:

Opening inventory on 1 March: 3,000 units

  100% complete for direct materials

  30% complete for conversion costs

  Cost $13,570 (= direct materials $12,600 + conversion costs $970)

Costs incurred during March:

  Direct materials: 7,000 units input, cost $28,000

  Conversion costs: $17,430

Completed units in the month: 8,000 units

Closing inventory: 2,000 units 100% complete for direct materials and 60% complete for conversion costs.

Answer

Statement of equivalent units (work done in the current period)

Equivalent units	Total units	Direct materials Equivalent units		Conversion costs Equivalent units
To complete opening inventory, finished first	3,000 (0%)	0	(70% × 3,000)	2,100
Units started and completed in the current period (8,000 – 3,000)	5,000	5,000		5,000
Finished output	8,000	5,000		7,100
Closing inventory	2,000	2,000	(2,000 × 60%)	1,200
Total equivalent units	10,000	7,000		8,300

Statement of cost per equivalent unit in the current period

Cost per equivalent unit	Direct materials	Conversion costs
Total cost in current period	$28,000	$17,430
Total equivalent units in the current period	7,000	8,300
Cost per equivalent unit (current period)	$4.00	$2.10

Statement of evaluation

	Direct materials		Conversion costs		Total cost
	$		$		$
Finished units:					
1. Opening WIP					
Cost b/f		12,600		970	13,570
Cost to complete		0	(2,100 × $2.1)	4,410	4,410
		12,600		5,380	17,980
2. Units started and finished	(5,000 × $4)	20,000	(5,000 × $2.1)	10,500	30,500
Finished units		32,600		15,880	48,480
Closing inventory	(2,000 × $4)	8,000	(1,200 × $2.1)	2,520	10,520
		40,600		18,400	59,000

These costs would be recorded in the process account as follows.

Process (WIP) account

	units	$		units	$
Opening WIP	3,000	13,570	Finished goods	8,000	48,480
Direct materials	7,000	28,000			
Conversion costs	–	17,430	Closing WIP	2,000	10,520
	10,000	59,000		10,000	59,000

(**Tutorial note**: If you compare this example using FIFO with the previous example using the weighted average cost method, you might notice that the cost of finished output and value of closing WIP is the same in each case. This is a coincidence. Normally, the two methods provide different costs for finished output and different closing WIP valuations).

6.4 FIFO method: summary

The first-in, first-out method for process costing with opening WIP can be summarised as follows.

- The cost of the opening units completed in the current period is calculated separately from the cost of the units that are started and finished in the current period.

- A cost per equivalent unit is calculated **for the current period,** as follows:

	Direct materials	Conversion costs
Costs incurred in the current period	TC_m	TC_c
Equivalent units of work in the current period to complete opening WIP	A	D
Number of units started and finished in the current period	B	E
Equivalent units of closing inventory at the end of the current period	C	F
Total equivalent units of work in this period	(A + B + C)	(D + E + F)
Cost per equivalent unit in the current period	$TC_m /(A + B + C)$	$TC_c /(D + E + F)$

- These costs are used to apportion the process costs in the current period between:
    - the cost of completing the opening WIP
    - the cost of units started and finished in the current period
    - the value of closing inventory.

- Having calculated costs for the current period, the valuation of output from the process is calculated as follows:

	Direct materials	Conversion costs	Total costs
Value of opening inventory b/f	M_1	C_1	$M_1 + C_1$
Costs to complete in the current period	M_2	C_2	$M_2 + C_2$
Total cost of opening inventory, finished first	$M_1 + M_2 = M_3$	$C_1 + C_2 = C_3$	$M_3 + C_3$
Units started and completed in the current period	M_4	C_4	$M_4 + C_4$
Total cost of finished output	$M_3 + M_4 = M_5$	$C_3 + C_4 = C_5$	$M_5 + C_5$

Exercise 4: FIFO cost method

From the following information relating to Process 2 in April:

(a) calculate the cost of finished output in the month and the value of the closing inventory, using the FIFO cost valuation method

(b) prepare the Process 2 account for the month.

Opening inventory on 1 April: 2,000 units:

  100% complete for direct materials

  80% complete for conversion costs

  Cost $20,900 (= direct materials $14,800 + conversion costs $6,100)

Costs incurred during April:

  Direct materials: 14,000 units input, cost $70,000

  Conversion costs: $34,200

  Completed units in the month: 11,000 units

Closing inventory: 5,000 units 100% complete for direct materials and 40% complete for conversion costs.

You will find the answer to the Exercises and practice multiple choice questions at the end of this book.

Chapter 14: Process costing

> **Losses and gains at different stages in the process**
>
> - Assumptions about when loss occurs
> - Equivalent units and abnormal loss part-way through the process
> - Equivalent units and abnormal gain part-way through the process

7 Losses and gains at different stages in the process

7.1 Assumptions about when loss occurs

In the earlier explanation of accounting for abnormal loss and abnormal gain, it was assumed that losses occur at the end of the production process. This assumption is not relevant for normal loss, but it is relevant for abnormal loss and abnormal gain, because these are given a value.

If it is assumed that losses occur at the end of a process, units of abnormal loss or gain are given a cost or value as if they are fully completed units – and so one equivalent unit each.

If losses occur at a different stage in the process, this assumption should not be applied. Instead, the concept of equivalent units should be used to decide the cost of the abnormal loss or the value of the abnormal gain. Equivalent units can be used provided that an estimate is made of the degree of completion of units at the time that loss occurs in the process. Differing degrees of completion might be used for direct materials and conversion costs.

7.2 Equivalent units and abnormal loss part-way through the process

When loss occurs part-way through a process, the cost of any abnormal loss should be calculated by:

- establishing the equivalent units of direct materials and conversion costs for the loss
- calculating a cost per equivalent units
- using the calculations of equivalent units and cost per equivalent unit to obtain a cost for finished output and abnormal loss in the period.

Example: abnormal loss and loss part-way through a process

The following information relates to a production process:

Input quantities of materials: 10,000 units

Direct materials cost: $27,000

Conversion costs: $13,200

Normal loss as % of input: 10%

Direct materials are added in full at the beginning of the process, and loss occurs 60% of the way through the process.

Actual output is 8,500 units.

Actual loss is 1,500 units. Normal loss is 1,000 units (= 10% of 10,000); therefore abnormal loss is 500 units.

The cost of finished output and abnormal loss can be calculated as follows.

Statement of equivalent units

Output	Direct materials		Conversion costs	
	Degree of completion	Equivalent units	Degree of completion	Equivalent units
Finished output	100%	8,500	100%	8,500
Abnormal loss	100%	500	60%	300
		9,000		8,800

Statement of cost per equivalent unit

	Direct materials	Conversion costs
Total costs	$27,000	$13,200
Equivalent units	9,000	8,800
Cost per equivalent unit	$3	$1.50

Statement of evaluation

		Finished output		Abnormal loss
		$		$
Direct materials	(8,500 × $3)	25,500	(500 × $3)	1,500
Conversion costs	(8,500 × $1.50)	12,750	(300 × $1.50)	450
Total cost		38,250		1,950

These costs would be recorded in the process account as follows.

Process (WIP) account

	units	$		units	$
Direct materials	10,000	27,000	Finished goods	8,500	38,250
Conversion costs	–	13,200	Normal loss	1,000	–
			Abnormal loss	500	1,950
	10,000	40,200		10,000	40,200

7.3 Equivalent units and abnormal gain part-way through the process

The same principles apply to the valuation of abnormal gain where the loss/gain occurs part-way through the process. However, there is one important difference. **Equivalent units of abnormal gain** are given a **negative value** and are **subtracted** from the total equivalent units of output in the period.

Perhaps the easiest way to think of the reason for this is that abnormal gain is on the opposite side of the process account (the debit side) from actual finished output (credit side) and abnormal gain equivalent units are subtracted because they offset the cost of the finished output.

Example: abnormal gain part-way through a process

The following information relates to a production process:

Input quantities of materials: 6,000 units

Direct materials cost: $27,000

Conversion costs: $11,040

Normal loss as % of input: 10%

Direct materials are added in full at the beginning of the process, and loss occurs 40% of the way through the process.

Actual output is 5,600 units.

Actual loss is 400 units. Normal loss is 600 units (= 10% of 6,000); therefore there is an abnormal gain of 200 units.

The cost of finished output and abnormal loss can be calculated as follows. Note in particular that abnormal gain is given a negative value for equivalent units.

Statement of equivalent units

Output	Total units	Direct materials		Conversion costs	
		Degree of completion	Equivalent units	Degree of completion	Equivalent units
Finished output	5,600	100%	5,600	100%	5,600
Abnormal gain	200	100%	(200)	40%	(80)
			5,400		5,520

Statement of cost per equivalent unit

	Direct materials	Conversion costs
Total costs	$27,000	$11,040
Equivalent units	5,400	5,520
Cost per equivalent unit	$5	$2

Statement of evaluation

Abnormal gain is given a value in the usual way based on equivalent units and cost per equivalent unit.

		Finished output $		Abnormal gain $
Direct materials	(5,600 × $5)	28,000	(200 × $5)	1,000
Conversion costs	(5,600 × $2)	11,200	(80 × $2)	160
Total cost		39,200		1,160

These costs would be recorded in the process account as follows.

Process (WIP) account

	units	$		units	$
Direct materials	6,000	27,000	Finished goods	5,600	39,200
Conversion costs	-	11,040	Normal loss	600	-
Abnormal gain	200	1,160			
	6,200	39,200		6,200	39,200

> **Process costing: joint products and by-products**
>
> - Definition of joint products
> - Apportioning common processing costs between joint products
> - Definition of by-products
> - Cost accounting treatment of by-products

8 Process costing: joint products and by-products

8.1 Definition of joint products

In some process manufacturing systems, two or more different products are produced. These are called **joint products** if they have a **substantial sales value** (or a substantial sales value after further processing).

Until the joint products are produced in the manufacturing process, they cannot be distinguished from each other. The same input materials and processing operation produces all the joint products together.

8.2 Apportioning common processing costs between joint products

The costs of the common process that produces the joint products are common costs. In order to calculate a cost for each joint product, these common costs must be shared (apportioned) between the joint products. The common costs of the process must be apportioned between the joint products on a fair basis, in much the same way that overhead costs are apportioned between cost centres.

One of the following three methods of apportionment is normally used:

- **Units basis**: Common costs are apportioned on the basis of the total number of units produced. The cost per unit is the same for all the joint products.

- **Sales value at the split-off point basis**: Common costs are apportioned on the basis of the sales value of the joint products produced, at the point where they are separated in the process (the 'split off point').

- **Sales value less further processing costs basis**: common costs are apportioned on the basis of their eventual sales value after they have gone through further processing to get them ready for sale.

Management Accounting (MA)

Example

Two joint products JP1 and JP2, are produced from a common process. During March, 8,000 units of materials were input to the process. Total costs of processing (direct materials and conversion costs) were $135,880.

Output was 5,000 units of JP1 and 3,000 units of JP2.

JP1 has a sales value of $40 per unit when it is output from the process.

JP2 does not have a sales value at the split-off point, but can be sold for $80 per unit after further processing costs of $15 per unit.

Required

Apportion the process costs between the joint products on the basis of:

- units produced
- sales value.

Answer

Units basis

$$\text{Process cost per unit} = \frac{\text{Process costs}}{\text{Number of units produced}} = \frac{\$135,880}{(5,000 + 3,000)} = \$16.985$$

Costs:	$
JP1: 5,000 units × $16.985	84,925
JP2: 3,000 units × $16.985	50,955
	135,880

Sales value basis (or sales value minus further processing costs)

	Sales value per unit	Sales value less further processing cost	Units	Total value
	$	$		$
JP1	40		5,000	200,000
JP2		65	3,000	195,000
				395,000

Common process costs		$135,880
Apportionment of costs as % of sales value		34.4%

Costs:	Total cost	Units	Cost per unit
	$		$
JP1: $200,000 × 34.4%	68,800	5,000	13.76
JP2: $195,000 × 34.4%	67,080	3,000	22.36
	135,880		

8.3 Definition of by-products

In some process manufacturing systems, when two or more different products are produced, any product that **does not have a substantial sales value** is called a **by-product**.

8.4 Cost accounting treatment of by-products

Since a by-product does not have any substantial value, there is no sense in charging it with a share of the common processing costs.

- Instead, the sales value of the by-product is deducted from the common processing costs.
- If there are joint products, the common processing costs are apportioned after deducting the sales value of the by-product from the total costs of the process.
- The sales value of the by-product is recorded as a credit entry in the process account, together with the cost of the finished joint products.

Example: by-product and joint products

Two joint products JP1 and JP2, are produced from a common process. During March, 9,000 units of materials were input to the process. Total costs of processing (direct materials and conversion costs) were $135,880.

- Output was 5,000 units of JP1 and 3,000 units of JP2 and 1,000 units of by-product BP3.
- JP1 has a sales value of $40 per unit when it is output from the process.
- JP2 does not have a sales value at the split-off point, but can be sold for $80 per unit after further processing costs of $15 per unit.
- BP3 has a sales value of $1.58 per unit.

Required

Apportion the process costs between the joint products on the basis of sales value.

Answer

Common process costs	$
Total process costs	135,880
Deduct: Sales value of by-product (1,000 × $1.58)	(1,580)
	134,300

Apportionment of cost between joint products on a sales value basis

	Sales value per unit	Sales value less further processing cost	Units	Total value
	$	$		$
JP1	40		5,000	200,000
JP2		65	3,000	195,000
				395,000

Common process costs	$134,300
Apportionment of costs as % of sales value	34.0%

Costs:	Total cost	Units	Cost per unit
	$		$
JP1: $200,000 × 34%	68,000	5,000	13.60
JP2: $195,000 × 34%	66,300	3,000	22.10
	134,300		

These costs would be shown in a process account as follows.

Process account

	Units	$		Units	$
Input costs	9,000	135,880	By-product (Bank account)	1,000	1,580
			JP1	5,000	68,000
	-	-	JP2	3,000	66,300
	9,000	135,880		9,000	135,880

Chapter 14: Process costing

Practice multiple choice questions

1   The input to a production process in one-month period was 12,000 units. There was no opening inventory. Output during the period was 11,000 units, and normal loss is expected to be 5% of input. Direct materials costs were $60,000 and conversion costs were $15,240. What was the cost of the abnormal loss in the month?

   A $2,508

   B $2,640

   C $3,960

   D $4,104   *(2 marks)*

2   The input to a production process in a one-month period was 3,600 units. There was no opening inventory. Output during the period was 3,200 units. Direct materials costs were $15,000 and conversion costs were $5,160. Normal loss is one-sixth of the quantity input. What was the value of the abnormal gain in the month?

   A $1,120

   B $1,260

   C $1,344

   D $1,440   *(2 marks)*

3   A company has a manufacturing process and uses the weighted average cost method of inventory valuation. In one month, opening inventory consisted of 500 units, 100% complete for direct materials and 60% complete for conversion costs. Its total value was $8,955, consisting of direct materials of $7,935 and conversion costs of $1,020.

During the month, a further 1,500 units of direct materials were input to the process, costing $25,605, and conversion costs in the month were $5,440. Direct materials are added in full at the start of the process. Closing work in process was 400 units, 100% complete for direct materials and 25% complete for conversion costs.

What was the value of the closing work-in-process at the end of the month?

   A $7,048

   B $7,088

   C $7,168

   D $10,000   *(2 marks)*

Management Accounting (MA)

4   A company has a manufacturing process and uses the FIFO method of inventory valuation. In one month, opening inventory consisted of 400 units, 100% complete for direct materials and 75% complete for conversion costs. Its total value was $2,920, consisting of direct materials of $2,200 and conversion costs of $720.

During the month, a further 2,000 units of direct materials were input to the process, costing $12,200, and conversion costs in the month were $3,060. Direct materials are added in full at the start of the process. Closing work in process was 500 units, 100% complete for direct materials and 40% complete for conversion costs.

What was the value of the finished output from the process during the month?

A $14,365
B $14,620
C $14,790
D $14,820   (2 marks)

5   The input to a production process in one-month period was 8,000 units. There was no opening inventory. Output during the period was 7,000 units. Direct materials costs were $30,400 and conversion costs were $11,040. Normal loss is 5% of input. All direct materials are input at the beginning of the process, and loss occurs 60% of the way into the process. What was the cost of the abnormal loss in the month?

A $2,940
B $3,272
C $3,300
D $5,672   (2 marks)

6   Two joint products JP1 and JP" are output from a common process, and a by-product BP1 is also produced from the same process. The by-product has a sales value of $1.50 per unit. Data for the current month are as follows:

Input 6,000 units: cost $57,000 (direct materials $42,000, conversion costs $15,000)

Output: 3,000 units of JP1, 2,000 units of JP2 and 1,000 units of BP1.

Common processing costs are shared on the basis of the quantities of joint products produced.

What is the cost of the output of JP2 in the month?

A $18,500
B $19,000
C $22,200
D $22,800   (2 marks)

You will find the answers to the practice multiple choice questions at the end of this book.

Applied Knowledge
Management Accounting (MA)

CHAPTER

15

Alternative costing systems

Contents
1 Activity based costing (ABC)
2 Target costing
3 Life cycle costing
4 Total quality management (TQM)

> ### Activity based costing (ABC)
>
> - Introduction to activity based costing
> - Activities
> - Cost drivers and cost pools
> - ABC and traditional absorption costing
> - When using ABC might be appropriate
> - Advantages and disadvantages of ABC

Both traditional absorption costing and marginal costing have weaknesses as a costing system for manufacturing companies, and neither of these costing systems is well-suited to costing in a modern manufacturing environment.

A number of alternative costing methods have been developed with a view to replacing the traditional methods.

1 Activity based costing (ABC)

1.1 Introduction to activity based costing

Activity based costing (ABC) is a form of absorption costing. However, it differs from traditional absorption costing, because it takes a different approach to the apportionment and absorption of production overhead costs.

Activity-based costing is based on the following assumptions:

- In a modern manufacturing environment, a large proportion of total costs are overhead costs, and direct labour costs are relatively small.

- Because overhead costs are large, it is appropriate to trace these costs as accurately as possible to the products that create the cost.

- In traditional absorption costing, production overheads are allocated or apportioned to production departments, and are then absorbed on the basis of the volume of production work, using a rate per direct labour hour or rate per machine hour. However many production overhead costs are not directly related to the production work that is carried out. For example:

    - The costs of quality control and inspection depend on the quality standards and inspection methods that are used: these do not necessarily relate to the number of hours worked in production.

    - The costs of processing and chasing customer orders through the factory relate more to the volume of customer orders rather than the hours worked on each job in production.

    - Costs of managing the raw materials inventories (storage costs) relate more to the volume of materials handled rather than hours worked on the material in production.

- The costs of production planning relate more to the volume and complexity of customer orders or the number of batch production runs, rather than hours worked in production.
- The traditional methods of absorbing production overhead costs on the basis of direct labour hours or machine hours do not have any rational justification and a better method is needed for charging overheads to different products or jobs.

1.2 Activities

Activity based costing (ABC) takes the view that many production overhead costs can be associated with particular activities that are not direct production work.

It is therefore appropriate to identify these activities and allocate overhead costs to them. Overhead costs can then be added to product costs by using a separate absorption rate for each activity. The costing of overheads and full production costs is therefore based on activities, rather than hours worked in production.

Identifying activities

A problem with introducing activity-based costing is deciding which activities create or 'drive' overhead costs.

They should be activities that use up a large amount of resources, such as labour time. However, there are many different activities within a manufacturing company, and it is not always clear which activities should be used for costing.

Activities might include, for example:

- Materials handling and storage
- Customer order processing and chasing
- Materials purchasing
- Quality control and inspection
- Production planning
- Repairs and maintenance.

These activities are not necessarily confined to single functional departments within the production department.

Although ABC is often concerned with production costs, it can also be applied to activities outside production, such as sales and distribution. Sales and distribution activities might include:

- selling activities
- warehousing and despatch
- after-sales service.

In a system of activity-based costing, it is preferable to select a fairly small number of activities. If a large number of activities are selected, the costing system could become too complex and time-consuming to operate.

The activities are selected on the basis of management judgement and experience, and their knowledge of the activities within manufacturing.

If only a small number of activities are identified and selected for use in the ABC system, it is likely that some overhead costs will not relate to those activities. An example might be the costs of rental of a factory and the running costs of the factory (heating and lighting costs, security costs and so on). These overhead costs not related to the selected activities might therefore be recorded as 'general overheads' and absorbed into product costs separately.

1.3 Cost drivers and cost pools

Cost drivers

For each activity, there should be a cost driver. (An activity might have more than one cost driver, but if an activity does have more than one cost driver the costing system becomes more complex. Just one cost driver per activity is desirable).

A cost driver for an activity can be defined as a factor that determines the cost of the activity. It is something that will cause the costs for an activity to increase as more of the activity is performed.

It is not always obvious what the cost driver for an activity might be. A cost driver might be unique to the activity. Here are some examples.

Activity	Possible cost driver
Materials handling and storage	Raw materials: purchases of materials
	Finished goods: volume of products made
Customer order processing	Number of customer orders
Materials purchasing	Number of purchase orders
Quality control and inspection	Number of inspections
Production planning	Number of production runs or batches
Repairs and maintenance	Number of machines, or machine hours operated
Selling	Number of sales orders
Warehousing and despatch	Number of deliveries made

Each cost driver must be a factor that can be measured, so that the number of units of the cost driver that have occurred during each period can be established.

Overhead costs are therefore caused by activities, and the costs of activities are driven by factors other than production volume.

In addition, it must be possible to relate the cost drivers for each activity to the products or services that the entity sells. For example:

Activity	Possible cost driver	Information needed for ABC
Customer order processing	Number of customer orders	Number of orders for each product
Materials purchasing	Number of purchase orders	Number of orders for materials for each finished product
Quality control and inspection	Number of inspections	Number of inspections of output of each product
Production planning	Number of production runs or batches	Number of runs or batches of each product
Repairs and maintenance	Number of machines, or machine hours operated	Number of machines or machine hours worked for each product
Selling	Number of sales orders	Number of orders for each product
Warehousing and despatch	Number of deliveries made	Number of deliveries for each product

Cost pools

Overhead costs are allocated (or allocated and apportioned) to each activity, and for each activity there is a 'cost pool'. A cost pool is simply the overhead expenditure allocated and apportioned to an activity.

In ABC, overheads are absorbed into the cost of products (or services) at a separate rate for each cost pool (each activity). The total production cost for each product or service is therefore direct production costs plus absorbed overheads for each activity. In addition, as mentioned earlier, there might also be an absorbed amount for general overheads, which cannot be attributed to any specific activity and cost pool.

Example

A manufacturing company has identified that a large part of its overhead costs are incurred in handling customer orders, and that the same effort goes into handling a small order as the effort required to deal with a large order. Order sizes differ substantially. The company makes four products, and the estimated costs of order handling are $250,000 per year.

The company uses ABC, and wants to establish an order-handling overhead cost for each product, based on the following budget:

Product	Number of orders	Total number of units ordered
W	15	60,000
X	22	33,000
Y	4	40,000
Z	9	27,000
	50	160,000

If the cost driver for order handling is the number of orders handled, the budgeted order handling cost will be $250,000/50 = $5,000 per order. Overhead costs will be charged to products as follows:

Product	Number of orders	Cost
		$
W	15	75,000
X	22	110,000
Y	4	20,000
Z	9	45,000
	50	250,000

Example

Menia Co makes three products, X, Y and Z using the same direct labour employees and the same machine for production. The company uses activity-based costing.

Production details for the three products for a typical period are as follows:

	Hours per unit		Materials	Production
	Labour hours	Machine hours	Cost per unit	units
			$	
Product X	0.25	0.75	10.0	1,500
Product Y	0.75	0.50	6.0	2,500
Product Z	0.50	1.50	12.5	14,000

Direct labour costs $16 per hour and production overheads are absorbed on a machine hour basis.

Total production overheads are $1,309,000 and further analysis shows that the total production overheads can be divided as follows:

	%
Costs relating to machinery	15
Costs relating to inspection	35
Costs relating to set-ups	30
Costs relating to materials handling	20
Total production overhead	100

The following total activity volumes are associated with each product for the period:

	Number of inspections	Number of set-ups	Number of movements of materials
Product X	360	80	40
Product Y	80	120	80
Product Z	960	500	280
	1,400	700	400

Required:

Calculate the cost per unit for each product using ABC principles.

Answer

Working: Machine hours per period = (1,500 × 0.75) + (2,500 × 0.5) + (14,000 × 1.5)

1,125 + 1,250 + 21,000 = 23,375 hours.

Activity	Cost allocated	Cost driver	Activity per period	Overhead absorption rate
	$			
Machinery operations (15%)	196,350	Machine hrs	23,375	$8.40 per machine hour
Inspection (35%)	458,150	Inspections	1,400	$327.25 per inspection
Set-ups (30%)	392,700	Set-ups	700	$561 per set-up
Materials handling (20%)	261,800	Movements	400	$654.50 per movement
Total	1,309,000			

Overheads per cost pool and per unit	X	Y	Z
Production overheads:	$	$	$
Machinery at $8.40 per machine hour	9,450	10,500	176,400
Inspection at $327.25 per inspection	117,810	26,180	314,160
Set-ups at $561 per set-up	44,880	67,320	280,500
Materials handling at $654.50 per movement	26,180	52,360	183,260
Overhead costs per product	198,320	156,360	954,320
Number of units	1,500	2,500	14,000
Overhead cost per unit	$132.21	$62.54	$68.17

Production cost per unit: ABC	X	Y	Z
	$	$	$
Direct materials	10.00	6.00	12.50
Direct labour	4.00	12.00	8.00
Production overhead	132.21	62.54	68.17
Full production cost per unit	146.21	80.54	88.67

1.4 ABC and traditional absorption costing

The difference between traditional absorption costing and ABC is shown by the following diagrams:

Traditional absorption costing

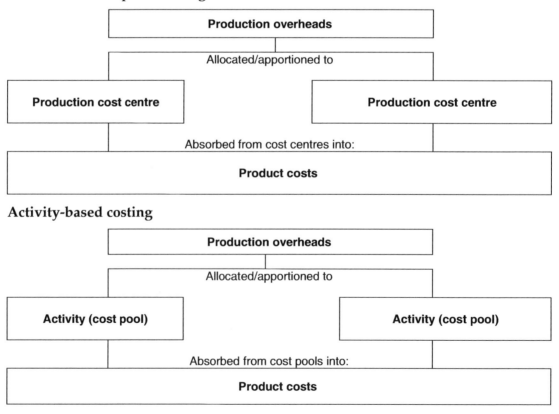

Activity-based costing

Although ABC is a form of absorption costing, the effect of ABC could be to allocate overheads in a completely different way between products. Product costs and product profitability will therefore be very different with ABC compared with traditional absorption costing.

Example

Entity Blue makes and sells two products, X and Y. Data for production and sales each month are as follows:

	Product X	Product Y
Sales demand	4,000 units	8,000 units
Direct material cost/unit	$20	$10
Direct labour hours/unit	0.1 hour	0.2 hours
Direct labour cost/unit	$2	$4

Production overheads are $500,000 each month. These are absorbed on a direct labour hour basis.

An analysis of overhead costs suggests that there are four main activities that cause overhead expenditure.

Activity	Total cost	Cost driver	Total number	Product X	Product Y
	$				
Batch setup	100,000	Number of set-ups	20	10	10
Order handling	200,000	Number of orders	40	24	16
Machining	120,000	Machine hours	15,000	6,000	9,000
Quality control	80,000	Number of checks	32	18	14
	500,000				

Required

Calculate the full production costs for Product X and Product Y, using:

(a) traditional absorption costing

(b) activity based costing.

Answer

Traditional absorption costing

The overhead absorption rate = $500,000/ (4,000 × 0.1 + 8,000 × 0.2) = $250

	Product X	Product Y	Total
	$	$	
Direct materials	20	10	
Direct labour	2	4	
Overhead (at $250 per hour)	25	50	
Cost per unit	47	64	
Number of units	4,000	8,000	
Total cost	$188,000	$512,000	$700,000

Activity based costing

Activity	Total cost	Cost driver		Product X	Product Y
	$		$	$	$
Batch setup	100,000	Cost/setup	5,000	50,000	50,000
Order handling	200,000	Cost/order	5,000	120,000	80,000
Machining	120,000	Cost/machine hour	8	48,000	72,000
Quality control	80,000	Cost/check	2,500	45,000	35,000
	500,000			263,000	237,000

	Product X	Product Y	Total
	$	$	$
Direct materials	80,000	80,000	
Direct labour	8,000	32,000	
Overheads	263,000	237,000	
Total cost	351,000	349,000	$700,000
Number of units	4,000	8,000	
Cost per unit	$87.75	$43.625	

Using ABC in this situation, the cost per unit of Product X is much higher than with traditional absorption costing and for Product Y the unit cost is much less.

The difference is caused by the fact that Product X uses only 20% of total direct labour hours worked, but much larger proportions of set-up resources, order handling resources, machining time and quality control resources. As a result, the overheads charged to each product are substantially different.

This is an important feature of activity-based costing. The overheads charged to products, and so the overhead cost per unit of product, can be significantly different from the overhead cost per unit that would be obtained from traditional absorption costing.

1.5 When using ABC might be appropriate

Activity based costing could be suitable as a method of costing in the following circumstances:

- In a manufacturing environment, where absorption costing is required for inventory valuations.
- Where a large proportion of production costs are overhead costs, and direct labour costs are relatively small.
- Where products are complex.
- Where products are provided to customer specifications.
- Where order sizes differ substantially, and order handling and despatch activity costs are significant.

1.6 Advantages and disadvantages of ABC

Advantages

- ABC provides useful information about the activities that drive overhead costs. Traditional absorption costing and marginal costing do not do this.
- ABC therefore provides information that could be relevant to long-term cost control and long-term product selection or product pricing.
- ABC can provide the basis for a management information system to manage and control overhead costs.
- With ABC, overheads are charged to products on the basis of the activities that are required to provide the product: Each product should therefore be charged with a 'fair share' of overhead cost that represents the activities that go into making and selling it.
- It might be argued that full product costs obtained with ABC are more 'realistic', although it can also be argued that full product cost information is actually of little practical use or meaning for management.
- There is also an argument that in the long run, all overhead costs are variable (even though they are fixed in the short-term). Measuring costs with ABC might therefore provide management with useful information for controlling activities and long-term costs.

Disadvantages

- The analysis of costs in an ABC system may be based on unreliable data and weak assumptions. In particular, ABC systems may be based on inappropriate activities and cost pools, and incorrect assumptions about cost drivers.

- ABC provides an analysis of historical costs. Decision-making by management should be based on expectations of future cash flows. It is incorrect to assume that there is a causal relationship between a cost diver and an activity cost, so that increasing or reducing the activity will result in higher or lower activity costs.

- In some cases, ABC may be little more than a sophisticated absorption costing system.

- Within ABC systems, there is still a large amount of overhead cost apportionment. General overhead costs such as rental costs, insurance costs and heating and lighting costs may be apportioned between cost pools. This reduces the causal link between the cost driver and the activity cost.

- Many ABC systems are based on just a small number of cost pools and cost drivers. More complex systems are difficult to justify, on grounds of cost.

- Many activities and cost pools have more than one cost driver. Identifying the most suitable cost driver for a cost pool/activity is often difficult.

- Traditional cost accounting systems may be more appropriate for the purpose of inventory valuation and financial reporting.

- It might be a costly system to design and use. The costs might not justify the benefits. It must be remembered that full product costing is of little relevance for management decision-making.

> **Target costing**
>
> - Origins of target costing
> - The purpose of target costing
> - The target costing method
> - Elements in the estimated cost and target cost
> - Closing the target cost gap
> - Advantages of target costing

2 Target costing

2.1 Origins of target costing

Target costing originated in Japan in the 1970s. It began with recognition that customers were demanding more diversity in products that they bought, and the life cycles of products were getting shorter. This meant that new products had to be designed more frequently to meet customer demands.

Companies then became aware that a large proportion of the costs of making a product are committed at the design stage, before the product goes into manufacture. The design stage was therefore critical for ensuring that new products could be manufactured at a cost that would enable the product to make a profit for the company.

2.2 The purpose of target costing

Target costing is a method of strategic management of costs and profits. As its name suggests, target costing involves setting a target or objective for the maximum cost of a product or service, and then working out how to achieve this target.

It is used for business strategy in general and marketing strategy in particular, by companies that operate in a competitive market where new products are continually being introduced to the market. In order to compete successfully, companies need to be able to:

- continually improve their existing products or design new ones
- sell their products at a competitive price; this might be the same price that competitors are charging or a lower price than competitors, and
- make a profit.

In order to make a profit, companies need to make the product at a cost below the expected sales price.

Target costing and new product development

Target costing is used mainly for new product development. This is because whenever a new product is designed and developed for a competitive market, a company needs to know what the maximum cost of the new product must be so that it will sell at a profit.

A company might decide the price that it would like to charge for a new product under development, in order to win a target share of the market. The company then decides on the level of profitability that it wants to achieve for the product, in order to make the required return on investment. Having identified a target price and a target profit, the company then establishes a target cost for the product. This is the cost at which the product must be manufactured and sold in order to achieve the target profits and return at the strategic market price.

Keeping the costs of the product within the target level is then a major factor in controlling its design and development.

New product design and development	$
Decide: The target sales price	X
Deduct: The target profit margin	(X)
Equals: The target cost (maximum cost in order to meet or exceed the target profit)	X

The reason that target costing is used for new products, as suggested earlier, is that the opportunities for cutting costs to meet a target cost are much greater during the product design stage than after the product development has been completed and the production process has been set up.

- Typically, when a new product is designed, the first consideration is to design a product that will meet the needs of customers better than rival products. However, this initial product design might result in a product with a cost that is too high, and which will therefore not be profitable.

- The estimated cost of a product design can be compared with the target cost. If the expected cost is higher than the target cost, there is a cost 'gap'.

- A cost gap must be closed by finding ways of making the product more cheaply without losing any of the features that should make it attractive to customers and give it 'value'. For example, it might be possible to simplify the product design or the production process without losing any important features of the product. It might also be possible to re-design the product using a different and cheaper material, without loss of 'value'.

- Having worked out how to reduce costs at the product design stage, management should try to ensure that the product is developed and the method of producing it is introduced according to plan, so that the target cost is achieved.

2.3 The target costing method

The principles of target costing may therefore be summarised as follows.

Target costing is based on the idea that when a new product is developed, a company will have a reasonable idea about:

- the price at which it will be able to sell the product, and
- the sales volumes that it will be able to achieve for the product over its expected life.

There may also be estimates of the capital investment required, and any incremental fixed costs (such as marketing costs or costs of additional salaried staff).

Taking estimates of sales volumes, capital investment requirements and incremental fixed costs over the life cycle of the product, it should be possible to calculate a target cost.

- The target cost for the product might be the maximum cost for the product that will provide at least the minimum required return on investment.
- However, an examination question might expect you to calculate the target cost from a target selling price and a target profit margin.

The elements in the target costing process are shown in the diagram below.

Target costing

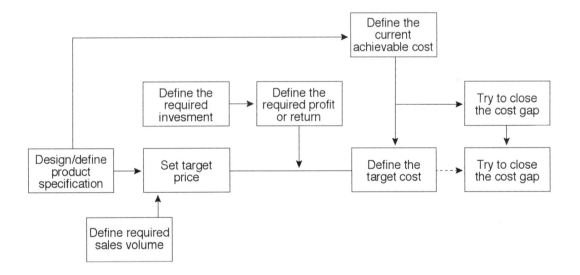

2.4 Elements in the estimated cost and target cost

A problem with target costing is to make sure that the estimates of cost are realistic. It is difficult to measure the cost of a product that has not yet been created, and the cost must include items such as raw material wastage rates and direct labour idle time, if these might be expected to occur in practice.

Raw materials costs

The target cost should allow for expected wastage rates or loss in processing. The price of materials should also allow for any possible increases up to the time when the new product development has been completed. Estimating prices of materials can be difficult when prices are volatile – such as commodity prices, which can be subject to large increases and falls within relatively short periods of time.

Direct labour

The target cost should allow for any expected idle time that will occur during the manufacture of the product. This might be the normal level of idle time in the company's manufacturing operations.

Production overheads

A target cost could be a target marginal cost. However production overhead costs are often a large proportion of total manufacturing costs, and it is therefore more likely that the target cost will be a full cost, including production overheads. If activity-based costing is used, it might be possible to identify opportunities for limiting the amount of production overheads absorbed into the product cost by designing the product in a way that limits the use of activities that drive costs, for example by reducing the need for materials movements or quality inspections.

Example

A company has designed a new product. NP8. It currently estimates that in the current market, the product could be sold for $70 per unit. A gross profit margin of at least 30% on the selling price would be required, to cover administration and marketing overheads and to make an acceptable level of profit.

A cost estimation study has produced the following estimate of production cost for NP8.

Cost item	
Direct material M1	$9 per unit
Direct material M2	Each unit of product NP8 will require three metres of material M2, but there will be loss in production of 10% of the material used. Material M2 costs $1.80 per metre.
Direct labour	Each unit of product NP8 will require 0.50 hour of direct labour time. However it is expected that there will be unavoidable idle time equal to 5% of the total labour time paid for. Labour is paid $19 per hour.
Production overheads	It is expected that production overheads will be absorbed into product costs at the rate of $60 per direct labour hour, for each active hour worked. (Overheads are not absorbed into the cost of idle time).

Required

Calculate:

(a) the expected cost of Product NP8

(b) the target cost for NP8

(c) the size of the cost gap.

Chapter 15: Alternative costing systems

 Answer

Expected cost per unit	$	$
Direct material M1		9.0
Direct material M2: 3 metres × 100/90 × $1.80		6.0
Direct labour: 0.5 hour × 100/95 × $19		10.0
Production overheads: 0.5 hour × $60		30.0
Expected full cost per unit		55.0
Target cost		
Sales price	70.0	
Minimum gross profit margin (30%)	21.0	
Target cost		49.0
Cost gap		6.0

The company needs to identify ways of closing this cost gap.

2.5 Closing the target cost gap

Target costs are rarely achievable immediately and ways must be found to reduce costs and close the cost gap.

Target costing should involve a multi-disciplinary approach to resolving the problem of how to close the cost gap. The management accountant should be involved in measuring estimated costs. Ways of reducing costs might be in product design and engineering, manufacturing processes used, selling methods and raw materials purchasing. Ideas for reducing costs can therefore come from the sales, manufacturing, engineering or purchasing departments.

Common methods of closing the target cost gap are:

- To re-design products to make use of common processes and components that are already used in the manufacture of other products by the company.

- To discuss with key suppliers methods of reducing materials costs. Target costing involves the entire 'value chain' from original suppliers of raw materials to the customer for the end-product, and negotiations and collaborations with suppliers might be an appropriate method of finding important reductions in cost.

- To eliminate non value-added activities or non-value added features of the product design. Something is 'non-value added' if it fails to add anything of value for the customer. The cost of non-value added product features or activities can therefore be saved without any loss of value for the customer. Value analysis may be used to systematically examine all aspects of a product cost to provide the product at the required quality at the lowest possible cost.

- To train staff in more efficient techniques and working methods. Improvements in efficiency will reduce costs.

- To achieve economies of scale. Producing in larger quantities will reduce unit costs because fixed overhead costs will be spread over a larger quantity of products. However, production in larger quantities is of no benefit unless sales demand can be increased by the same amount.

- To achieve cost reductions as a result of the learning curve or, more likely, the experience curve effect. The learning curve is described in a later chapter and is most likely to exist in a labour intensive environment. It results in cost savings as labour becomes more familiar with performing a new and complex task. The experience curve effect relates to cost savings made in costs other than labour costs as the company becomes more familiar with production of a new product. For example, management of the process and marketing may become more efficient as the company gains experience of making and selling the product.

2.6 Advantages of target costing

There are several possible advantages from the use of target costing.

- It helps to improve the understanding within a company of product costs.

- It recognises that the most effective way of reducing costs is to plan and control costs from the product design stage onwards.

- It helps to create a focus on the final customer for the product or service, because the concept of 'value' is important: target costs should be achieved without loss of value for the customer.

- It is a multi-disciplinary approach, and considers the entire supply chain. It could therefore help to promote co-operation, both between departments within a company and also between a company and its suppliers and customers.

- Target costing can be used together with other recognised methods for reducing costs, such as value analysis, value engineering, just-in-time purchasing and production, Total Quality Management and continuous improvement.

> **Life cycle costing**
>
> - The nature of life cycle costing
> - Asset acquisitions
> - Life cycle costing and the product life cycle

3 Life cycle costing

3.1 The nature of life cycle costing

Life cycle costing is sometimes called 'whole life costing' or 'whole life cycle costing'. It is a technique that attempts to identify the total cost associated with the ownership of an asset so that decisions can be made about asset acquisitions. It recognises that decisions made at the initial acquisition have the effect of locking in certain costs in the future.

The principles of LCC can be applied to both complex and to simple acquisitions.

- As a simple example if a person buys a new printer that person is committed to buying toner cartridges that are compatible to the printer. Thus in choosing between two printers the initial cost of one might be less than the other but its toner cartridges might be more expensive. Life cycle cost analysis would allow a choice to be made based on the total life time costs.

- A company will of course be concerned with cost when it buys a complex asset of some kind but it will also be concerned with reliability, servicing time, maintenance costs etc.

Life cycle costing can be applied to:

- Major asset acquisitions.
- Introduction of new products to the market.

3.2 Asset acquisitions

The cost of ownership of an asset is incurred throughout its life and not just at acquisition. A decision made at the purchase stage will determine future costs associated with an asset.

Life cycle costs

The costs of a product or asset over its life cycle could be divided into three categories:

- **Acquisition costs, set-up costs or market entry costs.** These are costs incurred initially to bring the product into production and to start selling it, or the costs incurred to complete the construction of a building or other major construction asset

- **Operational costs or running costs** throughout the life of the product or asset

- **End-of-life costs**. These are the costs incurred to withdraw a product from the market or to demolish the asset at the end of its life.

Acquisition costs or set-up costs are usually 'one-off' capital expenditures and other once-only costs, such as the costs of training staff and establishing systems of documentation and performance reporting. Similarly, end-of-life costs are 'one-off' items that occur just once.

Running costs or operational costs are regular and recurring annual costs throughout the life of the product or asset. However, these may vary over time: for example maintenance costs for an item of equipment, such as the maintenance costs of elevators in a building, are likely to increase over time as the asset gets older.

Although costs are incurred throughout the life of an asset, a large proportion of these costs are committed at a very early stage in the product's life cycle, when the decision to develop the new product or construct the new building is made.

Life cycle costing methodology

A proper purchasing decision requires that the costs of all available options should be taken into account. This involves cost identification and estimation and discounting. (Discounting is a technique that takes into account the time value of money. That is to say it recognises that $1 today is worth more than $1 in the future).

Benefits of LCC include:

- Improved evaluation of options
- Improved management awareness about the consequences of decisions
- Improved forecasting
- Improved understanding of the trade-off between performance of an asset and its cost.

Problems with using LCC

- Availability of data
- It is difficult and time consuming
- Often organisations are structured in a way that different managers are responsible for the purchase decision and the future operation of the asset. Thus, even though the purchase decision locks in future costs the manager making the acquisition has no incentive to consider LCC.

3.3 Life cycle costing and the product life cycle

Most products made in large quantities for selling to customers go through a life cycle which consists of several stages:

- product development stage
- product introduction to the market
- a period of growth in sales and market size
- a period of maturity
- a period of decline
- withdrawal from the market.

The diagram below indicates typical characteristics of sales revenue and profit at each stage.

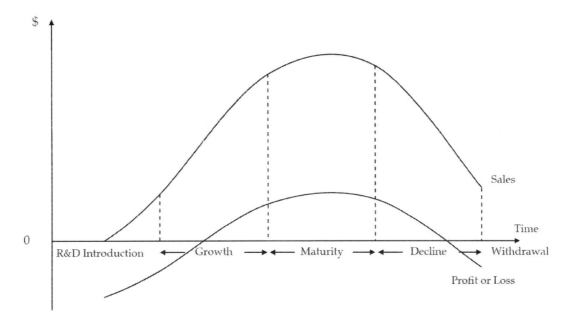

At each phase of a product's life cycle:

- selling prices will be altered
- costs may differ
- the amount invested (capital investment) may vary
- spending on advertising and other marketing activities may change

LCC can be important in new product launches as a company will of course want to make a profit from the new product and the technique considers the total costs that must be recovered. These will include:

- Research and development costs;
- Training costs
- Machinery costs
- Production costs
- Distribution and selling costs

- Marketing costs
- Working capital costs
- Retirement and disposal costs

Decisions made at the development phase impact later costs.

Stage	Costs
Product development	R&D costs
	Capital expenditure decisions
Introduction to the market	Operating costs
	Marketing and advertising to raise product awareness (strong focus on market share)
	Set up and expansion of distribution channels
Growth	Costs of increasing capacity
	Maybe learning effect and economies of scale
	Increased costs of working capital
Maturity	Incur costs to maintain manufacturing capacity
	Marketing and product enhancement costs to extend maturity
Decline	Close attention to costs needed as withdrawal decision might be expensive
Withdrawal	Asset decommissioning costs
	Possible restructuring costs
	Remaining warranties to be supported

Total Quality Management (TQM)
■ The importance of quality
■ Quality related costs
■ Managing quality related costs

4 Total Quality Management (TQM)

4.1 The importance of quality

Success in business depends on satisfying the needs of customers and meeting the requirements of customers. An essential part of meeting customer needs is to provide the quality that customers require. Quality is therefore an important aspect of product design and marketing.

Quality is also important in the control of production processes. Poor quality in production will result in losses due to rejected items and wastage rates, sales returns by customers, repairing products sold to customers (under warranty agreements) and the damaging effect on sales of a loss of reputation.

Total Quality Management

Total Quality Management (TQM) is an approach to improving quality in processes and products that originated in Japan in the 1950s. Manufacturing methods and quality management are credited with giving Japanese manufacturers the leading position in many global industries that many of them still enjoy today.

- TQM is 'an effective system for integrating the quality development, quality maintenance and quality improvement efforts of various groups in an organisation so as to enable production and service at the most economical levels which allow for full customer satisfaction' (Feigenbaum).

- TQM is 'the continuous improvement in quality, productivity and effectiveness obtained by establishing management responsibility for processes as well as outputs. In this every process has an identified process owner and every person in an entity operates within a process and contributes to its improvement' (CIMA).

The TQM approach to quality costs is to 'get things right the first time, every time'.

4.2 Quality-related costs

The CIMA's *Official Terminology* defines quality-related costs as: 'the expenditure incurred in defect prevention and appraisal activities and the losses due to internal and external failure of a product or service, through failure to meet agreed specification'.

An organisation must incur costs to deal with quality.

- It might incur costs to prevent poor quality, or detect poor quality items when they occur.

- It might incur costs in correcting the problem when poor quality does occur.

Quality costs can be classified as:

- prevention costs
- appraisal costs
- internal failure costs
- external failure costs.

Prevention costs

Prevention costs are the costs of action to prevent defects (or reduce the number of defects). They are costs incurred to prevent a quality problem from arising. Prevention costs include:

- designing products and services with in-built quality
- designing production processes of a high quality
- training employees to do their jobs to a high standard.

Appraisal costs

Appraisal costs are the costs of checking the quality of work that has been done. Appraisal costs include inspection and testing costs.

Internal failure costs

Internal failure costs are costs incurred when defective production occurs. They include:

- the cost of scrapped items
- the cost of re-working items to bring them to the required quality standard
- the cost of production time lost due to failures and defects.

External failure costs

External failure costs are costs incurred when the quality problem arises after the goods have been delivered to the customer. They include the costs of:

- dealing with customers' complaints
- the costs of carrying out repair work under a guarantee or warranty
- the costs of recalling all items from customers in order to correct a design fault
- legal costs, when a customer takes the organisation to court
- the cost of lost reputation: when an organisation gets a reputation for poor quality, customers will stop buying from it.

4.3 Managing quality-related costs

The traditional view of managing quality costs is that the total of all quality costs should be minimised. An organisation should spend more money on prevention and detection costs, if this reduces internal and external failure costs by a larger amount. On the other hand, there is no reason to spend more on preventing poor quality if the benefits do not justify the extra cost.

This traditional view is rejected by supporters of the Total Quality Management (TQM) principle. The TQM view is that it is impossible to identify and measure all quality costs. In particular, it is impossible to measure the costs of lost reputation, which will lead to a decline in sales over time. The aim should therefore always to be to work towards zero defects. To achieve zero defects, it will be necessary to spend more money on prevention costs.

Example

You are presented with the following list of performance measurements before the implementation of a Total Quality Management Programme (Pre-TQM) and after its implementation (Post-TQM).

	Pre-TQM performance	Post-TQM performance
	%	%
Returns by customers due to packaging defects	5	2
Rejections on final inspection	6	4
Losses in production	3	1

Required

Calculate how many units must be input to the process to achieve final sales of 1,000 units:

(a) before the TQM programme

(b) after the TQM programme.

Answer

	Performance Pre-TQM	Post-TQM
	units	units
Sales	1,000	1,000
Packaging failures	50	20
	1,050	1,020
Rejected units	67	43
	1,117	1,063
Process losses	35	11
Units to be input	1,152	1,074

The TQM improvements have led to a reduction of about 7% (78/1,152) in the quantity of units that need to be input to produce 1,000 units of output.

Applied Knowledge
Management Accounting (MA)

CHAPTER 16

Budgeting

Contents
1 The budgeting process
2 Preparing functional budgets
3 Cash budgets
4 Fixed, flexible and flexed budgets
5 Responsibility accounting
6 Behavioural aspects of budgeting

> **The budgeting process**
>
> - Planning framework
> - The nature of budgets
> - Purposes of budgeting
> - Preparing the budget
> - The master budget
> - Functional budgets
> - Principal budget factor
> - Stages in the budget process

1 The budgeting process

1.1 Planning framework

A business entity should plan over the long term, medium term and short term.

- Long term planning, or strategic planning, focuses on how to achieve the entity's long-term objectives.
- Medium-term or tactical planning focuses on the next year or two.
- Short-term or operational planning focuses on day-to-day and week-to-week plans.

Budgets are medium-term plans for the business, expressed in financial terms. A typical budget is prepared annually, and the overall budget is divided into control periods for the purpose of control reporting. The stages in the planning and control process are set out below.

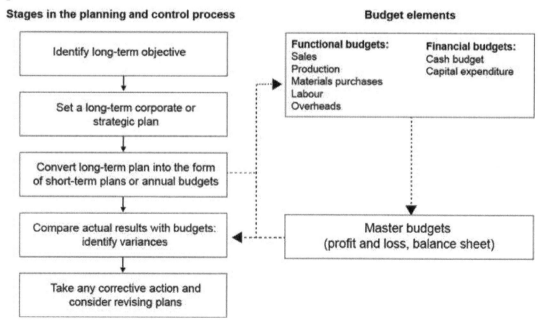

1.2 The nature of budgets

A budget is a formal plan, expressed mainly in financial terms and covering all the activities of the entity. It is for a specific period of time, typically one year. When budgets are prepared annually, they are for the next financial year.

The total budget period (one year) may be sub-divided into shorter control periods of one month or one quarter (three months).

1.3 Purposes of budgeting

Budgets have several purposes.

- To convert long-term plans (strategic plans) into more detailed shorter-term (annual) plans.
- To ensure that planning is linked to the long-term objectives and strategies of the organisation.
- To co-ordinate the actions of all the different parts of the organisation, so that they all work towards the same goals. (This is known as 'goal congruence'). One of the benefits of budgeting is that is covers all activities, so the plan should try to ensure that all the different activities are properly co-ordinated and working towards the same objective.
- To communicate the company's plans to the individuals (managers and other employees) who have to put the plans into action.
- To motivate managers and employees, by setting targets for achievement, and possibly motivating them with the incentive of bonuses or other rewards if the targets are met.
- To provide guidelines for authorising expenditure. Expenditure might not be permitted unless it has been planned in the budget or unless it is within the budgeted expenditure limits for the department.
- To identify areas of responsibility for implementing the plans. For each part of the budget, an individual manager should be made responsible for achieving the budget targets for performance.
- To provide a benchmark against which actual performance can be measured.
- To control costs. Costs can be controlled by comparing budgets with actual results and investigating any differences (or variances) between the two. This is known as **budgetary control**.

1.4 Preparing the budget

Preparing the annual budget is a major activity for many entities. In many medium-sized and large companies, there is a well-defined process for budget preparation, because a large number of individuals have to co-ordinate their efforts to prepare the budget plans. The budgeting process may take several months, from beginning to eventual approval by the board of directors.

The budget process might be supervised and controlled by a special committee (the **budget committee**). This consists of senior managers from all the main areas of the business. The committee co-ordinates the various functional budgets submitted to it for review, and gives instructions for changes to be made when the draft budgets are unsatisfactory or the functional budgets are not consistent with each other.

Although the budget committee manages the budget process, the functional budgets are usually prepared by the managers with responsibility for the particular aspect of operations covered by that functional budget.

Budget manual

To guide everyone involved in the budgeting process, there should be a budget manual or budget handbook. This should set out:

- the key objectives of the budget
- the planning procedures and the timetables to follow when preparing the budget
- instructions about the budget details that must be included in the functional budgets
- responsibilities for preparing the functional budgets (sales budget, production budget, materials budgets, labour budget and overhead expenditure budgets)
- details of the budget approval process. The budget must be approved by the budget committee and then by the board of directors.

1.5 The master budget

The 'master budget' is the final approved budget. It is usually presented in the form of financial statements - a budgeted income statement and a budgeted balance sheet for the end of the financial year.

However the master budget is the result of a large number of detailed plans, many of them prepared at a departmental or functional level. To prepare the master budget, it is therefore necessary to prepare functional budgets first.

1.6 Functional budgets

A functional budget is a budget for a particular aspect of the entity's operations. The functional budgets that are prepared vary with the type of business and industry. In a manufacturing company, functional budgets should include:

- a sales budget
- a production budget
- a budget for production resources and resource costs (such as a materials cost budget and a labour cost budget)
- a materials purchasing budget
- expenditure budgets for every overhead cost centre and general overhead costs.

1.7 Principal budget factor

The budgeting process begins with the preparation of functional budgets, which must be co-ordinated and consistent with each other. To make sure that functional budgets are co-ordinated and consistent, the first functional budget that should be prepared is the budget for the principal budget factor.

The principal budget factor (also called the key budget factor) is the factor in the budget that will set a limit to the volume and scale of operations.

Sales demand (sales volume) as the principal budget factor

Normally, the principal budget factor is the expected sales demand. When this happens, the expected sales demand should set a limit on the volume of production (or volume of services). A company might have the capacity to increase its production and output, but producing larger quantities has no purpose unless the extra quantities can be sold.

A company will therefore prepare a budget on the basis of the sales volumes that it hopes or expects to achieve. When sales demand is the principal budget factor, the sales budget is the first functional budget that should be prepared.

A principal budget factor other than sales volume

Sometimes, there is a different limitation on budgeted activity. There might be a shortage of a key resource, such as machine time or the availability of skilled labour. When there is a shortage of a resource that will set a limit on budgeted production volume or budgeted activity, the first functional budget to prepare should be the budget for that resource.

In government, the principal budget factor for each government department is often an expenditure limit for the department. The department must then prepare a budget for the year that keeps the activities and spending plans of the department within the total expenditure limit for the department as a whole.

1.8 Stages in the budget process

The budgeting process for a manufacturing company is probably more complex than for many other types of organisation, and manufacturing company budgets are more likely to be the subject of an examination question than budgets for companies in other industries. This chapter therefore describes the budgeting process for a manufacturing company.

The stages in setting the budget might be as follows.

- **Stage 1**: Identify the principal budget factor (or key budget factor). The principal budget factor is often sales volume.

- **Stage 2**: Prepare the functional budget or plan for the principal budget factor. Usually, this means that the first functional budget to prepare is the sales budget.

- All the other functional budgets should be prepared within the limitation of the principal budget factor. For example, even if the company has the capacity to produce more output, it should not produce more than it can sell (unless it formally decides to increase the size of the finished goods inventory, in which case the production volume will be higher than the sales volume).

- **Stage 3**: Prepare the other functional budgets, in logical sequence where necessary. When the sales budget has been prepared, a manufacturing organisation can then prepare budgets for inventories (= plans to increase or reduce the size of its inventories), a production budget, labour budgets and materials usage and purchasing budgets. Expenditure budgets should also be prepared for overhead costs (production overheads, administration overheads and sales and distribution overheads). Overhead costs budgets are usually prepared for each cost centre individually.

- **Stage 4**: Submit the functional budgets to the budget committee for review and approval. The functional budgets are co-ordinated by the budget committee, which must make sure that they are both realistic and consistent with each other.

- **Stage 5**: Prepare the 'master budget'. This is the budget statement that summarises the plans for the budget period. The master budget might be presented in the form of:
  - a budgeted income statement for the next financial year
  - a budgeted balance sheet as at the end of the next financial year
  - a cash budget or cash flow forecast for the next financial year.

- It should be possible to prepare the master budget statements from the functional budgets.

- **Stage 6**: The master budget and the supporting functional budgets should be submitted to the board of directors for approval. The board approves and authorises the budget.

- **Stage 7**: The detailed budgets are communicated to the managers responsible for their implementation.

- **Stage 8**: Control process. After the budget has been approved, actual performance should be monitored by comparing it with the budget. Actual results for the period should be recorded and reported to management. These results should be compared with the budget, and significant differences should be investigated. The reasons for the differences ('variances') should be established, and where appropriate control measures should be taken. Comparing actual results with the budget therefore provides a system of control. The managers responsible for activities where actual results differ significantly from the budget will be held responsible and accountable.

The planning process (budgeting) should therefore lead on to a management monitoring and control process (budgetary control).

Preparing functional budgets

- The sales budget
- Cost budgets
- The production budget
- The materials usage budget
- The materials purchases budget
- The labour budget
- Budgeted profit and loss account
- Overheads budgets

2 Preparing functional budgets

This section describes the approach used to prepare functional budgets for a manufacturing organisation. In practice, budgets are usually prepared with a computer model, such as a **spreadsheet**. However, you need to understand the logic of budget preparation.

2.1 The sales budget

The sales budget is the plan for the volume and value of sales in the budget period. It is prepared for each product individually, in units of sale and sales revenue, and for sales revenue in total.

It is calculated for each product simply by multiplying the volume of sales in units by the budgeted sales price per unit.

Example

A company makes and sells two products, Product P and Product Q.

The sales price and expected sales volume for each product next year are as follows:

	Product P	Product Q
Sales price per unit	$20	$30
Budgeted sales volume	20,000 units	30,000 units

A sales budget can be prepared as follows.

Product	Budgeted sales quantity	Budgeted sales price	Budgeted sales revenue
	units	$	$
P	20,000	20	400,000
Q	30,000	30	900,000
Total			1,300,000

Sometimes, a sales budget is prepared by making adjustments to actual sales in the current financial year.

Example

A company is preparing its sales budget for the year. In the current financial year it expects that total sales will be $2.6 million. Next year it hopes to raise its selling prices by 3% and to increase sales volume by 5%.

The sales budget for next year is therefore: $2.6 million × 1.03 × 1.05 = $2.8 million (to the nearest $100,000).

2.2 Cost budgets

When sales are a key factor, the cost budgets all flow from the number to be sold and must be prepared in the following order:

Production budget

This is the number of units to be produced in the period. This number starts with the number of units to be sold which is then adjusted for inventory movement. (For example, if 100 items are to be sold, in the absence of other information, the company would need to make 100 items. However, if 20 items can be taken from inventory, the company would only need to make 80 items).

Materials usage budge

This can only be constructed after the number of units to be made is known.

Materials purchases budget

This can only be constructed after the amount of raw material to be used is known.

Labour usage budget

This can only be constructed after the number of units to be made is known.

You can see from the above that the labour usage budget can be prepared before the materials usage budget if you prefer.

The various functional budgets can be combined to produce a profit or loss account for the period.

The process will be explained with a series of examples building the functional budgets and budgeted profit or loss account of X Plc limited.

2.3 The production budget

The production budget is calculated initially in units of output, although a budget for production costs can be prepared when production quantities have been decided.

The production budget for each product in units is the sales budget in units adjusted for any planned changes in finished goods inventories.

The production budget in units is prepared for each product, as follows:

Illustration: Production budget

	Units
Sales budget in units	X
Plus: Budgeted closing inventory	X
Minus: Opening inventory	(X)
Production budget	X

Example: Production budget

X Plc makes and sells two products, Product P and Product Q. Its sales budget for next year is to sell 2,000 units of Product P and 3,000 units of Product Q.

The following opening and closing inventories are budgeted:

	Opening	Closing
Finished goods:	Units	Units
P	200	300
Q	150	100

A production budget can be prepared as follows:

	Product P units	Product Q units
Sales budget	2,000	3,000
Plus: Budgeted closing inventory	300	100
	2,300	3,100
Minus: Opening inventory	(200)	(150)
Production budget	2,100	2,950

2.4 The materials usage budget

After the production budget has been prepared, budgets can be prepared for the resources required to achieve the production targets.

Production resources budgets will include a materials usage budget, a direct labour usage budget and possibly a machine hours budget.

Separate budgets can be prepared for each production centre, and these can be added together to create the total production budget. For example, if a manufacturing process consists of a machining department, a finishing department and an assembly department, production budgets will be prepared for each department separately, and these will then be combined to produce a total production department budget.

The materials usage budget is a budget for the quantities of materials that will be used. It is a statement of the quantities of direct materials required for production, and their cost.

The usage budget is prepared for each item of material separately, and a total cost of the materials used should also be shown.

Example: Materials usage budget

X Plc makes and sells two products, Product P and Product Q.

The company has determined that it will make 2,100 units of Product P and 2,950 units of Product Q next year.

The products are expected to use raw materials as follows:

	Product P	Product Q
Direct materials	Usage (kgs)	Usage (kgs)
Material A ($40 per kg)	2	0.5
Material B ($50 per kg)	0.5	3
Material C ($70 per kg)	1	-

A material usage budget can be prepared as follows:

	A (kgs)	B (kgs)	C (kgs)
Usage to make 2,100 units of P			
2,100 units × 2 kgs	4,200		
2,100 units × 0.5 kgs		1,050	
2,100 units × 1 kgs			2,100
Usage to make 2,950 units of Q			
2,950 units × 0.5 kgs	1,475		
2,950 units × 3 kgs		8,850	
Usage in kgs	5,675	9,900	2,100
Cost per kg	$40	$50	$70
Usage in dollars	227,000	495,000	147,000
Total cost			$869,000

2.5 The materials purchases budget

The budgeted cost of materials for use in production is not the same as the quantity and cost of materials that will be purchased. Material purchases and material usage will be different if there are plans to increase or reduce raw materials inventories.

The materials purchases budget is the budget for the purchase cost of materials that will be purchased in the budget period. The materials purchases budget might be prepared for all materials, direct and indirect, or for direct materials only.

The purchases budget differs from the materials usage budget by the amount of the planned increase or decrease in inventory levels of materials in the budget period.

The purchase quantities are calculated first. Purchase quantities are calculated as follows, for each item of material:

Illustration: Materials purchases budget

	kgs
Material usage	X
Plus budgeted closing inventory	X
Minus opening inventory	(X)
Purchases budget	X

The purchase quantities for each item of material are converted into a purchases cost at the budgeted purchase price for the item of material.

The total material purchases budget (in $) is the sum of the purchases budget for each of the individual items of material.

Example: Materials purchases budget

X Plc makes and sells two products, Product P and Product Q.

The company expects to use raw materials in the coming year as follows:

Direct materials	Usage (kgs)	
Material A	5,675	
Material B	9,900	
Material C	2,100	-

The following opening and closing inventories are budgeted:

Materials:	Cost per kg ($)	Opening kgs	Closing kgs
A	40	500	600
B	50	550	400
C	70	100	250

A material purchases budget can be prepared as follows:

	A (kgs)	B (kgs)	C (kgs)
Usage	5,675	9,900	2,100
Clsoing inventory	600	400	250
	6,275	10,300	2,350
Opening inventory	(500)	(550)	(100)
Purchases (kgs)	5,775	9,750	2,250
Cost per kg ($)	40	50	70
Purchases ($)	231,000	487,500	157,500
Total cost			$876,000

2.6 The labour usage budget

Direct labour usage budget

The direct labour usage budget is prepared in a similar way to the materials usage budget. It is a statement of the quantities of direct labour required for production, and its cost.

The budget is prepared for different grades of labour separately, but the total labour cost should also be shown.

The expected hours of work to make the budgeted production quantities of each product should be calculated separately for each grade of labour and then for all the products in total. The total budget in hours for each grade of labour is converted into a cost at the standard/budgeted rate per hour for the grade of labour.

Example: Labour usage budget

X Plc makes and sells two products, Product P and Product Q.

The company has determined that it will make 2,100 units of Product P and 2,950 units of Product Q next year.

The products are expected to require labour as follows:

Direct labour	Usage (hrs)	Usage (hrs)
Grade X ($100 per hr.)	0.25	0.5
Grade Y ($80 per hr.)	0.25	0.75

A labour usage budget can be prepared as follows:

	Grade X (hrs)	Grade Y (hrs)
Usage to make 2,100 units of P		
2,100 units × 0.25 hrs	525	
2,100 units × 0.25 hrs		525
Usage to make 2,950 units of Q		
2,950 units × 0.5 hrs	1,475	
2,950 units × 0.75 hrs		2,212.5
Usage in kgs	2,000	2,737.5
Cost per kg ($)	100	80
Usage in dollars	200,000	219,000
Total cost($)		419,000

2.7 Budgeted profit and loss account

The functional budgets can be combined to produce a budgeted profit and loss account for the period.

Full details from the X Plc examples are given below for your convenience.

Example: Preparing a functional budget

X Plc makes and sells two products, Product P and Product Q. Its sales budget for next year is to sell 2,000 units of Product P at a sales price of $400 per unit and 3,000 units of Product Q at a sales price of $500 per unit.

The following cost information is expected to apply in the next year:

	Product P		Product Q	
Direct materials	Usage (kgs)	Cost ($)	Usage (kgs)	Cost ($)
Material A ($40 per kg)	2	80	0.5	20
Material B ($50 per kg)	0.5	25	3	150
Material C ($70 per kg)	1	70	–	–
		175		170
Direct labour	Usage (hrs)		Usage (hrs)	
Grade X ($100 per hr.)	0.25	25	0.5	50
Grade Y ($80 per hr.)	0.25	20	0.75	60
		45		110
Unit cost		220		280

The following opening and closing inventories are budgeted:

		Opening		Closing	
Finished goods:	Cost ($)	Units	Total ($)	Units	Total ($)
P	220	200	44,000	300	66,000
Q	280	150	42,000	100	28,000
			86,000		94,000
Materials:	Cost	kgs		kgs	
A	40	500	20,000	600	24,000
B	50	550	27,500	400	20,000
C	70	100	7,000	250	17,500
			54,500		61,500
Total inventory			140,500		155,500

Example: Preparing a functional budget

The following additional information has been derived from the above during the budget process:

	Product	Sales price ($)	Units	$
Sales budget	P	400	2,000	800,000
	Q	500	3,000	1,500,000
				2,300,000
Purchases				876,000
Labour usage				419,000

The above figures can be used to produce a budgeted profit or loss account for the year as follows:

	$	$
Sales budget		2,300,000
Cost of sales:		
Opening inventory	140,500	
Purchases	876,000	
Labour usage	419,000	
	1,435,500	
Closing inventory	(155,500)	
		(1,280,000)
Budgeted gross profit		1,020,000

The budgeted gross profit can be checked as follows:

	(Units × (Sales price − Unit cost))	$
Profit from selling P	(2,000 units × (400 − 220))	360,000
Profit from selling Q	(3,000 units × (500 − 280))	660,000
		1,020,000

2.8 Overheads budgets

Overheads budgets are prepared for each department or cost centre, in production, administration and sales and distribution.

- To prepare expenditure budgets for each overhead cost centre, overhead expenditure is allocated and apportioned, using the methods described in the earlier chapter on overhead costs.

- In an absorption costing system, an overhead absorption rate should then be calculated from the total budgeted expenditure and the budgeted volume of activity.

When flexed budgets are prepared, overhead costs might be divided into variable and fixed costs.

Example

A company makes and sells one product, Product Z. The production budget is to make and sell 5,000 units of Product Z, but there is a possibility that sales demand might be less than expected; therefore management have decided to prepare a budget for 4,000 units of production and sales.

Production overhead costs are expected to be fixed costs of $360,000 plus variable overheads of $1.50 per direct labour hour. Product Z takes 2 hours to produce.

A production overheads budget can be prepared at production volumes of both 4,000 and 5,000 units, as follows.

	4,000 units $	5,000 units $
Variable overheads (2 hours × $1.50 = $3 per unit)	12,000	15,000
Fixed overheads	360,000	360,000
Total overheads	372,000	375,000
Overhead cost per unit	$93	$75

> **Cash budgets**
>
> - Format of a cash budget
> - Bank overdraft interest
> - Receipts from credit sales
> - Payments to suppliers and payments for running costs (overheads)

3 Cash budgets

3.1 Format of a cash budget

A cash budget is a budget of cash receipts and cash payments during each control period of the budget. Cash budgets might be prepared on a month-by-month basis. However, cash budgets might be prepared on a week-by-week basis, or even a day-by-day basis if required for short-term planning.

A recommended format for a monthly cash budget is as follows. Illustrative figures are included for January and February.

	January	February	and so on
	$	$	$
Cash receipts			
Cash sales	15,000	10,000	
Cash from trade receivables	80,000	85,000	
Other cash income	2,000	0	
Total cash receipts	97,000	95,000	
Cash payments			
To suppliers	40,000	28,000	
Wages and salaries	35,000	35,000	
Other running costs	12,000	12,000	
Capital purchases	70,000	0	
Other cash payments	1,000	2,000	
Total cash payments	158,000	77,000	
Cash receipts minus cash payments	(61,000)	18,000	
Cash at beginning of month	50,000	(11,000)	7,000
Cash at end of month	(11,000)	7,000	

The cash budget should show all cash items of receipt or payment, including:

- cash from issuing shares
- interest or dividends received from investments
- interest payments, but only in the months that interest is actually paid
- taxation payments but only in the months that tax is actually paid
- dividend payments.

3.2 Bank overdraft interest

In an examination question, you might be required to calculate bank overdraft interest. For example, you might be told that the bank overdraft interest is calculated at the end of the month on any opening negative bank balance at the beginning of the month.

You should include a line in the cash payments section for the overdraft interest each month, but you cannot work out the interest cost until you know what the bank balance is at the beginning of the month. It is therefore one of the last items you can enter in the cash budget.

3.3 Receipts from credit sales

One of the more difficult calculations in a cash budget is the cash receipts from trade receivables. When sales are on credit, payments will not be received until a later month. There might also be bad debts to allow for.

We recommend that you should prepare a table for your workings for cash received from credit sales.

Example

The previous example will be continued. Suppose the sales of the company were as follows:

	Product P	Product Q
	units	units
November	1,500	2,000
December	2,000	3,000
January	1,000	2,000
February	2,000	3,000
March	3,000	4,000

Product P is sold for $20 per unit, and Product Q for $30. All sales are on credit. 20% of total sales are paid for in the month of sale, and 40% in the following month. The rest, excluding bad debts, are paid at the end of the second month. Bad debts are 2% of total sales and are written off at the end of the second month following sale.

Required

Calculate the budgeted cash receipts from sales, for inclusion in the cash budget for January, February and March.

Answer

The total sales in each month must be calculated.

	Product P ($20)		Product Q ($30)		Total
	units	$	units	$	$
November	1,500	30,000	2,000	60,000	90,000
December	2,000	40,000	3,000	90,000	130,000
January	1,000	20,000	2,000	60,000	80,000
February	2,000	40,000	3,000	90,000	130,000
March	3,000	60,000	4,000	120,000	180,000

The pattern of payments must be established. Here, the pattern is:

20% in the month of sale

40% one month after sale

38% two months after sale

Bad debts = 2%

A table of workings for cash receipts can now be prepared, as follows:

	Sales in month	Received in		
		January	February	March
Month of sale	$	$	$	$
November	90,000	34,200	–	–
December	130,000	52,000	49,400	–
January	80,000	16,000	32,000	30,400
February	130,000	–	26,000	52,000
March	180,000	–	–	36,000
Total cash receipts		102,200	107,400	118,400

3.4 Payments to suppliers and payments for running costs (overheads)

Payments to suppliers

Payments to suppliers can be calculated in a similar way to cash receipts from credit sales. The starting point for calculating payments in each month should be the material purchases in each month. Having established total purchases, you can then work out when the payments will be made.

There will be no bad debts to worry about, because all purchases will be paid for.

Payments for running costs (overheads)

To work out the cash payments for running costs or overhead expenses:

- exclude any non-cash costs such as depreciation from the total of running costs
- if any specific payments are made in a particular month, deduct these from the total costs, and enter them in the cash budget in the month when the cash payment will be made.

It is usual to assume that all other cash payments for running costs will be an equal amount in every month, so the remaining costs can be divided by 12, and the monthly amount entered in the cash budget as payments in each month.

Example

In the example used earlier, the budgeted annual overhead costs were as follows.

Production overheads	$80,000	including depreciation charges of $20,000
Administration overheads	$120,000	including depreciation charges of $10,000
Selling and distribution overheads	$190,000	including depreciation charges of $10,000

Suppose that the administration overheads include office rental of $20,000 for the year, payable in February, and the selling and distribution overheads include annual bonuses for salesmen, $30,000, payable in December.

The budgeted cash payments for overheads in January, February and March would be calculated as follows.

	Production	Administration	Sales and distribution
	$	$	$
Total annual costs	80,000	120,000	190,000
Depreciation	(20,000)	(10,000)	(10,000)
Annual cash expenses	60,000	110,000	180,000
Rent	-	(20,000)	-
Sales bonuses	-	-	(30,000)
Other cash expenses	60,000	90,000	150,000
Regular monthly payments	5,000	7,500	12,500

The January to March cash budget for overhead costs is as follows:

	Payments in		
	January	February	March
	$	$	$
Rent	-	20,000	-
Production overheads	5,000	5,000	5,000
Administration overheads	7,500	7,500	7,500
Selling/distribution overheads	12,500	12,500	12,500
Total	25,000	45,000	25,000

> **Fixed, flexible and flexed budgets**
>
> - Budgetary control
> - Fixed budgets
> - Flexed budgets
> - Flexible budgets
> - What if" analysis and scenario planning

4 Fixed, flexible and flexed budgets

4.1 Budgetary control

One of the main purposes of budgeting is budgetary control and the control of costs. Costs can be controlled by comparing budgets with the results actually achieved.

Differences between expected results and actual results are known as variances. Variances can be either favourable (F) or adverse (A) depending on whether the results achieved are better or worse than expected. Favourable variances increase profits and adverse variances decrease profits.

There are three different types of budget that you need to know about.

- fixed budgets
- flexed budgets
- flexible budgets.

4.2 Fixed budgets

The original budget prepared at the beginning of a budget period is known as the fixed budget. A fixed budget is a budget for a specific volume of output and sales activity, and it is the 'master plan' for the financial year that the company tries to achieve.

The term 'fixed' in 'fixed budget' means that the output and sales volumes are for a fixed amount or quantity.

A fixed budget might be suitable as a plan, provided that the business environment is fairly stable and sales and production volumes should be predictable with reasonable accuracy. However, a fixed budget is not suitable for the purpose of budgetary control – reporting differences between actual costs and profits and what costs and profits should have been. Fixed budgets are not suitable for budgetary control reporting because the variances calculated with a fixed budget can provide misleading information

Example

A company makes and sells a single product. Its budget for the year was to make and sell 10,000 units of the product. Actual sales and production were 15,000 units.

The expected results in the fixed budget and actual results are set out and compared in the table below.

	Fixed budget	Actual results	Difference
Units	10,000	15,000	
	$	$	
Sales revenue	200,000	286,000	$86,000 Favourable
Materials costs	60,000	94,000	$34,000 Adverse
Labour costs	70,000	97,000	$27,000 Adverse
Variable overheads	20,000	23,000	$3,000 Adverse
Fixed costs	30,000	34,000	$4,000 Adverse
Total costs	180,000	248,000	

The total differences calculated in this way, comparing the fixed budget for 10,000 units with the actual results for 15,000 units, do not provide useful information for management. The differences do not compare 'like with like'. It should be expected that when sales and production volumes are higher than the budgeted quantities, sales revenues and costs will be higher, and profit will be higher.

Much more useful information would be provided by producing a revised budget based on the actual quantities produced and sold.

4.3 Flexed budgets

A flexed budget is a budget prepared to show the revenue, costs and profits that should have been expected from the actual volumes of production and sale. A flexed budget is prepared for the actual volume of sales and output, and it allows for the fact that sales revenues and variable costs should be expected to increase or fall with increases or falls in sales and output.

A flexed budget is prepared at the end of the budget period when the actual results are known. It is used to compare:

- the actual results with the flexed budget
- the fixed budget with the flexed budget.

If a flexed budget is compared with the actual results for a period, the differences between the two (variances) are much more meaningful than if the fixed budget and actual results are compared.

Example

Taking the previous example which shows a fixed budget and actual results, a flexed budget would be prepared as follows.

	Fixed budget	Flexed budget	Actual results	Difference
Units	10,000	15,000	15,000	
	$	$	$	
Sales revenue	200,000	300,000	286,000	$14,000 Adverse
Materials costs	60,000	90,000	94,000	$4,000 Adverse
Labour costs	70,000	105,000	97,000	$8,000 Favourable
Variable overheads	20,000	30,000	23,000	$7,000 Favourable
Fixed costs	30,000	30,000	34,000	$4,000 Adverse
Total costs	180,000	255,000	248,000	
Profit	20,000	45,000	38,000	

In the flexed budget, the expected sales revenue and all the expected variable costs are shown for output and sales of 15,000 units, which is the actual volume. A comparison of the flexed budget and actual results shows the differences (variances) between the actual performance and the results that should have been expected for the actual volume of output and sales.

The table also shows the expected profit in the fixed budget, the expected profit in the flexed budget and the actual profit obtained in the period.

- The expected profit in the fixed budget is $20,000 but in the flexed budget it is $45,000. By increasing sales from 10,000 units to 15,000 units, the company would have been expected to earn an additional profit of $25,000.

- However, actual profit was only $38,000, which is $7,000 less than in the flexed budget. This difference is explained by the sum of the variances in the right-hand column of the table. These variances add up to $7,000 Adverse.

A budgetary control report can be prepared as follows from this information. (F) represents a favourable variance and (A) represents an adverse variance.

	$	$
Original budgeted profit (fixed budget)		20,000
Sales volume variance		25,000 (F)
Flexed budget profit		45,000
Sales price variance		14,000 (A)
Actual sales minus flexed budget costs		31,000
Materials cost variance	4,000 (A)	
Labour cost variance	8,000 (F)	
Variable overhead cost variance	7,000 (F)	
Fixed overhead expenditure variance	4,000 (A)	
Total cost variances		7,000 (F)
Actual profit		38,000

Variances are explained in more detail in a later chapter.

4.4 Flexible budgets

Flexible budgets are not the same as flexed budgets, although they are similar.

- **Flexed budgets** are prepared at the end of a budget period and look back at what costs, revenues and profits should have been in a period (based on actual activity levels). They are used to calculate variances for the purpose of management control and control reporting (**budgetary control**).

- **Flexible budgets**, on the other hand, are forward-looking and are prepared at the beginning of a budget period when the fixed (original) budget is prepared. Flexible budgets are prepared to show the results that would be expected at different levels of activity, for example, at 75%, 80% and 85% of the full capacity. They might be prepared when there is uncertainty about what the actual volumes of sales and production will be, and several budgets are therefore prepared for a number of different possible outcomes.

Flexible budget	Level of activity			
	75%	80%	85%	100%
	$	$	$	$
Direct materials	7,500	8,000	8,500	10,000
Direct labour	22,500	24,000	25,500	30,000
Production overheads	27,500	28,000	28,500	30,000
Other overheads	8,000	8,000	8,000	8,000
Total cost	65,500	68,000	70,500	78,000

4.5 "What if" analysis and scenario planning

What if analysis

This is a technique used to determine how projected performance is affected by changes in the assumptions that those projections are based upon.

What if analysis is often used to compare different scenarios and their potential outcomes based on changing conditions.

For example, the functional budgets example above assumed that Material C would cost $70 per kg. X Plc could recalculate the figures based on a different assumption, for example, what if the cost of Material C was $80 per kg.

What if analysis is also described as sensitivity analysis. This is because it can be used to test the sensitivity of a decision to a change in a variable. For example, suppose a company planned to sell a product for $110 per unit and the product cost $100 per unit. The company would not want to sell the product for $110 if the cost of the product increased by $10 to $110. This would usually be expressed as a percentage increase (product cost sensitivity = 10%).

What if analysis enables a company to make better informed decisions. For example, if a company conducts sensitivity analysis before deciding to increase prices, its decision is less risky than if it did not perform the exercise.

Scenario management tools such as those built into Microsoft Excel can be used to perform what if analysis.

Scenario planning

Scenario planning has its roots in military planning and is now used by business and government to put plans in place to deal with possible (though maybe unlikely) future scenarios. For example:

- Local authorities in the UK have major incident plans in place. For example, if there is a major accident involving a large number of injuries, local hospitals will suspend routine operations and call extra staff into work.

- An oil company might have plans in place to allow it to respond quickly to an explosion on an oil platform.

Scenario planning is a technique which allows plans to be made to deal with possible situations that may arise in the future. It is not a prediction technique but a method of making contingency plans if certain scenarios arise.

Scenario planning involves developing different plausible representations of an organisation's future, based on assumptions about the forces driving the market and including different uncertainties (Kotler and Keller)

Scenarios have the following characteristics;

- a descriptive portrayal of some potential future situation; and
- an analysis of the impact of that situation on the company.

> **Responsibility accounting**
>
> - Controllable costs
> - Responsibility accounting
> - Performance reporting and responsibility accounting
> - Practical difficulties with responsibility accounting
> - Non-financial information for measuring performance

5 Responsibility accounting

5.1 Controllable costs

Revenues and costs might be classified as controllable or uncontrollable. A cost is controllable if a manager is able to take action that will alter its amount. Typically, a cost is controllable if action by a manager may result in a reduction in the cost.

However, a cost might be controllable by one manager in an organisation, but not by another. Management information should attribute costs to the managers who can control them.

A performance management system should try to identify costs, revenues and investments that are:

- directly attributable to a division or performance centre within the organisation, and
- controllable by the manager responsible for the division or performance centre.

However, there are some problems with identifying and measuring controllable costs.

- Costs that are directly attributable to a department or cost centre might not be controllable by the manager of the department or cost centre. For example, the rental costs of a building used by a department are a directly-attributable fixed cost of the department, but the manager of the department might have no control over the decision about whether the department remains in the building or not. The rental cost is therefore directly attributable, but non-controllable by the manager.

- Some costs are partly-controllable, not fully controllable. For example the quantity of materials used by a department might be controllable by its manager, but their purchase price is not controllable if the materials are purchased by a separate buying department. Total material costs depend on both the quantities used and their price. In this situation, quantities would be controllable by one manager and price by another.

Example

A business unit employs 10 staff who are paid a fixed annual salary. The salary costs are directly attributable to the business unit, and salaries are decided centrally by head office. The manager of the unit has no control over salary levels. However, he should be able to influence the efficiency and effectiveness of the employees who work for him. It is therefore appropriate that the manager should be held accountable for the salary costs of the business unit, and the results achieved by incurring those costs, even though he does not have full control.

5.2 Responsibility accounting

Responsibility accounting is a method of reporting based on measuring the performance of responsibility centres within an organisation. The manager of a responsibility centre is responsible and accountable for the performance of the centre.

Responsibility accounting is based on the principle that managers should be responsible – and so held accountable – for costs and other aspects of performance over which they have control. Managers should not be held accountable for costs and other matters over which they have no control.

Cost centres, profit centres and investment centres

This is why, for example, reporting units within an organisation may be:

- cost centres, where the manager is in a position to control costs, but not sales revenue
- profit centres, where the manager is in a position to control costs and sales revenue, but is not in a position to control the amount of investment and other investment decisions
- investment centres, where the manager is in a position to control costs and sales revenue, and also has control over investment decisions affecting the centre.

Within a system for reporting the costs of a centre, a system of responsibility accounting should also try to make a distinction between:

- costs over which the manager should have short-term control: these are often reported as variable costs and directly-controllable fixed costs (or directly attributable fixed costs)
- costs over which the manager has some control, but over the longer term rather than the short term
- costs over which the manager has no control: in some systems of responsibility accounting, centres are not charged at all with any share of general overhead costs that the centre manager cannot control.

There might be a hierarchy of responsibility centres.

- A business entity might be divided into several investment centres (strategic business units or operating subsidiaries).
- Within each investment centre there might be several profit centres.
- Within each profit centre there might be several cost centres and revenue centres.

Although the details of a responsibility accounting system may vary between different entities, the basic principle is consistent: the accounting system should identify performance that a manager should be able to control, and for which he or she should therefore be made responsible and held to account.

5.3 Performance reporting and responsibility accounting

Management information is provided to each responsibility centre manager, usually in the form of regular performance reports that the manager uses to:

- assess performance
- investigate any aspects of performance that seem poor (or very good), and
- take any appropriate control measures, depending on what the investigation reveals.

A management information system for responsibility centres should identify revenues, costs and investment that are directly attributable to each centre, for which the centre manager is responsible and that the centre manager is in a position to control.

Type of responsibility centre	Performance information required
Cost centre	Controllable costs
Revenue centre (for example, a sales team)	Sales revenue
Profit centre	Controllable costs Revenues Profits
Investment centre	Controllable costs Revenues Profit Controllable investment Return on investment

An effective management accounting system must be able to supply the managers of responsibility centres with the information that they need, in a suitable form and with sufficient regularity. Managers must be able to use the information to help them with managing their centre, and taking appropriate control decisions so that actual performance meets (or exceeds) expectations or target.

Example

The manager of an operating division has received the following report about the performance of the division for the financial year that has just ended.

	Current year	Previous year
	$	$
Sales	800,000	500,000
Operating costs excluding depreciation	600,000	390,000
Depreciation	200,000	80,000
Interest charges	40,000	20,000
Profit/(loss)	(40,000)	10,000

The manager is responsible for operations within the division, but has no control over decisions relating to capital expenditure or borrowing to finance expenditure. These decisions are taken by senior executives within the company.

The manager has been asked to explain the deterioration in the performance of the division in the current year. The manager has replied that as far as he is concerned, there has been a significant improvement in performance.

What is the most appropriate method of assessing performance?

 Answer

This performance report shows that although sales revenue has increased from $500,000 to $800,000 compared with the previous year, a $10,000 profit has turned into a $40,000 loss.

However, the division manager has no control over capital expenditure or borrowing. The decline in performance may be due to the increase in depreciation costs and interest charges since the previous year. If so, the decline in performance might be attributable wholly or partly to the buying and borrowing decisions of senior management.

A suitable measure of performance for the manager of the operating division might be operating profit, which is sales revenue minus operating costs. Operating profit may be referred to as:

- profit before interest and tax (PBIT), or possibly
- earnings before interest, tax, depreciation and amortisation (EBITDA).

Using this measure of performance, a performance report might be presented as follows:

	Current year	Previous year
	$	$
Sales	800,000	500,000
Operating costs excluding depreciation	600,000	390,000
Operating profit – manager's responsibility	200,000	110,000
Depreciation	200,000	80,000
Interest charges	40,000	20,000
Profit/(loss) for the division	(40,000)	10,000
Operating profit/sales ratio	25%	22%
Growth in annual sales revenue	60%	

This shows that sales revenue grew by 60% in the current year (presumably helped by new investment in non-current assets for the division) and the ratio of operating profit/sales went up from 22% to 25%. This lends support to the division manager's claim that performance has improved.

5.4 Practical difficulties with responsibility accounting

The principle of responsibility accounting is valid. In practice, however, it is often difficult to apply successfully. The main reason for this is that many costs are only partially controllable.

- A cost centre manager may be in a position to control the efficiency of resource utilisation (for example materials usage, wastage rates, machine utilisation and labour efficiency).

- However, the centre manager may not be able to control purchase prices for materials, the effectiveness of machine repairs by maintenance staff or wage rates for employees under his or her management.

There is a risk that managers will be held responsible for costs or other aspects of poor performance over which they did not have effective control, and so were not in a position to deal with. For example, a production centre manager may be held responsible for a fall in production output during a month, when the reason for the fall was a mistake in the purchasing department, which ordered the wrong materials and so caused a hold-up in production.

If managers are held responsible, within a system of responsibility accounting, for performance that they were unable to control, the reporting system will create problems of motivation. If so, the system may well have the opposite effect of what it was designed to achieve – better performance measurement as a means of giving managers an incentive to improve performance.

Another serious limitation of responsibility accounting systems is the short-term nature of the performance that they measure. Managers are usually held accountable on a monthly, quarterly or annual basis for costs, revenues or return on investment. By concentrating on specific aspects of short-term performance, the reporting system encourages managers to ignore other aspects of performance – including long-term performance.

When a new manager is appointed to manage a responsibility centre, he will inherit the 'legacy' left by his predecessor. For a considerable time, the short-term performance of the centre will be affected by decisions made by the previous manager at some time in the past. As a result, the new manager's performance will be judged – praised or criticised – partly on the basis of another manager's decisions and efforts.

5.5 Non-financial information for measuring performance

Management information systems for planning and measuring performance will often focus on non-financial performance measures as well as on financial performance.

Some business organisations use a 'balanced scorecard' approach to setting planning targets and measuring performance. The main target is a financial performance target, but it is also recognised that non-financial performance is also vitally important for long-term financial success. In a balanced scorecard approach, targets and performance measurements are therefore established for:

- a financial perspective
- an internal business perspective
- a customer perspective, and
- an innovation and learning perspective.

The balanced scorecard approach is described in more detail in a later chapter.

> **Behavioural aspects of budgeting**
>
> - Misunderstanding and worries about cost-cutting
> - Opposition to unfair targets set by senior management
> - Sub-optimisation
> - Budget slack (budget bias)
> - Corporate and individual aspirations
> - Budgets, incentives and performance level
> - Participation in budget setting
> - Top-down budgeting and bottom-up budgeting

6 Behavioural aspects of budgeting

The effectiveness of budgeting and budgetary control depends largely on the behaviour and attitudes of managers and (possibly) other employees.

- Budgets provide performance targets for individual managers. If managers are rewarded for achieving or exceeding their target, budgets could provide them with an incentive and motivation to perform well.

- It has also been suggested that budgets can motivate individuals if they are able to participate in the planning process. Individuals who feel a part of the planning and decision-making process are more likely to identify with the plans that are eventually decided. By identifying with the targets, they might have a powerful motivation to succeed in achieving them.

When budgeting helps to create motivation in individuals, the human aspect of budgeting is positive and good for the organisation.

Unfortunately, in practice human behaviour in the budgeting process often has a negative effect. There are several possible reasons why behavioural factors can be harmful:

- Misunderstanding and worries about cost-cutting
- Opposition to unfair targets set by senior management
- Sub-optimisation
- Budget slack or budget bias

6.1 Misunderstanding and worries about cost-cutting

Budgeting is often considered by the managers affected to be an excuse for cutting back on expenditure and finding ways to reduce costs. Individuals often resent having to reduce their spending, and so have a hostile attitude to the entire budgeting process. This fear and hostility can exist even when senior management do not have a cost-cutting strategy.

6.2 Opposition to unfair targets set by senior management

When senior managers use the budgeting process to set unrealistic and unfair targets for the year, their subordinates may unite in opposition to what the senior managers are trying to achieve. Senior managers should communicate and consult with the individuals affected by target-setting, and try to win their agreement to the targets they are trying to set. Targets need to be reasonable.

A distinction can be made between:

- **aspirational budgets**, which are budgets based on performance levels and targets that senior managers would like to achieve, and
- **expectational budgets**, which are budgets based on performance levels and targets that senior managers would realistically expect to achieve.

Aspirational budgets might be considered unfair, especially if the individuals affected have not been consulted. Expectational budgets, based on current performance levels, do not provide for any improvements in performance.

Ideally perhaps, budgets might be set with realistic targets that provide for some improvements in performance.

6.3 Sub-optimisation

There may be a risk that the planning targets for individual managers are not in the best interests of the organisation as a whole. For example, a production manager might try to budget for production targets that fully utilise production capacity. However, working at full capacity is not in the best interests of the company as a whole if sales demand is lower. It would result in a build-up of unwanted finished goods inventories. The planning process must be co-ordinated in order to avoid sub-optimal planning. In practice, however, effective co-ordination is not always achieved.

6.4 Budget slack (budget bias)

Budget slack has been defined as 'the intentional overestimation of expenses and/or underestimation of revenue in the budgeting process' (CIMA *Official Terminology*). Managers who prepare budgets may try to overestimate costs so that it will be much easier to keep actual spending within the budget limit. Similarly, managers may try to underestimate revenue in their budget so that it will be easier for them to achieve their budget revenue targets. As a result of slack, budget targets are lower than they should be.

When managers are rewarded for achieving their budget targets, the motivation to include some slack in the budget is even stronger.

An additional problem with budget slack is that when a manager has slack in his spending budget, he may try to make sure that actual spending is up to the budget limit. There are two reasons for this:

- If there is significant under-spending, the manager responsible might be required to explain why.

- Actual spending needs to be close to the budget limit in order to keep the budget slack in the budget for the next year.

The problem of budget slack is particularly associated with spending on 'overhead' activities and **incremental budgeting**. One of the advantages of **zero based budgeting** is that it should eliminate a large amount of slack from budgets.

In some cases, budget bias operates the other way. Some managers might prepare budgets that are too optimistic. For example, a sales manager might budget for sales in the next financial year that are unrealistic and unachievable, simply to win the approval of senior management.

6.5 Corporate and individual aspirations

The behavioural problems with budgeting arise because the corporate aims of an organisation are usually not the same as the aspirations of the individuals who work for it. For example, the aim of a company might be to maximise shareholder wealth, but there is no reason at all why this should be the aim of the company's employees and managers. Individuals have their own aims and ambitions, that working might (or might not) satisfy.

The potential conflict between corporate objective and the aspirations of the company's employees can become apparent in the budgeting process, when an organisation sets its targets for the next year.

The accepted wisdom is that there is a potential conflict between corporate and individual aspirations. Individuals will be inclined to do what they want for themselves, regardless of whether this is good for the organisation.

The solution to the problem should be to bring the aspirations of individual managers and other employees as closely as possible into line with the objectives of the organisation. This is the rationale for measures to motivate individuals, such as reward schemes and motivation through participation.

6.6 Budgets, incentives and performance level

Many entities have reward systems based on the achievement of budget performance targets. Rewards often take the form of a cash bonus for certain individuals if actual performance reaches or exceeds the budget target. The purpose of offering rewards for performance is to give managers an incentive to achieve their targets, and to provide goal congruence between the interests of the entity and the personal interests of the manager.

Although rewards such as cash bonuses should provide incentives to improve performance, behavioural problems may arise in the negotiation of targets. This is because the performance target can be set at various different levels. Performance levels can be grouped into three broad types:

- An **'ideal' level** of performance that will only be achieved through exceptional effort, and perhaps is unachievable in practice
- The **current level** of performance, which is the average level of performance that is being achieved at the moment

- A **target level** of performance, which is more challenging than the current level but not as challenging as an ideal level.

Individuals who are offered a bonus for achieving their performance target will probably argue that current performance levels should be used, and that they should be rewarded for performance that is better than this.

Senior managers may prefer to insist on a target level of performance that is higher than current levels of achievement.

Even if it is agreed that the target performance level should be higher than the current level, there is room for negotiation (and differences of opinion) about just how difficult the target ought to be.

6.7 Participation in budget setting

Rewards for performance are intended to motivate individuals to achieve the targets they have been set.

Another view is that individuals can be motivated to improve their performance and to set challenging budgets through their commitment to the work that they do. If individuals enjoy their work and feel committed to performing as well as possible, challenging budget targets can be agreed and better levels of actual performance should be achieved.

Personal motivation to improve performance, it may be argued, can be achieved if individuals are allowed to:

- participate meaningfully in the budget-setting or target-setting process
- be directly involved in negotiating performance targets for the budget period.

Advantages and disadvantages of participation

The **advantages** of participative budgeting are as follows:

- Stronger motivation to achieve budget targets, because individuals are involved in setting or negotiating the targets.
- There should be much better communication of goals and budget targets to the individuals involved, and a better understanding of the target-setting process.
- Involvement by junior managers in budgeting provides excellent experience for personal development
- Better planning decisions – participation might lead to better planning decisions, because 'local' managers often have a much better detailed knowledge of operations and local conditions than senior managers.

However, there are significant **disadvantages** with participation.

- It might be difficult for junior managers to understand the overall objectives of the organisation that budgets should be designed to meet.
- The quality of planning with participation depends on the skills, knowledge and experience of the individuals involved. Participation is not necessarily beneficial in all circumstances, particularly when individuals lack experience.

- There might be a danger that budget targets will be set at a level that is not ambitious. Participation on its own is not necessarily a sufficient incentive to raise standards and targets for achievement. Individuals might try to argue that performance targets should be set at current levels of achievement.

- Senior managers might pretend to be encouraging participation, but in practice they might disregard all the proposals and ideas of their subordinates. To be effective, participation must be 'real'.

- It is generally considered that participation is a good thing, but it needs to be strictly managed by senior management to make sure optimum decisions are taken that are in line with the company's goals.

Imposed budgets

The opposite of a participative budget is an imposed budget, where senior management dictates what the budget targets should be. Imposed budgets have certain advantages:

- Less time consuming. Line managers do not have to spend time on budgeting and so are not distracted from the task of running the business.

- Senior managers may have a greater appreciation of the constraints faced by the business, such as restrictions on cash and other resources, and shareholder expectations of profits and dividends.

- It may be easier to co-ordinate departmental budgets if they are prepared together by senior management.

However the disadvantages of imposed budgets are that:

- Targets may be set at a challenging level and so are unachievable. If unachievable targets are imposed, this will lead to de-motivation.

- Opportunities for exploiting the specialist knowledge of more junior managers may be lost if they are excluded from the budget-setting process.

6.8 Top-down budgeting and bottom-up budgeting

Top-down budgeting

In a system of **top-down budgeting**, the budget targets for the year are set at senior management level, perhaps by the board of directors or by the budget committee. Top-level decisions might be made, for example, about the amount of budgeted profit that will be achieved, the growth in sales, reductions in production costs and other functional department costs, and so on.

Divisions and departments are then required to prepare a budget for their own operations that is consistent with the budget imposed on them from above.

For example, the board of directors might state that in the budget for the next financial year, sales revenue will grow by 5% and profits by 8%. The sales director would then be required to prepare a more detailed sales budget in which the end result is a 5% growth in annual sales revenue. A production budget and other functional budgets will then be prepared that is consistent with the sales budget. The target for 8% growth in profits cannot be checked until all the functional budgets have been prepared in draft form. If the initial draft budgets fail to achieve 8% growth in profits, some re-drafting of the budgets will be required.

This process is called top-down budgeting because it starts at the top with senior management and works its way down to the most detailed level of budgeting within the management hierarchy. This might be departmental level or possibly an even smaller unit level, such as budgets for each work section within each department. A system of top-down budgeting would normally be associated with an entity where management control is highly centralised.

Bottom-up budgeting

In a system of **bottom-up budgeting**, budgeting starts at the lowest level in the management hierarchy where budgets are prepared. This may be at work section level or departmental level. The draft lower-level budgets are then submitted to the next level of management in the hierarchy, which combines them into a co-ordinated budget, for example a departmental budget. Departmental budgets might then be submitted up to the next level of management, which might be at divisional level, where they will be combined and co-ordinated into a divisional budget. Eventually budgets for each division will be submitted up to the budget committee or board of directors.

The budget committee or board of directors will consider the draft budgets they receive, and ask for changes to be made if the overall master budget is unsatisfactory. Re-drafting of budgets will then go on until the master budget is eventually approved.

In a system of bottom-up budgeting, lower levels of management are likely to have more input to budget decision-making than in a top-down budgeting system, and it is associated with budgeting in entities where management authority is largely decentralised.

Practice multiple choice questions

1 In the budgeting process, what is usually considered to be the principal budget factor?

- **A** Sales volume
- **B** Sales price
- **C** Machine capacity
- **D** Skilled labour capacity

(1 mark)

2 A manufacturing company makes and sells a single product, product X. Budgeted sales next year are 20,000 units of product X. Each unit of product X consumes 3 kilos of material. A decision has been taken that inventory of material B will be increased from 9,000 kilos to 18,000 kilos by the end of the year, and inventory of product X will be reduced from 5,000 to 4,000 units during the year.

What is the budgeted materials purchase quantity for material B?

- **A** 57,000 kilos
- **B** 66,000 kilos
- **C** 69,000 kilos
- **D** 72,000 kilos

(2 marks)

3 Which one of the following statements most accurately defines a fixed budget?

A fixed budget is a plan for the entire entity:

- **A** in which no changes are permitted to the plan
- **B** in which there is a specific quantity of output and sales volume
- **C** that can be adjusted for changes in the expected activity level
- **D** that provides useful control information through comparison of budget and actual results.

(1 mark)

4 A company manufactures Product Z. The sales budget for Product Z is 19,000 units. Each unit of product Z uses 2 kilos of a raw material, material T. The materials purchase budget for material T, which is used only in the manufacture of Product Z, is 40,000 kilos. The budget plans for a reduction in the inventory level of material T by 4,000 kilos during the year.

What is the planned change in inventory of Product Z during the year?

- **A** Reduction by 1,000 units
- **B** No change
- **C** Increase by 1,000 units
- **D** Increase by 3,000 units

(2 marks)

5   A company manufactures two products, Product A and Product B, using the same team of direct labour employees. The sales budget for Product A is 12,000 units and budgeted sales of Product B are 15,000 units. The company plans to reduce inventory of Product A from 2,000 units to 1,000 units by the end of the budget period, and to increase inventory of Product B during the same period from 3,000 to 5,000 units. Each unit of Product A requires 2 hours of direct labour and each unit of Product B requires 1.5 hours. Direct labour is paid $18 per hour.

What is the direct labour budget for the year?

A $747,000
B $819,000
C $855,000
D $927,000   *(2 marks)*

You will find the answers to the practice multiple choice questions at the end of this book.

Applied Knowledge
Management Accounting (MA)

CHAPTER 17

Capital budgeting and discounted cash flows

	Contents
1	Investment appraisal and capital budgeting
2	The time value of money: compounding and discounting
3	Net present value (NPV) method of investment appraisal
4	Internal rate of return (IRR) method of investment appraisal
5	Annuities and perpetuities
6	The payback method of investment appraisal
7	Relevant cash flows

> **Investment appraisal and capital budgeting**
>
> - Types of expenditure
> - Investment appraisal
> - Capital budgeting
> - Features of investment projects
> - Profit and cash flow
> - Methods of investment appraisal
> - The basis for making an investment decision

1 Investment appraisal and capital budgeting

1.1 Types of expenditure

Expenditure on assets

This includes expenditure on non-current assets, such as buildings and equipment, or investing in a new business (also known as capital expenditure). As a result of such spending, a new non-current asset appears on the statement of financial position, possibly as an 'investment in subsidiary'.

Expenditure on expense items

This refers to expenditure that does not create long-term assets, but is either written off as an expense in the statement of profit or loss in the period that it is incurred, or that creates a short-term asset (such as the purchase of inventory).

Capital expenditure initiatives are often referred to as investment projects, or 'capital projects'. They can involve just a small amount of spending, but in many cases involve substantial expenditure on new non-current assets.

1.2 Investment appraisal

Before capital expenditure projects are undertaken, they should be assessed and evaluated. As a general rule, projects should not be undertaken unless:

- they are expected to provide a suitable financial return, and
- the investment risk is acceptable.

Investment appraisal is the evaluation of proposed investment projects involving capital expenditure. The purpose of investment appraisal is to make a decision about whether the capital expenditure is worthwhile and whether the investment project should be undertaken.

1.3 Capital budgeting

Capital expenditure by a company should provide a long-term financial return, and spending should therefore be consistent with the company's long-term corporate and financial objectives. Capital expenditure should therefore be made with the intention of implementing chosen business strategies that have been agreed by the board of directors.

Many companies have a capital budget, and capital expenditure is undertaken within the agreed budget framework and capital spending limits. For example, a company might have a five-year capital budget, setting out in broad terms its intended capital expenditure for the next five years. This budget should be reviewed and updated regularly, typically each year.

Within the long-term capital budget, there should be more detailed spending plans for the next year or two.

- Individual capital projects that are formally approved should be included within the capital budget.

- New ideas for capital projects, if they satisfy the investment appraisal criteria and are expected to provide a suitable financial return, might be approved provided that they are consistent with the capital budget and overall spending limits.

Investment appraisal and capital budgets

Investment appraisal therefore takes place within the framework of a capital budget and strategic planning. It involves:

- Generating capital investment proposals in line with the company's strategic objectives

- Forecasting relevant cash flows relating to the project

- Evaluating the projects

- Implementing projects which satisfy the company's criteria for deciding whether the project will earn a satisfactory return on investment

- Monitoring the performance of investment projects to ensure that they perform in line with expectations.

1.4 Features of investment projects

Many investment projects have the following characteristics:

- The project involves the purchase of an asset with an expected life of several years, and involves the payment of a large sum of money at the beginning of the project. Returns on the investment consist largely of net income from additional profits over the course of the project's life.

- The asset might also have a disposal value (residual value) at the end of its useful life.

- A capital project might also need an investment in working capital. Working capital also involves an investment of cash.

Alternatively a capital investment project might involve the purchase of another business, or setting up a new business venture. These projects involve an initial capital outlay, and possibly some working capital investment. Financial returns from the investment might be expected over a long period of time, perhaps indefinitely.

1.5 Profit and cash flow

When a business makes a profit of $1,000, this does not mean that it receives $1,000 more in cash than it has spent. Profit and cash flow are different, for several reasons:

There are items of cost in the statement of profit or loss that do not represent a cash flow. Examples are:

- depreciation and amortisation charges
- the gain or loss on the disposal of non-current assets.

There are items of cash flow that do not appear in the statement of profit or loss. Examples are:

- Cash flows relating to the acquisition or disposal of investments, such as the purchase of new non-current assets, and cash from the sale of non-current assets. (The statement of profit or loss includes gains or losses on the disposal of non-current assets, but this is not the same as the cash proceeds from the sale).
- Cash flows relating to financial transactions, such as obtaining cash by issuing shares or obtaining loans, the repayment of loans and the payment of dividends to ordinary shareholders.

Some investment appraisal methods are based on profit and others on cash.

1.6 Methods of investment appraisal

There are different methods of evaluating a proposed capital expenditure project. Any or all of the methods can be used but which method is chosen depends on what the company is looking to achieve in buying the asset.

Common investment appraisal methods include:

- Payback method
- Payback method using discounted cash flows
- Discounted cash flow (DCF) methods:
    - Net Present Value (NPV) method
    - Internal Rate of Return (IRR) method

1.7 The basis for making an investment decision

When deciding whether or not to make a capital investment, management must decide on a basis for decision-making. The decision to invest or not invest will be made for **financial reasons** in most cases, although non-financial considerations could be important as well.

There are different financial reasons that might be used to make a capital investment decision. Management could consider:

- the time it will take to recover the cash invested in the project. If so, they might use the **payback period** as the basis for the investment decision.

- the expected investment returns from the project. If so, they should use **discounted cash flow (DCF)** as a basis for their decision. DCF considers both the size of expected future returns and the length of time before they are earned.

There are two different ways of using DCF as a basis for making an investment decision:

- **Net present value (NPV) approach.** With this approach, a present value is given to the expected costs of the project and the expected benefits. The value of the project is measured as the net present value (= the present value of income or benefits minus the present value of costs). The project should be undertaken if it adds value. It adds value if the net present value is positive (greater than 0).

- **Internal rate of return (IRR) approach.** With this approach, the expected return on investment over the life of the project is calculated, and compared with the minimum required investment return. The project should be undertaken if its expected return (as an average percentage annual amount) exceeds the required return.

NPV is believed to be the superior technique. This is because it takes account of cash flows (which are not affected by accounting policies) and the time value of money which is explained later in the chapter.

NPV also selects the projects which meet the most common corporate objective which is to maximise shareholders' wealth. Theoretically, the NPV of a project is the amount by which the market value of a business will increase. Therefore, if a company wants to increase its market value by as much as possible it should select projects with the highest NPV.

> **The time value of money: compounding and discounting**
>
> - Interest rates
> - The time value of money
> - Compounding
> - Discounting
> - Discount factors
> - Introduction to discounted cash flow (DCF) analysis

2 The time value of money: compounding and discounting

Discounted cash flow analysis (DCF) is a method of evaluating proposed capital investments, that:

- evaluates the expected cash flows of the investment, not accounting profits, and
- recognises the relevance of the time value of money.

2.1 Interest rates

When a person or entity borrows money the lender will usually charge interest.

Compound interest – this is where the annual interest is based on the amount borrowed plus interest accrued to date. For example if a person borrows $1,000 at 10% to be repaid after 3 years, interest in year 1 will be $100. Interest in year 2 will be $110 (10% of $1,000 + $100). Interest in year 3 will be $121 (10% of $1,000 + $100 + $110). Note that this assumes that there are no annual payments made to the lender.

Simple interest is interest that is not compounded.

Simple' interest is where the annual interest is a fixed percentage of the original amount borrowed. For example, if a person borrows $1,000 at 10% simple interest, they will have to pay $100 per annum interest over the duration of the loan. This implies that the interest is actually paid on an annual basis.

Nominal and effective rates

The nominal rate is the "face value" cost of a loan. However, this might not be the true annual cost because it does not take into account the way the loan is compounded.

Example

A company wants to borrow $1,000. It has been offered two different loans.

Loan A charges interest at 10% per annum and loan B at 5% per 6 months.

Which loan should it take?

The nominal interest rates are not useful in making the decision because they relate to different periods. They can be made directly comparable by restating them to a common period. This is usually per annum.

	Loan A	Loan B
Amount borrowed	1,000	1,000
Interest added:		
		50
		1,050
	100	52.5
	1,100	1,1025
Effective rate per annum	10%	10.25%

The effective annual rate can be calculated as:

$(1 + \text{period rate})^{\text{Number of times it fits into a year}} - 1$

For loan B

$(1.05)^{\text{number of times it fits into a year}} - 1$

$(1.05)^2 - 1 = 0.1025$ or 10.25% per annum

Therefore Loan A is preferable

2.2 The time value of money

Companies make investments in order to earn a return. They want to recover their investment, and in addition make a profit. However investments and investment returns should be measured by their cash flows, not their accounting profits. Companies that invest are no different in this respect from individuals who invest.

Money has a time value, because an investor expects a return that allows for the length of time that the money is invested. Larger cash returns should be required for investing for a longer term.

Example

If $1,000 is invested at 10% annual interest, the investor will want a return of:

$1,100 (= $1,000 × 1.10^1) if it is a one-year investment, but

$1,210 (= $1,000 × 1.10^2) if it is a two-year investment and

$1,331 (= $1,000 × 1.10^3) if it is a three-year investment.

Investment returns can be measured by compounding or discounting.

2.3 Compounding

Compounding is used to calculate the future value of an investment, where the investment earns a compound rate of interest. If an investment is made 'now' and is expected to earn interest at r% in each time period, for example each year, the future value of the investment can be calculated as follows.

Future return = Initial investment $\times (1 + r)^n$

The term 'future value' or 'FV' means the value of an investment or cash flow at a future date. 'Present value' or 'PV' refers to value now. The above compound interest formula can therefore be stated as:

$FV = PV \times (1 + r)^n$.

Notes

r = the return on the investment each time period (year). This might be an actual return or a required return.

n = the number of time periods (years) covered by the investment.

r is expressed as a proportion. For example:

- if the return is 12%, r = 0.12
- if the return is 7%, r = 0.07
- if the return is 8.5%, r = 0.085.

Example
A company is investing $200,000 to earn an annual return of 6% over three years. If there are no cash returns before the end of Year 3, what will be the return from the investment after three years?

Answer
$200,000 $\times 1.06^3$ = $238,203.

2.4 Discounting

Discounting is the reverse of compounding. Future cash flows from an investment can be converted to an equivalent present value amount.

Present value of future return = Future value of return $\times [1/(1 + r)^n]$

$PV = FV \times [1/(1 + r)^n]$.

The present value of a future cash flow from an investment is the amount that would have to be invested now, at the investment cost of capital, to earn that future cash flow.

Example

How much would an investor need to invest now in order to have $1,000 after 12 months, if the compound interest on the investment is 0.5% each month?

Answer

The future value of the investment return is $1,000 after 12 months. The investment 'now' would have to be the present value of $1,000 after 12 months, discounted at 0.5% per month.

Present value = $1,000 × [1/(1.005)^{12}] = $1,000 × 0.942 = $942.

Example

An investor wants to make a return on his investments of at least 7% per year. He has been offered the chance to invest in a bond that will cost $200,000 and will pay $270,000 at the end of four years. If there is no investment risk with the bond, should he undertake the investment?

Answer

If the investor could invest his money at 7% per year, then in order to earn $270,000 after four years the amount of his investment now would need to be:

PV = $270,000 × 1/(1.07)^4 = $270,000 × 0.763

= $206,010.

He is required to invest only $200,000 to earn $270,000 after 4 years. This indicates that the bond will provide a return in excess of 7% per year. It can also be suggested that the bond would give the investor an immediate increase in wealth of $6,010 because an investment costing $200,000 is actually 'worth' $206,010 to him.

2.5 Discount factors

A discount factor is $1/(1 + r)^n$. Future cash flows or investment values are multiplied by the appropriate discount factor to convert them into a present value.

Present value = Future cash flow × Discount factor

The discount factor is smaller for higher values of r and higher values of n.

2.6 Introduction to discounted cash flow (DCF) analysis

Discounted cash flow is a technique for evaluating proposed investments, to decide whether they are financially worthwhile.

The expected future cash flows from the investment (cash payments and cash receipts) are all converted to a present value by discounting them at the cost of capital r. The present value of investment costs and the present value of the investment returns (cash benefits or returns) can be compared.

There are two methods of DCF:

- **Net present value (NPV) method**: the cost of capital r is the return required by the investor or company
- **Internal rate of return (IRR) method**: the cost of capital r is the actual return expected from the investment.

> **Net present value (NPV) method of investment appraisal**
>
> - Calculating the NPV of an investment project
> - Assumptions about the timing of cash flows
> - Discount tables
> - Advantages and disadvantages of the NPV method

3 Net present value (NPV) method of investment appraisal

With the NPV method of investment appraisal, all the future cash flows from an investment are converted into a present value by discounting each future cash flow at the investment cost of capital. This cost of capital is the return required from the investment.

The present value of a future cash inflow from a capital project is the amount that would have to be invested now at the cost of capital to obtain that cash flow in the future. For example suppose that a project is expected to provide a cash return of $40,000 after two years and a further $50,000 after three years, and the company needs to make a return of 10% per year. The NPV approach to investment appraisal is to convert these expected future cash inflows into their present value equivalent.

- The present value of these future cash flows would be the amount that the company would need to invest now at 10% per year to obtain a return of $40,000 after two years and another $50,000 after three years.

- The present value of the expected cash flows is therefore the value to the company, in terms of 'today's value' of those cash flows in the future.

3.1 Calculating the NPV of an investment project

In NPV analysis, all future cash flows from a project are converted into a present value, so that the value of all the annual cash outflows and cash inflows can be expressed in terms of 'today's value'.

The net present value (NPV) of a project is the net difference between the present value of all the costs incurred and the present value of all the cash flow benefits (savings or revenues).

- If the present value of benefits exceeds the present value of costs, the NPV is positive.

- If the present value of benefits is less than the present value of costs, the NPV is negative.

- The NPV is 0 when the PV of benefits and the PV of costs are equal.

The **decision rule** is that, ignoring other factors such as risk and uncertainty, and non-financial considerations, a project is worthwhile financially if the NPV is positive or zero. It is not worthwhile if the NPV is negative.

The **net present value** of an investment project is also **a measure of the value of the investment**. For example, if a company invests in a project that has a NPV of $2 million, the value of the company should increase by $2 million.

3.2 Assumptions about the timing of cash flows

In DCF analysis, the following assumptions are made about the timing of cash flows during each year:

- All cash flows for the investment are assumed to occur at the end of the year
- If a cash flow will occur early during a particular year, it is assumed that it will occur at the end of the previous year. Therefore cash expenditure early in Year 1, for example, is assumed to occur in Year 0.

Year 0 cash flows

Cash flows at the beginning of the investment, in Year 0, are already stated at their present value.

The discount factor for a cash flow in Year 0 is $1/(1 + r)^0$.

Any value to the power of 0 is always = 1. Therefore the discount factor for Year 0 is always = 1.000, for any cost of capital.

This means that the present value of $1 in year 0 is always $1, for any cost of capital.

Example

A company estimates that its cost of capital is 10%. It is considering whether to invest in a project with the following cash flows and will make the decision on the basis of the net present value of the project:

Year	$
0	(10,000)
1	6,000
2	8,000

Should the project be undertaken?

Answer

The cash flow in each year must be converted into a present value, using a discount rate of 10%. Negative cash flows have a negative present value and positive cash flows have a positive present value. The sum of the present values in each year is the net present value of the investment.

Year	Cash flow	Discount factor at 10%	Present value
	$		$
0	(10,000)	1	(10,000)
1	6,000	1/(1.10)	5,456
2	8,000	1/(1.10)²	6,612
		NPV	2,068

The project should be accepted, ignoring other factors such as risk and uncertainty, because it has a positive NPV of $2,068.

(**Note:** The figures here are rounded to the nearest $1. It might be more appropriate to round to the nearest $100 or even the nearest $1,000, depending on the degree of accuracy that is required or that is appropriate, given the inevitable uncertainties in the cash flow estimates).

The positive NPV shows that in order to earn a cash return of $6,000 after one year and $8,000 after two years, for an investment return of 10%, the company would need to invest $12,068 now. Instead, by investing just $10,000 in the project, it will obtain the same returns so which is better: investing $10,000 or investing $12,068 in order to obtain exactly the same returns? Clearly, the answer is that it is better to invest $10,000. The project will provide a return in excess of 10% per year.

Example

A company is considering whether to undertake an investment. The cost of capital is 10%. The initial cost of the investment would be $50,000 and the expected annual cash flows from the project would be:

Year	Revenue	Costs	Net cash flow
	$	$	$
1	40,000	30,000	10,000
2	55,000	35,000	20,000
3	82,000	40,000	42,000

Required

(a) Use compounding arithmetic to calculate what the investment should be worth at the end of Year 3.

(b) Using discounting, calculate the NPV of the project.

(c) Reconcile the future value of the investment (calculated by compounding) with the NPV.

Answer

Compounding	$
Investment in Year 0	(50,000)
Interest required (10%), Year 1	(5,000)
Return required, end of Year 1	(55,000)
Net cash flow, Year 1	10,000
	(45,000)
Interest required (10%), Year 2	(4,500)
Return required, end of Year 2	(49,500)
Net cash flow, Year 2	20,000
	(29,500)
Interest required (10%), Year 3	(2,950)
Return required, end of Year 3	(32,450)
Net cash flow, Year 3	42,000
Future value, end of Year 3	9,550

Discounting: NPV method

Year	Cash flow	Discount factor at 10%	Present value
	$		$
0	(50,000)	1.0	(50,000)
1	10,000	$1/(1.10)^1$	9,091
2	20,000	$1/(1.10)^2$	16,529
3	42,000	$1/(1.10)^3$	31,555
Net present value			+7,175

Reconciliation of present value and future value

NPV × $(1 + r)^n$ = Future value: $7,175 × $(1.10)^3$ = $9,550

This example shows a simple capital project with an initial capital outlay in Year 0 and cash inflows for three years. The same technique can be applied to much bigger and longer capital projects, and projects with negative cash flows in years other than Year 0.

3.3 Discount tables

Discount tables are available. They take away the need to calculate the value of discount factors $[1/(1 + r)^n]$. Discount tables are included in the formula and tables sheets at the beginning of this study text.

Discount tables are provided in your examination, and the discount factors in the tables are rounded to three decimal places.

An extract from discount tables is shown below.

Discount rates (r)

Periods (n)	1%	2%	3%	4%	5%	6%	7%	8%	9%	10%
1	0.990	0.980	0.971	0.962	0.952	0.943	0.935	0.926	0.917	0.909
2	0.980	0.961	0.943	0.925	0.907	0.890	0.873	0.857	0.842	0.826
3	0.971	0.942	0.915	0.889	0.864	0.840	0.816	0.794	0.772	0.751
4	0.961	0.924	0.888	0.855	0.823	0.792	0.763	0.735	0.708	0.683
5	0.951	0.906	0.863	0.822	0.784	0.747	0.713	0.681	0.650	0.621

For example, suppose that you need to calculate the present value of $60,000 in Year 4 if the cost of capital (discount rate) is 7%.

You could use your calculator to calculate: $60,000 \times 1/(1.07)^4 = \$45,774$.

Alternatively, you could use discount tables to calculate: $60,000 \times 0.763 = \$45,780$.

The rounding difference is insignificant.

3.4 Advantages and disadvantages of the NPV method

The **advantages** of the NPV method of investment appraisal are that:

- NPV takes account of the timing of the cash flows by calculating the present value for each cash flow at the investor's cost of capital.

- DCF is based on cash flows, not accounting profits. It is therefore much more suitable than the Accounting Rate of Return (ARR) method for investment appraisal.

- It evaluates all cash flows from the project, unlike the payback method which considers only those cash flows in the payback period.

- It gives a single figure, the NPV, which can be used to assess the value of the investment project. The NPV of a project is the amount by which the project should add to the value of the company, in terms of 'today's value'.

- The NPV method provides a decision rule which is consistent with objective of maximisation of shareholders' wealth. In theory, a company ought to increase in value by the NPV of an investment project (assuming that the NPV is positive).

The main **disadvantages** of the NPV method are:

- The time value of money and present value are concepts are not easily understood.

- There might be some uncertainty about what the appropriate cost of capital or discount rate should be for applying to any project.

Internal rate of return (IRR) method of investment appraisal

- The investment decision rule with IRR
- Calculating the IRR of an investment project
- Advantages and disadvantages of the IRR method
- Summary: comparison of the three investment appraisal methods

4 Internal rate of return (IRR) method of investment appraisal

The internal rate of return method (IRR method) is another method of investment appraisal using DCF.

The internal rate of return of a project is the discounted rate of return on the investment.

- It is the average annual investment return from the project
- Discounted at the IRR, the NPV of the project cash flows must come to 0.

The internal rate of return is therefore the discount rate that will give a net present value = $0.

4.1 The investment decision rule with IRR

A company might establish the minimum rate of return that it wants to earn on an investment. If other factors such as non-financial considerations and risk and uncertainty are ignored:

- If a project IRR is equal to or higher than the minimum acceptable rate of return, it should be undertaken
- If the IRR is lower than the minimum required return, it should be rejected.

Since NPV and IRR are both methods of DCF analysis, the same investment decision should normally be reached using either method.

The internal rate of return is illustrated in the diagram below:

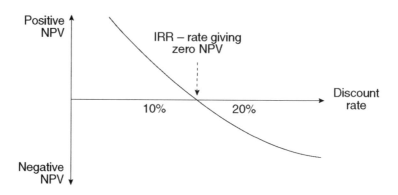

4.2 Calculating the IRR of an investment project

The IRR of a project can be calculated by inputting the project cash flows into a financial calculator. In you examination, you might be required to calculate an IRR without a financial calculator. An approximate IRR can be calculated using interpolation.

To calculate the IRR, you should begin by calculating the NPV of the project at two different discount rates.

- One of the NPVs should be positive, and the other NPV should be negative. (This is not essential. Both NPVs might be positive or both might be negative, but the estimate of the IRR will then be less reliable).
- Ideally, the NPVs should both be close to zero, for better accuracy in the estimate of the IRR.

When the NPV for one discount rate is positive NPV and the NPV for another discount rate is negative, the IRR must be somewhere between these two discount rates.

Although in reality the graph of NPVs at various discount rates is a curved line, as shown in the diagram above, using the interpolation method we **assume that the graph is a straight line** between the two NPVs that we have calculated. We can then use **linear interpolation** to estimate the IRR, to a reasonable level of accuracy.

The interpolation formula

If the NPV at A% is positive, + $P

and if the NPV at B% is negative, - $N

$$IRR = A\% + \left[\frac{P}{P+N} \times (B-A)\% \right]$$

Ignore the minus sign for the negative NPV. For example, if P = + 75 and N = - 30, then P + N = 105.

Example

A business requires a minimum expected rate of return of 12% on its investments. A proposed capital investment has the following expected cash flows.

Year	$
0	(80,000)
1	20,000
2	36,000
3	30,000
4	17,000

Required

Calculate the NPV at a cost of capital of 10% and a cost of capital of 15%. Use these NPV figures to estimate the IRR

Answer

Year	Cash flow	Discount factor at 10%	Present value at 10%	Discount factor at 15%	Present value at 15%
	$		$		$
0	(80,000)	1.000	(80,000)	1,000	(80,000)
1	20,000	0.909	18,180	0.870	17,400
2	36,000	0.826	29,736	0.756	27,216
3	30,000	0.751	22,530	0.658	19,740
4	17,000	0.683	11,611	0.572	9,724
NPV			+ 2,057		(5,920)

The IRR is above 10% but below 15%.

Using the interpolation method:

- The NPV is + 2,057 at 10%.
- The NPV is – 5,920 at 15%.
- The NPV therefore falls by 7,977 between 10% and 15%.

The estimated IRR is: $IRR = 10\% + \left[\dfrac{2,057}{(2,057 + 5,920)} \times (15 - 10)\% \right]$

= 10% + 1.3%

= 11.3%

Recommendation

The project is expected to earn a DCF return below the target rate of 12%, and on financial grounds it is not a worthwhile investment.

4.3 Advantages and disadvantages of the IRR method

The main **advantages** of the IRR method of investment appraisal are:

- As a DCF appraisal method, it is based on cash flows, not accounting profits.
- Like the NPV method, it recognises the time value of money.
- It is easier to understand an investment return as a percentage return on investment than as a money value NPV in $.
- For accept/reject decisions on individual projects, the IRR method will reach the same decision as the NPV method.

The **disadvantages** of the IRR method are:

- It is a relative measure (% on investment) not absolute measure in $. Because it is a relative measure, it ignores the absolute size of the investment. For example, which is the better investment if the cost of capital is 10%:
    - an investment $1m with an IRR of 15% or
    - an investment $1,000 with an IRR of 20%?
- If the investments are mutually exclusive, and only one of them can be undertaken the correct answer is that it depends on the size of each of the investments. This means that the IRR method of appraisal can give an incorrect decision if it is used to make a choice between mutually exclusive projects
- Unlike the NPV method, the IRR method does not indicate by how much an investment project should add to the value of the company.

Example

There are two mutually exclusive projects.

Year	Project 1	Project 2
	$	$
	(1,000)	(10,000)
	1,200	4,600
	-	4,600
	-	4,600
IRR	20%	18%
NPV at 15%	+ $43	+ $503

Which is better?

Answer

Project 2 is better, because it has the higher NPV. Project 2 will add to value by $503 but Project 1 will add value of just $43.

4.4 Summary: comparison of the three investment appraisal methods

A comparison of the three investment appraisal methods is given in the table below. The **key points to note** are that:

- DCF is superior to the payback method of investment appraisal
- It is often equally as good to use NPV or IRR
- However, NPV has two advantages over IRR
    - The NPV method indicates the value that the investment should add (if the NPV is positive) or the value that it will destroy (if the NPV is negative).
    - When there are two or more mutually exclusive projects, the NPV will always identify the project that should be selected. This is the project that will provide the highest value (NPV).
- The IRR method has the advantage of being more easily understood by non-accountants
- Another disadvantage of the IRR method is that a project might have two or more different IRRs, when some annual cash flows during the life of the project are negative. (The mathematics that demonstrate this point are not shown here.)

Payback	Discounted cash flow	
Advantages	*Advantages*	
Cash flows, not accounting values	Based on investment cash flows, not accounting profit	
	Recognises the time value of money	
Focus on recovering the cost of the investment	Recognises all cash flows, over the full life of the project	
	By far the best investment appraisal method	
	Required return is based on the organisation's cost of finance.	
Disadvantages	*NPV*	*IRR*
Choice of maximum payback period is arbitrary	Indicates the increase in the value of the company that should be expected if it were to undertake the investment.	More easily understood than NPV by a non-accountant.
Ignores cash from the project after payback	If a choice has to be made between two (or more) **mutually exclusive projects**, the **NPV method is more reliable** than IRR.	
Ignores the time value of money.		

Chapter 17: Capital budgeting and discounted cash flows

> **Annuities and perpetuities**
>
> - Definition of an annuity
> - Calculating the PV of an annuity
> - Annuity discount tables
> - Using annuities and annuity factors for investment appraisal
> - Definition of a perpetuity
> - Present value of a perpetuity

5 Annuities and perpetuities

5.1 Definition of an annuity

An annuity is a constant cash flow for a given number of time periods. A capital project might include estimated annual cash flows that are an annuity.

Examples of annuities are:

- $30,000 each year for years 1 – 5
- $20,000 each year for years 3 – 10
- $500 each month for months 1 – 24.

The present value of an annuity can be calculated using annuity factors, rather than using discount factors to calculate the present value of the cash flow for each individual year.

5.2 Calculating the PV of an annuity

If you need to calculate the present value of $50,000 per year for years 1 – 3 at a discount rate of 9%, you could calculate this as follows:

Year	Cash flow	Discount factor at 9%	Present value
	$		$
1	50,000	1/(1.09) = 0.917	45,850
2	50,000	$1/(1.09)^2$ = 0 842	42,100
3	50,000	$1/(1.09)^3$ = 0.772	38,600
		NPV	126,550

There is a formula for calculating the present value of an annuity. The formula is:

$$PV = \frac{A}{r} \times \left[1 - \frac{1}{(1+r)^n}\right]$$

Where:

A = the constant annual cash flow (the annuity)

r = discount rate, as a proportion

n = number of time periods

The present value of $50,000 per year for three years at a discount rate of 9% can therefore be calculated as:

$$\frac{\$50,000}{0.09} \times \left[1 - \frac{1}{(1.09)^3}\right] = [\$50,000/0.09] \times (1 - 0.0.77218) = \$555,555 \times 0.22782$$

= $126,567.

5.3 Annuity discount tables

Another way of calculating the PV of an annuity is to multiply the annuity by the sum of the discount factors for the years in which the cash flows occur. In the example above, the PV of $50,000 for years 1 – 3 at a discount rate of 9% could be calculated as:

$50,000 × (0.917 + 0.842 + 0.772) = $50,000 × 2.531 = $126,550.

The discount factors for annuities are simply the sum of the annual discount factors for each year of the annuity. Discount tables for annuities are included in the formula and tables sheets near the start of this text. These tables will be provided in your examination. An extract is shown below.

Extract from annuity tables

Periods (n)	\multicolumn{10}{c}{Discount rates (r)}									
	1%	2%	3%	4%	5%	6%	7%	8%	9%	10%
1	0.990	0.980	0.971	0.962	0.952	0.943	0.935	0.926	0.917	0.909
2	1.970	1.942	1.913	1.886	1.859	1.833	1.808	1.783	1.759	1.736
3	2.941	2.884	2.829	2.775	2.723	2.673	2.624	2.577	2.531	2.487
4	3.902	3.808	3.717	3.630	3.546	3.465	3.387	3.312	3.240	3.170
5	4.853	4.713	4.580	4.452	4.329	4.212	4.100	3.993	3.890	3.791

The annuity factors are for periods starting in period 1 (year 1). For example, the annuity factor for years 1 – 3 at 9%, from the table, is 2.531.

Examples

The annuity factor for years 1 – 2 at a cost of capital of 8% = 1.783 (n = 2, discount factor 8%. This is the sum of the discount factors at 8% for years 1, and 2 (0.926 + 0.857).

The annuity factor for years 1 – 5 at a cost of capital of 10% = 3.791 (n = 5, discount factor = 10%). This is the sum of the discount factors at 10% for years 1, 2, 3, 4 and 5 (0.909 + 0.826 + 0.751 + 0.683 + 0.621).

5.4 Using annuities and annuity factors for investment appraisal

Annuity discount factors can be used in DCF investment analysis, mainly to make the calculations easier and quicker.

Example
What is the present value of the cash flows for a project, if the cash flows are $60,000 each year for years 1 – 7, and the cost of capital is 15%?

Answer
$60,000 × 4.160 (annuity factor at 15%, n = 7) = $249,600.

Example
What is the present value of the following cash flows, when the cost of capital is 12%?

Year	Annual cash flow	Discount factor at 12%	Present value
	$		$
0	(100,000)		
1	10,000		
2	15,000		
3 – 15	20,000		
NPV			

Answer
Annuity factor at 12%, years 1 – 15 = 6.811

Annuity factor at 12%, years 1 – 2 = 1.690

Therefore annuity factor at 12%, years 3 – 15 = 6.811 – 1.690 = 5.121

Year	Annual cash flow	Discount factor at 12%	Present value
	$		$
0	(100,000)	1.000	(100,000)
1	10,000	0.893	8,930
2	15,000	0.797	11,955
3 – 15	20,000	5.121	102,420
NPV			+23,305

Example

A company is considering an investment of $70,000 in a project. The project life would be five years.

What must be the minimum annual cash returns from the project to earn a return of at least 9% per annum?

Answer

Investment = $70,000

Annuity factor at 9%, years 1 – 5 = 3.890

Minimum annuity required = $17,995 (= $70,000/3.890)

5.5 Definition of a perpetuity

A perpetuity is a constant annual cash flow 'forever', or into the long-term future.

In investment appraisal, an annuity might be assumed when a constant annual cash flow is expected for a long time into the future.

5.6 Present value of a perpetuity

The present value of a perpetuity is C/r, where:

- C is the constant annual cash flow in perpetuity
- r is the cost of capital, for example 0.08, 0.10 etcetera.

Examples

The present value of $2,000 in perpetuity, starting in Year 1, given a cost of capital of 8%, is: $2,000/0.08 = $25,000.

The present value of $5,500 in perpetuity, starting in Year 4, given a cost of capital of 11%, is calculated as follows:

- The perpetuity starts in Year 4, therefore the 'present value' as at the end of Year 3 = $5,500/0.11 = $50,000.
- At a discount rate of 11%, the present value (Year 0 value) of $50,000 as at the end of Year 3

    = $50,000 × discount factor for Year 3 at 11%

    = $50,000 × 0.731

    = $36,550.

Chapter 17: Capital budgeting and discounted cash flows

> **The payback method of investment appraisal**
>
> - Definition of payback
> - Decision rule for the payback method
> - Advantages and disadvantages of the payback method
> - Discounted payback period

6 The payback method of investment appraisal

6.1 Definition of payback

Payback is the length of time before the cash invested in a project will be recovered (paid back) from the net cash returns from the investment project.

For example, suppose that a project will involve capital expenditure of $80,000 and the annual net cash returns from the project will be $30,000 each year for five years. The expected payback period is:

$$\frac{\$80,000}{\$30,000} = 2.67 \text{ years.}$$

6.2 Decision rule for the payback method

Using the payback method, a maximum acceptable payback period is decided, as a matter of policy. The expected payback period for the project is calculated.

- If the expected payback is within the maximum acceptable time limit, the project is acceptable.
- If the expected payback does not happen until after the maximum acceptable time limit, the project is not acceptable.

The **time value of money** is ignored, and the total return on investment is not considered.

Example

A company requires all investment projects to pay back their initial investment within three years. It is considering a new project requiring a capital outlay of $140,000 on plant and equipment and an investment of $20,000 in working capital. The project is expected to earn the following net cash receipts:

Year	
1	$40,000
2	$50,000
3	$90,000
4	$25,000

Should the investment be undertaken?

Management Accounting (MA)

 Answer

Note that for the purpose of investment appraisal, 'now' is usually referred to as 'Year 0'.

The investment in working capital should be included as an outflow of cash at the beginning of the project. This is because when there is an increase in working capital, cash flows are lower than cash profits by the amount of the increase.

Similarly when working capital is reduced to $0 at the end of the project, the reduction is added to cash flows because when there is a reduction in working capital, cash flows are higher than cash profits by the amount of the reduction.

Year	Cash flow	Cumulative cash position at the end of the year	
	$	$	
0	(160,000)	(160,000)	(= $140,000 + $20,000)
1	40,000	(120,000)	
2	50,000	(70,000)	
3	90,000	20,000	
4	465,000	65,000	cash flow = $25,000 + $20,000

(a) If we assume that all cash flows occur at the end of each year, the payback period is three years.

(b) If we assume that cash flows arise evenly over the course of each year, then the payback period is:

2 years + (70,000/90,000) year

= 2.78 years = 2 years 9 months.

The investment should be undertaken.

Note: The payback period of 2 years 9 months is calculated as follow.

(1) Payback occurs during the third year. At the beginning of year 3 the cumulative cash flow is $(70,000). During the year there are net cash flows of $90,000. The cumulative cash flow therefore starts to become positive, assuming even cash flows through the year, after 70,000/90,000 of the year = 0.78 year.

(2) A decimal value for a year can be converted into months by multiplying by 12, or into days by multiplying by 365. So 0.78 years = 9 months (= 0.78 × 12) or 285 days (= 0.78 × 365).

6.3 Advantages and disadvantages of the payback method

The **advantages** of the payback method for investment appraisal are as follows:

- Simplicity – The payback is easy to calculate and understand.

- The method analyses cash flows, not accounting profits. Investments are about investing cash to earn cash returns. In this respect, the payback method is better than the ARR method.

- Payback is often used together with a DCF method, particularly by companies that have liquidity problems and do not want to tie up cash for long periods.

Payback can be used to eliminate projects that will take too long to pay back. Investments that pass the payback test can then be evaluated using one of the DCF methods.

The **disadvantages** of the payback method are as follows:

- It ignores all cash flows after the payback period, and so ignores the total cash returns from the project. This is a significant weakness with the payback method.

- It ignores the timing of the cash flows during the payback period. For example, for an investment of $100,000, cash flows of $10,000 in Year 1 and $90,000 in Year 2 are no different from cash flows of $90,000 in Year 1 and $10,000 in Year 2, because both pay back after two years. However it is clearly better to receive $90,000 in Year 1 and $10,000 in Year 2 than to receive $10,000 in Year 1 and $90,000 in Year 2.

6.4 Discounted payback period

Instead of using the ordinary payback to decide whether a project is acceptable, discounted payback might be used as an alternative. A maximum discounted payback period is established and projects should not be undertaken unless they pay back within this time.

A consequence of applying a discounted payback rule (and the same applies to ordinary payback) is that projects are unlikely to be accepted if they rely on cash profits in the long-term future to make a suitable financial return. Since longer-term estimates of cash flows are usually more unreliable than estimates in the shorter-term, using discounted payback as a criterion for project selection will result in the rejection of risky projects.

A discounted payback period is calculated in the same way as the 'ordinary' payback period, with the exception that the cash flows of the project are converted to their present value. The discounted payback period is the number of years before the cumulative NPV of the project reaches $0.

Year	Annual cash flow
	$
0	(200,000)
1	(40,000)
2	30,000
3	120,000
4	150,000
5	100,000
6	50,000

The discounted payback period is calculated as follows.

Year	Annual cash flow	Discount factor at 10%	PV of cash flow	Cumulative NPV
	$		$	$
0	(200,000)	1.000	(200,000)	(200,000)
1	(40,000)	0.909	(36,360)	(236,360)
2	30,000	0.826	24,780	(211,580)
3	120,000	0.751	90,120	(121,460)
4	150,000	0.683	102,450	(19,010)
5	100,000	0.621	62,100	43,090
6	50,000	0.564	28,200	71,290
NPV			**+ 71,290**	

The discounted payback period is Year 5, and we can estimate it in years and months as:

4 years + (19,010/62,100) × 12 months

= 4 years 4 months.

The discounted period for a capital investment is always longer than the 'ordinary' non-discounted payback period.

One criticism of the discounted payback method of project evaluation is the same as for the non-discounted payback method. It ignores the expected cash flows from the project after the payback period has been reached.

Relevant cash flows

- Introduction
- Relevant cost of materials
- Relevant cost of existing equipment
- Relevant cost of investment in working capital

7 Relevant cash flows

7.1 Introduction

Decisions must be based on relevant information. Therefore, it is necessary to identify those cash flows (both costs and revenues) which are relevant to a decision.

This applies to both the payback method DCF.

Relevant cash flows are all of the future incremental cash flows that arise as a result of the decision. In other words, relevant costs and benefits are future cash flows arising as a direct consequence of the decision under consideration.

- **Relevant cash flows.** Any items of cost or revenue that are not cash flows must be ignored for the purpose of decision. For example, depreciation expenses are not cash flows and must always be ignored.

- **Future incremental cash flows.** Costs that have already been incurred are not relevant to a decision that is being made now. The cost has already been incurred, whatever decision is made, and it should therefore not influence the decision. For example, a company might incur initial investigation costs of $20,000 when looking into the possibility of making a capital investment. When later deciding whether to undertake the project, the investigation costs are irrelevant, because they have already been spent.

- **Incremental cash flows.** In other words they arise as a direct consequence of the decision. If a cash flow will occur whatever decision is taken, it is not relevant to the decision.

7.2 Relevant costs of materials

When a company must buy new inventory for a project, the relevant cost is the purchase price.

When a company already owns inventory and this is to be used in a project, finding the relevant cost is more complicated.

- If the materials are in regular use, and quantities consumed for the investment project would be replaced in the normal course of trading operations, the relevant cost of the materials is their current replacement cost.

- If the materials will not be replaced if they are used for the investment project, their relevant cost is the higher of:
  - their net disposal value and
  - the net contribution that could be earned using the materials for another available use.

Example

A project requires 5,000 kilograms of material X. Material X is used regularly by the company. The company has 4,000 kilograms of material X currently in inventory, which cost $400 per kilogram. The price for material X has since risen to $420 per kilogram.

The project also needs 2,000 kilograms of material Y. There are 1,500 kilograms of material Y in inventory, but material Y is no longer in regular use by the company. The 1,500 kilograms originally cost $144,000, and have a scrap value of $36,000. New purchases of material Y would cost $100 per kilogram.

Relevant costs of the materials are as follows:

Material X

This is in regular use. Any units of the material that are held in inventory will have to be replaced for other work if they are used in the project. The relevant cost is their replacement cost.

Relevant cost = replacement cost = 5,000 kilograms × $420 = $2,100,000.

Material Y

This is not in regular use. There are 1,500 kilograms in inventory, and an additional 500 kilograms would have to be purchased. The relevant cost of material Y for the contract is:

	$
Material held in inventory (scrap value)	36,000
New purchases (500 × $100)	50,000
Total relevant cost of Material Y	86,000

7.3 Relevant cost of existing equipment

When new capital equipment will have to be purchased for a project, the purchase cost of the equipment will be a part of the initial capital expenditure, and so a relevant cost.

However, if an investment project will also make use of equipment that the business already owns, the relevant cost of the equipment will be the higher of:

- the current disposal value of the equipment, and
- the present value of the cash flows that could be earned by having an alternative use for the equipment.

7.4 Relevant cost of investment in working capital

Investment in working capital must also be included as a relevant cash flow.

The relevant cash flow is the movement on the working capital. It is assumed that all working capital becomes cash at the end of a project.

Example

A company is considering whether to invest in the production of a new product. The project would have a six-year life. Investment in working capital would be $30,000 at the beginning of Year 1 and a further $20,000 at the beginning of Year 2.

For the purpose of investment appraisal, it is usually assumed that a cash flow, early during a year, should be treated as a cash flow as at the end of the previous year.

The relevant cash flows for the working capital investment would therefore be as follows:

Year	$
1 (cash outflow)	(30,000)
2 (cash outflow)	(20,000)
6 (cash inflow)	50,000

Applied Knowledge
Management Accounting (MA)

CHAPTER 18

Standard costing and variance analysis

Contents

1. Standard costs
2. Cost variances
3. Direct materials: price and usage variances
4. Direct labour: rate and efficiency variances
5. Variable production overheads: expenditure and efficiency variances
6. Fixed production overhead cost variances: absorption costing
7. Sales variances: sales price and sales volume variances
8. Interrelationships between variances
9. Reconciling budgeted and actual profit: standard absorption costing
10. Standard marginal costing
11. Deciding whether to investigate a variance
12. Calculating actual costs or standard costs from variances

> **Standard costs**
>
> - Standard units of product or service
> - Standard cost defined and standard costing
> - Who sets standard costs?
> - The purposes of standard costing
> - Establishing a standard cost

1 Standard costs

1.1 Standard units of product or service

A standard costing system might be used when an organisation produces standard units of a product or service that are identical to all other similar units produced. Standard costing is usually associated with standard products, but can be applied to standard services too (for example standard costs of burgers and other items in a fast-food restaurant).

A standard unit should have exactly the same input resources (direct materials, direct labour time) as all other similar units, and these resources should cost exactly the same. Standard units should therefore have exactly the same cost. This is the standard cost for the item.

1.2 Standard cost defined and standard costing

A **standard cost is a predetermined unit cost** based on expected direct materials quantities and expected direct labour time, and priced at a predetermined rate per unit of direct materials and rate per direct labour hour and rate per hour of overhead.

- Standard costs are usually restricted to production costs only, not administration and selling and distribution overheads. This is because traditionally, standard costing has been used in manufacturing industries but much less so in service industries.

- Standard costing can be based on either absorption costing or marginal costing. When absorption costing is used with standard costs, overheads are normally absorbed into the standard cost per unit at a rate per direct labour hour.

Example

The standard cost of Product XYZ might be:

	$	$
Direct materials:		
Material A: 2 litres at $4.50 per litre	9.00	
Material B: 3 kilos at $2 per kilo	6.00	
		15.00
Direct labour		
Grade 1 labour: 0.5 hours at $10 per hour	5.00	
Grade 2 labour: 0.75 hours at $8 per hour	6.00	
		11.00
Variable production overheads: 1.25 hours at $4 per hour		5.00
Fixed production overheads: 1.25 hours at $20 per hour		25.00
Standard (production) cost per unit		56.00

Standard costing

Standard costing is a system of costing in which:

- all units of product (or service) are recorded in the cost accounts at their standard cost, and
- the value of inventory is based on standard production cost.

In the cost ledger, production costs are recorded at their standard cost. Differences between actual costs and standard costs are recorded as variances, which may be either favourable or adverse. Variances that occur during a costing period are used to adjust the reported profit at the end of the period.

When a standard cost system is used:

- finished goods inventory is always valued at standard production cost (which may be either a full cost with absorption costing or a variable cost only with marginal costing)
- raw materials inventory may be valued at either actual cost or standard cost: there is no 'rule' that either standard cost or actual cost should be used.

1.3 Who sets standard costs?

Standard costs are set by managers with the expertise to assess what the standard prices and rates should be. Standard costs are normally reviewed regularly, typically once a year as part of the annual budgeting process.

- Standard prices for direct materials should be set by managers with expertise in the purchase costs of materials. This is likely to be a senior manager in the purchasing department (buying department).

- Standard rates for direct labour should be set by managers with expertise in labour rates. This is likely to be a senior manager in the human resources department (personnel department).

- Standard usage rates for direct materials and standard efficiency rates for direct labour should be set by managers with expertise in operational activities. This may be a senior manager in the production or operations department, or a manager in the technical department.

- Standard overhead rates should be identified by a senior management accountant, from budgeted overhead costs and budgeted activity levels that have been agreed in the annual budgeting process.

1.4 The purposes of standard costing

Standard costing has three main purposes:

- It is an alternative system of cost accounting. In a standard costing system, all units produced are recorded in the cost ledger at their standard cost of production.

- It is a system of performance measurement. The differences between standard costs (= expected costs) and actual costs can be measured as variances. Variances can be reported regularly to management, in order to identify areas of good performance or poor performance.

- It is also a system of control reporting. When differences between actual results and expected results (the budget and standard costs) are large, this could indicate that operational performance is not as it should be, and that the causes of the variance should be investigated.

Management can therefore use variance reports to identify whether control measures might be needed, to improve poor performances or continue with good performances.

- When there are large adverse (unfavourable) variances, this might indicate that actual performance is poor, and control action is needed to deal with the weaknesses.

- When there are large favourable variances, and actual results are much better than expected, management should investigate to find out why this has happened, and whether any action is needed to ensure that the favourable results continue in the future.

1.5 Establishing a standard cost

A standard variable cost is established by building up the standard materials, labour and variable overhead costs for each standard unit.

In a standard absorption costing system, the standard fixed overhead cost is a standard cost per unit, based on budgeted data about fixed costs and the budgeted production volume. ('Normal' annual production volume is used as the volume of activity for deciding the absorption rate for overheads.)

Exercise 1

A company manufactures two products, X and Y. In Year 1 it budgets to make 2,000 units of Product X and 1,000 units of Product Y. The standard quantity of resources per unit are as follows:

	Product X	Product Y
Direct materials per unit:		
Material A	2 units of material	1.5 units of material
Material B	1 unit of material	3 units of material
Direct labour hours per unit	1.5 hours	2 hours

Standard rates and prices are as follows.

Direct material A	$4 per unit
Direct material B	$3 per unit
Direct labour	$10 per hour
Variable production overhead	$2 per direct labour hour

Fixed production overheads per unit are calculated by applying a direct labour hour absorption rate to the standard labour hours per unit, using the budgeted fixed production overhead costs of $60,000 for the year.

Required

Calculate the standard full production cost per unit of:

(a) Product X, and

(b) Product Y

You will find the answer to the Exercises and practice multiple choice questions at the end of this book.

> **Cost variances**
>
> - Adverse and favourable cost variances
> - Cost variances and measuring profit
> - Variances and performance reporting
> - Calculating cost variances
> - Total variable cost variances

2 Cost variances

2.1 Adverse and favourable cost variances

In a standard costing system, all units of output are valued at their standard cost. Cost of production and cost of sales are therefore valued at standard cost.

Actual costs will differ from standard costs. A cost variance is the difference between an actual cost and a standard cost.

- When actual cost is higher than standard cost, the cost variance is adverse [(A)] or unfavourable [(U)].
- When actual cost is less than standard cost, the cost variance is favourable [(F)].

Several different variances are calculated, relating to direct materials, direct labour, variable production overhead and fixed production overhead. (There are also some sales variances. These are explained in a later section).

2.2 Cost variances and measuring profit

In a cost accounting system, cost variances are adjustments to the profit in an accounting period.

- Favourable variances increase the reported profit.
- Adverse variances reduce the reported profit.

2.3 Variances and performance reporting

Variance reports are produced at the end of each control period (say, at the end of each month).

- Large adverse variances indicate poor performance and the need for control action by management.
- Large favourable variances indicate unexpected good performance. Management might wish to consider how this good performance can be maintained in the future.

Variances might be reported in a statement for the accounting period that reconciles the budgeted profit with the actual profit for the period. This statement is known as an **operating statement**.

2.4 Calculating cost variances

The method of calculating cost variances is similar for all variable production cost items (direct materials, direct labour and variable production overhead).

A different method of calculating cost variances is required for fixed production overhead.

There are several different techniques that can be used to calculate variances. Some people learn variances as formulae. The approach taken here is to present variance calculations in tables. The advantages of this approach are that:

- Presenting variances in tables helps to explain the logic of variances – both what they mean and how they are calculated

- Learning how to calculate variances in tables also teaches you how to work out a standard cost when you are given a variance and an actual cost, and how to work out an actual cost when you are given a variance and a standard cost. (This is a specific learning requirement in the syllabus!)

2.5 Total variable cost variances

In standard costing, variable cost variances can be calculated for all items of variable cost – direct materials, direct labour and variable production overhead. The method of calculating the variances is similar for each variable cost item.

- The total cost variance for the variable cost item is the difference between the actual variable cost of production and the standard variable cost of producing the items.

- However, the total cost variance is not usually calculated. Instead, the total variance is calculated in two parts, that add up to the total cost variance:

    - a price variance or rate variance or expenditure per hour variance.

    - a usage or efficiency variance.

However, if you are asked to calculate a total variable cost variance, the method to apply is as follows (for a variable production cost).

When Q units have been produced:

	$	(F) or (A)
Q units of output should cost		
(= Q units × Standard cost per unit)	X	
Q units of output did cost	(X)	
Difference = Total cost variance for the variable cost item	X	(F) or (A)

The variance is adverse (A) if actual cost is higher than the standard cost, and favourable (F) if actual cost is less than the standard cost.

Example

A unit of Product P123 has a standard cost of 5 litres of Material A at $3 per litre. The standard direct material cost per unit of Product P123 is therefore $15.

In a particular month, 2,000 units of Product P123 were manufactured. These used 10,400 litres of Material A, which cost $33,600.

The total direct material cost variance is calculated as follows:

	$
2,000 units of output should cost (× $15)	30,000
They did cost	33,600
Total direct materials cost variance	3,600 (A)

The variance is adverse, because actual costs were higher than the standard cost.

Exercise 2

The standard variable production overhead for Product Z is $3, representing 1.5 direct labour hours at $2 per hour. During September, 4,000 units of Product Z were produced in 5,500 hours. The variable production overhead cost was $11,700.

Required

Calculate the total variable production overhead variance for September.

You will find the answer to the Exercises and practice multiple choice questions at the end of this book.

> **Direct materials: price and usage variances**
>
> - Direct materials price variance
> - Direct materials usage variance
> - Direct materials: possible causes of variances

3 Direct materials: price and usage variances

The direct materials total cost variance can be analysed into a price variance and a usage variance.

- A price variance measures the difference between the actual price paid for materials and the price that should have been paid (the standard price).
- A usage variance measures the difference between the materials that were used in production and the materials that should have been used (the standard usage).

3.1 Direct materials price variance

The price variance is calculated by taking the **actual quantity** of:

- materials purchased or
- materials used.

For your examination, it is unlikely that you will need to decide whether to use the quantity purchased or the quantity used. Briefly, however:

- the price variance is calculated from the **quantities purchased** when closing inventory of direct materials is valued at standard cost
- the price variance is calculated from the **quantities used** when closing inventory of direct materials is valued at actual cost.

An examination question will often state that quantities of materials purchased and materials used were the same. However, if a question states that raw materials are valued at standard cost, the price variance must be calculated using actual quantities of materials purchased.

The actual cost of the actual quantity of materials is compared with the standard purchase price of the materials. The difference is the materials price variance.

A direct materials price variance is calculated as follows:

	$	
Units of materials purchased/used should cost		
(× standard price per unit of material)	X	
They did cost	(X)	
Material price variance	X	(F) or (A)

If there are two or more direct materials, a price variance is calculated separately for each material.

Example

A unit of Product P123 has a standard cost of 5 litres of Material A at $3 per litre. The standard direct material cost per unit of Product P123 is therefore $15. In a particular month, 2,000 units of Product P123 were manufactured. These used 10,400 litres of Material A, which cost $33,600.

The direct materials price variance is calculated as follows.

The price variance is calculated on the quantity of materials purchased/used.

Materials price variance

	$
10,400 litres of materials should cost (× $3)	31,200
They did cost	33,600
Material price variance	2,400 (A)

The price variance is adverse because the materials cost more to purchase than they should have done (i.e. actual cost was higher than the standard or expected cost).

3.2 Direct materials usage variance

The usage variance is calculated by taking the **actual quantity of units produced**.

For the actual number of units produced, the actual usage of materials is compared with the standard usage. The difference is the usage variance, measured as a quantity of materials. This is converted into a money value at the **standard price** for the material.

A direct materials usage variance is calculated as follows:

	Units of material	
Units produced should use	X	
(output × standard material usage per unit)		
They did use	(X)	
Material usage variance in quantities	X	(F) or (A)
× Standard price per unit of material	× $P	
Material price variance in $	X	(F) or (A)

 Example

A unit of Product P123 has a standard cost of 5 litres of Material A at $3 per litre. The standard direct material cost per unit of Product P123 is therefore $15. In a particular month, 2,000 units of Product 123 were manufactured. These used 10,400 litres of Material A, which cost $33,600.

The direct materials usage variance is calculated as follows.

The usage variance is calculated by taking the actual quantity of units produced. The usage variance in material quantities is then converted into a money value at the standard price per unit of the raw material.

Materials usage variance

	litres	
2,000 units of Product P123 should use (× 5 litres)	10,000	
They did use	10,400	
Material usage variance in litres	400	(A)
Standard price per litre of Material A	× $3	
Material usage variance in $	$1,200	(A)

The usage variance is adverse because more materials were used than expected, which has added to costs.

Exercise 3

The standard direct materials cost of Product P44 is:

2 kilos of material L at $3 per kilo: $6.

During February, 6,000 units of Product P44 were produced. These used 12,800 kilos of material L, which cost $35,900.

Required

(a) Calculate the direct materials total cost variance for the month.

(b) Analyse this total variance into a direct material price variance and a direct material usage variance.

You will find the answer to the Exercises and practice multiple choice questions at the end of this book.

3.3 Direct materials: possible causes of variances

When variances occur and they appear to be significant, management should investigate the reason for the variance. If the cause of the variance is something within the control of management, control action should be taken. Some of the possible causes of materials variances are listed below.

Materials price variance: causes

- Suppliers increased their prices by more than expected. (Higher prices might be caused by an unexpected increase in the rate of inflation).

- Different suppliers were used, and these charged a higher price (adverse price variance) or lower price (favourable price variance) than the usual supplier.

- Materials were purchased in sufficient quantities to obtain a bulk purchase discount (a quantity discount), resulting in a favourable price variance.

- Materials were bought that were of lower quality than standard (and so cheaper than expected) or better quality than standard (and more expensive than expected).
- There was a severe shortage of the materials, so that prices in the market were much higher than expected.

Materials usage variance: causes

- Poor materials handling resulted in a large amount of breakages (adverse usage variance). Breakages mean that a quantity of materials input to the production proves are wasted.
- Improvements in production methods resulted in more efficient usage of materials (favourable usage variance).
- Wastage rates were higher or lower than expected.
- Materials used were of cheaper quality than standard, with the result that more materials had to be thrown away as waste.

> **Direct labour: rate and efficiency variances**
>
> - Direct labour rate variance
> - Direct labour efficiency variance
> - Direct labour: possible causes of variances

4 Direct labour: rate and efficiency variances

The direct labour total cost variance can be analysed into a rate variance and an efficiency variance. These are calculated in a similar way to the direct materials price and usage variances.

- A rate variance measures the difference between the actual wage rate paid per labour hour and the rate that should have been paid (the standard rate of pay).

- An efficiency variance (or productivity variance) measures the difference between the time taken to make the production output and the time that should have been taken (the standard time).

4.1 Direct labour rate variance

The direct labour rate variance is calculated by taking the actual number of hours worked and paid for.

The actual labour cost of the actual hours worked is compared with the standard cost for those hours. The difference is the labour rate variance.

A direct labour rate variance is calculated as follows.

	$	
Hours worked/paid for should cost	X	
(× standard rate per hour)		
They did cost	(X)	
Direct labour rate variance	X	(F) or (A)

If there are two or more different types or grades of labour, each paid a different standard rate per hour, a rate variance is calculated separately for each labour grade.

4.2 Direct labour efficiency variance

The direct labour efficiency variance is calculated by taking the actual quantity of units produced.

For the actual number of standard units produced, the actual hours worked is compared with the standard number of hours that should have been worked to produce the actual output. The difference is the efficiency variance, measured in hours. This is converted into a money value at the standard direct labour rate per hour.

A direct labour efficiency variance is calculated as follows.

	Hours	
Units produced should take (× standard hours per unit)	X	
They did take	(X)	
Efficiency variance in hours	X	(F) or (A)
× Standard direct labour rate per hour	× $P	
Direct labour efficiency variance in $	X	(F) or (A)

Example

Product P234 has a standard direct labour cost per unit of:

0.5 hours × $12 per direct labour hour = $6 per unit.

During a particular month, 3,000 units of Product P234 were manufactured. These took 1,400 hours to make and the direct labour cost was $16,200.

Required

Calculate for the month:

- the total direct labour cost variance
- the direct labour rate variance
- the direct labour efficiency variance.

Answer

Total direct labour cost variance	$	
3,000 units of output should cost (× $6)	18,000	
They did cost	16,200	
Direct labour total cost variance	1,800	(F)

The variance is favourable, because actual costs were less than the standard cost.

The direct labour rate variance is calculated by taking the actual number of hours worked (and paid for).

Direct labour rate variance	$	
1,400 hours should cost (× $12)	16,800	
They did cost	16,200	
Direct labour rate variance	600	(F)

The rate variance is favourable because the labour hours worked cost less than they should have done.

The labour efficiency variance, like a materials usage variance, is calculated for the actual number of units produced. The variance in hours is converted into a money value at the standard rate of pay per hour.

Direct labour efficiency variance

	hours	
3,000 units of Product P234 should take (× 0.5 hours)	1,500	
They did take	1,400	
Efficiency variance in hours	100	(F)
Standard direct labour rate per hour	× $12	
Direct labour efficiency variance in $	$1,200	(F)

The efficiency variance is favourable because production took less time than expected, which has reduced costs.

Labour cost variances: summary	$	
Labour rate variance	600	(F)
Labour efficiency variance	1,200	(F)
Total direct labour cost variance	1,800	(F)

4.3 Direct labour: possible causes of variance

When labour variances appear significant, management should investigate the reason why they occurred, and take control measures where appropriate to improve the situation in the future. Possible causes of labour variances include the following.

Labour rate variance

- An increase in pay for employees.
- Working overtime hours, when overtime is paid at a premium above the basic rate.
- Using direct labour employees who were more skilled and experienced than the 'normal' and who are paid more than the standard rate per hour (adverse rate variance).
- Using direct labour employees who were relatively inexperienced and new to the job (favourable rate variance, because these employees would be paid less than 'normal').

Labour efficiency variance

- More efficient methods of working.
- Good morale amongst the workforce and good management with the result that the work force is more productive.
- If incentive schemes are introduced to the workforce, this may encourage employees to work more quickly and therefore give rise to a favourable efficiency variance.
- Using employees who are more experienced or less experienced than 'standard', resulting in favourable or adverse efficiency variances. Experienced employees might be able to complete their work more quickly than less-experienced colleagues.

> **Variable production overheads: expenditure and efficiency variances**
>
> - Variable production overhead expenditure variance
> - Variable production overhead efficiency variance
> - Variable production overheads: possible causes of variances

5 Variable production overheads: expenditure and efficiency variances

The variable production overhead total cost variance can be analysed, if required, into an expenditure variance (= spending rate per hour variance) and an efficiency variance.

- The expenditure variance is similar to a materials price variance or a labour rate variance. It is the difference between actual variable overhead spending in the hours worked and what the spending should have been (the standard rate).

- The variable overhead efficiency variance in hours is the same as the labour efficiency variance in hours and is calculated in a very similar way. It is the variable overhead cost or benefit from adverse or favourable direct labour efficiency variances.

5.1 Variable production overhead expenditure variance

It is normally assumed that variable production overheads are incurred during hours actively worked.

- The variable production overhead expenditure variance is calculated by taking the actual number of hours worked.

- The actual variable production overhead cost of the actual hours worked is compared with the standard cost for those hours. The difference is the variable production overhead expenditure variance.

A variable production overhead expenditure variance is calculated as follows. Like the direct labour rate variance, it is calculated by taking the actual number of labour hours worked, since it is assumed that variable overhead expenditure varies with hours worked.

	$	
Hours worked should cost		
(active hours of work × standard rate per hour)	X	
They did cost	(X)	
Variable production overhead expenditure variance	X	(F) or (A)

5.2 Variable production overhead efficiency variance

The variable production overhead efficiency variance in hours is exactly the same as the direct labour efficiency variance in hours.

It is converted into a money value at the standard variable production overhead rate per hour.

Example

Product P123 has a standard variable production overhead cost per unit of:

1.5 hours × $2 per direct labour hour = $3 per unit.

During a particular month, 2,000 units of Product P123 were manufactured. These took 2,780 hours to make and the variable production overhead cost was $6,550.

Required

Calculate for the month:

- the total variable production overhead cost variance
- the variable production overhead expenditure variance
- the variable production overhead efficiency variance.

Answer

Total variable production overhead cost variance	$
2,000 units of output should cost (× $3)	6,000
They did cost	6,550
Total variable production overhead cost variance	550 (A)

Variable production overhead expenditure variance	$
2,780 hours should cost (× $2)	5,560
They did cost	6,550
Variable production overhead expenditure variance	990 (A)

The expenditure variance is adverse because the expenditure on variable overhead in the hours worked was more than it should have been.

Variable production overhead efficiency variance	
	hours
2,000 units of Product P123 should take (× 1.5 hours)	3,000
They did take	2,780
Efficiency variance in hours	220 (F)
Standard variable production overhead rate per hour	× $2
Variable production overhead efficiency variance in	$440 (F)

The efficiency variance is favourable because production took less time than expected, which has reduced costs.

Variable production overhead cost variances: summary

	$	
Variable production overhead expenditure variance	990	(A)
Variable production overhead efficiency variance	440	(F)
Total variable production overhead cost variance	550	(A)

5.3 Variable production overhead: possible causes of variances

Possible causes of variable production overhead variances include the following:

- Incorrect budgets being set at the beginning of the year may give rise to expenditure variances.

- Variable production overhead efficiency variances arise for the same reasons as labour efficiency variances, for example: substituting one grade of labour for another; introducing incentive schemes; and the learning curve effect.

Chapter 18: Standard costing and variance analysis

> **Fixed production overhead cost variances: absorption costing**
>
> - Total fixed production overhead cost variance
> - Fixed production overhead expenditure variance
> - Fixed production overhead volume variance
> - Fixed production overhead efficiency and capacity variances
> - Fixed production overheads: possible causes of variances

6 Fixed production overhead cost variances: absorption costing

Variances for fixed production overheads are different from variances for variable costs. The variances reported differ according to whether standard absorption costing or standard marginal costing is used.

With standard absorption costing, the standard cost per unit is a full production cost, including an amount for absorbed fixed production overhead. Every unit produced is valued at standard cost.

This means that **production overheads are absorbed into production costs at a standard cost per unit produced**. This standard fixed cost per unit is derived from a standard number of direct labour hours per unit and a fixed overhead rate per hour.

- The **total fixed overhead cost variance** is the **total amount of under-absorbed or over-absorbed overheads**, where overheads are absorbed at the standard fixed overhead cost per unit.

- It was explained in an earlier chapter that the total under- or over-absorption of fixed overheads can be analysed into an **expenditure variance** and a **volume variance**. This applies to standard costing as well as to ordinary absorption costing.

- The total volume variance can be analysed even further in standard absorption costing, into a fixed overhead **capacity variance** and a fixed overhead **efficiency variance**.

Fixed overhead variances are as follows:

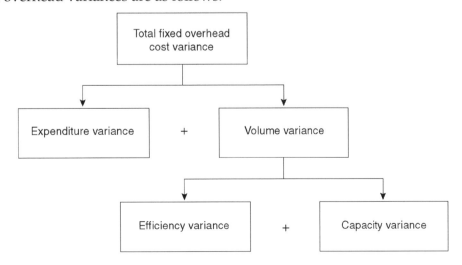

6.1 Total fixed production overhead cost variance

The total fixed production overhead cost variance is rarely calculated, because it is more usual to calculate the expenditure and volume variances.

However, the total fixed overhead cost variance is the amount of:

- under-absorbed fixed production overhead (= adverse variance) or
- over-absorbed fixed production overhead (= favourable variance).

Overheads are absorbed at a standard fixed cost per unit produced, not at standard rate per hour.

In standard absorption costing, the total fixed production overhead cost variance can be analysed into an expenditure variance and a volume variance. Together, these variances explain the reasons for the under- or over-absorption.

6.2 Fixed production overhead expenditure variance

A fixed production overhead expenditure variance is the difference between:

- budgeted fixed production overhead expenditure, and
- actual fixed production overhead expenditure.

Actual fixed overheads are expected to be the budgeted fixed expenditure. If actual fixed cost expenditure differs from the budget, there is an expenditure variance.

- An **adverse** expenditure variance occurs when actual fixed overhead expenditure exceeds the budgeted fixed overhead expenditure.
- A **favourable** expenditure variance occurs when actual fixed overhead expenditure is less than budget.

	$	
Budgeted fixed production overhead expenditure	X	
Actual fixed production overhead expenditure	(X)	
Fixed production overhead expenditure variance	X	(F) or (A)

Fixed overhead expenditure variances can be calculated, for control reporting, for other overheads as well as production overheads. For example:

- an administration fixed overheads expenditure variance is the difference between budgeted and actual fixed administration overhead costs
- a sales and distribution fixed overheads expenditure variance is the difference between budgeted and actual fixed sales and distribution overhead costs.

6.3 Fixed production overhead volume variance

In a system of standard absorption costing, the total cost variance for fixed overheads can be analysed as the sum of the fixed overhead expenditure variance and a fixed overhead volume variance.

The fixed production overhead volume variance measures the amount of fixed overheads under- or over-absorbed because of the fact that actual production volume differs from the budgeted production volume.

The volume variance is measured first of all in either:

- units of output or
- standard hours of the output units.

These are the same amount.

The volume variance in units (or standard hours of those units) is converted into a money value, as appropriate, at the standard fixed overhead cost per unit (or the standard fixed overhead rate per standard hour produced).

Fixed overhead volume variance	Units produced **	
Actual number of units produced **	X	
Budgeted production (units)	(X)	
Volume variance in units **	X	F or (A)
× Standard fixed overhead cost per unit	× $P	
Fixed production volume variance in $	X	F or (A)

** Instead of units, these measurements could be in **standard hours produced**. Standard hours produced = Actual units produced × Standard hours per unit.

Example

A company budgeted to make 5,000 units of a single standard product in Year 1. Budgeted direct labour hours are 10,000 hours. Budgeted fixed production overhead is $40,000. Actual production in Year 1 was 5,200 units, and fixed production overhead was $40,500.

Required

Calculate for Year 1:

- the total fixed production overhead cost variance
- the fixed overhead expenditure variance
- the fixed overhead volume variance

Answer

Standard fixed overhead cost per unit = $8 ($40,000/$5,000 units)

Fixed production overhead total cost variance

	$
5,200 units: standard fixed cost (× $8) = fixed overhead absorbed	41,600
Actual fixed overhead cost expenditure	40,500
Fixed production overhead total cost variance	1,100 (F)

The variance is favourable, because fixed overhead costs have been over-absorbed.

Fixed overhead expenditure variance

	$
Budgeted fixed production overhead expenditure	40,000
Actual fixed production overhead expenditure	40,500
Fixed overhead expenditure variance	500 (A)

This variance is adverse because actual expenditure exceeds the budgeted expenditure.

Fixed overhead volume variance

	units of production
Budgeted production volume in units	5,000
Actual production volume in units	5,200
Fixed overhead volume variance in units	200 (F)
Standard fixed production overhead cost per unit	$8
Fixed overhead volume variance in $	$1,600 (F)

This variance is favourable because actual production volume exceeded the budgeted volume.

Summary

	$
Fixed overhead expenditure variance	500 (A)
Fixed overhead volume variance	1,600 (F)
Fixed overhead total cost variance	1,100 (F)

Exercise 4

A company has budgeted to make 6,000 units of Product P345 in Year 2. Total budgeted fixed production costs are $72,000. Each unit of Product P345 has a standard direct labour time of 0.5 hours.

Actual output in Year 2 was 5,600 units of Product P345 and actual fixed production overhead expenditure was $71,200.

Required

Calculate for Year 2:

- the fixed production overhead expenditure variance
- the fixed production overhead volume variance.

You will find the answer to the Exercises and practice multiple choice questions at the end of this book.

6.4 Fixed production overhead efficiency and capacity variances

A fixed production overhead volume variance can be analysed, if required, into a fixed overhead efficiency variance and a fixed overhead capacity variance.

There are two reasons why actual production volume might differ from the budgeted production volume:

- Production operations were either more or less efficient than budgeted, so that more units or less units than expected were produced in the available time. This causes an **efficiency variance**.

- Actual hours worked were either more or less than budgeted, which means that either more units or less units than budgeted should be expected. This causes a **capacity variance**. (It might help you to think of the capacity variance as an 'hours worked' variance).

Fixed production overhead efficiency variance

This is exactly the same, in hours, as the direct labour efficiency variance and the variable production overhead efficiency variance.

It is converted into a money value at the standard fixed overhead rate per hour.

Fixed production overhead capacity variance

This is the difference between the budgeted and actual hours. It is converted into a money value at the standard fixed overhead rate per hour.

Fixed overhead capacity variance	hours	
Actual number of hours worked	X	
Budgeted hours	(X)	
Capacity variance in hours	X	F or (A)
× Standard fixed overhead rate per hour	× $P	
Fixed production capacity variance in $	X	F or (A)

Example

A company budgeted to make 5,000 units of a single standard product in Year 1. Budgeted direct labour hours are 10,000 hours. Budgeted fixed production overhead is $40,000. Actual production in Year 1 was 5,200 units in 10,250 hours of work, and fixed production overhead was $40,500.

This same example was used earlier to calculate the fixed overhead volume variance, which is $1,600 (F).

Required

Calculate for Year 1:

- the fixed overhead efficiency variance
- the fixed overhead capacity variance.

Answer

The standard direct labour hours per unit = 10,000 hours/5,000 units = 2 hours per unit.

The standard fixed overhead rate per hour = $40,000/10,000 hours = $4 per hour.

The standard fixed overhead cost per unit is 2 hours × $4 per hour = $8 (or $40,000/5,000 units).

Fixed overhead efficiency variance

	hours	
5,200 units should take (× 2 hours)	10,400	
They did take	10,250	
Efficiency variance in hours	150	(F)
Standard fixed overhead rate per hour	$4	
Fixed overhead efficiency variance in $	$600	(F)

Fixed overhead capacity variance

	hours	
Budgeted hours of work	10,000	
Actual hours of work	10,250	
Capacity variance in hours	250	(F)
Standard fixed overhead rate per hour	$4	
Fixed overhead capacity variance in $	$1,000	(F)

The capacity variance is favourable because actual hours worked exceeded the budgeted hours (therefore more units should have been produced).

Summary	$	
Fixed overhead efficiency variance	600	(F)
Fixed overhead capacity variance	1,000	(F)
Fixed overhead volume variance	1,600	(F)

Exercise 5

A company manufactures widgets. These are expected to take 0.25 hours each to make.

Budgeted production volume in Year 3 was 16,000 units and budgeted fixed production costs were $96,000.

Actual production volume in Year 3 was 15,700 units in 4,200 hours of work. Actual fixed overhead expenditure was $98,500.

Required

(a) For Year 3, calculate:

- the fixed overhead expenditure variance
- the fixed overhead volume variance.

(b) Analyse the volume variance into an efficiency and a capacity variance.

You will find the answer to the Exercises and practice multiple choice questions at the end of this book.

6.5 Fixed production overheads: possible causes of variances

Some of the possible causes of fixed production overhead variances include the following.

Fixed overhead expenditure variance

- Poor control over overhead spending (adverse variance) or good control over spending (favourable variance).
- Poor budgeting for overhead spending. If the budget for overhead expenditure is unrealistic, there will be an expenditure variance due to poor planning rather than poor expenditure control.
- Unplanned increases or decreases in items of expenditure for fixed production overheads, for example, an unexpected increase in factory rent.

Fixed overhead volume variance

A fixed overhead volume variance can be explained by anything that made actual output volume different from the budgeted volume. The reasons could be:

- Efficient working by direct labour: a favourable labour efficiency variance results in a favourable fixed overhead efficiency variance.
- Working more hours or less hours than budgeted (capacity variance).
- An unexpected increase or decrease in demand for a product, with the result that longer hours were worked.
- Strike action by the workforce, resulting in a fall in output below budget.
- Extensive breakdowns in machinery, resulting in lost production.

> **Sales variances: sales price and sales volume variances**
>
> - Sales price variance
> - Sales volume variance
> - Sales: possible causes of variances

7 Sales variances: sales price and sales volume variances

Sales variances, unlike cost variances, are not recorded in a standard costing system of cost accounts (in the cost ledger). However, sales variances are included in variance reports to management.

- They help to reconcile actual profit with budgeted profit.
- They help management to assess the sales performance.

There are two sales variances:

- a sales price variance, and
- a sales volume variance.

7.1 Sales price variance

A sales price variance shows the difference between:

- the actual sales prices achieved for items that were sold, and
- their standard sales price.

To calculate this variance, you should take the **actual items sold**, and compare the actual sales revenue with the standard selling prices for the items.

	$	
Actual units sold should sell for	X	
(units sold × standard sales price/unit)		
They did sell for (actual sales revenue)	(X)	
Sales price variance	X	F or (A)

There is a favourable sales price variance if units were sold for more than their standard sales price, and an adverse variance if sales prices were below the standard price.

7.2 Sales volume variance

A sales volume variance shows the effect on profit of the difference between the actual sales volume and the budgeted sales volume. The sales volume variance is calculated differently in standard absorption costing compared with standard marginal costing.

In a **standard absorption costing system**, the sales volume variance might be called a sales volume **profit** variance. A method for calculating the sales volume variance is as follows:

Sales volume variance: usual method of calculation

	units of sale	
Actual sales volume (units)	X	
Budgeted sales volume (units)	(X)	
Sales volume variance in units	X	F or (A)
× Standard profit per unit	× $P	
Sales volume variance in $	X	F or (A)

The volume variance is favourable if actual sales volume is higher than the budgeted volume, and adverse if the actual sales volume is below budget.

There is an alternative method of calculating the sales volume variance, which produces exactly the same figure for the variance.

Sales volume variance: alternative method of calculation

	$	
Actual sales at standard selling price	X	
Budgeted sales revenue	(X)	
Sales volume variance in $ revenue	X	F or (A)
Standard profit/sales price ratio	X%	
Sales volume variance (profit variance)	X	F or (A)

Example

A company budgets to sell 7,000 units of Product P456. It uses a standard absorption costing system. The standard sales price of Product P456 is $50 per unit and the standard cost per unit is $42.

Actual sales were 7,200 units, which sold for $351,400.

The sales price variance and sales volume variance would be calculated as follows.

Sales price variance	$	
7,200 units should sell for (× $50)	360,000	
They did sell for	351,400	
Sales price variance	8,600	(A)

The sales price variance is adverse because actual sales revenue from the units sold was less than expected.

Sales volume variance: usual method of calculation

	units	
Actual sales volume (units)	7,200	
Budgeted sales volume (units)	7,000	
Sales volume variance in units	200	(F)
Standard profit per unit ($50 − $42 = $8)	$8	
Sales volume variance (profit variance)	$1,600	(F)

The sales volume variance is favourable because actual sales exceeded budgeted sales.

Sales volume variance: alternative method of calculation

	$
Actual sales at standard selling price (7,200 × $50)	360,000
Budgeted sales (7,000 units × $50)	350,000
Sales volume variance in $ revenue	10,000 (F)
Standard profit/sales price ratio ($8/$50)	16%
Sales volume variance (profit variance)	$1,600 (F)

Both methods of calculating the sales volume variance produce the same answer.

Exercise 6

A company budgets to sell 42,000 units of Product P567. The standard sales price of Product P567 is $20 per unit and the standard cost per unit is $16. Actual sales were 39,200 units, which sold for $802,300.

Required

Calculate the sales price variance and the sales volume variance (profit variance) for the period. The company uses a standard absorption costing system.

You will find the answer to the Exercises and practice multiple choice questions at the end of this book.

7.3 Sales: possible causes of variances

Possible causes of sales variances include the following:

Sales price variance

- Actual increases in prices charged for products were higher or less than expected due to market conditions.
- Actual sales prices were less than standard because major customers were given an unplanned price discount.
- Competitors reduced their prices, forcing the company to reduce the prices of its own products.

Sales volume variance

- Actual sales demand was more or less than expected.
- The sales force worked well and achieved more sales than budgeted.
- An advertising campaign had more success than expected.
- A competitor went into liquidation, and the company attracted some of the former competitor's customers.
- The products that the company makes and sells are going out of fashion earlier than expected; therefore the sales volume variance was adverse.

Chapter 18: Standard costing and variance analysis

> **Interrelationships between variances**
>
> - The nature of interrelationships between variances
> - Sales price and sales volume
> - Materials price and usage
> - Labour rate and efficiency
> - Footnote: the importance of reliable standard costs

8 Interrelationships between variances

8.1 The nature of interrelationships between variances

In your examination, you might be required to show an understanding of the possible causes of variances. Some causes of individual variances have already been listed.

The reasons for variances might also be connected, and two or more variances might arise from the same cause. This is known as an interrelationship between two variances.

For example, one variance might be favourable and another variance might be adverse. Taking each variance separately, the favourable variance might suggest good performance and the adverse variance might suggest bad performance. However, the two variances might be inter-related, and the favourable variance and the adverse variance might have the same cause. When this happens, management should look at the two variances together, in order to assess their significance and decide whether control action is needed.

Examples of interrelationships between variances are given below.

8.2 Sales price and sales volume

A favourable sales price variance and an adverse sales volume variance might have the same cause. If a company increases its selling prices above the standard price, the sales price variance will be favourable, but sales demand might fall and the sales volume variance would be adverse.

Similarly, in order to sell more products a company might decide to reduce its selling prices. There would be an adverse sales price variance due to the reduction in selling prices, but there should also be an increase in sales and a favourable sales volume variance.

© Emile Woolf International Limited

8.3 Materials price and usage

A materials price variance and usage variance might be inter-related. For example, if a company decides to use a material for production that is more expensive than the normal or standard material, but easier to use and better in quality, there will be an adverse price variance. However a consequence of using better materials might be lower wastage. If there is less wastage, there will be a favourable material usage variance. Therefore, using a different quality of material can result in an adverse price variance and a favourable usage variance.

8.4 Labour rate and efficiency

If there is a change in the grade of workers used to do some work, both the rate and efficiency variances may be affected.

For example, if a lower grade of labour is used instead of the normal higher grade:

- there should be a favourable rate variance because the workers will be paid less than the standard rate

- however the lower grade of labour may work less efficiently and take longer to produce goods than the normal higher grade of labour would usually take. If the lower grade of labour takes longer, then this will give rise to an adverse efficiency variance.

Therefore the change in the grade of labour used results in two 'opposite' variances, an adverse efficiency variance and a favourable rate variance.

When inexperienced employees are used, they might also waste more materials than more experienced employees would, due to mistakes that they make in their work. The result might be not only adverse labour efficiency, but also **adverse materials usage**.

8.5 Footnote: the importance of reliable standard costs

It is important to remember that the value of variances as control information for management depends on the reliability and accuracy of the standard costs. If the standard costs are inaccurate, comparisons between actual cost and standard cost will have no meaning. Adverse or favourable variances might be caused by inaccurate standard costs rather than by inefficient or efficient working.

9 Reconciling budgeted and actual profit: standard absorption costing

9.1 Purpose of an operating statement

A management report called an operating statement might be prepared, showing how the difference between budgeted and actual profit is explained by the sales variances and cost variances. An operating statement reconciles the profit that was expected in the budget with the actual profit that was achieved.

The purpose of an operating statement is to report all variances to management, so that management can assess the effect they are having on profitability. Senior management can also use an operating statement to assess the success of junior managers in controlling costs and achieving sales.

9.2 Format of an operating statement

In a standard absorption costing system, an operating statement can be set out as follows. You should try to familiarise yourself with this type of statement.

Operating statement (standard absorption costing)

	(F)	(A)	$	
Budgeted profit			BP	
Sales price variance			X	(F) or (A)
Sales volume variance			X	(F) or (A)
Actual sales minus the standard production cost of sales			X	
	(F)	(A)		
Cost variances	$	$		
Direct materials price	X			
Direct materials usage		X		
Direct labour rate		X		
Direct labour efficiency	X			
Variable production o'head expenditure	X			
Variable production o'head efficiency	X			
Fixed production overhead expenditure		X		
Fixed production overhead efficiency	X			
Fixed production overhead capacity		X		
Other overhead expenditure variances (see note)		X		
Total cost variances	X	X	X	(F) or (A)
Actual profit			AP	

Note: Other overhead expenditure variances, assuming administration overheads and selling and distribution overheads are all fixed costs, are the difference between:

- budgeted other overheads expenditure, and
- actual other overheads expenditure.

In a system of absorption costing:

- The operating statement begins with the budgeted profit.

- The sales variances are shown next. These are added to (favourable variances) or subtracted from (adverse variances), and the resulting figure is shown as a sub-total. This figure is the actual sales revenue in the period minus the standard production cost of sales.

- The cost variances are listed next. They can be listed in any format, but showing separate columns for favourable variances and adverse variances helps to make the statement clear to the reader. Adverse variances reduce the profit and favourable variances add to profit.

- The cost variances are added up and then shown as a total.

- The actual profit is shown as the final figure, at the bottom of the operating statement.

Standard marginal costing

- Standard marginal costing and standard absorption costing compared
- Fixed production overhead variances in standard marginal costing
- Sales volume variance in standard marginal costing
- Standard marginal costing operating statement
- Standard absorption costing and standard marginal costing: differences in profit

10 Standard marginal costing

10.1 Standard marginal costing and standard absorption costing compared

When a company uses standard marginal costing rather than standard absorption costing:

- units produced and finished goods inventory are valued at standard variable production cost, not standard full production cost
- variances are calculated and presented in exactly the same way as for standard absorption costing, but with two important differences:
    - fixed production overhead variances
    - sales volume variances.

10.2 Fixed production overhead variances in standard marginal costing

In standard marginal costing, there is a fixed production overhead expenditure variance, but no fixed production overhead volume variance.

The fixed production overhead expenditure variance is calculated in the way already described and is the same amount in a standard marginal costing system as in a standard absorption costing system.

10.3 Sales volume variance in standard marginal costing

In standard absorption costing, the sales volume variance is calculated by applying the standard profit per unit to the volume variance in units.

In standard marginal costing, the sales volume variance is calculated using standard contribution, and the variance might be called the sales volume contribution variance. Contribution is the difference between the selling price and the variable cost.

- Standard contribution is therefore the difference between the standard selling price per unit and the standard variable cost.

- Standard contribution can also be expressed as a contribution to sales ratio, which is the ratio of the standard contribution per unit to the standard selling price per unit. The standard contribution to sales ratio is a constant value.

A sales volume contribution variance is calculated in either of the following ways. (Both methods produce the same variance).

Sales volume variance: usual method of calculation

	units	
Actual sales volume (units)	X	
Budgeted sales volume (units)	(X)	
Sales volume variance in units	X	(F) or (A)
Standard contribution per unit	$C	
Sales volume variance (contribution variance)	$X	(F) or (A)

Sales volume variance: alternative method of calculation

	$	
Actual sales at standard selling price	X	
Budgeted sales	X	
Sales volume variance in $ revenue	X	(F) or (A)
Standard contribution / sales ratio	C%	
Sales volume variance (contribution variance)	$X	(F) or (A)

Both methods of calculating the sales volume (contribution) variance produce the same answer.

10.4 Standard marginal costing operating statement

With standard marginal costing, an operating statement is presented in a different way from an operating statement with standard absorption costing. Budgeted contribution can be reconciled with actual contribution, by means of the sales price variance, sales volume variance and variable cost variances. Fixed cost expenditure variances should be presented in a separate part of the operating statement.

Operating statement: standard marginal costing

	$	
Budgeted profit	X	
Add budgeted fixed costs	(X)	
Budgeted contribution (BP + BF)	X	
Sales price variance	X	(F) or (A)
Sales volume variance	X	(F) or (A)
Sales less standard variable cost of sales	X	

Operating statement: standard marginal costing

	(F)	(A)	$
	$	$	
Direct materials price	X		
Direct materials usage		X	
Direct labour rate		X	
Direct labour efficiency	X		
Variable production overhead rate	X		
Variable production o'head efficiency	X		
Total variable cost variances	Totals		X (F) or (A)
Actual contribution			X
Budgeted fixed overhead expenditure	X		
Fixed overhead expenditure variance	X (F) or (A)		
Actual fixed production overheads			(X)
Actual profit			X

Try to familiarise yourself with the format of an operating statement with standard marginal costing.

- The operating statement begins with budgeted profit. However, most variances in standard marginal costing should show the effect of variances on total contribution. The budgeted profit should therefore be 'converted' into budgeted contribution, by adding back the budgeted fixed costs.

- The sales variances are shown next, which is the same as in an operating statement with standard absorption costing.

- The variances for variable costs only are listed next, and the total of all variances for variable cost items is shown.

- The actual contribution is the difference between the budgeted contribution and the sum of the sales variances and the variable cost variances. Adverse variances reduce the profit and favourable variances add to profit.

- Actual fixed costs are deducted from actual contribution to arrive at the actual profit at the bottom of the operating statement. Actual fixed cost expenditure should be shown as the budgeted fixed overheads plus the adverse fixed overhead expenditure variance or minus the favourable fixed overhead expenditure variance.

10.5 Standard absorption costing and standard marginal costing: differences in profit

A previous chapter explains the difference in the reported profit using absorption costing compared with marginal costing. The same principles apply in standard costing.

The reported profit using standard absorption costing will differ from the reported profit using standard marginal costing, and the difference in the reported profit can be explained entirely by differences in the increase or decrease in inventory valuation during the period.

Example

A company uses standard absorption costing. It manufactures a single product, which has a standard full production cost of $20 per unit. This consists of $12 of standard variable costs and $8 per unit of fixed production costs.

During a financial period, the company made 25,000 units of the product and sold 23,000 units. The actual reported profit for the period, using standard absorption costing, was $55,000.

If standard marginal costing had been used, the reported profit would have been different.

- There was an increase in inventory of 2,000 units. When finished goods inventory increases, the reported profit with absorption costing is higher than with marginal costing.

- The difference in profit is the amount of fixed overhead in the increase (or reduction) in inventory. In this example, this is $16,000 (= 2,000 units × $8).

- Reported profit would therefore be $16,000 lower using standard marginal costing – i.e. the reported profit would be $39,000 (= $55,000 - $16,000).

> **Deciding whether to investigate a variance**
>
> - Management responses to reported variances
> - Factors to consider

11 Deciding whether to investigate a variance

11.1 Management responses to reported variances

When a variance is reported, the manager responsible must decide whether it should be investigated. The purpose of investigating a variance is to:

- find out the cause or causes of the variance

- decide whether the variance is 'controllable': a variance is controllable if management control action can be taken that will affect the amount of the variance in future periods

- if the variance is controllable, to decide whether any control action should be taken to deal with its cause.

Investigating the cause of a variance takes management time and can be costly. Management should not spend time and money on an investigation if the expected benefits are unlikely to exceed the costs.

The size of a reported variance can be misleading. For example, if a reported labour efficiency variance is $4,000 adverse, this does not necessarily mean that $4,000 can be saved by taking action to correct the cause of the adverse variance.

- The reported variance is a historical variance, and any control action can only affect the future, not what has already happened in the past.

- The reported variance shows how much actual costs were higher than expected because actual efficiency was worse than the expected standard of efficiency. However, this does not mean that control action will enable the entity to achieve standard efficiency in the future. For example, the standard might be an ideal standard, which means that the reported efficiency variance will almost certainly always be adverse.

- Control action should affect all periods in the future, so the effect of taking control action in response to a reported variance in one period could have an effect that lasts for several periods, or even years, into the future.

11.2 Factors to consider

Before making a decision whether to investigate a variance, the following factors should be considered:

- **Size of the variance.** As a general rule, the cause of a variance is more likely to be significant when the variance is large. For example, a sales volume variance that is $40,000 adverse will be considered more significant than a sales volume variance of $400 adverse. The larger the variance, the greater the potential benefit from investigation and control measures.

- **Favourable or adverse variance.** Significant controllable favourable variances should be investigated as well as adverse variances. However, more significance might be given by management to adverse variances than to favourable variances. Management might take the view that if a reported variance is favourable, no action is needed and the variance might continue to be favourable in future periods – and this is desirable. However, using the same logic, unless control action is taken to correct the cause of an adverse variance, adverse variances will continue in the future – and this is undesirable. For this reason, a fairly small adverse variance might be investigated, but a favourable variance of the same amount might not be investigated.

- **Probability that the cause of the variance will be controllable.** A decision whether or not to investigate the cause of a variance will also depend on the expectation of management that the cause of the variance will be controllable. For example, management might be aware that there has recently been a significant increase in the market price of a raw material, or an increase in pay rates for employees. If so, they might decide that reported adverse material price and labour rate variances shouldn't be investigated, because the main cause is already known and it is unlikely that any control measures can be taken that will be effective in reducing adverse price and rate variances in the future.

- **Costs and benefits of control action.** Investigating a variance has a cost in terms of both management time and expenditure. A variance should not be investigated unless the expected benefits exceed the costs of investigation and control. The benefits are the cost savings or other benefits that will be obtained in the future if the variance is found to have a controllable cause and control action is therefore taken.

- **Random variations in reported variances.** Management might take the view that a favourable or adverse variance in one month is due to random factors that will not recur next month. A decision might therefore be taken to do nothing in the current month about the variance, but to wait and see whether the same variance occurs again next month. If the variance is due to random factors, it should not happen again next month, and management can probably ignore it without risk.

- **Reliability of budgets and measurement systems.** Management might have a view about whether the variance is caused by poor planning and poor measurement systems, rather than by operational factors. If so, investigating the variance would be a waste of time and would be unlikely to lead to any cost savings.

Calculating actual costs or standard costs from variances

- Calculating actual cost from variances and standard cost
- Calculating standard cost from variances and actual cost

12 Calculating actual costs or standard costs from variances

In your examination, you might be given a question where you are required to:

- calculate actual costs, given information about variances and standard costs, or
- calculate a standard cost, given information about variances and actual costs.

This type of problem does not occur in practice, but it is a useful way of testing knowledge of variances.

12.1 Calculating actual cost from variances and standard cost

This type of problem can be solved by using the tables to calculate variances, described in this chapter. You can enter into a table all the data given by the question. The 'missing figure' for actual cost or standard cost can then be calculated.

Some examples will be used to illustrate the technique.

Example

The standard direct materials cost of making Product B is $20, consisting of 4 kilos of material at $5 per kilo. During one period, 1,250 kilos of the material were purchased and the direct materials price variance was $250 (A).

Required

Calculate the actual costs of direct materials purchased and used in the period.

Answer

A table should be prepared showing how the total materials cost variance is calculated, and the figures that are available should be entered in the table.

	$
1,250 kilos of material should cost (× $5)	6,250
The materials did cost	?
Total materials cost variance	250 (A)

Actual purchase costs were higher than standard cost because the price variance is adverse. Actual purchase costs were therefore $6,250 + $250 = $6,500.

Example

The standard direct material cost of Product C is $21 (6 kilos of material at $3.50 per kilo). During a period when 400 units of Product C were made, the direct material usage variance was $630 (F).

Required

Calculate the actual quantity of direct materials used in the period.

Answer

A table should be prepared showing how the materials usage variance is calculated, and the figures that are available should be entered in the table.

Materials usage variance

	kilos
400 units of Product C should use (× 6 kilos)	2,400
They did use	?
Material usage variance in kilos	?
Standard price per kilo	× $3.50
Material usage variance in $	$630 (F)

From this information we can **calculate the material usage variance in kilos**. A usage variance is valued at the standard cost per unit of material; therefore the usage variance in $ can be converted into a usage variance in kilos:

Usage variance = $630(F)/$3.50 per kilo = 180 kilos (F).

The variance is favourable, which means that actual usage was less than the standard (expected) usage. We know that the standard usage is 2,400 kilos.

Actual material usage was therefore:

2,400 kilos – 180 kilos = 2,220 kilos.

Example

In the standard cost of Product D, the cost of Grade A labour is $24 per unit (= 1.5 hours per unit at $16 per hour). During a month when 500 units of Product D were made and 780 hours were worked, the labour rate variance for Grade A labour was $1,500 (F).

Required

Calculate the actual cost of Grade A labour in the month.

Answer

A table should be prepared showing how the labour rate variance is calculated, and the figures that are available should be entered in the table.

Direct labour rate variance	$
780 hours should cost (× $16)	12,480
They did cost	?
Direct labour rate variance	1,500 (F)

The rate variance was favourable, which means that actual costs were less than standard.

Actual cost of Grade A labour = $12,480 − $1,500 = $10,980.

Example

In a standard absorption costing system, the standard fixed production overhead cost per unit of Product E is $36. This represents 3 direct hours at $12 per hour.

The budgeted production volume in the period was 6,000 units of Product E. The fixed production overhead volume variance was $12,600 (F).

Calculate the actual quantity of Product E that was produced.

Answer

A table should be prepared showing how the production overhead volume variance is calculated, and the figures that are available should be entered in the table.

Fixed overhead volume variance	
	units of production
Budgeted production volume in units	6,000
Actual production volume in units	?
Fixed overhead volume variance in units	? (F)
Standard fixed production overhead cost per unit	× $36
Fixed overhead volume variance in $	$12,600 (F)

We know the volume variance in $. The volume variance is valued at the standard fixed overhead cost per unit. The volume variance in $ can therefore be converted into a volume variance in units as follows:

$12,600(F)/$36 per unit = 350 units (F).

Actual production volume is higher than the budgeted volume, because the volume variance is favourable. The budgeted production volume was 6,000 units.

Actual production volume = 6,000 units + 350 units = 6,350 units.

12.2 Calculating standard cost from variances and actual cost

The same approach can be used to calculate a standard cost or budget amount if you are given a variance and data about actual costs (or sales revenues). Some further examples will illustrate the technique.

Example

Product F uses a direct material, material M. The standard price of material M is $4 per kilo. During one month, 2,500 units of Product F were manufactured. These required 12,000 kilos of material M and the material usage variance was $2,000 (A).

Required

Calculate the standard direct material cost per unit of Product F.

Answer

We know the standard price of material M, but we need to calculate the standard material usage. This can be obtained from the data provided. A table should be prepared showing how the material usage variance is calculated, and the figures that are available should be entered in the table.

Materials usage variance

	kilos
2,500 units of Product F should use	?
They did use	12,000
Material usage variance in kilos	?
Standard price per kilo	× $4
Material usage variance in $	2,000 (A)

We know the material usage variance in $. The variance is valued at the standard price per unit of material. From the information provided we can therefore calculate the material usage variance in kilos:

Usage variance = $2,000(A)/$4 per kilo = 500 kilos (A).

The variance is adverse, which means that actual usage was more than the standard (expected) usage. The standard material usage is therefore:

12,000 kilos − 500 kilos = 11,500 kilos.

This is the standard usage for 2,500 units of Product F, so the standard usage per unit is 11,500/2,500 = 4.60 kilos per unit.

The standard material cost for Product F is therefore:

4.6 kilos of material M at $4 per kilo = $18.40.

Chapter 18: Standard costing and variance analysis

Example

The standard time required to make one unit of Product G is 1.25 hours of direct labour. During one month, total direct labour costs were $119,000. The company made 6,800 units of Product G. These took 9,100 direct labour hours and the direct labour rate variance was $8,400 (F).

Required

Calculate the standard direct labour cost per unit of Product G.

Answer

We know the standard direct labour time, which is 1.25 hours per unit, but we need to calculate the standard direct labour rate per hour. This can be obtained from the data provided. A table should be prepared showing how the labour rate variance is calculated, and the figures that are available should be entered in the table.

Direct labour rate variance	$
9,100 hours should cost	?
They did cost	119,000
Direct labour rate variance	8,400 (F)

The rate variance is favourable, which means that actual costs were lower than standard costs. The actual labour cost for the 9,100 hours was $119,000. Expected costs are higher.

The 9,100 hours should therefore cost $119,000 + $8,400 = $127,400.

The standard rate per hour is $127,400/9,100 hours = $14 per hour.

The standard direct labour cost of Product G is:

1.25 hours at $14 per hour = $17.50

Tutorial note

It is easy to get confused about whether variances should be added or subtracted in this type of calculation. You need to think carefully and logically, to avoid making a mistake.

Exercise 7

A company makes a single product. The standard direct labour cost of one unit of the product is $24 (= 1.5 hours at $16 per hour).

During a month when 900 units of the product were manufactured, 1,240 hours were worked and the direct labour rate variance was $1,700 (F).

Required

Calculate actual cost of direct labour during the month.

You will find the answer to the Exercises and practice multiple choice questions at the end of this book.

Exercise 8

During one month, a factory produced 3,200 units of Product H and these took 5,150 direct labour hours. The standard direct labour rate per hour is $18 per unit, and the direct labour efficiency variance for the month was $8,100 (F).

Required

Calculate the standard direct labour cost per unit of Product H.

You will find the answer to the Exercises and practice multiple choice questions at the end of this book.

Practice multiple choice questions

1 A company uses standard costing. Last month 18,000 direct labour hours were worked at an actual cost of $328,500. The production output measured in standard hours was 17,700 standard hours. The standard direct labour cost per hour was $18.50.

What was the direct labour rate variance?

- **A** $1,050 (A)
- **B** $1,050 (F)
- **C** $4,500 (A)
- **D** $4,500 (F). *(2 marks)*

2 A company uses standard costing. It makes a single product, and it should take 2 direct labour hours to make each unit. Last month 18,000 direct labour hours were worked at an actual cost of $18 per hour. Actual output measured was 8,800 units of product. The standard direct labour cost per hour is $18.50.

What was the direct labour efficiency variance?

- **A** $7,200 (A)
- **B** $7,200 (F)
- **C** $7,400 (A)
- **D** $7,400 (F). *(2 marks)*

3 A company uses standard marginal costing. Last month, the budgeted sales were 6,000 units. The standard sales price is $15 per unit and the contribution to sales ratio is 80%. Actual sales in the month were 6,450 units and total sales revenue was $92,880.

What were the adverse sales price and favourable sales volume contribution variances?

	Sales price $	Sales volume contribution $
A	1,800	5,400
B	3,870	5,400
C	1,800	6,750
D	3,870	6,750

(2 marks)

Management Accounting (MA)

4 A company uses standard marginal costing. Last month, actual fixed overhead expenditure was 3% below budget and the fixed overhead expenditure variance was $4,800.

What was the actual fixed overhead expenditure last month?

A $155,200
B $159,856
C $160,000
D $164,800

(2 marks)

5 A company uses standard absorption costing. The following data relates to the previous costing period.

	Budget	Actual
Sales and production (units)	1,500	1,600

	Standard $	Actual $
Selling price per unit	48	46
Total production cost per unit	34	33

What was the favourable sales volume profit variance for the period?

A $1,200
B $1,300
C $1,400
D $1,500

(2 marks)

6 Who should a materials price variance be reported to?

A Factory department manager
B Senior buying manager
C Human resources department manager

(1 mark)

7   A company manufactures a single product. The standard material cost of the product is 0.5 kilos of direct material at $8 per kilo. During last month 20,000 units of the product were made and these used 10,500 kilos of material. Purchases and usage of materials were the same quantity and purchases cost $82,500.

What was the direct materials price variance for the month?

A $1,500 (F)
B $1,500 (A)
C $2,500 (F)
D $2,500 (A)   *(2 marks)*

8   A company uses standard absorption costing. It manufactures a single product and the standard fixed production cost is $36 per unit, consisting of 3 hours per unit at a fixed overhead rate of $12 per hour. The following data relates to the previous costing period.

	Budget	Actual
Sales and production (units)	35,000	36,000

The fixed overhead capacity variance for the month was $7,200 favourable.

How many hours were worked in the month?

A   104,400
B   105,600
C   107,400
D   108,600   *(2 marks)*

You will find the answers to the practice multiple choice questions at the end of this book.

Applied Knowledge
Management Accounting (MA)

CHAPTER 19

Performance measurement

Contents
1 Performance measurement and mission
2 Financial performance indicators (FPIs)
3 Non-financial performance indicators (NFPIs)
4 The balanced scorecard approach
5 Unit costs
6 Resource utilisation
7 Return on investment
8 Residual income
9 Performance measurement in service industries
10 Performance measurement in not-for-profit organisations and the public sector
11 Value for money
12 Other aspects of performance measurement

> **Performance measurement and mission**
>
> - Reasons for measuring performance
> - Mission statement
> - Objectives
> - Long-term, medium-term and short-term performance
> - Economic and market conditions
> - Impact of government regulation on performance measurement

1 Performance measurement and mission

1.1 Reasons for measuring performance

Performance in business should be measured and reported back to:

- the individuals most directly responsible for the performance
- their boss or bosses.

The purpose of measuring performance is to:

- inform individuals whether the planning targets or standards (for which they are responsible) are being met
- inform senior managers about the performance of each of their subordinates, as well as their own performance
- indicate the risk that targets will not be met, so that action to correct the situation can be considered
- indicate poor performance, so that individuals and their managers can take whatever corrective action seems appropriate
- reward the successful achievement of targets or standards, for example by means of cash bonuses or other incentives.

A business entity must have management information systems that are capable of providing reliable and relevant information about all the important aspects of performance.

1.2 Mission statement

Some organisations have a formal mission statement. The purpose of a mission statement is to provide a clear expression of the reason why the organisation is in existence and what it is seeking to achieve.

The content of mission statements varies between different organisations, but common elements are:

- a statement of the purpose of the organisation
- a statement of its broad strategy for achieving its purpose
- a statement of the values and culture of the organisation.

A mission statement can have several useful purposes including helping managers to formulate their business strategy. Managers should consider new strategies in the context of whether it is consistent with the organisation's purpose.

Mission statements do not have a time scale for achievement. An organisation must establish specific targets and time scales for achievement to convert a mission statement into objectives or goals.

Mission statements may be useful for formulating strategies, but they are of limited value for monitoring actual performance.

1.3 Objectives

An organisation should have high level 'strategic' objectives that are consistent with its mission. For companies, the highest corporate objective is likely to be the aim of providing benefits to their shareholders. This objective may be expressed in general terms as 'maximising the wealth of shareholders over the long term'.

High-level corporate objectives must be converted into more specific plans or targets. The targets clarify the objectives of the organisation. A target should be a clear statement of what an entity wants to achieve within a specified period of time. Targets are usually quantified, but may be expressed in qualitative terms.

Companies tend to construct a hierarchy of objectives for each level of management.

A common approach to analysing levels of management and management decision-making is to identify three levels:

- strategic management
- tactical management
- operational management.

In a well-designed performance management system, all planning targets are consistent with each other, at the strategic, tactical and operational levels.

1.4 Long-term, medium-term and short-term performance

Performance measurement should cover the long-term, medium-term and short-term.

Long-term performance

Long-term performance measures should be linked to the long-term objectives and the strategies of the organisation. The most significant long-term objectives might be called **critical success factors** or **CSFs**. In order to achieve its long-term and strategic objectives, the critical success factors must be achieved.

For each critical success factor, there should be a way of measuring performance, in order to check whether the CSF targets are being met. Performance measurements for CSFs might be called **key performance indicators (KPIs)** or possibly **key risk indicators** (KRIs).

Medium-term performance

Medium-term performance measurement is perhaps most easily associated with the annual budget, and meeting budget targets. Targets, whether financial or non-financial, can be set for a planning period such as the financial year, and actual results should be compared against the planning targets.

Short-term performance

Short-term performance should be monitored by means of operational performance measures. For example, quality might be measured by the percentage of rejected units in production, or the rate of customer returns or customer complaints. Speed might be measured by the average time required to meet a customer order.

1.5 Economic and market conditions

This refers to any factors that influence the state of the market or markets in which a company operates. These include:

- the state of the economy
- innovation and technological change.

Companies will usually hope to achieve growth in sales and profits, and economic conditions may be either favourable or adverse. When the economy is growing, demand for goods and services generally should be increasing, and market conditions are favourable for the development and growth of business. When the economy is in recession, the opposite is true: companies may even struggle to survive.

Other financial conditions may affect a company's performance, such as changes in rates of taxation, interest rates or foreign exchange rates.

Performance measurement should take the economic and market conditions into account. For example:

- sales growth of 10% in a period in which there was no growth in a market might be considered to be a good performance;
- sales growth of 10% in a period in which the market grew by 30% might be considered to be a good performance.

1.6 Impact of government regulation on performance measurement

Government regulation can have profound effect on performance reporting in both the private and public sectors.

Governments can enact regulations which require performance of a certain type, set targets and specify performance measures which must be used in assessing progress in achieving such targets.

Private sector

The government in the UK has introduced mandatory greenhouse gas (GHG) reporting regulations for quoted companies in the UK

The government also encourages other organisations to make voluntary reports on a range of environmental matters, including voluntary GHG reporting and through the use of key performance indicators (KPIs).

It is left to companies to decide on the detail of the report the performance measurements systems of all quoted companies will be affected as they must:

- determine the key environmental impacts of the company and set key performance indicators in those areas;
- set up a system to gather information; and
- prepare and publish reports.

Public sector

Government expenditure within the public sector involves very large numbers and often represents a significant percentage of the gross national product of a country.

A government will need to ensure that its policies and directions in particular areas are being executed and whether they are successful or not. A government might introduce performance measures that must be used.

For example, in the UK the government requires the publication of "league tables" of exam results for schools in each area.

Another UK example is the requirement for local health authorities to publish average patient waiting times for types of operation or for attention at accident and emergency facilities.

> **Financial performance indicators (FPIs)**
>
> - Aspects of financial performance
> - Using financial ratios: comparisons
> - FPIs for measuring profitability
> - FPIs for measuring liquidity
> - FPIs for measuring financial risk
> - Activity ratios

2 Financial performance indicators (FPIs)

2.1 Aspects of financial performance

A common method of analysing and measuring the financial performance of an organisation is by means of ratio analysis. Although profitability is a very important aspect of business performance, it is not the only aspect of financial performance that should be monitored. The main aspects of financial performance are usually:

- profitability
- liquidity
- financial risk.

Information for measuring financial performance is obtained largely from internal sources – financial statements produced by the entity and its accounting systems.

Each financial ratio should be of potential significance. Remember that it is not good enough simply to know how to calculate a ratio. You need to understand what the ratio might tell you about financial performance.

2.2 Using financial ratios: comparisons

Financial ratios can be used to make comparisons:

- Comparisons over a number of years. By looking at the ratios of a business entity over a number of years, it might be possible to detect improvements or deterioration in the financial performance or financial position. For example, changes over time can be used to measure rates of growth or decline in sales or profits. Ratios can therefore be used to make comparisons over time, to identify changes or trends, and (perhaps) to assess whether the rate or direction of change is 'good' or 'bad'.

- Comparisons with the similar ratios of other, similar companies for the same period.

- In some cases, perhaps, comparisons with 'industry average' ratios.

2.3 FPIs for measuring profitability

Profitability depends on sales revenues and costs. Financial performance indicators that may be relevant for assessing performance therefore include ratios for sales and costs, as well as profit.

Profitability may also be assessed by relating profit to the amount of capital employed by the business. Return on investment (ROI) and other similar financial ratios are explained in a later section.

Percentage annual growth in sales

Business entities will monitor their annual growth (or decline) in sales, measured as a percentage of sales in the previous year.

For example, if sales in the year just ended were $5,800,000 and sales in the previous year were $5,500,000, the annual growth in sales has been ($300,000/$5,500,000) × 100% = 5.45%.

Sales growth can be a very important measure of financial performance for a number of reasons.

- If a company wishes to increase its annual profits, it will probably want to increase its annual sales revenue. Sales growth is usually necessary for achieving a sustained growth in profits over time.

- The rate of growth can be significant. For example, suppose that the annual rate of growth in a particular market is 7%. If a company achieves sales growth in the year of 15%, it will probably consider this to be a good performance. If sales growth is 3%, this would probably be considered poor performance – although sales have increased, they have not increased in line with growth in the market.

Sales growth (or a decline in sales) can usually be attributed to two causes:

- sales prices and
- sales volume.

Any growth in sales should be analysed to identify whether it has been caused by changes in sales prices, changes in sales volume or a combination of both.

Profit margin

Profit margin is the profit as a percentage of sales revenue. It is therefore the ratio of the profit that has been achieved for every $1 of sales.

Profit margin = Profit/sales × 100%

It is wrong to conclude, without further analysis, that a high profit margin means 'good performance' and a low profit margin means 'bad performance'. To assess performance by looking at profit margins, it is necessary to look at the circumstances in which the profit margin has been achieved.

There are several ways of measuring profit margin. If you are required to measure profit margin in your examination, the most suitable ratio is likely to be:

- Gross profit margin (= gross profit/sales). Gross profit is sales revenue minus the cost of sales.

- Net profit margin (= net profit/sales). Net profit = gross profit minus all other costs, such as administration costs and selling and distribution costs.

Any change in profit margin from one year to the next will be caused by:

- changes in selling prices, or
- changes in costs as a percentage of sales, or
- a combination of both.

Changes in costs as a percentage of sales may be caused by a growth or fall in sales volumes, where there are fixed costs in the entity's cost structure.

Example

Sobco makes and sells footwear. Its profits and sales revenue for the past three years are as follows

	Current year (just ended)	Year – 1 (previous year)	Year – 2
Sales revenue	$20 million	$22 million	$24 million
Items sold	1 million	1.1 million	1.2 million
Gross profit	$5.8 million	$6.6million	$6.8 million
Net profit	$0.4 million	$1.2 million	$1.4 million

Required

Analyse profitability and costs.

Answer

Profit margins are as follows:

	Current year (just ended)	Year – 1 (previous year)	Year – 2
Gross profit margin (%)	29.0%	30.0%	28.3%
Net profit margin (%)	2.0%	5.5%	5.8%

The gross profit margin has fallen slightly in the current year, but is higher than the gross profit margin two years ago. There is insufficient information to assess performance, except to conclude that the gross profit margin has been fairly stable over the three-year period.

(This means that the ratio of cost of sales as a percentage of sales has also been fairly constant. The cost of sales/sales ratio is simply 100% minus the gross profit margin.)

The net profit margin has fallen from 5.8% two years ago to 2.0% in the current year. The actual net profit has fallen from $1.4 million to $0.4 million. The reason for the fall in net profit margin is attributable to either changes in selling prices or changes in costs (as a percentage of sales).

- The average selling price per unit has been $20 in each of the three years, suggesting that the fall in net profit margin is not caused by changes in selling prices.

- The fall in net profit margin is therefore due to changes in costs. Although there has been some variability in the ratio of cost of sales to sales revenue, the main problem appears to be changes in 'other costs' as a percentage of sales.

- Other costs = the difference between gross profit and net profit. Two years ago these were $5.4 million (= $6.8 million - $1.4 million), one year ago they were $5.4 million (= $6.6 million - $1.2 million) and in the current year they were also $5.4 million (= $5.8 million - $0.4 million). This suggests that other costs are all fixed costs.

- Fixed costs have remained constant each year, but sales revenue has fallen due to falling sales volume. The reduction in the net profit margin can therefore be attributed mainly to the higher ratio of other fixed costs to sales revenue – in other words, to falling sales.

Cost/sales ratios

Profitability may also be measured by cost/sales ratios, such as:

- Ratio of cost of sales/sales
- Ratio of administration costs/sales
- Ratio of sales and distribution costs/sales
- Ratio of total labour costs/sales.

Performance may be assessed by looking at changes in these ratios over time. A large increase or reduction in any of these ratios would have a significant effect on profit margin.

2.4 FPIs for measuring liquidity

Liquidity for a business entity means having enough cash, or having ready access to additional cash, to meet liabilities when they fall due for payment. The most important sources of liquidity for non-bank companies are:

- operational cash flows (cash from sales)
- liquid investments, such as cash held on deposit or readily-marketable shares in other companies
- a bank overdraft arrangement or a similar readily-available borrowing facility from a bank.

Cash may also come from other sources, such as the sale of a valuable non-current asset (such as land and buildings), although obtaining cash from these sources may need some time.

Liquidity is important for a business entity because without it, the entity may become insolvent even though it is operating at a profit. If the entity is unable to settle its liabilities when they fall due, there is a risk that a creditor will take legal action and this action could lead on to insolvency proceedings.

In December 2008 a long-established retail company, Woolworths, became insolvent. Although the company was operating at a loss, a major factor in the collapse was lack of sufficient cash to pay for leases on premises that fell due for payment in the month, and which the company did not have the cash to pay.

On the other hand a business entity may have too much liquidity, when it is holding much more cash than it needs, so that the cash is 'idle', earning little or no interest. Managing liquidity is often a matter of ensuring that there is sufficient liquidity, but without having too much.

Changes in the cash balance or bank overdraft balance

A simple method of monitoring liquidity is to keep the cash balance at the bank under continual review, and look for any deterioration (or improvement) in the cash position. If the entity has a bank overdraft facility, the cash position should be monitored to makes sure that the overdraft does not get too close to the limit.

When there is a big change in the cash position, it is important to investigate its cause and judge whether liquidity has become a matter for concern. If you are familiar with statements of cash flows, you should be aware of the various sources of cash and reasons for payments of cash. A large fall in cash (or a big increase in the bank overdraft) may be caused by:

- Operating losses
- Increases in working capital (inventory plus receivables, minus trade payables)
- Expenditures on investments, such as purchases of new non-current assets
- Repayments of debt capital (bank loans) or payments of dividends.

A reduction in cash caused by operating losses would be the most serious reason for a loss of liquidity, but when a business entity is short of liquidity anything that uses up cash may be significant.

Liquidity ratios

Liquidity may also be monitored by looking at changes in a liquidity ratio over time. There are two ratios for measuring liquidity that could be used:

- current ratio
- quick ratio, also called the acid test ratio.

The more suitable ratio for use depends on whether inventory is considered a liquid asset that will soon be used or sold, and converted into cash from sales.

The **current ratio** is the ratio of current assets to current liabilities.

$$\text{Current ratio} = \frac{\text{Current assets}}{\text{Current liabilities}}$$

It is sometimes suggested that there is an 'ideal' current ratio of 2.0 times (2:1). However, this is not necessarily true and in some industries, much lower current ratios are normal. It is important to assess a current ratio by considering:

- changes in the ratio over time
- the liquidity ratios of other companies in the same industry.

The **quick ratio or acid test ratio** is the ratio of 'current assets excluding inventory' to current liabilities. Inventory is excluded from current assets on the assumption that it is not a very liquid item.

$$\text{Quick ratio} = \frac{\text{Current assets excluding inventory}}{\text{Current liabilities}}$$

This ratio is a better measurement of liquidity than the current ratio when inventory turnover times are very slow, and inventory is not a liquid asset.

It is sometimes suggested that there is an 'ideal' quick ratio of 1.0 times (1:1). However, this is not necessarily true and in some industries, much lower quick ratios are normal. As indicated earlier, it is important to assess liquidity by looking at changes in the ratio over time, and comparisons with other companies and the industry norm.

When there is a significant change in liquidity, the reason should be investigated. Liquidity ratios will deteriorate (i.e. get smaller) when:

- there is an increase in current liabilities without an increase in current assets
- there is a reduction in current assets without a reduction in current liabilities (for example, writing off inventory or bad debts).

Examples of reasons for a reduction in liquidity are:

- operating losses
- using cash to purchase new non-current assets.

2.5 FPIs for measuring financial risk

Financial risk is the risk to a business entity that arises for reasons related to its financial structure or financial arrangements

Debt ratios

Debt ratios can be used to assess whether the total debts of the entity are within control and are not excessive.

Gearing ratio (leverage)

Gearing, also called leverage, measures the total long-term debt of a company as a percentage of either:

- the equity capital in the company, or
- the total capital of the company.

$$\text{Gearing} = \frac{\text{Long-term debt}}{\text{Share capital and reserves}} \times 100\%$$

Alternatively:

$$\text{Gearing} = \frac{\text{Long-term debt}}{\text{Share capital and reserves} + \text{Long-term debt}} \times 100\%$$

When there are preference shares, it is usual to include the preference shares within long-term debt, not share capital.

A company is said to be **high-geared** or **highly-leveraged** when its debt capital exceeds its share capital and reserves. This means that a company is high-geared when the gearing ratio is above either 50% or 100%, depending on which method is used to calculate the ratio.

A company is said to be **low-geared** when the amount of its debt capital is less than its share capital and reserves. This means that a company is low-geared when the gearing ratio is less than either 50% or 100%, depending on which method is used to calculate the ratio.

The gearing ratio can be used to monitor changes in the amount of debt of a company over time. It can also be used to make comparisons with the gearing levels of other, similar companies, to judge whether the company has too much debt, or perhaps too little, in its capital structure.

Interest cover ratio

Interest cover measures the ability of the company to meet its obligations to pay interest.

$$\text{Interest cover} = \frac{\text{Profit before interest and tax}}{\text{Interest charges in the year}}$$

An interest cover ratio of less than 3.0 times is considered very low, suggesting that the company could be at risk from too much debt in relation to the amount of profits it is earning.

The risk is that a significant fall in profitability could mean that profits are insufficient to cover interest charges, and the entity will therefore be at risk from any legal action or other action that lenders might take.

2.6 Activity ratios

Activity ratios measure an organisation's ability to convert balance sheet items into cash or sales. They measure the efficiency of the business in managing its assets.

Asset turnover ratio

The asset turnover ratio' measures the amount of sales achieved during the period for each $1 of investment in assets.

$$\text{Asset turnover} = \frac{\text{Sales}}{\substack{\text{Total equity + long term liabilities} \\ \text{(=total assets less current liabilities)}}}$$

It is measured as a multiple (x times a year).

Example

The following figures relate to the revenue and capital of a company.

	Current year (just ended)	Year – 1 (previous year)
Sales revenue	$25 million	$22 million
Total equity + long term liabilities	$10 million	$10 million

Required

Analyse asset turnover.

Answer

Asset turnovers are as follows:

	Current year (just ended)	Year – 1 (previous year)
$25m/£10	× 2.5	
$22m/£10		× 2.2

Last year every $1 invested managed to generate $2.2 of revenue. This year every $1 invested generated $2.5 of revenue. This implies that efficiency has improved in this area. The asset base is being managed to provide more opportunity to earn margin than it did last year.

Receivables days (average time to collect receivables)

This estimates the time that it takes on average to collect the payment from customers after the sale has been made. It could be described as the average credit period allowed to customers or the 'average collection period'.

$$\text{Average days to collect} = \frac{\text{Trade receivables}}{\text{Sales}} \times 365 \text{ days}$$

Trade receivables should be the average value of receivables during the year. This is the average of the receivables at the beginning of the year and the receivables at the end of the year.

However, the value for receivables at the end of the year is also commonly used.

Sales are usually taken as total sales for the year. However, if sales are analysed into credit sales and cash sales, it is more appropriate to use the figure for credit sales only.

The average time to collect money from credit customers should not be too long. A long average time to collect suggests inefficient collection of amounts due from receivables.

Inventory days (average time for holding inventory)

This is an estimate of the average time that inventory is held before it is used or sold.

$$\text{Average Inventory days} = \frac{\text{Inventory}}{\text{Cost of sales}} \times 365 \text{ days}$$

In theory, inventory should be the average value of inventory during the year. This is the average of the inventory at the beginning of the year and the inventory at the end of the year.

However, the value for inventory at the end of the year is also commonly used, particularly in examinations.

Payables days (average time to pay suppliers)

The average time to pay suppliers may be calculated as follows:

$$\text{Average time to pay} = \frac{\text{Trade payables}}{\text{Cost of purchases}} \times 365 \text{ days}$$

Trade payables should be the average value of trade payables during the year. This is the average of the trade payables at the beginning of the year and the trade payables at the end of the year.

However, the value for trade payables at the end of the year is also commonly used

When the cost of purchases is not available, the **cost of sales** should be used instead. This figure is obtained from the profit and loss information in the statement of profit or loss and other comprehensive income.

Example

The following information is available for The Brush Company for Year 1.

	1 January Year 1	31 December Year 1
	$	$
Inventory	300,000	360,000
Trade receivables	400,000	470,000
Trade payables	150,000	180,000

Sales in Year 1 totalled $3,000,000 and the cost of sales was $1,800,000.

Required

Calculate the working capital turnover ratios.

Answer

Average inventory = [$300,000 + $360,000]/2 = $330,000

Average trade receivables = [$400,000 + $470,000]/2 = $435,000

Average trade payables = [$150,000 + $180,000]/2 = $165,000.

Activity ratios

Average days to collect = [435,000/3,000,000] × 365 days = 52.9 days

Average inventory period = [330,000/1,800,000] × 365 days = 66.9 days

Average time to pay = [165,000/1,800,000] × 365 days = 33.5 days.

> **Non-financial performance indicators (NFPIs)**
>
> - Introduction to NFPIs
> - Non-financial aspects of performance
> - Common areas in which companies adopt NFPIs
> - NFPIs for departments or functions
> - NFPIs in different types of industry

3 Non-financial performance indicators (NFPIs)

3.1 Introduction to NFPIs

Non-financial performance refers to every aspect of operations within a business except the financial aspect.

Variability in the circumstances of different businesses

With financial performance measurement, there are a limited number of financial ratios that are used, which can be applied to all types of business. For example, the ratios discussed in the previous section can be used to provide insight to the performance many different types of company (though interpretation would be carried out in the light of knowledge of the relevant sector).

With NFPIs, the key measures of performance vary between different types of business, and depend on the nature of the business. For example, the key non-financial measures of performance for a chemical manufacturer will differ from those of a passenger transport company such as a bus or train company.

Also, non-financial performance indicators might differ between companies within the same industry. This is because the companies might operate on different business models or might be trying to achieve different objectives or might simply have a different view of what is important to the success of their business.

Time scale for achievement

Financial performance targets are often set for a budget period, and actual performance is compared against budget. Non-financial performance targets need not be restricted to one year, and in some cases it may be sensible to establish targets for a longer term (or possibly a shorter term) than one year.

Unfortunately, if some employees are awarded cash bonuses for achieving non-financial performance targets, there will be a tendency to set annual targets in order to fit in with the annual budget cycle.

3.2 Non-financial aspects of performance

For the purpose of assessing the performance of the entity as a whole, it is necessary to identify which aspects of non-financial performance are the most important in terms of the entity achieving its corporate objectives. The problem is to decide which aspects of performance are critically important. An entity might identify a number of critical aspects of performance across its different departments within the business.

The whole process would involve:

- Identification of objective
- Identification of the critical aspects of performance necessary to achieve the objective
- Setting targets to drive behaviour towards addressing these critical aspects of performance
- Measuring actual performance so that it can be compared to the desired level of performance
- Communicating results to managers of responsibility centres.
- Identifying performance indicators

An entity would need to carry out some form of analysis to identify suitable non-financial performance indicators. An analysis to identify NFPIs for a railway company might be as follows:

Objective	To increase passenger revenue by improving the utilisation of each train
How will we do this?	By attracting more passengers
How?	By giving them what they value
What do they value?	Trains being on time
	Cleanliness and comfort
Possible NFPIs	
Overall	Percentage utilisation
Trains being on time	Percentage of trains that arrive late
	Number of cancellations
Cleanliness and comfort	Level of customer satisfaction (from surveys)

For each of the NFPIs identified above the company would need to establish suitable targets, systems for measuring the performance and systems for communicating results to managers.

3.3 Common areas in which companies adopt NFPIs

Many companies identify non-financial performance indicators in the following areas.

- Human resources: A motivated and well trained workforce of adequate size is often vital to an organisation achieving its objectives.

- Customer satisfaction: It is customers that ultimately determine the level of profits. Companies often analyse what is important to their customers and structure their marketing offering in line with this and

- Quality: Quality is linked closely to customer satisfaction. Resolving quality issues has a direct cost (e.g. the cost of replacing an item) and indirect costs (e.g. lost goodwill leading to future lost sales).

In all cases suitable indicators and associated targets would be established as a result of analysis similar to that illustrated above.

The following table suggests possible NFPIs in these areas.

Area	Possible NFPIs
Human resources	Labour turnover rate;
	Training days per year;
	Absenteeism rates (e.g sick days) often used as a measure of staff morale;
	Average hours worked;
	Idle time;
	Proportion billable hours;
	Head count by grade of labour.
Customer satisfaction	Measures of customer satisfaction might include:
	Percentages of new and returning customers;
	Results of customer satisfaction surveys;
	Number of complaints;
	Speed of complain resolution;
	Subsequent sales to customers who registered a complaint previously.
Quality	Possible quality measures include:
	Proportion of re-worked items during production;
	Proportion of returns;
	Proportion of fails;
	Number of successful inspections.

3.4 NFPIs for departments or functions

Performance targets can be set for an entity's departments or in respect of its functions.

Possible non-financial performance indicators might be as follows for different departments:

Department	Possible NFPIs
Sales and customer service	Calls per hour
	Conversion rates calls to orders
	Proportion of returning customers
	Proportion of 'very satisfied' customers
	Average waiting time
	Number of advertising campaigns run
On-line sales	Number of visits to web-site
	Conversion rates (number of sales as a percentage of the number of visits)
	Number of return visits
	Number of sales to returning customers
	Customer satisfaction (number of return visits/number of complaints)
	Website down time
	Delivery times (time between an order being placed and filled)
Inventory control	Average inventory holding
	Proportion wastage
	Number of stock outs
	Number of returns to suppliers
Sustainability measures	Proportion of components sourced from 'green materials';
	Annual percentage reduction in CO_2 emissions;
	Proportion of packaging that is recyclable.
Research and development	Number of new invention/ideas
	Conversion rate of invention ideas to production

3.5 NFPIs in different types of industry

As mentioned previously, the key measures of performance vary between different types of business, and depend on the nature of the business. It is impossible to provide examples for all industries but the following are some possible examples of NFPIS that might be important in certain industries.

Type of industry	Possible NFPIs
Manufacturing operations	Average build time
	Average production line down-time
	Capacity utilisation
Airline	Average utilisation rates (i.e. percentage of aircraft occupied);
	Average non-availability;
	Planes - proportion of time in the air;
	Average turnaround time for when plane is on the ground.
Hotels	Occupancy;
	Customer satisfaction measures.

> **The balanced scorecard approach**
>
> - The concept of the balanced scorecard
> - The balanced scorecard: four perspectives of performance
> - Using the balanced scorecard

4 The balanced scorecard approach

4.1 The concept of the balanced scorecard

The balanced scorecard approach was developed by Kaplan and Norton in the 1990s as an approach to measuring performance in relation to long-term objectives. They argued that for a business entity, the most important objective is a financial objective. However, in order to achieve financial objectives over the long term, it is also necessary to achieve goals or targets that are non-financial in nature, as well as financial.

The concept of the balanced scorecard is that there are several aspects of performance ('perspectives on performance') and targets should be set for each of them. The different 'perspectives' may sometimes appear to be in conflict with each other, because achieving an objective for one aspect of performance could mean having to make a compromise with other aspects of performance. The aim should be to achieve a satisfactory balance between the targets for each of the different perspectives on performance. These targets, taken together, provide a balanced scorecard, and actual performance should be measured against all the targets in the scorecard.

The reason for having a balanced scorecard is that by setting targets for several key factors, and making compromises between the conflicting demands of each factor, managers will take a more balanced and long-term view about what they should be trying to achieve. A balanced scorecard approach should remove the emphasis on financial targets and short-term results.

However, although a balanced scorecard approach takes a longer-term view of performance, it is possible to set shorter-term targets for each item on the scorecard. In this way it is possible to combine a balanced scorecard approach to measuring performance with the annual budget cycle, and any annual incentive scheme that the entity may operate.

4.2 The balanced scorecard: four perspectives of performance

In a balanced scorecard, critical success factors are identified for four aspects of performance, or four 'perspectives':

- customer perspective
- internal perspective
- innovation and learning perspective
- financial perspective.

Of these four perspectives, three are non-financial in nature.

For each perspective, Kaplan and Norton argued that an entity should identify key performance measures and key performance targets. The four perspectives provide a framework for identifying what those measures should be, although the specific measures used by each entity will vary according to the nature of the entity's business.

For each perspective, the key performance measures should be identified by answering a key question. The answer to the question indicates what the most important issues are. Having identified the key issues, performance measures can then be selected, and targets set for each of them.

Perspective	The key question
Customer perspective	**What do customers value?**
	By recognising what customers value most, the entity can focus its performance targets on satisfying the customer more effectively. Targets might be developed for several aspects of performance such as cost (value for money), quality or place of delivery.
Internal perspective	**To achieve its financial and customer objectives, what processes must the organisation perform with excellence?**
	Management should identify the key aspects of operational performance and seek to achieve or maintain excellence in this area. For example, an entity may consider that customers value the quality of its service, and that a key aspect of providing a quality service is the effectiveness of its operational controls in preventing errors from happening.
Innovation and learning perspective	**How can the organisation continue to improve and create value?**
	The focus here is on the ability of the organisation to maintain its competitive position, through the skills and knowledge of its work force and through developing new products and services, or making use of new technology as it develops.
Financial perspective	**How does the organisation create value for its owners?**
	Financial measures of performance in a balanced scorecard system might include share price growth, profitability and return on investment.

Several measures of performance may be selected for each perspective, or just one. Using a large number of different measures for each perspective adds to the complexity of the performance measurement system.

4.3 Using the balanced scorecard

The focus should be on strategic objectives and the critical success factors necessary for achieving them. The main focus is on what needs to be done now to ensure continued success in the future.

The main performance report for management each month is a balanced scorecard report, not budgetary control reports and variance reports.

Examples of measures of performance for each of the four perspectives are as follows. This list is illustrative only, and entities may use different measurements.

Perspective	Outcome measures
Critical financial measures	Return on investment
	Profitability and profitability growth
	Revenue growth
	Productivity and cost control
	Cash flow and adequate liquidity
	Avoiding financial risk: limits to borrowing
Critical customer measures	Market share and market share growth
	Customer profitability: profit targets for each category of customer
	Attracting new customers: number of new customers or percentage of total annual revenue obtained from new customers during the year
	Retaining existing customers
	Customer satisfaction, although measurements of customer satisfaction may be difficult to obtain
	On-time delivery for customer orders
Critical internal measures	Success rate in winning contract orders
	Effectiveness of operational controls, measured by the number of control failures identified during the period
	Production cycle time/throughput time
	Amount of re-working of defective units
Critical innovation and learning measures	Revenue per employee
	Employee productivity
	Employee satisfaction
	Employee retention or turnover rates
	Percentage of total revenue earned from sales of new products
	Time to develop new products from design to completion of development and introduction to the market

Example

Kaplan and Norton described the example of Mobil in the early 1990s, in their book *The Strategy-focussed Organisation*. Mobil, a major supplier of petrol, was competing with other suppliers on the basis of price and the location of petrol stations. Its strategic focus was on cost reduction and productivity, but its return on capital was low.

The company's management re-assessed their strategy, with the aim of increasing market share and obtaining stronger brand recognition of the Mobil brand name. They decided that the company needed to attract high-spending customers who would buy other goods from the petrol station stores, in addition to petrol.

As its high-level financial objective, the company set a target of increasing return on capital employed from its current level of about 6% to 12% within three years.

From a **financial perspective**, it identified such key success factors as productivity and sales growth. Targets were set for productivity (reducing operating costs per gallon of petrol sold) and 'asset intensity' (ratio of operational cash flow to assets employed).

From a **customer perspective**, Mobil carried out market research into the identity of its customers and the factors that influenced their buying decisions. Targets were set for providing petrol to customers in a way that would satisfy the customer and differentiate Mobil's products from rival petrol suppliers. Key issues were found to be having petrol stations that were clean and safe, and offering a good quality branded product and a trusted brand. Targets were set for cleanliness and safety, speedy service at petrol stations, helpful customer service and rewarding customer loyalty.

From an **internal perspective**, Mobil set targets for improving the delivery of its products and services to customers, and making sure that customers could always buy the petrol and other products that they wanted, whenever they visited a Mobil station.

> **Unit costs**
>
> - Performance measures for process costing
> - Performance measures for contract costing

5 Unit costs

5.1 Performance measures for process costing

Process costing was covered in detail in an earlier chapter.

Process costing is appropriate for a manufacturing process in which output is continually produced from the process and output is normally measured in total quantities, such as tonnes or litres produced, or in very large quantities of small units (such as the number of cans or tins).

Often there are losses in a process. Process costing identifies normal and abnormal losses. Abnormal losses are the difference between expected output and actual output.

Possible performance measures for process costing include the following:

- Amount of abnormal loss (it should be zero if the process operates as planned).

- Actual process duration compared to expected process duration. Management would be concerned to ensure that any one process did not cause a bottleneck in the system.

Standard costing could be used in a process costing system. In that case, variances could be calculated and used in the performance measurement system.

5.2 Performance measures for contract costing

Contract accounting is not included in the Management Accounting syllabus.

However, the syllabus does require knowledge of performance measurement in a contract accounting environment. Therefore, this section provides a brief explanation of contract accounting as a basis for describing possible performance measures.

Contract costing is a form of specific order costing in which costs are attributed to individual contracts. It is used to account for major construction projects which often take several years to complete. For example, building hospital, ships, dams would all be accounted for using contract costing.

Contract costing is superficially similar to job costing. The difference between a contract and a job is one of size and time-span. Contract costing is used by businesses undertaking building or other constructional contracts which take months or years to complete.

Each contract is a separately identifiable cost unit, so that costs will be accumulated in a separate ledger account for each contract. The various elements of cost are as follows:

- direct materials;
- direct wages;
- direct expenses; and
- indirect costs.

In the case of large contracts, where the work involved may spread over many months or even years, the contractor will expect interim payments from the client in respect of the contract price. Such payments are related to the work done so far on the contract. This is often established by an independent consultant who certifies how much work has been performed to date. This figure is known as work certified (not surprisingly).

Another feature of large construction contracts is that the contract might contain a penalty if the contract (or a phase of a contract) is completed later than an agreed date. The penalty would mean that the contractor is paid less for the contract than he would have been had the contract been completed on time. The size of the deduction is related to the length of the delay.

Possible performance measures

These include:

- Actual costs incurred compared to expected costs for the level of completion (Actual costs/work certified)
- Expected costs to complete
- Overall profit (contract revenue − (costs to date + costs to complete).
- Time overruns (Time spent/Total time × Contract revenue compared to work certified)
- Time to complete

> **Resource utilisation**
>
> - Introduction
> - The three ratios

6 Resource utilisation

6.1 Introduction

Resource utilisation is about how effectively resources have been used to generate output. It is also described as productivity.

Three ratios are used to provide information on resource utilisation. These ratios are related to some of the fixed overhead variances which were explained in an earlier chapter. (They are the same ratios which were explained in Chapter 6 as the labour efficiency ratio, capacity utilisation ratio and production volume ratio).

The three ratios are:

- Efficiency ratio: This is concerned with how well the actual hours worked have been used to generate output.

- Capacity ratio: This is concerned with how many hours were worked compared to the hours that should have been worked.

- Volume ratio: This is a function of the other two ratios. Differences between efficiency of the hours worked compared to budgeted efficiency and the number of the hours worked compared to the budgeted hours, result in volume of output being different to that budgeted.

6.2 The three ratios

Efficiency ratio

$$\text{Efficiency ratio} = \frac{\text{Expected hours to produce the actual output}}{\text{Actual hours to produce the actual output}} \times 100$$

or (restated in terms of standard hours)

$$\text{Efficiency ratio} = \frac{\text{Standard hours to produce the actual output}}{\text{Actual hours to produce the actual output}} \times 100$$

Capacity ratio

$$\text{Capacity ratio} = \frac{\text{Actual hours worked}}{\text{Total hours available for work}} \times 100$$

Volume ratio

$$\text{Volume ratio} = \frac{\text{Expected hours to produce the actual output}}{\text{Total hours available for work}} \times 100$$

Example

A business planned to make 1,200 units at a standard time of 2 hours per unit.

Actual production was 1,100 units.

The actual time taken was 2,250 hours.

Therefore:

	Hours
Actual hours to make actual production	2,250
Expected time to make the actual production (1,100 units should have used 2 hours per unit)	2,200
Total number of hours expected to be used (1,200 units should have used 1 hours per unit)	2,400

$$\text{Efficiency ratio} = \frac{(1,100 \times 2 \text{ hours}) = 2,200 \text{ hours}}{2,250 \text{ hours}} \times 100 = 97.78\%$$

$$\text{Capacity ratio} = \frac{2,250 \text{ hours}}{(1,200 \times 2 \text{ hours}) = 2,400 \text{ hours}} \times 100 = 93.75\%$$

$$\text{Volume ratio} = \frac{(1,100 \times 2 \text{ hours}) = 2,200 \text{ hours}}{2,400 \text{ hours}} \times 100 = 91.67\%$$

Link between the ratios

Efficiency ratio × Capacity ratio = Volume ratio

 Example

Using answers obtained above

Labour efficiency ratio	97.78%
Capacity utilisation ratio	× 93.75%
Production volume ratio	91.67%

> **Return on Investment (ROI)**
>
> - The reason for using ROI as a financial performance indicator
> - Measuring ROI
> - ROI and investment decisions
> - Advantages and disadvantages of ROI for measuring performance

7 Return on Investment (ROI)

7.1 The reason for using ROI as a financial performance indicator

Return on investment (ROI) is a measure of the return on capital employed for an investment centre. It is also called the accounting rate of return (ARR).

It is often used as a measure of divisional performance for investment centres because:

- the manager of an investment centre is responsible for the profits of the centre and also the assets invested in the centre, and
- ROI is a performance measure that relates profit to the size of the investment.

Profit is not a suitable measure of performance for an investment centre. It does not make the manager accountable for his or her use of the net assets employed (the investment in the investment centre).

Example

A company has two divisions which are treated as investment centres for the purpose of performance reporting. Centre 1 has net assets of $5 million and made a profit of $250,000. Centre 2 has net assets of $1 million and made a profit of $150,000.

If the performance of the centres is compared on the basis of profits, the performance of Centre 1 ($250,000) is better than the performance of Centre 2 ($150,000). However Centre 1 employed assets of $5 million to earn its profit and its ROI was just 5% ($250,000/$5 million). Centre 2 employed assets of just $1 million and its ROI was 15%. Comparing performance on the basis of ROI, Centre 2 performed better.

7.2 Measuring ROI

Performance measurement systems could use ROI to evaluate the performance of both the manager and the division. ROI is the profit of the division as a percentage of capital employed.

$$\text{ROI} = \frac{\text{Profit}}{\text{Capital employed (size of investment)}}$$

ROI can be measured in different ways, but the following is often used:

- **Profit.** This should be the annual accounting profit of the division, without any charge for interest on capital employed. This means that the profit is after deduction of any depreciation charges on non-current assets.
- **Capital employed/investment.**
    - This should be the sum of the non-current assets used by the division plus the working capital that it uses. Working capital = current assets minus current liabilities, which for a division will normally consist of inventory plus trade receivables minus trade payables.
    - An examination question may ignore working capital in the figures that it provides. If so, capital employed will consist of non-current assets only.
    - Non-current assets could be measured at their initial cost. However, it is more usual to measure non-current assets at their carrying value, which in an examination question is likely to be at cost less accumulated depreciation.
    - Capital employed may be the capital employed at the beginning of the financial year, the end of the financial year or the average capital employed for the year. Check an examination question carefully to establish which of these is required.

Link between ROI, profit margin and asset turnover

ROI = Profit margin × Asset turnover ratio

Example

A company achieved the following results in Year 1.

	$
Capital employed	1,200,000
Sales	5,800,000
Profit	145,000

ROI	=	Profit/sales	×	Sales/capital employed
$\dfrac{240,000}{1,200,000}$	=	$\dfrac{240,000}{5,800,000}$	×	$\dfrac{5,800,000}{1,200,000}$
20%	=	4.14%	×	4.83

7.3 ROI and investment decisions

The performance of the manager of an investment centre may be judged on the basis of ROI – whether the division has succeeded or not in achieving a target ROI for the financial year, or whether ROI has improved since the previous year.

If an incentive scheme is in operation, a divisional manager may receive a bonus on the basis of the ROI achieved by the division.

Investment centre managers may therefore have a strong incentive to improve the ROI of their division and to avoid anything that will reduce the ROI. This can be a serious problem when investment decisions are involved. When an investment centre manager's performance is evaluated by ROI, the manager will probably be motivated to make investment decisions that increase the division's ROI in the current year, and reject investments that would reduce ROI in the current year.

The problem is that investment decisions are made for the longer term, and a new investment that reduces ROI in the first year may increase ROI in subsequent years. An investment centre manager may therefore reject an investment because of its short-term effect on ROI, without giving proper consideration to the longer term.

Example

A division has net assets of $800,000 and makes an annual profit of $120,000. It should be assumed that if the investment described below is not undertaken, the division will continue to have net assets of $800,000 and an annual profit of $120,000 for the next four years.

The division is considering an investment in a new item of equipment that would cost $80,000. The estimated life of the equipment is four years with no residual value. The estimated additional profit before depreciation from the investment is as follows:

Year	$
1	20,000
2	25,000
3	35,000
4	40,000

The asset will be depreciated on a straight-line basis.

Required

What would be the ROI on this investment? ROI should be measured on the basis of the average net assets employed during the year.

Would the investment centre manager decide to undertake this investment or not?

Answer

The annual profit from the investment, allowing for depreciation of $20,000 per year, and the annual ROI of the division would be as follows:

Year	Profit without the investment	Extra profit from the investment	Total profit	Net assets	ROI
	$	$	$	$	
1	120,000	0	120,000	870,000	13.8%
2	120,000	5,000	125,000	850,000	14.7%
3	120,000	15,000	135,000	830,000	16.3%
4	120,000	20,000	140,000	810,000	17.3%

Note: Net assets are $800,000 plus the net assets for the new investment. The net asset value of the new investment is $80,000 at the beginning of Year 1, $60,000 at the beginning of Year 2 and so on down to $0 at the end of Year 4. Average net assets are therefore $70,000 in Year 1, $50,000 in Year 2, $30,000 in Year 3 and $10,000 in Year 4.

Without the new investment, the annual ROI would be 15% (= $120,000/$800,000).

The new investment would therefore reduce ROI in the first and second years, and increase ROI in Year 3 and Year 4. It is therefore probable that the divisional manager, if he is more concerned about financial performance in the short term, will decide that the investment should not be undertaken, even though over a four-year period the investment may be worthwhile.

Note. Investment decisions should not be taken on the basis of ROI, even though divisional managers are often tempted to do so. We can, however, calculate the average ROI from this proposed investment:

	$
Total 4-year profits before depreciation	120,000
Depreciation over four years	80,000
Total profit over 4 years	40,000
Average annual profit from the investment	10,000

Average asset carrying value over 4 years: $\dfrac{80,000+0}{2} = \$40,000$

Average ROI = $10,000/$40,000 = 25%.

This is higher than the ROI of 15% achieved from the division's other assets.

7.4 Advantages and disadvantages of ROI for measuring performance

Advantages of using ROI

There are several advantages in using ROI as a measure of the performance of an investment centre.

- It relates the profit of the division to the capital employed, and the division manager is responsible for both profit and capital employed.
- ROI is a percentage measure and can be used to compare the performance of divisions of different sizes.
- It is an easily understood measure of financial performance.
- It focuses attention on capital as well as profit, and encourages managers to sell off unused assets and avoid excessive working capital (inventory and receivables).

Disadvantages of using ROI

There are also disadvantages in using ROI as a measure of the performance of an investment centre.

- As explained above, investment decisions might be affected by the effect they would have on the division's ROI in the short term, and this is inappropriate for making investment decisions.
- There are different ways of measuring capital employed. ROI might be based on the net book value (carrying value) of the division at the beginning of the year, or at the end of the year, or the average for the year. Comparison of performance between different organisations is therefore difficult.
- When assets are depreciated, ROI will increase each year provided that annual profits are constant. The division's manager might not want to get rid of ageing assets, because ROI will fall if new (replacement) assets are purchased.
- ROI is an accounting measure of performance. An alternative system of performance measurement that includes non-financial performance indicators, such as a balanced scorecard approach, might be more appropriate.

> **Residual income (RI)**
>
> - Measuring residual income
> - Imputed interest (notional interest) and the cost of capital
> - Residual income and investment decisions
> - Advantages and disadvantages of residual income

8 Residual income (RI)

8.1 Measuring residual income

Residual income (RI) is another way of measuring the performance of an investment centre. It is an alternative to using ROI.

Residual income = Divisional profit minus imputed interest charge.

Note

Divisional profit is an accounting measurement of profit, after depreciation charges are subtracted. It is the same figure for profit that would be used to measure ROI.

8.2 Imputed interest (notional interest) and the cost of capital

Residual income is calculated by deducting an amount for imputed interest (also called notional interest) from the accounting profit for the division.

The **interest charge** is calculated by applying a cost of capital to the division's net investment (net assets). The most appropriate measure of net investment is the average investment during the period, although an exam question may instruct you to calculate the interest charge on net assets at the beginning of the year.

Imputed interest (notional interest) is the division's capital employed, multiplied by:

- the organisation's cost of borrowing, or
- the weighted average cost of capital of the organisation, or
- a special risk-weighted cost of capital to allow for the special business risk characteristics of the division. A higher interest rate would be applied to divisions with higher business risk.

Chapter 19: Performance measurement

Example

An investment centre has reported the following results.

	Current year	Previous year
	$000	$000
Sales	600	600
Gross profit	180	210
Net profit	24	30
Net assets at beginning of year	200	180

The division has a cost of capital of 10%, which is applied to net assets at the beginning of the year to calculate notional interest.

Required

How would the financial performance of the investment centre be assessed if residual income is used as the main measure of performance?

Answer

The residual income of the division in each year is calculated as follows.

	Current year		Previous year	
		$000		$000
Profit		24,000		30,000
Notional interest	(10% × $200,000)	(20,000)	(10% × $180,000)	(18,000)
Residual income		4,000		12,000

Residual income has fallen from $12,000 in the previous year to $4,000 in the current year. This indicates deterioration in divisional performance, although the residual income is still positive. This means that the division's profits exceed its cost of capital.

An analysis of gross profit margin, net profit margin and sales growth (0%) will indicate the causes of the fall in residual income.

8.3 Residual income and investment decisions

One reason for using residual income instead of ROI to measure a division's financial performance is that residual income has a money value, whereas ROI is a percentage value. A company may prefer to measure performance in money terms. In most other respects, however, residual income is similar to ROI as a measure of divisional performance.

Example

The difference between ROI and residual income can be illustrated by returning to the previous example that was used to illustrate the effect of ROI on investment decision-making.

A division has net assets of $800,000 and makes an annual profit of $120,000. It should be assumed that if the investment described below is not undertaken, the division will continue to have net assets of $800,000 and an annual profit of $120,000 for the next four years. The division's financial performance is measured using residual income, and the division's cost of capital is 12%.

The division is considering an investment in a new item of equipment that would cost $80,000. The estimated life of the equipment is four years with no residual value. The estimated additional profit before depreciation from the investment is as follows:

Year	$
1	20,000
2	25,000
3	35,000
4	40,000

The asset will be depreciated on a straight-line basis.

Required

What would be the annual residual income on this investment? Notional interest should be calculated on the basis of the average net assets employed during the year.

Would the investment centre manager decide to undertake this investment or not?

Answer

	Year 1	Year 2	Year 3	Year 4
Workings: notional interest	$	$	$	$
Average investment	870,000	850,000	830,000	810,000
Notional interest at 12%	104,400	102,000	99,600	97,200
Calculation of residual income	$	$	$	$
Profit without investment	120,000	120,000	120,000	120,000
Additional profit before depreciation	20,000	25,000	35,000	40,000
Additional depreciation	(20,000)	(20,000)	(20,000)	(20,000)
Divisional profit	120,000	125,000	135,000	140,000
Notional interest (see workings)	(104,400)	(102,000)	(99,600)	(97,200)
Residual income	15,600	23,000	35,400	42,800

If the investment is not undertaken, the residual income in each year would be:

	$
Profit without investment	120,000
Notional interest (12% × $800,000)	(96,000)
Residual income	24,000

If the investment is undertaken, residual income would fall in Year 1 and Year 2, but increase in Year 3 and Year 4. If the divisional manager is most concerned about short-term financial performance, he would decide that the investment should not be undertaken, in spite of the longer-term addition to residual income.

8.4 Advantages and disadvantages of residual income

Advantages of residual income

There are several advantages in using residual income as a measure of the performance of an investment centre.

- It relates the profit of the division to the capital employed, by charging an amount of notional interest on capital employed, and the division manager is responsible for both profit and capital employed.

- Residual income is a flexible measure of performance, because a different cost of capital can be applied to investments with different risk characteristics.

Disadvantages of residual income

There are also disadvantages in using residual income as a measure of the performance of an investment centre.

- Residual income is an accounting-based measure, and suffers from the same problem as ROI in defining capital employed and profit.

- Its main weakness is that it is difficult to compare the performance of different divisions using residual income. Larger divisions should earn a bigger residual income than smaller divisions. A small division making residual income of $50,000 might actually perform much better than a much larger division whose residual income is $100,000. This point is illustrated in the example below.

- Residual income is not easily understood by management, especially managers with little accounting knowledge.

Example

A company has two divisions, Small and Big. Big Division has net assets of $8 million and makes an annual profit of $900,000. Small Division has net assets of $400,000 and makes an annual profit of $90,000. The cost of capital for both divisions is 10%.

Required:

Compare the performance of the two divisions using:

(a) ROI

(b) Residual income.

Answer

	Big	Small
Profit	$900,000	$90,000
Net assets	$8 million	$400,000
ROI	11.25%	22.5%

	$	$
Profit	900,000	90,000
Notional interest	800,000	40,000
Residual income	100,000	50,000

Using ROI as a measure of performance, Small Division has performed better than Big Division. However Big Division has made a higher residual income, and it could therefore be argued that it has performed better than Small Division.

> **Performance measurement in service industries**
>
> - The characteristics of services and service industries
> - NFPIs in service industries

9 Performance measurement in service industries

9.1 The characteristics of services and service industries

Many organisations provide services rather than manufacture products. There are many examples of service industries: hotels, entertainment, the holiday and travel industries, professional services, banking, cleaning services, and so on.

Performance measurement for services may differ from performance measurement in manufacturing in several ways:

- **Simultaneity.** With a service, providing the service ('production') and receiving the service ('consumption' by the customer) happen at the same time. In manufacturing, the making of the product happens before the customer buys it.

- **Perishability.** It is impossible to store a service for future consumption: unlike manufacturing and retailing, there is no inventory of unused services. The service must be provided when the customer wants it.

- **Heterogeneity.** A product can be made to a standard specification. With a service provided by humans, there is variability in the standard of performance. The service is different in some way each time that it is provided. For example, even if they perform the same songs at several concerts, the performance of a rock band at a series of concerts will be different each time.

- **Intangibility.** With a service, there are many intangible elements of service that the customer is given, and that individual customers might value. For example, a high quality of service in a restaurant is often intangible, but noticed and valued by the customer.

Since services differ to some extent from products, should performance setting and performance measurement be different in service companies, compared with manufacturing companies?

9.2 NFPIs in service industries

Management accounting has its origins in manufacturing and construction industries. Over time, service industries have become a much more significant aspect of business, especially in countries with developed economies.

Performance measures – both financial and non-financial – are needed for service industries, but the key measures that are best suited to service industries are often very different from the key NFPIs in manufacturing.

Even some of the key financial performance measures in service industries may be a combination of both financial and non-financial performance, such as:

- Annual sales revenue per cubic metre of shelf space (ratio used by supermarkets and other stores)
- Cost per tonne-mile carried (road haulage companies)
- Cost per passenger-mile carried (transport companies)
- Average income per consultant day (management consultancy company).

> **Performance measurement in not-for-profit organisations and the public sector**
>
> - The special characteristics of not-for-profit organisations and the public sector
> - Identifying performance targets in not-for-profit and public sector organisations
> - Problems with measuring performance in this sector

10 Performance measurement in not-for-profit organisations and the public sector

10.1 The special characteristics of not-for-profit organisations and the public sector

The public sector refers to the sector of the economy that is owned or controlled by the government in the interests of the general public. It includes all government departments and government-financed bodies, including nationalised industries. In the UK, this includes the National Health Service, state-owned schools, the police and fire services, and so on.

Not-for-profit organisations are entities that are not government-owned or in the public sector, but which are not in existence to make a profit. They include charitable organisations and professional bodies.

A common feature of public sector organisations and not-for-profit organisations is that their main objective is not financial. The main objective of any such organisation depends on the purpose for which it exists: to administer the country (government departments), to provide education (schools and universities), provide medical care (hospitals), do charitable work, and so on.

A not-for-profit organisation will nevertheless have some financial objectives:

- State-owned organisations must operate within their spending budget.

- Charitable organisations may have an objective of keeping running costs within a certain limit, and of raising as much funding as possible for their charity work.

Although the main objective of not-for-profit and public sector organisations is not financial, they need good management, and their performance should be measured and monitored. In many countries, including the UK, public sector organisations are given a range of performance targets, against which actual performance is compared.

Since the main objective of these organisations is not financial, the main performance targets and measurements of performance should not be financial either. Performance measurement should be related to achieving targets that will help the organisation to achieve its objectives, whatever these may be.

10.2 Identifying performance targets in not-for-profit and public sector organisations

The broad principle is that any not-for-profit organisation should have:

- strategic targets, mainly non-financial in nature
- operational targets, which may be either financial (often related to costs and keeping costs under control) or non-financial (related to the nature of operations).

10.3 Problems with measuring performance in this sector

A good performance measurement system seeks to monitor the success of an organisation in achieving its objectives. To do this it must

- have clear objectives
- set targets which are linked to objectives
- measure performance against these targets.

However, there are several reasons why the problems with performance measurement in the public sector are greater than those in commercial business organisations including:

- An organisation in the public sector (and also not-for-profit organisations) may have a number of different 'main objectives', and they are required to achieve all these objectives within the constraint of limited available finance.

- In the public sector, the interests of different stakeholder groups are often important, and each group may have different expectations of what the organisation should be trying to achieve.

- In the public sector the government decides what the strategic objectives and targets should be and with a change of government, there may well be a change of priorities and targets.

Chapter 19: Performance measurement

> **Value for money**
>
> - The three Es
> - Performance measurement
> - Quantitative measures of efficiency

11 Value for money

11.1 The three Es

The performance of not-for-profit organisations or departments of government may be assessed on the basis of value for money 'VFM'. Value for money is often referred to as the '3Es':

- economy;
- efficiency; and
- effectiveness.

Economy

Economy means keeping spending within limits, and avoiding wasteful spending. It also means achieving the same purpose at a lower expense. A simple example of economy is found in the purchase of supplies. Suppose that an administrative department buys items of stationery from a supplier, and pays $2 each for pens. It might be possible to buy pens of the same quality to fulfil exactly the same purpose for $1.50 each. Economy would be achieved by switching to buying the $1.50 pens, saving $0.50 per pen with no loss of operating efficiency or effectiveness.

Efficiency

Efficiency means getting more output from available resources. Applied to employees, efficiency is often called 'productivity'. Suppose that an employee in the government's tax department processes 20 tax returns each day. Efficiency would be improved if the same individual increases the rate of output, and processes 25 tax returns each day, without any loss of effectiveness.

Effectiveness

Effectiveness refers to success in achieving end results or success in achieving objectives. Whereas efficiency is concerned with getting more outputs from available resources, effectiveness is concerned with achieving outputs that meet the required aims and objectives. For example, the effectiveness of treatment of a particular medical condition will be improved if the proportion of patients who are treated successfully rises from 80% to 90%.

Management accounting systems and reporting systems may provide information to management about value for money. Has VFM been achieved, and if so, how much and in what ways?

The link between the 3 Es

These refer to aspects of financial performance by looking at the outcome achieved by amount of cash input.

- Economy refers to the cost of inputs. Economy focuses on the need to avoid wasteful expenditure on items, and to keep spending within limits. It also helps to ensure that the limited finance available is spent sensibly.

- Efficiency refers to how the inputs have been used to generate outputs. It focuses on the need to make full use of available resources.

- Effectiveness refers to whether the outputs have met the objectives of the organisation. It focuses on the need to use resources for their intended purpose and achieve the objectives of the organisation.

11.2 Performance measurement

Performance measures need to be established so that employees operate in a way that meets the organisation's objectives for economy, efficiency and effectiveness.

The exact nature of such performance indicators would vary from case to case.

Example

State-owned schools may be given a target that their pupils (of a specified age) must achieve a certain level of examination grades or 'passes' in a particular examination.

Economy

This would be concerned with whether there any unnecessary spending and whether the same value could have been obtained for lower spending?

- Targets could be set for the prices paid for various items from external suppliers and actual performance measured against the targets.

- Quality targets could be set for goods purchased (e.g. number of returns to suppliers) and the standard of service from suppliers (number of late deliveries, number of incorrect deliveries, mistakes in invoicing).

Efficiency

This would be concerned with whether the school's resources been used efficiently. In particular whether more output could have been obtained from the available resources or whether the same results could have been achieved with fewer resources.

Performance indicators might include:

- teaching time per teacher per week; and

- utilisation of resources (e.g. science equipment and computer-based training materials, language laboratories);

Effectiveness

This would be concerned with whether pass rates have improved:

Performance indicators might include:

- total number of exams passed and by subject;
- grades achieved by subject;
- number of students passing exams by number passed;
- number of students achieving different levels of grade;
- number of students who continue to the next level of education (perhaps university).

11.3 Quantitative measures of efficiency

The syllabus requires you to understand the meaning and be able to calculate efficiency, capacity and activity ratios in a given situation. These were covered in chapter 6 (section 3).

Other quantitative measures of efficiency

Efficiency relates the quantity of resources to the quantity of output. This can be measured in a variety of ways

- $\text{Actual output} / \text{Maximum output for a given resource} \times 100\%$
- $\text{Minimum input to achieve required level of output} / \text{actual input} \times 100\%$
- $\text{Actual output} / \text{actual input} \times 100\%$ compared to a standard or target

Example

A hospital has an operating theatre which can be utilised for 20 hours per day.

The maximum number of operations that can be performed in any day is 40.

If on a particular day 35 operations were performed, this represents

$35/40 \times 100\% = 87.5\%$ efficiency

Example

A local authority must ensure that the refuse of all residents is collected each week for re-cycling. This normally requires 1,000 man hours.

If in a particular week 900 man hours were used this represents:

$1,000/900 \times 100\% = 111.1\%$ efficiency

Example

Schools may have a standard pupil to teacher ratio of 27.

If a particular school has 550 pupils and 21 teachers then the actual ratio is 26.2 which represents:

$^{27}/_{26.2} \times 1005 = 103.05\%$ efficiency.

> **Other aspects of performance measurement**
>
> - Benchmarking
> - Cost control, cost reduction and value analysis

12 Other aspects of performance measurement

12.1 Benchmarking

It may be useful to be aware of benchmarking as a method of assessing performance. Benchmarking involves comparing performance with the performance of another, similar organisation or operation. In other words, another organisation or department is used as a 'benchmark for comparison'.

Performance can be assessed in terms of whether it has been better or worse than the selected benchmark. By making such comparisons, it should be possible to identify strengths and weaknesses in performance.

There are three main types of benchmarking.

- **Internal benchmarking**. An entity may have many similar operations, such as regional or area branches. For example, a bank may have a network of branches, and a retail company may have a network of retail stores. The best-performing branches or departments can be used as a benchmark, and the performance of other branches compared against it.

- **Competitive benchmarking**. This involves comparing the performance of the organisation against the performance of its most successful competitors. In this way, the areas of performance where the competitor is better can be identified, and measures can then be planned for reducing the gap in performance.

  The practical difficulty with competitive benchmarking is that the competitor will not willingly act as a benchmark, and allow its competitors to make a detailed study of its operations. Competitive benchmarking is therefore usually done without the competitor's knowledge. For example, a company might buy a product of a successful competitor and analyse its qualities and features in detail, perhaps by taking it apart in a laboratory and investigating its structure and components.

- **Operational benchmarking**. A company might use benchmarking to assess the performance of a particular aspect of its operations, such as customer order handling, handling e-commerce orders from the Internet, or warehousing and despatch operations. It might be able to identify a company in a completely different industry that carries out similar operations successfully. The other company might be prepared to act as a benchmark, and allow its operations to be studied and its staff interviewed. The benefit of this type of benchmarking is that a business is able to learn from world-class companies how to improve its operations and raise its performance levels.

12.2 Cost control, cost reduction and value analysis

Cost control is different from cost reduction.

Cost control

Cost control is the process of monitoring and regulating expenditure. Cost control should be an ongoing activity for all companies. An organisation is willing to spend money but does not want to waste it. The term cost control implies control of costs to achieve a certain level of activity.

Cost control is an ongoing management process which should commence from the start of the business.

Cost control is achieved through setting targets against which actual performance can be compared. Differences can then be investigated and action taken as necessary.

Variance analysis is an effective cost control technique. Both positive and negative variances should be investigated.

- Negative variances might indicate that something is going wrong and corrective action should be taken

- Positive variances might indicate that a manager has found a new and more efficient method of carrying out a task. It might be possible to spread this new approach throughout the business, thus reducing costs.

Cost reduction

Cost reduction is the process of identifying and eliminating unnecessary costs to improve profitability.

Cost reduction is a reaction to a problem. An organisation might find itself in financial difficulties and so tries to reduce costs. It could try to do this by closing departments or dismissing staff.

Cost reduction techniques include:

- Investment in digital technology (email instead of printing, communication with skype instead telephone)

- Outsourcing involves contracting out of business process to another party. For example, a company might close its payroll department and outsource this function to a specialist provider of payroll services. Many different business processes might be outsourced including routine data processing, debt collection, distribution, component manufacturing etc.

- Target costing

- Lifecycle costing

- Benchmarking

Value analysis

Value analysis is an approach which attempts to improve the return from a product by understanding its components and their associated costs. The idea is to improve the components by reducing their cost or by improving their quality.

Value analysis is defined as "the systematic inter-disciplinary examination of factors affecting the cost of a product or service, in order to devise means of achieving the specified purpose most economically at the required standard of quality and reliability".

The aim of value analysis is to maintain or improve the value and quality of a product at a reduced cost.

Target costing is value analysis technique.

Applied Knowledge
Management Accounting (MA)

Answers to exercises and practice multiple choice questions

Chapter 1: The nature and purpose of cost and management accounting

1 **True**

2 **D**

Management accountants provide information for decision-making but do not make the decisions themselves. A cost accounting system gathers data, not information. Management accounting systems provide some but not all the information needed for strategic and tactical planning. Information should be timely and relevant: it should also be reliable but need not be 100% accurate.

3 **B**

Budgets are a form of tactical plan, even when they do not extend over a one-year financial period.

Chapter 2: Cost classification

1 **True**

Inspectors and testers are indirect labour. They work in the production department and so are production overhead costs.

2 **C**

Workers in a stores department are indirect labour. The other employees in the question are all engaged in the direct production of the items produced or the direct provision of the services sold by the entity.

3   A

A writer's fee is a direct expense of publishing. The cost of a copy editor is a direct labour cost if the editor is employed by the publisher or a direct expense if an external editor is used. The cost of copies sent for review is a marketing overhead cost. The cost of buying printed copies of the book fro a printer is a direct material cost.

4   A

The factory manager does not appear to have responsibility for revenues (or profits) since all output is transferred to a processing centre. The manager is also not responsible for capital investment. The factory is therefore likely to be a cost centre.

5   C

Weekly cost reports are likely to be too frequent to be useful – especially since many costs such as salaries and rent are incurred on a monthly basis. Monthly cost reporting is the most probable frequency.

6   B

Chapter 5: Forecasting techniques

Exercise

	P		$
High: Total cost of	16,100 units	=	107,450
Low: Total cost of	12,600 units	=	(91,700)
Difference: Variable cost of	3,500 units	=	15,750

Therefore variable cost per unit = $15,750/3,500 units = $4.50 per unit.

(Tutorial note: take the highest volume of activity (= 16,100 units), not the volume of activity with the highest cost, which in this exercise was 16,000 units.)

Substitute in high or low equation	Cost
	$
Total cost of 12,600 units	91,700
Variable cost of 12,600 units (× $4.50)	(56,700)
Therefore fixed costs per month	35,000

Cost estimate for August	Cost
	$
Fixed costs	35,000
Variable cost (15,000 units × $4.50)	67,500
Estimated total costs	102,500

Answers to exercises and practice multiple choice questions

1 C

Adjust cost of 'low' activity level: adjusted cost = $960,000 + $36,000 = $996,000

Variable cost per unit = $(1,104,000 − 996,000)/(72,000 − 60,000) units = $9 per unit.

Fixed costs = $1,104,000 − (72,000 × $9) = $456,000.

Total cost of 70,000 units = (70,000 × $9) + $456,000 = $1,086,000.

2 D

Variable cost (above 15,000 units) = $(1,104,000 − 960,000)/(72,000 − 60,000) units = $12 per unit.

Variable cost per unit below 15,000 units = $\$12/0.9$

Fixed costs = $960,000 − (60,000 × $12) = $240,000.

Total costs of 14,000 units = (14,000 × $\$12/0.9$) + $240,000 = $426,667.

3 A

4 A

$$b = \frac{5(138{,}546) - (258)(2{,}670)}{5(13{,}732) - (258)^2}$$

$$= 3{,}870/2{,}096 = 1.846$$

$$a = \frac{2{,}670}{5} - \frac{1.846(258)}{5}$$

$$= 439$$

5 B

The correlation coefficient must have a value in the range − 1 to + 1.

6 C

Spreadsheets can be used to prepare any table of figures, and this includes calculating a line of best fit from data entered into the spreadsheet model. Spreadsheets are not suitable for the recording and storage of large quantities of data.

Chapter 8: Accounting for materials

Exercise 1

Remember that holding costs and usage quantities should refer to the same length of time. In this example, holding costs are 8% of $60 = $4.80 per unit per year. Usage is 5,000 units in three months, which is 20,000 units per year.

$$EOQ = \sqrt{\frac{2C_oD}{C_H}}$$

Where:

$C_o = 250$

$D = 20,000$

$C_H = 4.80$

$$= \sqrt{\left(\frac{2 \times 20,000 \times 250}{4.80}\right)} = 1,443 \text{ units}$$

1 D

$EOQ = \sqrt{(2 \times 240 \times 8,000)/0.54} = 2,667$ units

2 A

An increase in the holding cost of inventory means that the EOQ will become smaller (since the holding cost is 'below the line' in the EOQ formula). A smaller EOQ means more orders on average each year; therefore annual ordering costs will increase.

3 C

$EOQ = \sqrt{(2 \times 500 \times 10,000)/2.50} = 2,000$ units.

Costs will be minimised by purchasing either 2,000 units (the EOQ) or the minimum quantity required to obtain the large order discount (5,000 units).

	Order size 2,000	Order size 5,000
	$	$
Purchase costs (10,000 units)	250,000	230,000
Holding costs (at $2.50)	2,500	6,250
Ordering costs ($500 per order)	2,500	1,000
Total costs	255,000	237,250

4 **C**

$$\sqrt{\frac{2 \times 800 \times (200 \times 50)}{2\left(1 - \frac{200}{1,000}\right)}}$$

= 3,162 units, or 3,200 units to the nearest 100 units.

5 **B**

Reorder level = Demand per day × Maximum supply lead time = 150 units × 10 days = 1,500 units.

Chapter 9: Accounting for labour

Exercise

Average number of employees = (600 + 630)/2 = 615.

Labour turnover rate = (35/615) × 100% = 5.7%.

1 **B**

Actual output = 2,100 units.

Capacity = 15 employees × 36 hours per week = 540 hours.

These two measurements need to be put on to the same basis, hours or units.

Actual output of 2,100 units is the equivalent of 525 hours of work at the standard rate of efficiency.

Production volume ratio = (525/540) × 100% = 97.2%.

Check: Capacity utilisation ratio = 500/540 = 92.6%.

Productivity or efficiency ratio = 2,100/(500 × 4) = 105%

Production volume ratio = 92.6% × 105% = 97.2%.

2 **A**

Employees at the beginning of the year = 5,700 − 360 + 600 = 5,940

Average number of employees = (5,700 + 5,940)/2 = 5,820

Labour turnover − (600/5,820) × 100% = 10.3%

Chapter 10: Accounting for overheads

Exercise 1

Reciprocal method of cost apportionment of service department costs

	Total	P1	P2	S1	S2
	$	$	$	$	$
Allocated/apportioned overhead costs	92,000	32,520	22,000	15,000	22,480
Apportion costs of service departments:					
S1 (20:60:20)		3,000	9,000	(15,000)	3,000
				0	25,480
S2 (70:20:10)		17,836	5,096	2,548	(25,480)
Now repeat:					
S1 (20:60:20)		510	1,529	(2,548)	509
S2 (70:20:10)		356	102	51	(509)
Repeat again					
S1 (20:60:20)		10	31	(51)	10
S2 (70:20:10)		7	2	1	(10)
Repeat again					
S1 (20:60:20)		0	1	(1)	0
	92,000	54,239	37,761	0	0

Exercise 2

(a)

	Machine hours
Product A: (3,000 units × 0.2 hours)	600
Product B: (4,000 units × 0.1 hours)	400
Product C: (1,000 units × 0.2 hours)	200
Total machine hours	1,200
Production overhead expenditure	$24,000
Absorption rate per machine hour	$20
Overheads absorbed by each product:	$
Product A: (600 hours × $20)	12,000
Product B: (400 hours × $20)	8,000
Product C: (200 hours × $20)	4,000
Total	24,000

	Product A	Product B	Product C
	$	$	$
Prime cost per unit	3.00	4.00	5.00
Absorbed overhead at $20/machine hour	4.00	2.00	4.00
Full production cost/unit	7.00	6.00	9.00

(b)

	Labour cost
Product A	$3,500
Product B	$8,000
Product C	$4,500
Total direct labour cost	$16,000
Production overhead expenditure	$24,000
Absorption rate as % of labour cost	150%

Overheads absorbed by each product:	$
Product A: ($3,500 × 150%)	5,250
Product B: ($8,000 × 150%)	12,000
Product C: ($4,500 × 150%)	6,750
Total	24,000

Exercise 3

(a)

Absorption rate = Budgeted overheads/Budgeted direct labour hours

= $240,000/30,000 hours = $8 per direct labour hour.

The overheads charged to the cost of production in Year 7 were 33,000 hours × $8 = $264,000.

(b)

	$
Overheads absorbed (see above)	264,000
Actual overhead expenditure	(258,000)
Over-absorbed overhead	6,000

Exercise 4

(a)

Absorption rate = Budgeted overheads/Budgeted direct labour hours

= $720,000/120,000 hours = $6 per direct labour hour.

The overheads charged to the cost of production in the year were 106,000 hours × $6 = $636,000.

	$
Overheads absorbed (see above)	636,000
Actual overhead expenditure	704,000
Under-absorbed overhead	68,000

Reasons for the under-absorbed overhead

Expenditure variance

	$	
Budgeted (expected) overhead expenditure	720,000	
Actual overhead expenditure	704,000	
Expenditure variance	16,000	Favourable

Volume variance

	Hours	
Budgeted direct labour hours	120,000	
Actual direct labour hours	106,000	
Volume variance in hours	14,000	Adverse
Absorption rate per hour	$6	
Volume variance in $	$84,000	Adverse

The volume variance and the expenditure variance together add up to the under-absorbed overhead of $68,000.

(b)

		Job 123		Job 124
		$		$
Prime costs		270,000		360,000
Production overhead	(50,000 × $6)	300,000	(56,000 × $6)	336,000
Full production cost		570,000		696,000

Exercise 5

The fixed overhead absorption rate = $800,000 / 100,000 direct labour hours = $8 per direct labour hour.

Absorbed overheads	$
Fixed overheads (97,000 hours × $8)	776,000
Variable overheads (97,000 hours × $4)	388,000
Total absorbed overheads	1,164,000
Actual overhead expenditure	1,120,000
Over-absorbed overheads	44,000

Explaining the over-absorbed overhead

Expected overhead expenditure	$	
Fixed overheads (= Budgeted fixed overhead)	800,000	
Variable overheads (97,000 × $4)	388,000	
Total expected overhead expenditure	1,188,000	
Actual overhead expenditure	1,120,000	
Expenditure variance	68,000	Favourable

	hours	
Budgeted volume (direct labour hours)	100,000	
Actual volume (direct labour hours)	97,000	
Volume variance (direct labour hours)	3,000	Adverse
Fixed overhead absorption rate/direct labour hour	$8	
Volume variance in $ (fixed overhead only)	$24,000	Adverse

Summary	$	
Expenditure variance	68,000	Favourable
Volume variance	24,000	Adverse
Total over-absorbed overhead	44,000	Favourable

1 C

	Basis of apportionment	P1	P2	S1	S2
		$	$	$	$
Initial costs		300,000	450,000	320,000	350,000
Apportion S2	(30:40:30)	105,000	140,000	105,000	(350,000)
				425,000	
Apportion S1	(30:70)	127,500	297,500	(425,000)	
		532,500	887,500		

2 A

	CC1	CC2
	hours	hours
Product Y	80,000	100,000
Product Z	40,000	80,000
Total hours	120,000	180,000
Cost	$660,000	$540,000
Absorption rate per hour	$5.50	$3

Cost per unit of Product Z = (2 hours × $5.50) + (4 hours × $3) = $23.

3 A

	C1	C2
	hours	hours
Product P	30,000	75,000
Product Q	60,000	45,000
Total hours	90,000	120,000
Cost	$324,000	$583,200
Absorption rate per hour	$3.60	$4.86

Cost per unit of Product Q	$
C1: 4 hours × $3.60	14.40
C2: 3 hours × $4.86	14.58
Total cost	28.98

4 D

If actual labour hours are less than budget, overhead will be under-absorbed. If actual overhead spending is more than budget, overhead will be under-absorbed.

5 D

Overhead absorption rate = $144,000/36,000 hours = $4 per direct labour hour

	$
Overhead absorbed (37,500 × $4)	150,000
Actual overhead expenditure	157,500
Under-absorbed overhead	7,500

6 A

Overhead absorption rate = $300,000/24,000 hours = $12.50 per direct labour hour.

	$
Overhead absorbed (26,000 × $12.50)	325,000
Actual overhead expenditure	318,500
Over-absorbed overhead	6,500

Chapter 11: Accounting for costs: ledger entries

Exercise 1

Materials

	$		$
Opening balance	1,000		
Financial ledger control	20,000		

Wages and salaries

	$		$
Financial ledger control	25,000		

Production overheads

	$		$
Financial ledger control	4,000		

Answers to exercises and practice multiple choice questions

Other overheads

	$		$
Financial ledger control	7,000		

Sales

	$		$
		Financial ledger control	90,000

Financial ledger control account

	$		$
Sales	90,000	Opening balances	5,000
		Materials	20,000
		Wages and salaries	25,000
		Production overheads	4,000
		Other overheads	7,000

Exercise 2

Materials

	$		$
Opening balance	7,000	Work-in-progress	33,000
Financial ledger control	50,000	Production overheads	17,000
(purchases)		Other overheads	2,000
		Closing balance c/f	5,000
	57,000		57,000
Opening balance b/f	5,000		

Wages and salaries

	$		$
Financial ledger control	45,000	Work-in-progress	28,000
		Production overheads	7,000
		Other overheads	10,000
	45,000		45,000

Production overheads

	$		$
Materials	17,000	Work-in-progress (absorbed)	50,000
Wages and salaries	7,000		
Financial ledger control	24,000		
(expenses)			
Over-absorbed overhead	2,000		
	50,000		50,000

Work-in-progress

	$		$
Opening balance	3,000	Finished goods	106,000
Materials	33,000	(balancing figure)	
Wages and salaries	28,000		
Production overhead	50,000	Closing balance c/f	8,000
	114,000		114,000
Opening balance b/f	8,000		

Finished goods

	$		$
Opening balance	4,000	Cost of sales	109,000
Work-in-progress	106,000	Closing balance c/f	1,000
	110,000		110,000
Opening balance b/f	1,000		

Other overheads

	$		$
Materials	2,000	Cost of sales	27,000
Wages and salaries	10,000		
Financial ledger control (expenses)	15,000		
	27,000		27,000

Sales

	$		$
Income statement	160,000	Financial ledger control	160,000

Cost of sales

	$		$
Finished goods	109,000	Income statement	136,000
Other overheads	27,000		
	136,000		136,000

Under- or over-absorbed overhead account

	$		$
Income statement	2,000	Production overhead	2,000

Costing income statement

	$		$
Cost of sales	136,000	Sales	160,000
Profit (financial ledger control account)	26,000	Over-absorbed overhead	2,000
	162,000		162,000

Financial ledger control account

	$		$
Sales	160,000	Opening balance	14,000
		Materials	50,000
		Wages and salaries	45,000
		Production overheads	24,000
		Other overheads	15,000
Closing balance c/f	14,000	Income statement (profit)	26,000
	174,000		174,000
		Opening balance b/f	14,000

Statement of closing balances

	Debit	Credit
	$	$
Materials	5,000	
Work-in-progress	8,000	
Finished goods	1,000	
Financial ledger control		14,000
	14,000	14,000

Chapter 12: Marginal costing and absorption costing

Exercise 1

Contribution per unit:

Product X: $8 – $3 = $5

Product Y: $6 – $2 = $4

	$
Contribution from Product X: (40,000 × $5)	200,000
Contribution from Product Y: (30,000 × $4)	120,000
Total contribution per month	320,000
Fixed costs	(250,000)
Profit per month	70,000

Exercise 2

Income statement, marginal costing	$	$
Sales (40,000 × $11)		440,000
Variable cost of sales (40,000 × $5)		(200,000)
Contribution		240,000
Fixed costs:		
Production fixed costs	110,000	
Other fixed costs	80,000	
Total fixed costs		(191,000)
Profit		49,000

	units
Sales volume	40,000
Production volume	37,000
Reduction in inventory	(3,000)

Fixed production overhead cost per unit = $111,000/37,000 units = $3 per unit

Since sales are more than production volume, there will be a fall in inventory and the marginal costing profit will be higher than the absorption costing profit.

	$
Marginal costing profit	49,000
Difference in profit (3,000 units × $3)	(9,000)
Absorption costing profit (lower)	40,000

1   A

	$000	$000
Sales		250
Direct materials	24	
Direct labour	36	
Direct expenses	5	
Variable production overheads	6	
Variable selling overheads	8	
Total variable costs		79
Contribution		171

2   B

There is a reduction in inventory by 1,000 units, since production volume (24,000 units) is less than sales volume (25,000 units).

If absorption costing is used, the fixed production overhead cost per unit is $4 (= $96,000/24,000 units).

The difference between the absorption costing profit and marginal costing profit is therefore $4,000 (= 1,000 units × $4).

Absorption costing profit is lower, because there has been a reduction in inventory.

Absorption costing profit would therefore be $65,000 – $4,000 = $61,000.

3   B

There is an increase in inventory by 2,000 units, since production volume (32,000 units) is more than sales volume (30,000 units).

If absorption costing is used, the fixed production overhead cost per unit is $5 (= $160,000/32,000 units).

The difference between the absorption costing profit and marginal costing profit is therefore $10,000 (= 2,000 units × $5).

Absorption costing profit is higher, because there has been an increase in inventory.

Marginal costing profit would therefore be $101,000 – $10,000 = $91,000.

4   D

Fixed production cost per unit = $5 (= $125,000/25,000 units).

Difference between marginal and absorption costing profits = $15,000.

Therefore difference between sales volume and production volume = $15,000/$5 = 3,000 units.

Absorption costing profit is lower, which means that sales volume is higher than production volume.

Expected sales volume = 25,000 units + 3,000 units = 28,000 units.

Chapter 13: Job costing, batch costing and service costing

1   B

Job cost	$
Direct materials	125
Direct labour (4 hours at $20)	80
Direct expenses	25
Prime cost	230
Production overhead (4 hours at $35)	140
Production cost of the job	370
Non-production overheads (60% of prime cost)	138
Total job cost	508

2   D

Job costing is appropriate where each cost unit (job) differs in some respects from other cost units. Installing elevators differs between each job (with the location of the building, the layout and height of the building, number of elevators to install, type of elevator and so on).

3   A

Number of tonne/kilometres = 80,000 kilometres carrying an average of 3 tonnes = 240,000.

Cost per tonne-kilometre = $720,000/240,000 = $3.

Chapter 14: Process costing

Exercise 1

Normal loss = 5% × 6,000 units = 300 units

Expected output = 95% × 6,000 units = 5,700 units

	$
Direct materials	21,600
Direct labour	8,000
Production overheads	16,000
	45,600
Scrap value of normal loss (300 × $3.80)	(1,140)
	44,460
Expected output	5,700 units
Cost per unit	$7.80

Process account

	units	$		units	$
Direct materials	6,000	21,600	Finished goods (at $7.80)	5,500	42,900
Direct labour		8,000	Normal loss (300 at $3.80)	300	1,140
Production overheads		16,000	Abnormal loss (at $7.80)	200	1,560
	6,000	45,600		6,000	45,600

Abnormal loss account

	units	$		units	$
Process account	200	1,560	Scrap (200 at $3.80)	200	760

Exercise 2

Normal loss = 4% × 10,000 units = 400 units

Expected output = 96% × 10,000 units = 9,600 units

	$
Direct materials	35,200
Conversion costs	29,600
	64,800
Expected output	9,600 units
Cost per unit	$6.75

Process account

	units	$		units	$
Direct materials	10,000	35,200	Finished goods (at $6.75)	9,750	65,813
Conversion costs		29,600	Normal loss	400	0
Abnormal gain (at $6.75)	150	1,013			
	10,150	65,813		10,150	65,813

Exercise 3

Statement of equivalent units

Equivalent units	Total	Direct materials		Conversion costs	
	Total units	Equivalent units		Equivalent units	
Completed units	11,000	11,000		11,000	
Closing inventory	5,000	5,000	(5,000 × 40%)	2,000	
Total equivalent units	16,000	16,000		13,000	

Statement of cost per equivalent unit

Costs	Direct materials	Conversion costs
	$	$
Opening inventory	14,800	6,100
Costs incurred in the period	70,000	34,200
Total costs	84,800	40,300
Equivalent units	16,000	13,000
Cost per equivalent unit	$5.30	$3.10

Statement of evaluation

Statement of evaluation	Direct materials		Conversion costs		Total cost
		$		$	$
Completed units	(11,000 × $5.3)	58,300	(11,000 × $3.1)	34,100	92,400
Closing inventory	(5,000 × $5.3)	26,500	(2,000 × $3.1)	6,200	32,700

The **process account** is prepared as follows:

Process account

	units	$		units	$
Opening inventory	2,000	20,900	Finished goods	11,000	92,400
Direct materials	14,000	70,000			
Conversion costs		34,200	Closing inventory c/f	5,000	32,700
	16,000	125,100		16,000	125,100

Exercise 4

Statement of equivalent units (work done in the current period)

Equivalent units	Total units	Direct materials Equivalent units		Conversion costs Equivalent units
To complete opening inventory, finished first	2,000	(0%)	0	(20% × 2,000) 400
Units started and completed in the current period	9,000		9,000	9,000
Finished output	11,000		9,000	9,400
Closing inventory	5,000	(40% × 5,000)	5,000	2,000
Total equivalent units	16,000		14,000	11,400

Statement of cost per equivalent unit (work in the current period)

Cost per equivalent unit	Direct materials	Conversion costs
Total cost in current period	$70,000	$34,200
Total equivalent units in the current period	14,000	11,400
Cost per equivalent unit	$5.00	$3.00

Statement of evaluation

	Direct materials		Conversion costs		Total cost
		$		$	$
Finished units					
Opening WIP					
Cost b/f		14,800		6,100	20,900
Cost to complete		0	(400 × $3)	1,200	1,200
		14,800		7,300	22,100
Units started and finished	(9,000 × $5)	45,000	(9,000 × $3)	27,000	72,000
Finished units		59,800		34,300	94,100
Closing inventory	(5,000 × $5)	25,000	(2,000 × $3)	6,000	31,000
		84,800		40,300	125,100

The process account is prepared as follows:

Process 2 account

	units	$		units	$
Opening inventory	2,000	20,900	Finished goods	11,000	94,100
Direct materials	14,000	70,000			
Conversion costs		34,200	Closing inventory c/f	5,000	31,000
	16,000	125,100		16,000	125,100
Opening inventory b/f	5,000	31,000			

Answers to exercises and practice multiple choice questions

1 B

Actual loss = 1,000 units (= 12,000 – 11,000). Normal loss = 600 units (= 5% of 12,000). Therefore, abnormal loss = 400 units.

Total costs = $60,000 + $15,240 = $75,240.

Expected output = 12,000 units less 5% = 11,400 units.

Cost per unit of expected output = $75,240/11,400 = $6.60

Therefore, cost of abnormal loss = 400 × $6.60 = $2,640.

2 C

Actual loss = 400 units (= 3,600 – 3,200). Normal loss = 600 units (= 1/6 of 3,600). Therefore, abnormal gain = 200 units.

Total costs = $15,000 + $5,160 = $20,160.

Expected output = 3,600 units × 5/6 = 3,000 units.

Cost per unit of expected output = $20,160/3,000 = $6.72

Therefore, cost of abnormal loss = 200 × $6.72 = $1,344.

3 B

Statement of equivalent units

	Direct materials equivalent units		Closing WIP equivalent units
Finished output	1,600		1,600
Closing WIP	400	(400 × 25%)	100
	2,000		1,700

Statement of cost per equivalent unit

		Direct materials		Conversion costs
Cost	(7,935 + 25,605)	$33,540	(1,020 + 5,440)	$6,460
Equivalent units		2,000		1,700
Cost per equivalent unit		$16.77		$3.80

Valuation of closing WIP = (400 × $16.77) + (100 × $3.80) = $7,088

4 C

	Direct materials equivalent units		Closing WIP equivalent units
Opening WIP finished	0	(400 × 25%)	100
Other finished output	1,500		1,500
Total finished output	1,500		1,600
Closing WIP	500	(500 × 40%)	200
	2,000		1,800

Statement of cost per equivalent unit in the current period

	Direct materials	Conversion costs
Cost	$12,200	$3,060
Equivalent units	2,000	1,800
Cost per equivalent unit	$6.10	$1.70

Valuation of finished output

	$
Opening WIP: cost brought forward	2,920
Costs in current period	
Direct materials (1,500 × $6.10)	9,150
Conversion costs (1,600 × $1.70)	2,720
Total cost of finished output	14,790

5 A

Actual loss = 1,000 units. Normal loss = 400 units. Therefore abnormal loss is 600 units.

Statement of equivalent units

	Direct materials equivalent units		Abnormal loss equivalent units
Finished output	7,000		7,000
Abnormal loss	600	(600 × 60%)	360
	7,600		7,360

Statement of cost per equivalent unit

	Direct materials	Conversion costs
Cost	$30,400	$11,040
Equivalent units	7,600	7,360
Cost per equivalent unit	$4	$1.50

Valuation of abnormal loss = (600 × $4) + (360 × $1.50) = $2,940

6 C

Cost of output net of by-product revenue = $(42,000 + 15,000 − 1,500) = $55,500

Units of joint product = 2,000 + 3,000 = 5,000

Cost per unit of joint product output = $55,500/5,000 = $11.10

Cost of output units of JP2 = 2,000 × $11.10 = $22,200

Chapter 16: Budgeting

1 A

2 B

Budgeted production = 20,000 + 4,000 − 5,000 units of product X = 19,000 units

Budgeted usage of material B = 19,000 units × 3 kilos per unit = 57,000 kilos

Budgeted purchase quantity of material B = 18,000 + 57,000 − 9,000 = 66,000 kilos

3 B

A fixed budget is for a fixed quantity of sales and output. It is not necessarily correct to state that no changes are permitted to a fixed budget.

4 D

Budgeted purchases of material T = 40,000 kilos

Budgeted usage of material T = 40,000 + 4,000 = 44,000 kilos

Budgeted production of Product Z = 22,000 units (= 44,000 kilos/2 kilos per unit)

Budgeted sales of Z = 19,000 units.

Therefore, an increase of 3,000 units in Product Z inventory is planned.

5   C

	Product A	Product B
	units	units
Sales budget	12,000	15,000
Closing inventory	1,000	5,000
Opening inventory	(2,000)	(3,000)
Production budget	11,000	17,000
	hours	hours
Hours per unit	2	1.5
Total direct labour hours	22,000	25,500

Direct labour budget = 22,000 + 25,500 = 47,500 hours at $18 per hour = $855,000

Chapter 18: Standard costing and variance analysis

Exercise 1

Budgeted direct labour hours	hours
Product X: (2,000 units × 1.5 hours)	3,000
Product Y (1,000 units × 2 hours)	2,000
	5,000
Budgeted fixed production overheads	$60,000
Fixed overhead absorption rate/hour	$12

	Product X		Product Y	
		$		$
Direct materials				
Material A	(2 units × $4)	8	(1.5 units × $4)	6
Material B	(1 unit × $3)	3	(3 units × $3)	9
Direct labour	(1.5 hours × $10)	15	(2 hours × $10)	20
Variable production overhead	(1.5 hours × $2)	3	(2 hours × $2)	4
Standard variable prod'n cost		29		39
Fixed production overhead	(1.5 hours × $12)	18	(2 hours × $12)	24
Standard full production cost		47		63

Exercise 2

Note: In standard costing, output is valued at the standard cost per unit produced. Output in this example is therefore costed as 4,000 units at $3 each, not as 5,500 hours at $2 each.

	$
4,000 units of output should cost (× $3)	12,000
They did cost	11,700
Variable overhead total cost variance	300 (F)

The variance is favourable, because actual costs were lower than the standard cost.

Exercise 3

Direct materials total cost variance:	$
6,000 units of output should cost (× $6)	36,000
They did cost	35,900
Total direct materials cost variance	100 (F)

Materials price variance	$
12,800 kilos of materials should cost (× $3)	38,400
They did cost	35,900
Materials price variance	2,500 (F)

Materials usage variance	kilos
6,000 units of Product P44 should use (× 2 kilos)	12,000
They did use	12,800
Materials usage variance in kilos	800 (A)
Standard price per kilo of material L	× $3
Materials usage variance in $	$2,400 (A)

The materials price variance and the materials usage variance add up to the materials total cost variance.

Exercise 4

Standard fixed production overhead cost per unit = $72,000/6,000 units = $12 per unit.

Fixed production overhead expenditure variance	$
Budgeted fixed overhead expenditure	72,000
Actual fixed overhead expenditure	71,200
Fixed overhead expenditure variance	800 (F)

Fixed production overhead volume variance	units	
Budgeted production volume	6,000	
Actual production volume	5,600	
Volume variance in units	400	(A)
Standard fixed overhead rate per unit	× $12	
Fixed production overhead volume variance in $	$4,800	(A)

Exercise 5

Standard fixed production overhead cost per unit = $96,000/16,000 units = $6 per unit.

Standard fixed production overhead rate per hour = $6 per unit/0.25 hours per unit = $24 per hour.

Budgeted hours of work = $96,000/$24 per hour = 4,000 hours.

(Alternatively: Budgeted hours of work = 16,000 units × 0.25 hours per unit = 4,000 hours).

Fixed production overhead expenditure variance	$	
Budgeted fixed overhead expenditure	96,000	
Actual fixed overhead expenditure	98,500	
Fixed overhead expenditure variance	2,500	(A)

Fixed production overhead volume variance	units	
Budgeted production volume	16,000	
Actual production volume	15,700	
Volume variance in units	300	(A)
Standard fixed overhead rate per unit	× $6	
Fixed production overhead volume variance in $	$1,800	(A)

Fixed overhead efficiency variance	hours	
15,700 units should take (× 0.25 hours)	3,925	
They did take	4,200	
Efficiency variance in hours	275	(A)
Standard fixed overhead rate per hour	× $24	
Fixed overhead efficiency variance in $	$6,600	(A)

Fixed overhead capacity variance	hours	
Budgeted hours of work	4,000	
Actual hours of work	4,200	
Capacity variance in hours	200	(F)
Standard fixed overhead rate per hour	× $24	
Fixed overhead capacity variance in $	$4,800	(F)

Exercise 6

Sales price variance	$
39,200 units should sell for (× $20)	784,000
They did sell for	802,300
Sales price variance	18,300 (F)

Sales volume profit variance	units
Actual sales volume (units)	39,200
Budgeted sales volume (units)	42,000
Sales volume variance in units	2,800 (A)
Standard profit per unit ($20 – $16 = $4)	× $4
Sales volume profit variance	$11,200 (A)

Exercise 7

Direct labour rate variance	$
1,240 hours should cost (× $16)	19,840
They did cost	?
Direct labour rate variance	1,700 (F)

The rate variance was favourable, which means that actual costs were less than standard.

Actual cost of labour = $19,840 - $1,700 = $18,140.

Exercise 8

Labour efficiency variance	hours
3,200 units of Product H should take	?
They did take	5,150
Labour efficiency variance in hours	?
Standard rate per hour	× $18
Labour efficiency variance in $	$8,100 (F)

Labour efficiency variance in hours = $8,100 (F)/$18 per hour = 450 hours (F).

The variance is favourable. This means that actual hours were less than standard hours (and so standard hours are more than actual hours).

Standard hours to make 3,200 units = 5,150 + 450 = 5,600 hours.

Standard time per unit = 5,600 hours/3,200 units = 1.75 hours per unit.

Standard direct labour cost of Product H =

1.75 hours at $18 per hour = $31.50.

1   D

	$
18,000 hours should cost (× $18.50)	333,000
They did cost	328,500
Direct labour rate variance	4,500 (F)

The variance is favourable because actual costs were lower than standard cost.

2   C

	hours
8,800 units of Product P234 should take (× 2 hours)	17,600
They did take	18,000
Efficiency variance in hours	400 (A)
Standard direct labour rate per hour	× $18.50
Direct labour efficiency variance in $	$7,400 (A)

The efficiency variance is adverse because the output took longer to make than it should have done.

3   B

	$
6,450 units should sell for (× $15)	96,750
They did sell for	92,880
Sales price variance	3,870 (A)

	units
Actual sales volume (units)	6,450
Budgeted sales volume (units)	6,000
Sales volume variance in units	450 (F)
Standard contribution per unit (80% × $15)	× $12
Sales volume variance (contribution variance)	5,400 (F)

4   A

Budgeted expenditure = 100%

Actual expenditure = 97% of budget

Expenditure variance = $4,800 which is 3% of budget

Budgeted expenditure = $4,800/0.03 = $160,000

Actual expenditure = 97% of budget = $155,200

Answers to exercises and practice multiple choice questions

5 C

	units
Actual sales volume (units)	1,600
Budgeted sales volume (units)	1,500
Sales volume variance in units	100 (F)
Standard profit per unit ($48 – $34)	× $14
Sales volume profit variance	1,400 (F)

6 B

The senior buying manager is the person most responsible for the prices paid for raw materials. Variances should be reported to the manager who is in the best position to explain or control their causes.

7 A

	$
10,500 kilos should cost (× $8)	84,000
They did cost	82,500
Material price variance	1,500 (F)

The variance is favourable because actual purchase costs were lower than expected.

8 B

	hours
Actual hours worked	?
Budgeted hours worked (35,000 units × 3)	105,000
Capacity variance in hours	?
Standard fixed overhead rate per hour	× $12
Fixed overhead capacity variance	7,200 (F)

The capacity variance is $7,200 (F), and at $12 per hour, this means that the capacity variance was 600 hours (F). When the capacity variance is favourable, actual hours worked were more than budgeted hours. Budgeted hours were 105,000. Therefore actual hours were 105,000 + 600 = 105,600 hours.

Applied Knowledge
Management Accounting (MA)

Practice questions

Contents		
		Page
Accounting for management		
1	Income statement	539
Cost behaviour and cost estimation		
2	Cost behaviour	539
3	High/low analysis	539
4	Maintenance and repair costs	540
Accounting for materials and labour		
5	Stock items 6786 and 6787	540
6	Inventory control	541
7	Economic batch quantity	541
8	Piece work	541
9	Labour cost	542
Accounting for overheads		
10	Overhead cost per unit	542
11	Apportionment	543
12	Service departments	544
13	Volume and expenditure variances	544

Contents	
	Page
Marginal costing and absorption costing	
14 Plack Company	545
15 Differences	545
16 Marginal and absorption	546
Process costing and other costing methods	
17 Job 6789	547
18 Process costing: the basic rules	547
19 Process 1 and Process 2	548
20 Equivalent units	549
21 Joint process	550
Budgeting	
22 Sales budget	550
23 Production budget	550
24 Labour budget	550
25 Materials budget	551
Business mathematics	
26 Regression	551
27 Time series	552
Standard costing and variance analysis	
28 Simple variances	553
29 Overhead variances	554
30 Standard cost sheet	554

Practice questions

1 Income statement

From the following information, prepare a budgeted income statement for the year to 31 December Year 6.

	$
Purchases of direct materials	243,000
Production overheads	270,000
Administration overheads	150,000
Marketing overheads	220,000
Sales	1,200,000
Direct labour cost	187,500
Inventories at 1 January Year 6:	
Direct materials	21,000
Work in progress	5,000
Finished goods	34,000
Inventories at 31 December Year 6:	
Direct materials	19,000
Work in progress	7,500
Finished goods	50,000

2 Cost behaviour

From the information in this cost behaviour graph, describe the behaviour of this item of cost, and calculate the total cost at 10,000 units of output.

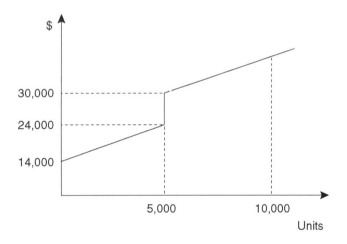

3 High/low analysis

A manufacturing company has budgeted to operate for 110,500 hours in the year, which is 85% capacity. Expected total costs for the year are $615,200.

The management accountant has also estimated that at 100% capacity, total annual costs would be $662,000.

Required

Using high/low analysis, estimate the variable cost per hour worked and the total annual fixed costs.

4 Maintenance and repair costs

Entity Z is trying to obtain a cost estimate for the costs of repairs. The following monthly repair costs have been recorded for the past six months.

Month	Number of machines repaired	Cost of repairs
		$
1	38	31,000
2	41	32,700
3	25	26,500
4	21	23,600
5	36	29,900
6	32	28,900

Required

Use high/low analysis to estimate the fixed costs of repairs each month and the variable cost per machine repaired.

Estimate the expected costs of repairs in a month when 30 machines are repaired.

5 Stock items 6786 and 6787

(a) A company uses 15,000 units of stock item 6786 each year. The item has a purchase cost of $4 per unit. The cost of placing an order for re-supply is $220. The annual holding cost of one unit of the item is 10% of its purchase cost.

Required

(i) What is the economic order quantity for item 6786, to the nearest unit?

(ii) What would be the effect of an increase in the annual holding cost per unit on (1) the EOQ and (2) total annual ordering costs?

(b) Data relating to stores item 6787 are as follows.

Daily use:	300 units
Lead time for re-supply:	5 – 20 days
Reorder quantity:	10,000 units

Required

What should be the reorder level for this stock item, to avoid the possibility of inventory-outs?

6 Inventory control

Entity G uses 105 units of an item of inventory every week. These cost $150 per unit. They are stored in special storage units and the variable costs of holding the item is $4 per unit each year plus 2% of the inventory's cost.

Required

(a) If placing an order for this item of material costs $390 for each order, what is the optimum order quantity to minimise annual costs? Assume that there are 52 weeks in each year.

(b) Suppose that the supplier offers a discount of 1% on the purchase price for order sizes of 2,000 units or more. What will be the order size to minimise total annual costs?

7 Economic batch quantity

A machine has the capacity to operate for 40 weeks each year during a 50-week year. It is used to manufacture several items, including component 3456. Component 3456 is produced in batches.

The machine is able to produce 8,000 units of item 3456 per hour. The cost of set-up for each batch is $6,000. Demand for the component occurs at an even rate throughout the year, and totals 2.5 million units per year. The cost of holding one unit of component 3456 in inventory is $1.50 per unit per year.

Required

(a) Calculate the economic batch production quantity for component 3456 to the nearest 10,000 units.

(b) Calculate the total costs per year of setting up the batches and inventory holding costs for this component, assuming the item is produced in batches of the size calculated in your answer to part (a).

8 Piece work

A production company pays the workers in a production department on a piece work basis. The workers produce a standard item, and the standard time allowed for the purpose of calculating pay is five minutes per unit. The company also guarantees these workers 75% of a time-based rate of pay, based on a rate of $24 per hour for a 7.5 hour day, and a five-day week. Piece work is paid at the rate of $20 per standard hour.

Required

What will be the weekly pay for a worker who produces:

(a) 444 units per week

(b) 400 units per week?

9 Labour cost

Two grades of direct labour workers are employed to produce units of Product 1234. There are 40 Grade 1 employees and 20 Grade 2 employees. All employees work a basic week of 40 hours. Grade 1 employees are paid $10 per hour and Grade 2 employees are paid $15 per hour. If employees work any overtime, they are paid at time-and-one-third (a premium of one third over the basic rate). There are also five 'support workers', such as maintenance engineers, who are paid $12 per hour for a basic 40-hour week.

During Week 23, the Grade 1 employees and support workers each worked 40 hours, and the Grade 2 employees worked 46 hours. Due to difficulties with some equipment, 250 hours of Grade 1 labour and 100 hours of Grade 2 labour were recorded as idle time in the week.

During Week 23, 4,000 units of Product 1234 were manufactured.

Required

(a) Calculate the direct labour costs and the indirect labour costs in Week 23.

(b) Calculate the direct labour cost per unit of Product 1234 in Week 23.

10 Overhead cost per unit

A company makes two products, Product X and Product Y. Each product is processed through two cost centres, CC1 and CC2. The following budgeted data is available.

	CC1	CC2
Allocated and apportioned overheads	$126,000	$180,000
(All overheads are fixed costs.)		
Direct labour hours per unit		
Product X	1.5	2.0
Product Y	1.2	2.6

The budgeted production is 12,000 units of Product X and 10,000 units of Product Y. Fixed overheads are absorbed into costs on a direct labour hour basis.

Required

Calculate the budgeted total fixed overhead cost per unit for Product X and for Product Y.

11 Apportionment

A production centre has three production departments, A, B and C.

Budgeted production overhead costs for the next period are as follows:

	$
Factory rent	60,000
Equipment depreciation	80,000
Insurance	20,000
Heating and lighting	18,000
Indirect materials:	
Department A	7,000
Department B	6,600
Department C	9,400
Indirect labour:	
Department A	40,000
Department B	27,000
Department C	20,000

Insurance costs relate mainly to health and safety insurance, and will be apportioned on the basis of the number of employees in each department. Heating and lighting costs will be apportioned on the basis of volume.

Other relevant information is as follows:

	Total	Department A	Department B	Department C
Direct labour hours	18,000	8,000	6,000	4,000
Number of employees	50	20	16	14
Floor area (square metres)	1,200	300	400	500
Cost of equipment ($000s)	1,000	200	600	200
Volume (cubic metres)	18,000	8,000	6,000	4,000

Required

(a) Calculate the overhead costs for each production department.

(b) Calculate an overhead absorption rate for the period for each department, assuming that a separate direct labour hour absorption rate is used for each department.

(c) Calculate an overhead absorption rate for the period, assuming that a single factory-wide direct labour hour absorption rate is used.

12 Service departments

In a factory with four production departments and two service departments, the operating costs for the month of October were as shown below.

	$
Production Department 1	700,000
Production Department 2	300,000
Production Department 3	400,000
Service departments	
Canteen	78,000
Boiler house	100,000
	1,578,000

The costs of running the canteen are apportioned to each department on the basis of the estimated use of the canteen by employees in each department.

The costs of the boiler house are apportioned on the basis of the estimated consumption of power by each department.

The service departments' costs are therefore apportioned as follows:

	Canteen	Boiler house
	%	%
Production Department 1	40	30
Production Department 2	20	30
Production Department 3	30	20
Service departments		
Canteen	–	20
Boiler house	10	–

Required

Prepare a statement showing the allocation of costs to the production departments using:

(a) the repeated distribution method

(b) the algebraic method or simultaneous equations method.

13 Volume and expenditure variances

A production manager is studying the cost report for the six-month period that has just ended. The production department incurred overhead costs of $680,000 and had under-absorbed overheads of $46,400. The actual direct labour hours worked in the department were 48,000 hours, which was 2,000 hours less than budgeted.

Required

(a) Calculate the budgeted absorption rate per direct labour hour.

(b) Calculate the budgeted overhead expenditure.

(c) Calculate the overhead expenditure and overhead volume variances in the period.

14　Plack Company

Plack Company is a manufacturing company that makes and sells a single product. The following information relates to the company's manufacturing operations in the next financial year.

Opening and closing stock:	Nil
Production:	18,000 units
Sales:	15,000 units
Fixed production overheads:	$117,000
Fixed sales overheads:	$72,000

Using absorption costing, the company has calculated that the budgeted profit for the year will be $43,000.

Required

What would be the budgeted profit if marginal costing is used, instead of absorption costing?

15　Differences

Entity T manufactures a single product, and uses absorption costing. The following data relates to the performance of the entity during October.

Profit	$37,000
Over-absorbed overhead	$24,000
Sales (48,000 units)	$720,000
Non-production overheads (all fixed costs)	$275,000
Opening inventory	$144,000
Closing inventory	$162,000

Units of inventory are valued at $9 each, consisting of a variable cost (all direct costs) of $3 and a fixed overhead cost of $6. All overhead costs are fixed costs.

Required

Calculate:

(a) the actual production overhead cost for October

(b) the profit that would have been reported in October if Entity T had used marginal costing.

16 Marginal and absorption

Entity RH makes and sells one product. Currently, it uses absorption costing to measure profits and inventory values. The budgeted production cost per unit is as follows:

		$
Direct labour	3 hours at $6 per hour	18
Direct materials	4 kilograms at $7 per kilo	28
Production overhead	(Fixed cost)	20
		66

Normal output volume is 16,000 units per year and this volume is used to establish the fixed overhead absorption rate for each year.

Costs relating to sales, distribution and administration are:

- Variable 20% of sales value
- Fixed $180,000 per year.

There were no units of finished goods inventory at 1 October Year 5.

The fixed overhead expenditure is spread evenly throughout the year.

The selling price per unit is $140.

For the two six-monthly periods detailed below, the number of units to be produced and sold are budgeted as follows:

	Six months ending 31 March Year 6	Six months ending 30 September Year 6
Production	8,500 units	7,000 units
Sales	7,000 units	8,000 units

The entity is considering whether to abandon absorption costing and use marginal costing instead for profit reporting and inventory valuation.

Required

(a) Calculate the budgeted fixed production overhead costs each year.

(b) Prepare statements for management showing sales, costs and profits for each of the six-monthly periods, using:

    (i) marginal costing

    (ii) absorption costing

(c) Prepare an explanatory statement reconciling for each six-monthly period the profit using marginal costing with the profit using absorption costing.

17 Job 6789

A company operates a job costing system. Job number 6789 will require $345 of direct materials and $210 of direct labour, which is paid $14 per hour. Production overheads are absorbed at the rate of $30 per direct labour hour and non-production overheads are absorbed at the rate of 40% of prime cost.

Required

What is the total expected cost of the job?

18 Process costing: the basic rules

The following examples take you through the basic rules for process costing.

Required

For each of the following examples, calculate:

(a) the cost of completed output from the process, and

(b) if there is any, the cost of any abnormal loss or the value of any abnormal gain

Example 1

1,500 litres of a liquid were input to a process at a cost of $7,200. Normal loss is 20% of the input quantity. Actual loss was equal to the normal loss.

Example 2

1,500 litres of liquid were input to a process at a cost of $7,200. A normal loss of 20% of the input is expected. The actual output for the period was only 1,100 litres.

Example 3

1,500 litres of liquid were input to a process at a cost of $7,200. A normal loss of 20% of the input is expected. Loss is sold as scrap, for a net sales price of $0.40 per litre. The actual output from the process was 1,200 litres.

Example 4

1,500 litres of liquid were input to a process at a cost of $7,200. The output from the process was 1,100 litres. Normal loss is 20% of the input quantity. Any lost units have a scrap value of $0.40 per litre.

Example 5

1,500 litres of liquid were input to a process at a cost of $7,200. Normal loss is 20% of the input quantity but the actual output for the period was 1,250 litres. Loss has no scrap value.

Example 6

1,500 litres of liquid were input to a process at a cost of $7,200. The output from the process was 1,250 units. Normal loss is 20% of the input quantity. Any lost units have a scrap value of $0.40 per litre.

19 Process 1 and Process 2

A manufacturing company operates two processes. Output from Process 1 is transferred as input to Process 2. Output from Process 2 is the finished product.

Data for the two processes in January are as follows:

Process 1

Opening work in process	Nil
Units introduced into the process	14,000
Units completed and transferred to the next process (Process 2)	10,000
Closing work-in-progress	4,000
Material cost added during the period	$70,000
Conversion cost added during the period	$48,000

Materials are input into Process 1 at the start of the process and conversion costs are incurred at a constant rate throughout processing. The closing work-in-progress in Process 1 at the end of January is estimated to be 50% complete for the conversion work.

Process 2

Opening work-in-process	Nil
Units transferred into the process from Process 1	10,000
Closing work-in-progress	1,000
Units completed and transferred to finished goods inventory	9,000
Costs for the period:	
Cost of production transferred from Process 1	$90,000
Conversion cost added during the period	$57,000
Added materials during Process 2	$36,000

The materials from Process 1 are introduced at the start of processing in Process 2, but the added materials are introduced at the end of the process. Conversion costs are incurred at a constant rate throughout processing. The closing work-in-progress in Process 2 at the end of January is estimated to be 50% complete.

Required

Calculate:

(a) the cost of completed output from Process 1 and Process 2

(b) the cost of the closing work-in-process in each process at the end of January.

(c) Prepare the Process 1 account and the Process 2 account for January.

20 Equivalent units

XYZ operates several process production systems.

(a) For Process 5, the FIFO method of valuing opening work-in-progress is used and the following details relate to September Year 5.

Opening work-in-process was 600 units, each 80% processed as to materials and 60% processed as to conversion costs.

Finished output was 14,500 units. There were no abnormal losses or gains.

Closing work-in-process was 800 units, each 70% processed as to materials and 40% processed as to conversion costs.

Costs of processing during the current period were:

Materials: $36,450

Conversion costs: $17,352.

Required

Calculate the cost per equivalent unit of output produced during September (= one unit started and completed during the month).

(b) The following details relate to Process 16 in September Year 5.

Opening work-in-progress	2,000 litres, fully complete as to materials and 40% complete as to conversion. The cost of materials in the opening WIP was $9,860 and conversion costs in the opening WIP were $4,700.
Material input	24,000 litres, cost $130,540
Conversion costs in the month	$82,960
Output to process 2	23,000 litres
Closing work-in-progress	3,000 litres, fully complete as to materials and 45% complete as to conversion.

The weighted average cost system is used for inventory valuation in Process 16.

Required

Calculate the cost per unit of output from this process during September.

Management Accounting (MA)

21 Joint process

In a joint process, two joint products are made, Product A and Product B. There are no inventory of work-in-process. Information relating to last month's production is set out in the table below.

Joint product	Opening inventory	Closing inventory	Sales
	units	units	units
A	800	1,200	8,000
B	700	300	10,000

The costs of the joint process in the month were $144,000. These are apportioned between the joint products on the basis of units produced.

Required

Calculate the joint processing costs for the month that are charged to each product.

22 Sales budget

A company makes and sells two products, Product A and Product B. The sales price and expected sales volume for each product next year are as follows:

	Product A	Product B
Sales price per unit	$2.50	$4.00
Budgeted sales volume	50,000	80,000

Required

Prepare the sales budget for the company for next year.

23 Production budget

A company produces Product L. Budgeted sales for Product L are 20,000 units for next year. Opening inventory is 2,500 units and planned closing inventory is 2,000 units.

Required

Prepare the production budget for Production L for next year.

24 Labour budget

A company makes Product DOY which requires two grades of labour, Grade I and Grade II.

Product DOY requires 4 hours of Grade I labour and (at $12 per hour) and 7 hours of Grade II labour (at $15 per hour).

Budgeted production of Product DOY is 25,000 units for the forthcoming year.

Required

Prepare the labour budget for Product DOY for the forthcoming year.

25 Materials budget

A company manufactures a single product. A single direct material, material X, is used in its manufacture. A budget is being prepared for next year. Opening inventory is expected to be 2,000 units of finished goods and 30,000 kilos of direct material X. Each unit of the product requires 5 kilos of material X.

Budgeted sales next year are 25,000 units of the product. It is also planned to increase finished goods inventory to 4,000 units before the end of the year and to reduce inventories of direct material X by 50%.

Required

Prepare a materials usage budget and a material purchase budget for material X

26 Regression

Total production costs each week in a production department have been measured for the past five weeks, as follows.

Week	Units produced	Total cost
		$000
1	5	20
2	9	27
3	4	17
4	5	19
5	6	23

Required

(a) Use linear regression analysis to obtain an estimate of fixed costs per week and the variable cost of production per unit.

(b) Use your results to estimate total costs in a week when 8 units are produced.

(c) Calculate the correlation coefficient and comment on the value of r that you have obtained.

(d) Estimate a value for fixed costs and variable costs from the same data, using the high/low analysis, and use the values that you obtain to estimate total costs in a week when 8 units are produced.

27 Time series

Seasonal Sales Company is preparing sales forecasts. It has used historical records of sales in every three months to establish the following trend line for sales and seasonal variations. Sales in each quarter are higher or lower than trend because seasonal factors affect sales demand.

Derived from historical sales data

Quarter	Trend in quarterly sales	Seasonal variation for the quarter
	$000	$000
3	1,200	− 12
4	1,240	− 20
5	1,281	+ 26
6	1,323	+ 6
7	1,357	− 14
8	1,400	− 17
9	1,435	+ 22
10	1,476	0
11	1,520	− 7
12	1,568	− 17
13	1,604	+ 30
14	1,638	+ 3

The trend line data has been used to establish a forecast trend in quarterly sales. This is (in $000) $1,080 + 40P$ where P is the period number.

Required

Prepare a sales forecast for quarters 17 – 20, and comment briefly on the reliability of your forecast.

28 Simple variances

(a) Z plc uses a standard costing system and has the following labour cost standard in relation to one of its products:

4 hours of skilled labour at $6.00 per hour: $24.00

During October, 3,350 units of this products were made, which was 150 units less than budgeted. The labour cost incurred was $79,893 and the number of direct labour hours worked was 13,450.

Required

Calculate the direct labour rate and efficiency variances for the month.

(c) Entity J uses a standard costing system and has the following data relating to one of its products:

	$ per unit	$ per unit
Selling price		9.00
Variable cost	4.00	
Fixed cost	3.00	
		7.00
Profit		2.00

The budgeted sales for October Year 5 were 800 units, but the actual sales were 850 units. The revenue earned from these sales was $7,480.

Required

Calculate the sales price and sales volume variances for October using:

(i) standard absorption costing

(ii) standard marginal costing.

The standard fixed production cost of a product is $20, which is 4 hours at a rate of $5 per direct labour hour.

(c) The budget was to produce 15,000 units. The standard fixed production cost of a product is $20, which is 4 hours at a rate of $5 per direct labour hour. Actual production was 14,600 units and actual fixed production overhead expenditure was $325,000. The production output was manufactured in 58,000 hours of work.

Required

Calculate:

(i) the fixed production overhead total cost variance

(ii) the fixed production overhead expenditure variance and volume variance

(iii) the fixed production overhead efficiency variance and capacity variance

29 Overhead variances

A company operates a standard overhead absorption costing system. The standard fixed overhead rate per hour is $25. The following data relate to last month:

Actual hours worked	8,250
Budgeted hours	9,000
Standard hours of actual production	7,800
Actual fixed overhead expenditure	$211,000

Required

Calculate for the month:

(a) the fixed overhead capacity variance

(b) the fixed overhead efficiency variance

(c) the fixed overhead expenditure variance.

30 Standard cost sheet

The following data relates to actual output, actual costs and variances for the four-weekly accounting period number 4 of a company which makes only one product.

The value of work-in-progress at the end of period 4 was the same as the value of work-in-progress at the beginning of the month.

Actual production of Product XY	18,000 units
Actual costs incurred:	$000
Direct materials purchased and used (150,000 kg)	210
Direct labour costs (32,000 hours)	136
Variable production overhead	38

Variances:	$000	
Direct materials price	15	Favourable
Direct materials usage	9	Adverse
Direct labour rate	8	Adverse
Direct labour efficiency	16	Favourable
Variable production overhead expenditure	6	Adverse
Variable production overhead efficiency	4	Favourable

Variable production overhead varies with labour hours worked.

A standard marginal costing system is operated.

Required

Present a standard product cost sheet for one unit of Product XY, showing how the standard marginal production cost of the product is made up.

Applied Knowledge
Management Accounting (MA)

Answers to practice questions

Contents

		Page
Accounting for management		
1	Income statement	557
Cost behaviour and cost estimation		
2	Cost behaviour	557
3	High/low analysis	557
4	Maintenance and repair costs	558
Accounting for materials and labour		
5	Stock items 6786 and 6787	558
6	Inventory control	559
7	Economic batch quantity	559
8	Piece work	560
9	Labour cost	560
Accounting for overheads		
10	Overhead cost per unit	561
11	Apportionment	561
12	Service departments	562
13	Volume and expenditure variances	563

Contents

Page

Marginal costing and absorption costing

14	Plack Company	563
15	Differences	564
16	Marginal and absorption	565

Process costing and other costing methods

17	Job 6789	567
18	Process costing: the basic rules	567
19	Process 1 and Process 2	569
20	Equivalent units	570
21	Joint process	571

Budgeting

22	Sales budget	571
23	Production budget	571
24	Labour budget	571
25	Materials budget	572

Business mathematics

26	Regression	572
27	Time series	574

Standard costing and variance analysis

28	Simple variances	575
29	Overhead variances	576
30	Standard cost sheet	577

Answers to practice questions

1 Income statement

Income statement for the year to 31 December Year 6

	$	$
Sales		1,200,000
Opening inventory, direct materials	21,000	
Purchases	243,000	
	264,000	
Closing inventory, direct materials	(19,000)	
Direct materials used in production	245,000	
Direct labour	187,500	
Production overheads	270,000	
Production costs in the period	702,500	
Opening inventory, work-in-progress	5,000	
Closing inventory, work-in-progress	(7,500)	
Cost of finished production	700,000	
Opening inventory, finished goods	34,000	
Closing inventory, finished goods	(50,000)	
Production cost of sales	684,000	
Administration overheads	150,000	
Sales and distribution overheads	220,000	
Cost of sales		(1,054,000)
Profit		146,000

2 Cost behaviour

The cost item is a mixed cost. Up to 5,000 units of output, total fixed costs are $14,000 and the variable cost per unit is $(24,000 – 14,000)/5,000 units = $2 per unit.

At the 5,000 units of output, there is a step increase in fixed costs of $6,000 (from $24,000 total costs to $30,000 total costs). Total fixed costs therefore rise from $14,000 to $20,000. The variable cost per unit remains unchanged.

At the 10,000 units level, total costs are therefore:

	$
Variable costs (10,000 × $2)	20,000
Fixed costs	20,000
Total costs	40,000

3 High/low analysis

110,500 hours = 85% capacity.

Therefore 100% capacity = 110,500 hours/85% = 130,000 hours.

	hours		$
High: Total cost of	130,000	=	662,000
Low: Total cost of	110,500	=	615,200
Difference: Variable cost of	19,500	=	46,800

Therefore the variable cost per hour = $46,800/19,500 hours = $2.40.

Substitute in high equation	Cost
	$
Total cost of 130,000 hours	662,000
Variable cost of 130,000 hours (× $2.40)	(312,000)
Therefore fixed costs	350,000

4 Maintenance and repair costs

	Units		$
High: Total cost of	41	=	32,700
Low: Total cost of	21	=	23,600
Difference: Variable cost of	20	=	9,100

Therefore variable cost per unit repaired = $9,100/20 hours = $455.

Substitute in low equation	Cost
	$
Total cost of 21 units	23,600
Variable cost of 21 units (≥ $455)	9,555
Therefore fixed costs per month	14,045

Cost estimate for 30 units	Cost
	$
Fixed costs	14,045
Variable cost of 30 units (x $455)	13,650
Estimated total costs	27,695

If this estimate is used to prepare a budget for a period, it might be rounded to a convenient number, say $27,700.

5 Stock items 6786 and 6787

(a) (i) $EOQ = \sqrt{\dfrac{2 \times 220 \times 15,000}{0.40}} = 4,062$ units

(ii) If the annual holding cost per unit increases to more than $0.40 per unit, the EOQ will become smaller.

If the EOQ is smaller, there will be more orders each year; therefore total annual ordering costs will increase.

(b) Reorder level to avoid inventory-outs

= Daily demand × Maximum lead time

= 300 units × 20 days

= 6,000 units.

Answers to practice questions

6 Inventory control

(a) The annual holding cost per unit of inventory = $4 + (2% × $150) = $7.

Annual demand = 52 weeks × 105 units = 5,460 units.

$$EOQ = \sqrt{\frac{2 \times 390 \times 5,460}{7}} = 780 \text{ units.}$$

(b) A discount on the price is available for order sizes of 2,000 units or more, which is above the EOQ.

The order size that minimises cost is therefore either the EOQ or the minimum order size to obtain the discount, which is 2,000 units.

Annual costs	Order size 780 units	Order size 2,000 units
	$	$
Purchases		
(5,460 × $150): ((5,460 × $150 × 99%)	819,000	810,810
Holding costs	2,730	7,000
($7 × 780/2): ($7 × 2,000/2)		
Ordering costs	2,730	1,065
($390 × 5,460/780): ($390 × 5,460/2,000)		
Total costs	824,460	818,875

Conclusion

The order size that will minimise total annual costs is 2,000 units.

7 Economic batch quantity

(a) Production capacity of the machine = 8,000 per hour × 40 hours per week × 50 weeks per year = 16 million units. Economic batch quantity =

$$\sqrt{\frac{2 \times 6,000 \times 2.5 \text{ million}}{1.50 \left(1 - \frac{2.5 \text{ million}}{16 \text{ million}}\right)}} = 153,960 \text{ units.}$$

To the nearest 10,000 units, this is 150,000 units.

(b) Average inventory = Q (1 − D/R)/2

= 150,000 [1 − (2.5 million/16 million)]/2

= 126,562.5/2 units = 63,281.25 units

		$
Annual holding costs	63,281.25 units × $1.50	94,922
Annual set-up costs	(2.5 million/150,000) × $6,000	100,000
		194,922

(With the economic batch quantity formula, the total annual holding costs and total annual set-up costs are not equal unless the order quantity used is the

EBQ. This is not the case here as the order quantity used is 150,000 but the EBQ was 153,960.

The answer to b would be as follows if the order quantity used = the EBQ.

b) Average inventory = Q (1 − D/R)/2

= 153,960 [1 − (2.5 million/16 million)]/2

= 129,903.75/2 units = 64,951.88 units

		$
Annual holding costs	64,951.88 units × $1.50	97,428
Annual set-up costs	(2.5 million/153,960) × $6,000	97,428
		194,856

8 Piece work

The minimum guaranteed wage = 75% of (7.5 hours × 5 days × $24 per hour) = 75% of $900 = $675 per week.

For piece work calculations, 1 unit = 5/60 standard hours.

(1) Piecework value of 444 units per week = 444 × 5/60 × $20 per hour = $740

(2) Piecework value of 400 units per week = 400 × 5/60 × $20 per hour = $666.67

(a) If output is 444 units in the week, pay will be $740.

(b) If output is 400 units per week, pay will be $675 (the guaranteed minimum).

9 Labour cost

(a)

		Total worked hours	Idle time hours	Worked on production hours		Overtime hours
Grade 1	(40 × 40)	1,600	250	1,350		
Grade 2	(20 × 46)	920	100	820	(20 × 6)	120

	Direct labour		Indirect labour (overhead)	
		$		$
Grade 1 basic wages	(1,350 × $10)	13,500	(250 × $10)	2,500
Grade 2 basic wages	(820 × $15)	12,300	(100 × $15)	1,500
Overtime premium			(120 × $15 × 1/3)	600
Support staff			(5 × 40 × $12)	2,400
Total		25,800		7,000

(b)

Units produced	4,000	
Direct labour cost/unit = $25,800/4,000 =	$6.45	per unit

10 Overhead cost per unit

		CC1			CC2	
			Total hours			Total hours
Product X		12,000 × 1.5	18,000	12,000 × 2.0		24,000
Product Y		10,000 × 1.2	12,000	10,000 × 2.6		26,000
			30,000			50,000
Total overheads			$126,000			$180,000
Absorption rate per hour			$4.20			$3.60

Fixed overhead cost/unit		Product X		Product Y	
		$		$	
CC1	1.5 × $4.20	6.30	1.2 × $4.20	5.04	
CC2	2.0 × $3.60	7.20	2.6 × $3.60	9.36	
Total		13.50		14.40	

11 Apportionment

Tutorial note: The answers to all three parts of the question are shown here, but are not labelled.

	Basis of apportionment	Total	A	B	C
		$	$	$	$
Indirect materials	Allocation	23,000	7,000	6,600	9,400
Indirect labour	Allocation	87,000	40,000	27,000	20,000
Rent	Floor area	60,000	15,000	20,000	25,000
Depreciation	Equipment cost	80,000	16,000	48,000	16,000
Insurance	Employee numbers	20,000	8,000	6,400	5,600
Heating, lighting	Volume	18,000	8,000	6,000	4,000
Total		288,000	94,000	114,000	80,000
Direct labour hours			8,000	6,000	4,000
Absorption rate	(per direct labour hour)		$11.75	$19	$20

If a single factory-wide absorption rate is used instead of separate absorption rates for each department, the absorption rate would be $16 per direct labour hour (= $288,000/18,000 hours).

12 Service departments

(a) Repeated distribution method

C = Canteen

BH = Boiler house

	Dept 1	Dept 2	Dept 3	C	BH
	$	$	$	$	$
Initial overheads	700,000	300,000	400,000	78,000	100,000
Apportion:					
BH (30:30:20:20)	30,000	30,000	20,000	20,000	(100,000)
				98,000	
C (40:20:30:10)	39,200	19,600	29,400	(98,000)	9,800
BH (30:30:20:20)	2,940	2,940	1,960	1,960	(9,800)
C (40:20:30:10)	784	392	588	(1,960)	196
BH (30:30:20:20)	59	59	39	39	(196)
C (40:20:30:10)	15	8	12	(39)	4
BH (30:30:20:20)	1	1	1	1	(4)
C (40:20:30:10)	1	0	0	(1)	0
Total overhead	773,000	353,000	452,000		

(b) Simultaneous equations method

Let X = the total overheads apportioned from the Canteen

Let Y = the total overheads apportioned from the Boiler House

This gives us the simultaneous equations:

$$X = 78,000 + 0.2Y \quad \ldots (1)$$
$$Y = 100,000 + 0.1X \quad \ldots (2)$$

Re-arrange:

$$78,000 = X - 0.2Y \quad \ldots (1)$$
$$100,000 = -0.1X + Y \quad \ldots (2)$$

Multiply (2) by 10

$$1,000,000 = -X + 10Y \quad \ldots (3)$$

Add (1) and (3)

$$1,078,000 = 9.8Y$$

$$Y = 110,000$$

Therefore, from (1) and substituting Y = 110,000:

X = 78,000 + 0.2 (110,000) = 100,000.

	Dept 1	Dept 2	Dept 3
	$	$	$
Initial overheads	700,000	300,000	400,000
Apportion:			
BH (30%, 30% and 20% of 110,000)	33,000	33,000	22,000
C (40%, 20% and 30% of 100,000)	40,000	20,000	30,000
Total overhead apportionment	773,000	353,000	452,000

Answers to practice questions

13 Volume and expenditure variances

(a)

	$
Actual overhead expenditure	680,000
Under-absorbed overhead	(46,400)
Absorbed overhead	633,600
Hours worked	48,000
Therefore budgeted absorption rate per hour ($633,600/48,000)	$13.20

(b)

	hours
Actual hours worked	48,000
This was less than budget by	2,000
Budgeted hours	50,000
Absorption rate per hour	$13.20
Budgeted overhead expenditure (50,000 hours × $13.20)	$660,000

(c)

Volume variance in hours	2,000 hours	Adverse
Absorption rate per hour	$13.20	
Volume variance in $	$26,400	Adverse

	$	
Actual overhead expenditure	680,000	
Budgeted overhead expenditure	660,000	
Expenditure variance	20,000	Adverse

14 Plack Company

Production overhead per unit, with absorption costing:

= $117,000/18,000 units

= $6.50 per unit.

The budgeted increase in inventory = 3,000 units (18,000 − 15,000).

Production overheads in the increase in inventory = 3,000 × $6.50 = $19,500.

With marginal costing, profit will be lower than with absorption costing, because there is an increase in inventory levels.

Marginal costing profit = $43,000 - $19,500 = $23,500.

15 Differences

(a)

	units
Opening inventory ($144,000/$9)	16,000
Closing inventory ($162,000/$9)	18,000
Increase in inventory in October	2,000
Sales	48,000
Production in October	50,000

	$
Absorbed production overhead (50,000 × $6)	300,000
Over-absorbed overheads	24,000
Actual production overhead expenditure	276,000

(b) Inventory increased during October; therefore the reported profit will be higher with absorption costing than with marginal costing.

	$
Absorption cost profit	37,000
Increase inventory × fixed production overhead per unit	
(2,000 × $6)	12,000
Marginal costing profit	25,000

Proof:

	$	$
Sales		720,000
Variable cost of sales (48,000 × $3)		144,000
Contribution		576,000
Fixed production overheads (see above)	276,000	
Other fixed overheads	275,000	
Total fixed overheads		551,000
Marginal costing profit		25,000

16 Marginal and absorption

(a) Budgeted production overhead expenditure =

Normal production volume × Absorption rate per unit

= 16,000 units × $20 = $320,000.

Since expenditure occurs evenly throughout the year, the budgeted production overhead expenditure is $160,000 in each six-month period.

(b)

Workings	$ per unit
Direct material	18
Direct labour	28
	46
Sales, distribution, administration (20% × $140)	28
Marginal cost of sale	74

(i) **Marginal costing**

	Six months to 31 March		Six months to 30 September	
Units sold		7,000		8,000
	$	$	$	$
Sales at $140		980,000		1,120,000
Marginal cost of sales (at $74)		518,000		592,000
Contribution		462,000		528,000
Fixed costs				
Production ($320,000/2)	160,000		160,000	
Other ($180,000/2)	90,000		90,000	
Total fixed costs		250,000		250,000
Profit		212,000		278,000

(ii) Absorption costing

The fixed overhead absorption rate is based on the normal volume of production. Since budgeted output in each six-month period is different from the normal volume, there will be some under- or over-absorption of production overhead in each six-month period.

		Six months to 31 March		Six months to 30 September
Units sold		7,000		8,000
	$	$	$	$
Sales at $140		980,000		1,120,000
Production cost of sales (at $66)		462,000		528,000
		518,000		592,000
Production overhead absorbed (8,500 × $20: 7,000 × $20)	170,000		140,000	
Actual production overhead	160,000		160,000	
Over-/(under-) absorbed overheads		10,000		(20,000)
		528,000		572,000
Sales, distribution, admin costs				
Variable (7,000 × $28: 8,000 × $28)	196,000		224,000	
Other	90,000		90,000	
		286,000		314,000
Profit		242,000		258,000

(c) Reconciliation of profit figures

Six months to 31 March Year 6

Increase in inventory	(8,500 – 7,000 units)	1,500 units
Production overhead absorbed in these units (absorption costing)		$20 per unit
Therefore absorption costing profit higher by		$30,000

Six months to 31 March Year 6

Reduction in inventory	(7,000 – 8,000 units)	1,000 units
Production overhead absorbed in these units (absorption costing)		$20 per unit
Therefore absorption costing profit lower by		$20,000

The difference in reported profits is due entirely to differences in the valuation of inventory (and so differences in the increase or reduction in inventory during each period).

17 Job 6789

	$
Direct materials	345
Direct labour (15 hours)	210
Prime cost	555
Production overheads (15 hours × $30)	450
Full production cost	1,005
Non-production overheads (40% × $555)	222
Full cost of sale for the job	1,227

18 Process costing: the basic rules

Example 1

	litres
Input	1,500
Normal loss (20%)	300
Expected output	1,200

Cost per unit of expected output = $7,200/1,200 litres = $6 per litre.

Actual output = 1,200 litres.

Cost of actual output = 1,200 litres × $6 = $7,200.

There is no abnormal loss or abnormal gain.

Example 2

	litres
Input	1,500
Normal loss (20%)	300
Expected output	1,200
Actual output	1,100
Abnormal loss	100

Cost per unit = same as in Example 1, $6 per litre.

Cost of actual output = 1,100 litres × $6 = $6,600.

Cost of abnormal loss = 100 litres × $6 = $600.

Example 3

	$
Input cost	7,200
Scrap value of normal loss (300 × $0.40)	120
Net cost of the process	7,080

Cost per unit of expected output = $7,080/1,200 litres = $5.90 per litre.

Actual output = 1,200 litres.

Cost of actual output= 1,200 litres × $5.90 = $7,080.

There is no abnormal loss or abnormal gain.

Example 4

Cost per unit = same as in Example 3, $5.90 per litre.

Cost of actual output = 1,100 litres × $5.90 = $6,490.

Cost of abnormal loss = 100 litres × $5.90 = $590.

This cost of abnormal loss is the amount recorded in the process account.

The net cost of abnormal loss is reduced (in the abnormal loss account) by the scrap value of the lost units.

	$
Cost of abnormal loss in the process account	590
Scrap value of abnormal loss (100 × $0.40)	(40)
Net cost of abnormal loss (= expense in the income statement)	550

Example 5

	litres
Input	1,500
Normal loss (20%)	300
Expected output	1,200
Actual output	1,250
Abnormal gain	50

Cost per unit = same as in Example 1, $6 per litre.

Cost of actual output = 1,250 litres × $6 = $7,500.

Value of abnormal gain = 50 litres × $6 = $300 (= debit entry in the process account).

Example 6

	litres
Input	1,500
Normal loss (20%)	300
Expected output	1,200
Actual output	1,250
Abnormal gain	50

Cost per unit = same as in Example 3, $5.90 per litre.

Cost of actual output = 1,250 litres × $5.90 = $7,375.

Value of abnormal gain = 50 litres × $5.90 = $295.

This value of abnormal gain is the amount recorded in the process account (as a debit entry).

The value cost of abnormal gain is reduced (in the abnormal gain account) by the scrap value of the units that have not been lost.

	$
Value of abnormal gain in the process account	295
Scrap value forgone: (50 × $0.40)	(20)
Net value of abnormal gain (= income in the income statement)	275

19 Process 1 and Process 2

There is no opening inventory in either process; therefore there is no difference between the weighted average cost and FIFO valuation methods.

Process 1

Equivalent units	Total		Direct materials		Conversion costs	
	Total units		Equivalent units		Equivalent units	
Completed units	10,000		10,000			10,000
Closing inventory	4,000		4,000	(4,000 × 50%)		2,000
Total equivalent units	14,000		14,000			12,000
Cost			$70,000			$48,000
Cost per equivalent unit			$5			$4

Statement of evaluation		Direct materials		Conversion costs	Total cost
		$		$	$
Completed units	(10,000 × $5)	50,000	(10,000 × $4) 40,000		90,000
Closing inventory	(4,000 × $5)	20,000	(2,000 × $4) 8,000		28,000
		70,000		48,000	118,000

The process account is prepared as follows:

Process 1 account

	units	$		units	$
Direct materials	14,000	70,000	Process 2 account	10,000	90,000
Conversion costs		48,000	Closing inventory c/f	4,000	28,000
	14,000	118,000		14,000	118,000

Process 2

Equivalent units	Total	Materials from Process 1	Conversion costs	Added materials
	Total units	Equivalent units	Equivalent units	Equivalent units
Completed units	9,000	9,000	9,000	9,000
Closing inventory	1,000	1,000	500	0
Total equivalent units	10,000	10,000	9,500	9,000
Cost		$90,000	$57,000	$36,000
		$9	$6	$4

Note: The added materials are added at the end of the process, which means that there are no added materials in the (unfinished) closing inventory.

Statement of evaluation	Materials from Process 1	Conversion costs	Added materials	Total cost
	$	$	$	$
Completed units	81,000	54,000	36,000	171,000
Closing inventory	9,000	3,000	0	12,000
	90,000	57,000	36,000	183,000

The process account is prepared as follows:

Process 2 account

	units	$		units	$
Materials from Process 1	10,000	90,000	Finished goods	9,000	171,000
Conversion costs		57,000			
Added materials		36,000	Closing inventory c/f	1,000	12,000
	10,000	183,000		10,000	183,000

20 Equivalent units

(a) FIFO method

Equivalent units	Total Units	Direct materials Equivalent units		Conversion costs Equivalent units	
Completion of opening WIP	600	(20%)	120	(40%)	240
Other completed units	13,900		13,900		13,900
	14,500		14,020		14,140
Closing inventory	800	(70%)	560	(40%)	320
Total equivalent units	15,300		14,580		14,460
Costs in the current period			$36,450		$17,352
Cost per equivalent unit			$2.5		$1.2

Cost per equivalent unit of fully completed units in the current period = $2.50 + $1.20 = $3.70.

(b) Weighted average cost

Equivalent units	Total Total units	Direct materials Equivalent units		Conversion costs Equivalent units	
Completed units	23,000		23,000		23,000
Closing inventory		(100%)	3,000	(45%)	1,350
	3,000				
Total equivalent units	26,000		26,000		24,350
Costs:			$		$
Opening WIP			9,860		4,700
Current period costs			130,540		82,960
Total costs			140,400		87,660
Cost per equivalent unit			$5.40		$3.60

Cost per equivalent unit of fully completed units in the current period
= $5.40 + $3.60 = $9.00.

21 Joint process

	Production
	units
Joint product A: (1,200 + 8,000 – 800)	8,400
Joint product B: (300 + 10,000 – 700)	9,600
Total production	18,000
Joint processing costs	$144,000
Joint processing costs per unit	$8

Apportionment of joint costs

	$
To Joint product A: (8,400 × $8)	67,200
To Joint product B: (9,600 × $8)	76,800
	144,000

22 Sales budget

Product	Sales quantity	Sales price	Sales revenue
A	50,000	$2.50	$125,000
B	80,000	$4.00	$320,000
Total			$445,000

23 Production budget

	Units
Sales budget in units	20,000
Plus budgeted closing inventory	2,000
Less closing inventory	(2,500)
	19,500

24 Labour budget

	Grade I	Grade II	Total
	hours	hours	
To make 25,000 units DOY	100,000	175,000	275,000
Labour cost per hour	$12	$15	
Total labour cost	$1,200,000	$2,625,000	$3,825,000

25 Materials budget

Production budget	Units
Closing inventory	4,000
Sales	25,000
	29,000
Opening inventory	(2,000)
Budgeted production	27,000

Materials usage budget, material X

= 27,000 units of product × 5 kilos per unit = 135,000 kilos.

Materials purchases budget	Kilos of material X
Closing inventory	15,000
Usage in production	135,000
	150,000
Opening inventory	(30,000)
Budgeted production	120,000

26 Regression

Workings

Output	Total cost			
units	$000			
x	y	Σx^2	Σxy	Σy^2
5	20	25	100	400
9	27	81	243	729
4	17	16	68	289
5	19	25	95	361
6	23	36	138	529
29	106	183	644	2,308
= Σx	= Σy	= Σx^2	= Σxy	= Σy^2

There are five pairs of data, so n = 5.

$$b = \frac{n\Sigma xy - \Sigma x \Sigma y}{n\Sigma x^2 - (\Sigma x)^2}$$

$$b = \frac{5(644) - (29)(106)}{5(183) - (29)^2} = \frac{3,220 - 3,074}{915 - 841} = \frac{146}{74}$$

b (in $000) = 1.97

$$a = \frac{\Sigma y}{n} - \frac{b \Sigma x}{n}$$

$$a = \frac{106}{5} - \frac{1.97(29)}{5} = 21.2 - 11.4$$

a (in $000) = 9.8

Answer

(a) The estimate of monthly fixed costs and the variable cost per unit is therefore:

y = 9,800 + 1,970x.

(b) When output is expected to be 8 units, the expected total costs will be:

	$
Fixed	9,800
Variable (8 x $1,970)	15,760
Total costs	25,560

(c) The value of the correlation coefficient, r, in this example is:

$$r = \frac{146}{\sqrt{(74)[5(2,308)-(106)^2]}}$$

$$= \frac{146}{\sqrt{(74)(11,540-11,236)}}$$

$$= \frac{146}{\sqrt{(74)(304)}}$$

$$= \frac{146}{150} = +0.97$$

The correlation coefficient is + 0.97. This is high, indicating a high degree of positive correlation and suggesting that the estimates of costs based on the formula should be reliable.

(d) **Using the high/low analysis:**

	units		$000
High: Total cost of	9	=	27
Low: Total cost of	4	=	17
Difference: Variable cost of	5	=	10

Therefore variable cost per unit produced = $10,000/5 units = $2,000.

Substitute in low equation	Cost
	$
Total cost of 4 units	17,000
Variable cost of 4 units (× $2,000)	8,000
Therefore fixed costs per week	9,000

Cost estimate for 8 units	Cost
	$
Fixed costs	9,000
Variable cost of 8 units (× $2,000)	16,000
Estimated total costs	25,000

27 Time series

Sales are recorded for each quarter. We can therefore assume that seasonal variations are quarterly, which means that there are four 'seasons' in each cycle.

A trend line has already been calculated. Seasonal variations can be estimated by taking the average of historical variations. The total of all variations in one cycle must add up to 0.

Periods	Quarter 1 variation	Quarter 2 variation	Quarter 3 variation	Quarter 4 variation	Total
	$000	$000	$000	$000	$000
3 – 6	– 12	– 20	+ 26	+ 6	
7 – 10	– 14	– 17	+ 22	0	
11 - 14	– 7	– 17	+ 30	+ 3	
Average	– 11	– 18	+ 26	+ 3	0

The average seasonal variations add up to 0 exactly; therefore no further adjustments are needed. These average variations will be used for the purpose of sales forecasting.

Period	Trend (1,080 + 40P)	Seasonal variation	Forecast sales
	$000	$000	$000
17	1,760	+ 26	1,786
18	1,800	+ 3	1,803
19	1,840	—11	1,829
20	1,880	– 18	1,865

The sales forecast should be reliable only if the trend in sales that has happened in the past continues into the future, and that the estimates of seasonal variations are reasonably accurate. Some error in forecasting is inevitable even if these assumptions are valid.

There is also some risk of error in the estimate of the trend line, but this can be evaluated using a correlation coefficient, assuming that the trend line was calculated using linear regression analysis.

There is also some risk of a small error in the estimate of seasonal variations, where simple arithmetical averages of variations in the past three years have been used.

28 Simple variances

(a)

Direct labour rate variance

	$
13,450 hours should cost (× $6)	80,700
They did cost	79,893
Labour rate variance	807 (F)

Direct labour efficiency variance

	hours
3,350 units should take (× 4 hours)	13,400
They did take	13,450
Efficiency variance in hours	50 (A)
Standard rate per hour	× $6
Direct labour efficiency variance in $	$300 (A)

(b)

Sales price variance

	$
850 units should sell for (× $9)	7,650
They did sell for	7,480
Sales price variance	170 (A)

Sales volume variance, absorption costing

	units
Actual sales volume (units)	850
Budgeted sales volume (units)	800
Sales volume variance in units	50 (F)
Standard profit per unit	× $2
Sales volume variance (profit variance)	$100 (F)

Sales volume contribution variance, marginal costing

Sales volume variance in units	50 (F)
Standard contribution per unit ($9 - $4)	× $5
Sales volume variance (contribution variance)	$250 (F)

(c) (i)

Fixed production overhead total cost variance

	$
Standard fixed overhead cost of 14,600 units (× $20)	292,000
Actual fixed overhead expenditure	325,000
Fixed overhead total cost variance (under absorption)	33,000 (A)

(ii)

Fixed production overhead expenditure variance

	$	
Budgeted fixed overhead expenditure (15,000 × $20)	300,000	
Actual fixed overhead expenditure	325,000	
Fixed overhead expenditure variance	25,000	(A)

Fixed production overhead volume variance

	units	
Budgeted production volume	15,000	
Actual production volume	14,600	
Volume variance in units	400	(A)
Standard fixed overhead rate per unit	× $20	
Fixed production overhead volume variance in $	$8,000	(A)

(iii)

Fixed production overhead efficiency variance

	hours	
14,600 units should take (× 4 hours)	58,400	
They did take	58,000	
Efficiency variance in hours	400	(F)
Standard fixed overhead rate per hour	× $5	
Fixed production overhead efficiency variance in $	$2,000	(F)

Fixed production overhead capacity variance

	hours	
Budgeted hours of work (15,000 × 4 hours)	60,000	
Actual hours of work	58,000	
Capacity variance in hours	2,000	(A)
Standard fixed overhead rate per hour	× $5	
Fixed production overhead capacity variance in $	$10,000	(A)

29 Overhead variances

Fixed production overhead capacity variance

	hours	
Budgeted production hours of work	9,000	
Actual production hours of work	8,250	
Capacity variance in hours	750	(A)
Standard fixed overhead rate per hour	× $25	
Fixed production overhead capacity variance in $	$18,750	(A)

Fixed production overhead efficiency variance

	hours
Standard hours produced	7,800
Actual hours worked	8,250
Efficiency variance in hours	450 (A)
Standard fixed overhead rate per hour	× $25
Fixed production overhead efficiency variance in $	$11,250 (A)

Fixed production overhead expenditure variance

	$
Budgeted fixed overhead expenditure (9,000 hours × $25)	225,000
Actual fixed overhead expenditure	211,000
Fixed overhead expenditure variance	14,000 (F)

30 Standard cost sheet

Tutorial note: This problem tests your understanding of the formulae for calculating variances. Here, you are given the actual costs and the variances, and have to work back to calculate the standard cost. The answer can be found by filling in the balancing figures for each variance calculation.

Materials price variance

	$
150,000 kilos of materials did cost	210,000
Material price variance	15,000 (F)
150,000 kilos of materials should cost	225,000

(The variance is favourable, so the materials did cost less to buy than they should have cost).

Therefore the standard price for materials is $225,000/150,000 kilograms = $1.50 per kilo.

Materials usage variance

Materials usage variance in $ = $9,000 (A)
Standard price for materials = $1.50
Materials usage variance in kilograms = 9,000/1.50 = 6,000 kilos (A)

	kilos
18,000 units of the product did use	150,000
Material usage variance in kilos	6,000 (A)
18,000 units of the product should use	144,000

Therefore the standard material usage per unit of product = 144,000 kilos/18,000 units = 8 kilos per unit.

Direct labour rate variance

	$
32,000 hours of labour did cost	136,000
Direct labour rate variance	8,000 (A)
32,000 hours of labour should cost	128,000

Therefore the standard direct labour rate per hour = $128,000/32,000 hours = $4 per hour.

Direct labour efficiency variance

Labour efficiency variance in $ = $16,000 (F)
Standard rate per hour = $4
Labour efficiency variance in hours = 16,000/4 = 4,000 hours (F)

	hours
18,000 units of the product did take	32,000
Labour efficiency variance in hours	4,000 (F)
18,000 units of the product should take	36,000

Therefore the standard time per unit of product = 36,000 hours/18,000 units = 2 hours per unit.

This number of hours per unit also applies to variable production overheads.

Variable overhead expenditure variance

	$
32,000 hours did cost	38,000
Variable overhead expenditure variance	6,000 (A)
32,000 hours should cost	32,000

Therefore the variable production overhead rate per hour = $32,000/32,000 hours = $1 per hour.

Standard marginal production cost – Product XY

		$
Direct materials	(8 kilos at $1.50 per kilo)	12.0
Direct labour	(2 hours at $4 per hour)	8.0
Variable production overhead	(2 hours at $1 per hour)	2.0
Standard marginal production cost		22.0

Applied Knowledge
Management Accounting (MA)

Index

A

Abnormal	
gain	287
loss	283
and loss with a scrap value	285
Absorbed production overheads	
cost ledger	245
Absorption costing	194, 198, 256
advantages and disadvantages	263
criticisms	196
definition	195
purpose	196
rate	214
Accounting	
for	
abnormal gain	287
abnormal loss	283
labour costs	186
normal loss	280
cost ledger	281
Accounting rate of return (ARR)	487
Accounts in the cost ledger	234
Acid test ratio	469
Activity based costing (ABC)	314, 324
Activity ratios	192, 470
Additive model	91
Administration costs	28
Adverse variances	416
Allocation	198

B

Annuity discount tables	399, 400
Apportioning common processing costs	307
Apportionment	198, 201
Appraisal costs	336
Aspirational budgets	371
Asset turnover ratio'	470
AVCO (weighted average cost)	157

Balance on an account	235
Balanced scorecard approach	369, 479
Bank overdraft balance	468
Bar charts	58
Base number for indices	106
Basis of apportionment	202
Batch	
costing	271
production	168, 271
Benchmarking	505
Benefits of LCC	332
Big data	17
characteristics	17
types	18
use	18
Bin card	150
Bottom-up budgeting	375
Budget	220, 341
committee	342
manual	342

period	341
process	343
slack (budget bias)	371
Budgetary control	341, 359
Budgeting	340
Buffer inventory	173
By-products	309

C

Capacity	
utilisation ratio	192
variance	433
Capital	
budgeting	381
expenditure	380
projects	380
Categorical data	3
Class interval	124
Closing inventory	240
Cluster sampling	23
Coefficient of determination r2	85
Competitive benchmarking	505
Component bar charts	59
Composite cost units	274
Compounding	386
Computerised inventory control system	150
Continuous variables	4, 121
Continuous weighted average method	157
Contribution	252
per unit	253
Control	6
Controllable costs	364
Conversion costs	278
Correlation coefficient	81
Correlation coefficient r	84
Cost(s)	
accounting	8
income statement	248
and management accounting	10
behaviour	48
graph(s)	49, 51
centre(s)	39, 198, 365
codes	37
drivers	316
estimation	64
gap	326
ledger	234
control account	242
object	41
partly controllable	364
pools	317
unit	41
variances	416
Cost of production and the WIP account	236
Cost of sales account	247
Cost/sales ratios	467
Costing system income statement	241
Credit	235
Critical success factors (CSFs)	461
Current ratio	468
Customer perspective	479

D

Data	2
analytics	19
organising and summarising	122
semi-structured	18
structured	18
types	120
unstructured	18
DCF	
assumptions about timing of cash flows	390
Debit	235
Debt ratios	469
Degrees of correlation	82
Delivery note	149
Descriptive analysis	4
Differential piecework systems	188
Direct	
costs	33
expenses	34
Direct labour	34
efficiency variance	423
employees	184
rate and efficiency variances	423
rate variance	423
usage budget	350
Direct materials	33
price and usage variances	419
usage variance	420
Discount factors	387
Discount tables	393

Discounted cash flow (DCF)	
analysis	384, 387
assumptions about timing of cash flows	394
Discounted payback period	405
Discounting	386
Discrete variables	4, 121
Double entry	
accounting for costs - overheads	244
cost accounting system	235

E

Earnings before interest, tax, depreciation and amortisation (EBITDA)	367
Economic and market conditions	462
Economic batch quantity (EBQ)	168
Economic environment: impact on costs and revenues	15
Economic order quantity (EOQ)	162
changes in the variables in the formula	164
price discounts for large orders	166
Economy	501
Effectiveness	501
Efficiency	501
Efficiency variance	424, 433
Equivalent units	291
FIFO method	298
weighted average cost method	294
Estimates based on judgement and experience	94
Expectational budgets	371
Expected values	137
Expenditure variance	223, 426
External failure costs	336

F

Favourable variances	416
FIFO method of process costing	298
Finance costs	28
Financial	
accounting	9
ledger control account	242
performance indicators (FPIs)	464
for measuring financial risk	469
for measuring liquidity	467
for measuring profitability	465

perspective	479
risk	469
Finished goods	235
account	247
Fixed	
budgets	359
costs	49
overhead(s)	227
absorption costing	227
variances - causes	435
production overhead	
capacity variance	433
cost variances	429
efficiency variance	433
expenditure variance	430
volume variance	430
Flexed budgets	360, 362
Flexible budgets	362
Frequency distributions	124
Full cost	37
Full of sale	195
production cost	195, 214
Functional	
budgets	342, 345
costs	29

G

Gearing ratio (leverage)	469
Goods received note	149
Gradual replenishment of inventory	168
Graph	61
Gross profit margin	465

H

High/low analysis	65
advantages and disadvantages	68
change in variable cost	71
step change in fixed costs	68
method	64
Holding costs	161, 163
Human/social data	13

I

Idle time 184

Imputed interest	492
Incentive	372
Incentive schemes	188
Income statement	241
Index numbers	106
construction	107
Indirect costs	35, 194
Inferential analysis	4
Information	2
attributes	5
external sources	13
Innovation and learning perspective	479
Interest cover ratio	470
Internal	
benchmarking	505
failure costs	336
perspective	479
Internal rate of return (IRR)	
method	394
advantages	397
disadvantages	397
Interpolation formula	395
Interrelationships between variances	439
Inventory	
accounts	234
days	472
ledger record	150
records	149, 150
monitoring physical inventory	151
Investigating variances	447
Investment	
appraisal	380
centre	39
centres	365
projects	380, 381
IRR method	
advantages	396
disadvantages	396

J

Job	
account	270
card	270
costing	268
sheet	270
Joint products	307

K

Key	
performance indicators (KPIs)	461
risk indicators (KRIs)	461

L

Labour	
costs	27, 184, 186
efficiency	
ratio	191
variance	423
rate variance	423
turnover	
causes	195
rate	195
usage budget	350
variances - causes	425
Laspeyre	
price index	112
quantity index	116
Life cycle costing	331
Linear	
function for total costs	64
regression analysis	75
forecasting	87
advantages and disadvantages	80
Liquidity	467
ratios	468
Long-term performance	461
Losses and gains at different stages of the process	303

M

Machine/sensor data	12
Management	
accounting	8
control systems	8
information system	2, 366
Manufacturing costs	27
Marginal	
cost	48, 250
costing	194
advantages and disadvantages	264
and absorption costing	256

assumptions	251
reporting profit	253
uses	251
Marketing costs	28
Master budget	342
Material(s)	
costs	26
procedures and documentation	148
inventory account	152
price variance	419
purchases budget	349
requisition note	150
return note	150
usage budget	348
usage variance	420
variances - causes	421
Maximum inventory level	174
Mean - ungrouped data	128
Measures of	
central tendency	
compared	131
dispersion	132
coefficient of variation	135
compared	136
standard deviation - grouped data	133
standard deviation - ungrouped data	132
variance	134
Median - ungrouped data	128
Medium-term performance	462
Minimum inventory level	174
Mission statement	460
Mixed costs	50
Mode - ungrouped data	128
Moving averages	88
Multiple bar charts	60
Multi-stage sampling	23

N

Negative correlation	83
Net present value (NPV) method	389
advantages	393
disadvantages	393
Net profit margin	466
New product development	326
Nominal data	3
Non-financial information	369

Non-financial performance indicators (NFPIs)	474
Non-production	
costs	27
overheads	
absorption costing	218
cost ledger	239
Normal	
distribution	141
loss	280
Not-for-profit organisations	499
Notional interest	492
Numerical data	4

O

One-off decision making	6
Opening inventory	240
Operating statement	441
standard marginal costing	444
Operational	
benchmarking	505
planning	7
Ordering costs	162, 163
Ordinal data	3
Organisation structure	38
Over-absorbed	
fixed production overhead	430
overhead	221
Over-absorption	221
Overhead(s)	35, 194
absorption	214
rate	214
apportionment	201
cost allocation	199
costs	316
expenditure variances	430
recovery rate	214
budgets	354
Overtime premium	185

P

Paasche	
price index	114
quantity index	117
Participation in budget setting	373
Payables days	472

Payback method	403
advantages	404
decision rule	403
disadvantages	404
Payroll records	186
Pay-off	
matrix	138
table	138
Percentage annual growth in sales	465
Perfect	
negative correlation	82
positive correlation	82
Performance	
measurement in service industries	497
measures for	
contract costing	483
process costing	483
reporting and responsibility accounting	366
reporting	416
Period costs	37
Periodic weighted average cost method	159
Perpetual inventory	150
Perpetuity	402
Pie charts	60
Piecework systems	187
Planning	6, 7
Positive correlation	83
Predetermined overhead rate	220
Present value of a perpetuity	402
Prevention costs	336
Price discounts for large orders	166
Price indices	
Laspeyre	112
Paasche	114
variance	419
Prime cost	35
Principal budget factor	343
Process costing	278
abnormal gain	287
inventory valuation	291
joint products and by-products	307
losses	280
Product lifecycle	333
impact on forecasting	95
Production	
and non-production costs	30
budget	347
costs	27
overhead expenditure variance	430
volume ratio	192
Productivity ratio	191
Profit	
and cash flow	382
before interest and tax (PBIT)	367
centre(s)	39, 365
margin	465
Proportional model	93
Purchase	
invoice	149
order	149
requisition	149
Purchasing procedures	149
PV of an annuity	399

Q

Quality-related costs	335
managing	337
Quantitative measures of efficiency	503
Quantity	
index	107
indices	116
Laspeyre	116
Paasche	117
Quick ratio	469
Quota sampling	23

R

Random sampling	21
Rate variance	423
Ratio analysis	464
Rebasing an index	108
Receivables days	471
Reciprocal method	205
simultaneous equations technique	211
Reconciling budgeted and actual profit	441
Recovery	198
rate	214
Relevant cash flows	407
Remuneration methods	187
Reorder level	172, 173
Repeated distribution technique	208
Reports	56
Residual income (RI)	492
Resource utilisation	485

Responsibility accounting	365, 368
Return on Investment (ROI)	487
investment decisions	489
Revenue	
centre	39
expenditure	380

S

Sales	
account	247
budget	345
price variance	436
value	
at the split-off point basis	307
less further processing costs basis	307
variances	436
causes	438
volume	
contribution variance	444
variance	436
Sampling	20
frame	21
Scrap value of normal loss	282
Seasonal variations	90
Selling and distribution costs	28
Semi-fixed cost	50
Semi-structured data	19
Semi-variable cost	50
Sensitivity analysis	102
Sensor data	12
Service	
centres	201
costing	273
department(s)	199
costs - apportionment	205
industries	497
Set-up costs	168, 272
Short-term performance	462
Simple	
aggregate price index	109
bar charts	58
index numbers	107
Social data	13
Spreadsheet	96, 345
Standard	
costing	412, 413
costs	412
hours produced	431
marginal costing - variances	443
Statement of	
cost per equivalent unit	292
equivalent units	292
evaluation	292
Stepped fixed cost	51
Strategic	
objectives	461
planning	7
Stratified sampling	22
Structured data	19
Supply lead time	172
Systematic sampling	22

T

Tables, charts and graphs	57
Tactical planning	7
Target costing	325
Time series analysis	86
advantages and disadvantages	94
Time sheets	186
Time value of money	385
Time-based systems	187
Top-down budgeting	374
Total	
contribution	253
fixed	
overhead cost variance	429
production overhead cost variance	430
Total Quality Management (TQM)	335
Transactional data	12
Trend line	87
Types of data	3

U

Under-absorbed	
fixed production overhead	430
overhead	221
Under-absorption	221
Usage variance	420

V

Value for money (VFM)	501

Variable cost	48
variances	417
Variable overhead	227
absorption costing	227
costs	250
efficiency variance	426
Variable production overhead	
efficiency variance	427
expenditure variance	426
Variance(s)	134
interrelationships	439
Volume variance	224, 431

W

Weighted	
average cost (AVCO)	
methods	157, 294
index numbers	112
What if analysis	102
Work-in-progress (WIP)	235

Y

Year 0 cash flows	390

Printed in France by Amazon
Brétigny-sur-Orge, FR